MW00910494

The Lost War

"ONE POWERFUL VOICE"

The Church Of The Early Morning

Our Days of Military Service Upon The Earth begin in the Discipline of the Mystical Darkness of the early morning hours in the Vault of Silence between Man and his Creator in Contemplation of the Sunrise awaiting in expectation of another day of duty, and perhaps the end of days, beneath the canopy of Stars for the first gray dim perceptions of Faint Light and to the appearance of the Sun upon the horizon regaled with many hues of splendid colors and to the realization that we are standing upon, and live in wonder of, a place called Earth, in all the charms of its elements and through the changing of the seasons of the year; a Wobbly World spinning in outer-space, circling a lone Star, among unfathomed Galaxies of Stars in a vast and inconceivable Universe; that is for us our Home in Heaven, as we know it to be, and with humbleness, to embrace the blessed toil of Combat of our days, secure in the knowledge that somehow and miraculously, We, and All There Is, Have Come To Exist; and to the Religious Sacrifice of each of our lives for it, the Call of Duty.

To Understand Our Place IN The Moral Mind Of God, of what it means to surrender our lives to Combat and for our sense of Duty, To Realize That We Exist In A Fusion Of Souls And Mind-Thought With "All Things" Sentient, Who Exist IN The Mind Of The Creator TO Be A Part Of. And That All Of This Interlacing of the Soul Of Everything Has Thought Upon Us, Involving Us With Itself, And We With Itself, Depending On Our Perceptions Of It, and Its Perceptions Of Us, To Relate To. And Always It Is With The Understanding About Everything, "To Be Mindful," And To Have Respect And Reverence And Cherishment For Everything, In Harmony To The Creator; Whose Dream, All Alone In The Timeless Darkness, It Was, For All Things To Exist. Prayer Alone Will Not Take Us There. It is only by Diligent Application and By Doing What Is Right That We Can Survive the Eternity that cannot endure a flaw. Duty Is Our Salvation. Duty Redeems Us And Sustains Us. Our Sacrifice of Duty Defines Us in our Holy Heritage as a Nation.

"Sooner or later one has to take sides."

The Quiet American
Graham Greene

THE LOST WAR - C 24 891 327   317/VSC/SPOPS/LJD
Copyright ©June 21, 2013 by Gary L. Koniz
ISBN: 978-1-304-16194-9

All Rights Reserved With Appreciation To **Wikipedia, CBS Evening News, The New York Times,** and Other Internet Public Domain Information Sources for their contributions. Published by Lulu Publishing, Inc. by arrangement with the author Gary L. Koniz

This complete work is dedicated to, **Dr. Dillie Warren, PhD,** Compensation and Pension Clinic, Veterans Health Administration, Gainesville, FL; for her Genuine Integrity of Profession; "A Caring Light In The Darkness" for the Safekeeping of our Veterans, to whom we are indebted.

Lulu Inc.
860 Aviation Parkway
Morrisville, NC 27560

"ONE POWERFUL VOICE"

The Eisenhower Memorial at West Point, NY

Dwight David "Ike" Eisenhower (October 14, 1890 – March 28, 1969) was a <u>five-star general</u> in the <u>United States Army</u> and the <u>34th</u> President of the American United States, whose Indomitable Commanding Spirit is the Eternal Guardian of the American People.

"ONE POWERFUL VOICE"

THIS IS AN IMPORTANT RECORD
SAFEGUARD IT

PERSONAL DATA	1. LAST NAME, FIRST NAME, MIDDLE NAME	2. SERVICE NUMBER	3. SOCIAL SECURITY NUMBER
	KONIZ, GARY LEE	RA 12 710 307	115 36 5132

4. DEPARTMENT, COMPONENT AND BRANCH OR CLASS	5a. GRADE RATE OR RANK	b. PAY GRADE	6. DATE OF RANK
ARMY-RA-ENGR	SP4 (T) (See 30)	E-4	17 Mar 67

7. U.S. CITIZEN	8. PLACE OF BIRTH (City and State or Country)	9. DATE OF BIRTH
[X] YES [ ] NO	Ft Meade, Md	1 May 46

SELECTIVE SERVICE DATA

10a. SELECTIVE SERVICE NUMBER	b. SELECTIVE SERVICE LOCAL BOARD NUMBER, CITY, COUNTY, STATE AND ZIP CODE	c. DATE INDUCTED
30 21 46 251	LB #21, Poughkeepsie, N.Y. 12602	NA

TRANSFER OR DISCHARGE DATA

11a. TYPE OF TRANSFER OR DISCHARGE	b. STATION OR INSTALLATION AT WHICH EFFECTED	d. EFFECTIVE DATE
Transferred to USAR (See 16)	Fort Stewart, Ga	11 Aug 67

c. REASON AND AUTHORITY
AR 635-200 SPN 201 Expiration of Term of Service

12. LAST DUTY ASSIGNMENT AND MAJOR COMMAND	13a. CHARACTER OF SERVICE	b. TYPE OF CERTIFICATE ISSUED
Co B, 575th Engr Bn (Const) US ARMY THIRD	HONORABLE	None

14. DISTRICT, AREA COMMAND OR CORPS TO WHICH RESERVIST TRANSFERRED	15. REENLISTMENT CODE
USAR Control Group (Reinf) USAAC, St Louis, Mo 63132	RE-1

16. TERMINAL DATE OF RESERVE/UNITMIL OBLIGATION	17. CURRENT ACTIVE SERVICE OTHER THAN BY INDUCTION a. SOURCE OF ENTRY	b. TERM OF SERVICE (Years)	c. DATE OF ENTRY
13 Aug 70	[X] ENLISTED (First Enlistment) [ ] ENLISTED (Prior Service) [ ] REENLISTED [ ] OTHER	3	14 Aug 64

18. PRIOR REGULAR ENLISTMENTS	19. GRADE RATE OR RANK AT TIME OF ENTRY INTO CURRENT ACTIVE SVC	20. PLACE OF ENTRY INTO CURRENT ACTIVE SERVICE (City and State)
None	PVT (P) E-1	Albany, N.Y.

SERVICE DATA

21. HOME OF RECORD AT TIME OF ENTRY INTO ACTIVE SERVICE (Street, RFD, City, County, State and ZIP Code)	22. STATEMENT OF SERVICE	YEARS	MONTHS	DAYS
6 Fulton Ct, Poughkeepsie, Dutchess, N.Y. 12603	CREDITABLE FOR BASIC PAY PURPOSES (1) NET SERVICE THIS PERIOD	2	11	28
	(2) OTHER SERVICE	0	0	0
	(3) TOTAL (Line (1) plus Line (2))	2	11	28
23a. SPECIALTY NUMBER & TITLE	b. RELATED CIVILIAN OCCUPATION AND D.O.T. NUMBER	b. TOTAL ACTIVE SERVICE	2	11	28
62E30 Const Mach Operator	7-72.580 Air-Compressor Operator	c. FOREIGN AND/OR SEA SERVICE	1	2	1

24. DECORATIONS, MEDALS, BADGES, COMMENDATIONS, CITATIONS AND CAMPAIGN RIBBONS AWARDED OR AUTHORIZED
Expert (Rifle M-14), VSM, VCM, 1 O/S Bar, NDSM

25. EDUCATION AND TRAINING COMPLETED
Ft Leonard Wood, Mo - 8 Weeks 1964 - Tractor Scraper Operator USAFI (GED) 1 Year College Equivalent Certified 1965 Code of Conduct Mil Jus CBR

VA AND CHP SERVICE DATA

26a. NON-PAY PERIODS TIME LOST (Preceding Two Years)	b. DAYS ACCRUED LEAVE PAID	27a. INSURANCE IN FORCE (NSLI or USGLI)	b. AMOUNT OF ALLOTMENT	c. MONTH ALLOTMENT DISCONTINUED
None	12	[ ] YES [X] NO	$ NA	NA

28. VA CLAIM NUMBER	29. SERVICEMEN'S GROUP LIFE INSURANCE COVERAGE
c. None	[X] $10,000 [ ] $5,000 [ ] NONE

REMARKS

30. REMARKS
Blood Group: "O" Item 5a: PFC (P) E-3 Appointed 9 Nov 66

Record Liber 31 of Discharges
P 271 on 12-8-67
Dutchess County Clerk's Office
J. John Hautmann, Co. Clerk

AUTHENTICATION

31. PERMANENT ADDRESS FOR MAILING PURPOSES AFTER TRANSFER OR DISCHARGE (Street, RFD, City, County, State and ZIP Code)	32. SIGNATURE OF PERSON BEING TRANSFERRED OR DISCHARGED
6 Fulton Ct, Poughkeepsie, Dutchess, N.Y. 12603	

33. TYPED NAME, GRADE AND TITLE OF AUTHORIZING OFFICER	34. SIGNATURE OF OFFICER AUTHORIZED TO SIGN
D. M. BOWEN, CPT, AGC, Asst AG	

DD FORM 214
1 JUL 66
PREVIOUS EDITIONS OF THIS FORM ARE OBSOLETE EFFECTIVE 1 JAN 67
GPO : 1966 O - 233-125
ARMED FORCES OF THE UNITED STATES
REPORT OF TRANSFER OR DISCHARGE

Standard Form 507   o43—16—81472p-3   opo

CLINICAL RECORD	Report on _____ DISCHARGE SUMMARY _____
	or
	Continuation of S. F. _____ 10-1000

(Strike out one line) (Specify type of examination or data)

(*Sign and date*)

with these activities was quite marginal, ~~and he complained his~~
~~problems were so dull.~~

The patient was discharged on 5/13/82 with 1 week supply of
Trilafon 8 mg. po qid, with recommendation that he should be
followed by a daily program from local mental health facilities on
a long term basis.

He is felt to be competent to handle his funds, but considered ∨for *disabled*
an undetermined period. Diet-regular diet. *Condition on discharge is improved.*

BYUNG KIM, M.D.
Staff Psychiatrist

(*Continue on reverse side*)

PATIENT'S IDENTIFICATION (*For typed or written entries give: Name—last, first, middle; grade; date; hospital or medical facility*)	REGISTER NO. 36 5132	WARD NO. 10D

KONIZ, Gary
AVAMC #500 ALBANY, NY

D-5/14/82 T-5/21/82 jed

REPORT ON _____ or CONTINUATION OF _____

STANDARD FORM 507
General Services Administration and
Interagency Committee on Medical Records
FPMR 101-11.80 6-8
October 1975 507-106
☆U.S. Government Printing Office: 1981—341-488/4638

C 24 891 327

317/VSC/SPOPS/LJD

A National Security Advisory Intelligence Gathering Report On Psychotropic Warfare

By Author Correspondent Gary L. Koniz

Anti-Veteran Sabotage Propaganda

From:**Gary Koniz** (gary.koniz@hotmail.com)
Sent: Wed 1/29/14 5:55 AM

To: Scott Pelley (evening@cbsnews.com); Dana McClintock (dlmcclintock@cbs.com); Eric Holder (askdoj@usdoj.gov) jacksvonville@ic.fbi.gov

Cc: Bill Cotterell (bcotterell@tallahassee.com); Bob Woodward (woodwardb@washpost.com); Chicago Tribune (ctc-tribletter@tribune.com); Cindy Holifield (cindy.holifield@jacksonville.com); Congressman Joe Wilson (wilson@mail.house.gov); Deborah Pueschel (pueschel@cxp.com); editorial@nytimes.com (editorial@nytimes.com); Felicia Steiger (fsteiger@postnewsweek.com); fns@foxnews.com (fns@foxnews.com); Frank Denton (frank.denton@jacksonville.com); Gerould W. Kern (ctc-editor@tribune.com); Jim Dao (dao@nytimes.com); Kevin Lenihan (klenihan@poughkee.gannett.com); klwilliams@wtlv.gannett.com (klwilliams@wtlv.gannett.com); Letters (letters@seattletimes.com); Lou Dobbs (lou@loudobbs.com); Matt Dixon (matt.dixon@jacksonville.com); Max Lederer, Jr. (lederer.max@stripes.com); mediadesk@centcom.mil (mediadesk@centcom.mil); Mike Garber (news@firstcoastnews.com); national@nytimes.com (national@nytimes.com); news@wftv.com (news@wftv.com); Nick Waller (nick.waller@wctv.tv); ontherecord@foxnews.com (ontherecord@foxnews.com); oped@seattletimes.com (oped@seattletimes.com); oped@nytimes.com (oped@nytimes.com); opinion@seattletimes.com (opinion@seattletimes.com); Pam Bondi (pam.bondi@myfloridalegal.com); Paul Flemming (pflemming@tallahassee.com); Paul Tash (timespresident@tampabay.com); pb_metro@pbpost.com (pb_metro@pbpost.com); Peter Faucher (pfaucher@ideastations.org); Rev. Terry Jones (info@doveworld.org); Richard Trumka (rtrumka@aflcio.org); Rick Scott (rick.scott@eog.myflorida.com); Sally Baptiste (sallylbaptiste@att.net); Senator Bill Nelson (bill@billnelson.senate.gov); senator@rockefeller.senate.gov (senator@rockefeller.senate.gov); Sergio Bustos (sbustos@miamiherald.com); Tim Cox (tim@gooh.com); Travis Bridges (chair@duvaldemocrats.org)

The Waiting Time with The V.A. on Post Traumatic Stress Claims and for Catastrophic Thorazine Compensation Damages, that has left our Veterans disabled and unable to work, is into Three Years to the date; from the time of application their Rejection Ex Parte without Counsel Representation, and with many incidents of lost and mishandled paperwork and with no consideration provided for Veterans testimony and supporting documentation. That now, (according to a V.A. Spokesperson,) is in a Waiting Period of over one year backlogged 376 Day on the average to hear appeals of Notice Of Disagreement. Please take head to adopt the "Proper Legislation" here reasoned for, to be funded based on "Full Faith Certificate," as needed, as the only way out of the Financial Deficit Troubles that the V.A. is having to be able to properly expedite the care of our Veterans.

"ONE POWERFUL VOICE"

Conspiracy

To prevail in an action for civil conspiracy, one must allege and prove two or more persons acted in concert to cause a wrong for their own advantage.

- two or more conspirators
- acting in concert
- to cause a wrong
- for their own advantage

They don't even have to communicate with each other!

At least one of them must commit at least one wrongful overt act with a shared goal to disadvantage the plaintiff!

Each must seek advantage for himself to be liable for plaintiff's damages.

The overt act(s) must be unlawful, willful, or malicious (a broad range of behavior).

When pleading conspiracy, one must also plead at least one additional count seeking damages for the wrongful act(s). That is to say there must be some "underlying wrongful act", such as tortious interference with an advantageous business relationship. An action for conspiracy alone is without basis and will be dismissed.

Plaintiff must sue for one or more other causes of action, adding a final count for conspiracy in which he alleges the wrongs were committed in concert by multiple defendants seeking their own advantage.

Elements

1. Intentional commission of an unlawful act or a lawful act by unlawful means by the combined effort of more than one actor. The acts need not be criminal, so long as they are forbidden by civil or criminal law. An intentional tort like fraud, for example, is sufficiently unlawful.
2. The acts complained of must be in furtherance of the conspiracy. Any act that does not advance the goal of the conspiracy is not conspiratorial.
3. Overt acts by each conspirator. Mere agreement or consent to the act of another isn't enough.
4. Damage to plaintiff resulting proximately from the conspiratorial act(s).

The gist of conspiracy is not the conspiracy itself, for the conspiracy alone causes no damage. It is the damage, accomplished by the conspired acts of multiple persons acting in concert to further the conspiracy that gives rise to this cause of action.

One person cannot conspire.

Comments

Civil conspiracy arises from an agreement, confederation, or other combination of two or more persons. Each must intend some benefit to himself resulting from the intended wrongful act. The meeting of two or more independent minds must be intent on one purpose, and those two (or more) must perform overt acts in furtherance of the conspiracy.

The benefit need not be money or property. The benefit could be advantage over or destruction of a circumstance previously enjoyed by the plaintiff, such as a business advantage or opportunity.

The benefit proves intent … *an essential element of this cause of action.*

If Harry and Bob conspire to destroy Sam's business, and Bob does the dirty work while Harry sits back in his office participating by nothing more than letting Bob use his car, Harry is responsible for every act Bob commits *just as if he were there in person.* By Harry's agreement and the overt act of supplying Bob with a car, the law will hold both Bob and Harry liable for Sam's damages. It is as if Bob and Harry each acted alone. The law deems that each conspirator is jointly and severally liable for all damages caused by acts of the co-conspirators.

The act of one is the act of all!

A mafia boss who orders a hit commits murder, though he is nowhere near when the killing occurs. If he furthers the act of the hit man by promising to pay for the kill (by money, property, or any advantage) the law treats him as if he pulled the trigger in person.

The same applies in a civil conspiracy.

A businessman, who promises to pay officers of a competitor firm to walk out and take the competitor's business records, thereby destroying the competitor's business, is liable for civil conspiracy. His over act is the promise to pay for wrongful acts of co-conspirators. The damaged plaintiff would sue for the damages he suffered by the underlying act of the walkout and theft of his records and would add a count for civil conspiracy that could result in punitive damages in addition to his actual money damages.

Assumption of Duty

An action taken for the benefit of another, whether for payment or not, imposes a duty and imputes knowledge of that duty on the person taking action to do so with reasonable care. Failure to exercise reasonable care when assuming a duty to assist another gives rise to a cause of action for Assumption of Duty. Defendant undertook, gratuitously or for consideration, to render services to another in circumstances a reasonable man would recognize as necessary for protection of the other person or the other person's property. Plaintiff suffered physical harm resulting from defendant's failure to exercise reasonable care to perform the services he undertook to perform in reasonable and justifiable reliance on defendant's undertaking.

9480 Princeton Square Blvd. S., #815
Jacksonville, FL 32256
January 25, 2014

Ira Katz, MD, PhD
Deputy Chief Patient Care Services Officer
For Mental Health
Veterans Health Administration
810 Vermont Avenue, N.W.
Washington, D.C. 20420

Dear Doctor Katz,

This issue has to do with the recent Season 4 Episode 13 Friday Night 1/17/2014 10:00 P.M airing of the **CBS TV Series Blue Bloods**, entitled, **"Unfinished Business."** That depicts **an Ex-Marine** who served three tours of duty in Afghanistan who is suffering from Post-Traumatic Stress Disorder, PTSD. And who (according to the narrative of the show,) **"thinks that he is still in combat,"** and is depicted while in a fugue state, to have beat up his wife and abducted his eight year old son and gone up to a roof top ready to jump off with the boy and commit suicide; and which the veteran did after letting his boy be rescued. The episode then ended with a tearful appeal to the nation from the Show's Co-Star **Tom Selleck** concerning the tragic reality of PTSD for the returning Combat Veterans and urging Veterans who are suffering from PTSD, and with their families' intervention of involvement, to get themselves to their nearest V.A. Medical Centers for counseling and treatment, and pleaded with the concerned voice of, **CBS Cares**.

What is wrong with this drama is, that this depiction of our Returning Combat Veterans -- as being unable to differentiate between being in Combat and the reality of civilian life -- is patently false, and constitutes Illegal Malicious Propaganda Slander against, and causing great harm to, a singled out Group of Americans, our Nation's Veterans, who are protected, (as all Groups of People Are, from malicious slander,) under **Title 47 of the United States Code** that defines the role and structure of the <u>Federal Communications Commission</u> against **"the communication of a statement that makes a claim, expressly stated or implied to be factual, that may give an individual, business, product, group, government, or nation a negative image."**

In the United States, the **Federal Defamation Law** is closely tied to the First Amendment. That being said, false statements of fact, Defamation—also called calumny, vilification, or traducement---that harms the reputation of an <u>individual</u>, <u>business</u>, <u>product</u>, <u>group</u>, <u>government</u>, <u>religion</u>, or <u>nation</u>, are not protected under Constitutional Free Speech provisions. Most U.S. Jurisdictions allow criminal legal action to deter various kinds of defamation and retaliate against groundless criticism. 47 U.S. Code § 230 defends our democratic ideals and protects our Internet civil rights from statements that are completely fabricated and possibly result in harm to others.

WE have been pointing this out to you for over a decade of our involvement with you; that this type of **Negative Propaganda Against our Combat Veterans** is being depicted "over and over again" by our Nation's Public Media who with malice portray Deranged Irrational Veterans to the American Public, **"With the Grave Intent,"** to **Discredit and Cause Harm to them personally and as a Body of Men**, and to cast disgrace upon their proud Military Careers and upon our Nation's Military Service in the overall. This has caused our returning from war soldiers en masse to be feared and looked upon as being irrational and dangerous to be around, and as portrayed to the Nation's Public that way to be the norm of the deadly scenario; **Which It Is Not**; and

"ONE POWERFUL VOICE"

constituting a patently a false depiction of what PTSD actually is; (that the subject of **"Black Out Fugue States,"** is not a part of, and has no documented medical evidence of in fact.)

This **"Get-Help at the V.A." Anti-Veteran Propaganda Appeal using the nation's media**, has been re-enacted relentlessly in defaming our returning home from War Veterans through the Vietnam War Era in recent history, and in exactly the same manner, and **that is being Put Out "Methodically" By Some Unknown Entity**, **who needs to be identified and put-an-end-to**.

This Propaganda has caused, and is causing a great Holocaust in Damage Toll to our Soldiers and is responsible for the maiming ruination and suicide deaths of tens of thousands of Veterans:

1. (In first Instance:) by the ensuing mass-public hysterias resulting to be thereby presumed unable to differentiate the between being in combat and the reality of civilian life; and who in such deranged fugue states of posing a decided threat to themselves and their families, (who fear being murdered in their sleep,) and so to involve the rest of society also in damaging the Veterans' Employability, to be thereof outcast and rejected by their close family members, (who mistrust and fear them,) and by society in the whole that way alienated to become homeless men. And what is Life-Threatening setting of being Homeless falling below the Threshold of Survival.

2. That (in the second instance:) of the Veterans reporting to their **presumed safeguarding V.A. Health Care Centers to get help**, (from the resulting ensuing homelessness and social alienation and depressed psychological states that they have been engulfed in as a result of such villainous propaganda,) who are thereby (and heavily documented about,) **betrayed by the V.A. Medical Staff** (under your direct Supervision,) **to be given needless Permanent Psychiatric History Stigmas** about, as a matter of **Standard Policy,** and **thereupon To Be Murdered with Anti-Psychotic Drugs** (having deadly consequences as documented,) from which our Veterans will never recover to be wholly functioning human beings again, and left abandoned To Suicide.

Our Nation's Veterans and their families need to be assured of a **Benign War Recovery Setting**, of; **Convalescent Bed Rest, Good Nutrition, Compassionate Counselling, and Therapy**, **free of Psychiatric Stigmas and from all Destructive Chemicals**; as it relates to their safekeeping; and safe from the damaging effects of Anti-Psychotic Medications, and from the prevailing real Social Stigma associated to the Diagnosis and Treatment of Mental Disorders to be Legally Clarified; as to what constitutes a Legal Diagnosis and concerning a person's Right To Refuse Treatment, and with appropriate protection of Legal Counsel to be provided for by The Veterans Administration as to The Rights of our Veterans to be covered under the Ninth and Fourteenth Amendments by Legal Due Process in the event of their being falsely Psychiatrically Accused, and to their Safeguard of Beneficial Treatment Under The Law. There are indeed situations of persons posing a threat to themselves and to others, on whom Strong Tranquilizer Drugs like Thorazine and others in its class of Psychotropic Chemicals are lawfully permitted; but the effects of this drug and others like it on otherwise Normal Veterans, renders them Totally Disabled and of such Diminished Capacity as to not be able to function "Normally" in society. We feel that neither you nor The Secretary has taken the necessary steps to defend our Veterans.

With All Due Respect,
Gary L. Koniz – Correspondent
Veterans of the Vietnam War

CC: David N. Donahue
Office of the General Counsel

We started working on this project together as an MOAA agenda in National Alarms several years ago; with The Veterans Administration, The U.S. Military, The Federal Government, and The F.B.I., in the need for dramatic intervention; and coinciding to the urgent Removal of the Heroin and other Dangerous Drugs from our society, and for the resulting Drug Warfare occurring in peril causing psychiatric conditions to the population particularly to our returning from war Veterans, and our first line of homeland defense to be eliminated; and to our suffering the loss of our American Nation over it, the trafficking in drugs, (of the American United States of the WWII generations,) for the aggressions of the many ways of wars having been allowed to overtake us; of corrupt, irrational, and immoral ideologies, and for the allowing of decidedly foreign peoples to politically and economically overrun us here, in the malaise of a drugged and corrupt society, to be left defenseless against. That we do at this time need to be intervening to the War Crimes involved with psychiatric coinciding to the Opium/Heroin Trafficking from Afghanistan, formerly from Vietnam.

It takes years in many cases for our Veterans Claims to get processed. What our Nation Needs at this time is To Make Use of a <u>Fiat Money Resolution Bill</u> based to "Full Faith Certificate," to Fund V.A. Facilities and Government Payrolls To better assist our Veterans and to Provide Work for them and for all the nation's unemployed, and as well to shore up and bolster the critical matters of; Aviation Safety issues, National Defense, (involving Border Invasion Overrun,) Pandemic Drug Trafficking-Addiction, Organized Crime, Prostitution and Pornography, (going general public now and an evil subversive industry beyond comprehension of murder-mayhem preying on the destitute, involved with drug trafficking, thrill killing snuff movies, the degradation exploitation of women, child molestation, and ensuing drug chemical warfare sabotage to the public;) in all concerns that WE need to be strengthening our manpower resources to defend against and not left weakened. The heroin-drug-trafficking porno mafia people love this kind of non-intervention economic climate; and otherwise; that once the mafia becomes public body-politic in size, (if they have not already and openly contributing to the economic collapse,) that WE Are In For It! I would appreciate your backing and support in this. Let's pull hard together and get the nation on a **Mature War Footing.**

These Forces Against Us, and as we have described them, need to be intervened to, and not for The Authorities In Charge to continue "to eliminate us" by Psychiatric Intake. To what purposes then, on the matters of the current problems facing us as Americans, in the immediacy of those times of the past and as carry-over into the current times of the year 2013, that is upon us now and fleeting as all time is, to hasten with the work of The Father about, in Terms of State, and concerning The Nation of The United States to resolve and as that we have influence over it, the Affairs of Other Nations about the World, to the World at large to what WE as loyal Americans and under The Creator's Advising Influence, have sway to remedy; which is in imminent terms of peril to do with the collapse of our U.S. economy and the overrun and conquest of our U.S. Territory by Enemy Forces. To comment about it that WE just cannot keep Borrowing ourselves into tremendous National Debt to pay off our Bills that WE can never hope in good time to ever repay, and to the other way of drastic Budget Reductions to Repay our loans and to Balance The Budget, that the more budget cuts they make, the less available resources WE are going to have to Maintain the functions of our Government by and to care for our Infrastructure, and to combat the forces of crime and terror prevention. To what purposes of a Purpose Drive Life that WE need to come up with a New and Better Plan to replace our current outdated Economic System in order to serve our Veterans better.

"ONE POWERFUL VOICE"

DEPARTMENT OF VETERANS AFFAIRS
St. Petersburg Regional Office
P.O. BOX 1437
St. Petersburg FL 33731

FEB 2 4 2014

Mr. Gary L. Koniz
9480 Princeton Square Blvd. #815
Jacksonville, FL 32256

In Reply Refer To: 317/VSC/21PC/NK
C 24 891 327
KONIZ, Gary L.

Dear Mr. Koniz:

    This is in reply to your inquiry submitted through the Office of General Counsel received on January 25, 2014. The Office of Congressional and Legislative Affairs referred your correspondence to our VA Regional Office, St. Petersburg, Florida on February 12, 2014 because we have jurisdiction of your pending appeal.

    Our VA Regional Office received your Notice of Disagreement (NOD) on June 12, 2013. You are appealing the Rating Decision of May 21, 2013 which denied service connection for post traumatic stress disorder (PTSD); individual unemployability (IU) and also denied entitlement to compensation under 38 U.S.C. 1151 for crippled nervous system; amnesia; impotency; crippled muscular system and incontinence.

    The Decision Review Officer (DRO) will review the materials in your VA claims folder, including arguments and statements from your representative if applicable. If appropriate, the DRO will then render a decision. You will be notified of the decision by a letter or provided a Statement of the Case (SOC) with instructions on how to continue your appeal.

    Our system records indicate on or about July 18 to the 30th, 2013 we received your letters, records, pictures and medical records from the Albany VA Medical Center. We also received the documents you submitted with your inquiry.

    We apologize for the delay. We understand the disappointment with an unfavorable decision. No rating assignment or denial of benefits should be seen as disrespect to your service as a veteran. The appeals are completed in the date order in which they are received, working the oldest one first.

    For further assistance, you may call our VA National Call Center toll-free at 800-827-1000, weekdays from 7:00 A.M. to 7:00 P.M. (except Federal holidays). You may send an electronic inquiry through the Internet at https://iris/va/gov. You may also contact the County Veterans Service Officer for assistance, found under each County Government Offices listing in the phone directory.

Sincerely yours,

KERRIE I. WITTY
Director

"ONE POWERFUL VOICE"

9480 Princeton Square Blvd. S., #815   317/VSC/21PC/NK
Jacksonville, FL 32256   C 24 891 327
March 10, 2014   Koniz, Gary L.

Kerrie I. Witty - Director
Department of Veterans Affairs
St. Petersburg Regional Office
P.O. Box 1437
St. Petersburg, FL 33731

Dear Director Witty:

I respectfully appreciate your effort to be in touch with me regarding the standing of my V.A. Appeal pending with **my claim for Compensation for Thorazine Disablement** while in the care of V.A. Medical Center at Albany, NY in 1982 related to Post Traumatic Stress Disorder and a Homeless State that I was experiencing then at that time and with severe complications arising from Loxitane and Cogentine Treatment that I was crippled by in the previous weeks during a recent 21 day commitment at the G. Werber Brian Psychiatric Hospital in Columbia, SC where I was taken by the Sheriff's men in handcuffs, after asking me if I was a Vietnam Veteran, for my complaining to the authorities about the dangerous situation of Drug Chemical Warfare occurring there in the deep South at the time. And to what, on top of the Contraindications from the effects of the Loxitane and Cogentine, that I was given the drug Thorazine for by the V.A..

And to understand here that my case as it stands **"is retroactive"** concerning the lost years of my life due to un-employability in direct result of the disabling Thorazine Treatment I received.

And here, I do not mean, as has been stated for by the Medical Examiner who denied me my claim to what I am appealing, concerning the term "employability," that this has anything to do with menial and low wage paying jobs taken subsequently to be considered as "employable;" but to conceive of my Professional Credentials; as a Summa Cum Laude Graduate, and regarding my professional career as Journalist News Reporter, my history of employment as a Government Supervisor working for the C.E.T.A. Program (Comprehensive Employment and Training Act,) my Commercial Multi-Engine Pilot License, and my Union Career with the International Union of Operating Engineers as a Heavy Equipment Operator; and along with **"the high income potential"** to be expected from such work, which "was lost," (and along with my **"Retirement Savings Potential,"** to include a higher Social Security rate,) due to the disabling effects of this Drug Thorazine; that left me; Physically, Mentally, Emotionally, and Psychologically Invalid for a period of several years, and which along with the Psychiatric Stigma associated, that cost me twenty years of my life, as I fell below the threshold of survival and became unemployable.

Most Respectfully,
Gary L. Koniz
Veterans of the Vietnam War

"ONE POWERFUL VOICE"

Superintendent
United States Military Academy
West Point, New York 10996-5000

February 12, 2009

Dear Mr. Koniz,

ank you for your note and for continuing to support our Nation's
erans. Unfortunately, I am not in a position to financially assist your cause
l I am prohibited by the Joint Ethics Regulations from asking the West
int staff for donations. General Shinseki is a great Soldier and leader;
will do an incredible job heading the

Veterans Administration as they strive to meet the needs of all
who served. All the best.

Sincerely,

F. L. Hagenbeck
Lieutenant General, US Army
Superintendent

Mr. Gary L. Koniz
9480 Princeton Square Blvd S.
Jacksonville, FL 32256

"ONE POWERFUL VOICE"

DEPARTMENT OF THE ARMY
UNITED STATES ARMY FLIGHT TRAINING CENTER
FORT STEWART, GEORGIA 31313

AJSCG   13 August 1967

Specialist Gary L. Koniz
575th Engineer Battalion (Construction)
Fort Stewart, Georgia   31313

Dear Specialist Koniz:

On the occasion of your separation from active duty, I wish to
extend to you my personal thanks and the sincere appreciation of the
United States Army for the outstanding service which you have given to
our country. You have helped to maintain the security of this nation
during a most critical period in its history.

I share your pride in the contributions you have made to the
Army and hope you will maintain an active interest in its objectives
in the future.

You take with you my best wishes and those of your comrades for
happiness and success in the years that lie ahead.

Sincerely,

FRANK MESZAR
Brigadier General, USA
Commanding

"ONE POWERFUL VOICE"

UNITED STATES CIVIL SERVICE COMMISSION

NEW YORK CITY AREA OFFICE

FEDERAL BUILDING, 26 FEDERAL PLAZA
NEW YORK, N. Y. 10007

IN REPLY PLEASE REFER TO

YOUR REFERENCE

Dear Candidate:

Congratulations on your successful performance on the written test of the Professional and Administrative Career Examination. Your numerical ratings and the grade levels for which you qualify and are available are indicated on the enclosed form. PACE is used to fill a wide variety of positions which offer challenge, advancement, and rewarding experience.

Please read the back of the enclosed form carefully. As explained in paragraph 8, we cannot provide definite information about your prospects for referral to Federal agencies, but we can tell you that competition is keen. Prospects are generally good for candidates with ratings above 90. You may also be referred for employment consideration if you have lower ratings, particularly if you have specialized education or experience required by some jobs. Regardless of your ratings you should not be discouraged if you are not contacted by an agency immediately. The number of referrals made varies from month to month and is dependent on fluctuating staffing needs.

We appreciate your interest in Federal employment and hope that your application through the PACE examination leads to a satisfying career.

Sincerely yours,

Kenneth P. Riley
Kenneth P. Riley
Area Manager

THE MERIT SYSTEM—A GOOD INVESTMENT IN GOOD GOVERNMENT

"ONE POWERFUL VOICE"

UNITED STATES CIVIL SERVICE COMMISSION
NEW YORK CITY AREA OFFICE
FEDERAL BUILDING
26 FEDERAL PLAZA
NEW YORK NY 10007

NOTICE OF RESULTS

Professional and Administrative Career Examination

KONIZ GARY L   OCTOBER 1975
31C COLONIAL ARMS   ID NO. 447598
NEW PALTZ   NY 12561

We appreciate your interest in a career with the Federal Government. Your results in the Professional and
Administrative Career Examination are shown below. Numerical ratings for *eligible* candidates are in Block
1. Please see Block 2 if you did not receive a numerical rating for any occupational category.

---

1. You are eligible to receive consideration for the occupational categories and grade levels shown, in
   accordance with the numerical ratings indicated. *(See back of this notice for explanation of test results
   and description of occupational categories).* SUBJECT TO MEETING MEDICAL
   REQUIREMENTS OF THE POSITION

Occupational Categories	GS-5	GS-7
A	097	097
B	097	097
C	096	096
D	098	098
E	098	098
F	097	097

For Consideration In NEW YORK REGION   Eligibility Expires:
WASHINGTON, D.C.   DECEMBER 1976

'YOUR NUMERICAL SCORES INCLUDE 05 POINTS
'VETERANS PREFERENCE

'YOUR NUMERICAL SCORES INCLUDE ADDITIONAL POINTS
ALLOWED UNDER THE OUTSTANDING SCHOLAR PROVISION

---

2. If you did not receive a numerical rating in the first block above, for one or more grade levels, the
   reason is:

BE SURE TO READ IMPORTANT MESSAGES ON BACK OF THIS FORM

CSC Form 4008 B(x)
September 1975

"ONE POWERFUL VOICE"

U.S. Department
of Transportation

**Federal Aviation
Administration**

1991 JUN -6 AM 11: 18

Eastern Region

Fitzgerald Federal Building
John F. Kennedy
International Airport
Jamaica, New York 11430

JUN 4 1991

The Honorable Daniel P. Moynihan
United States Senator
28 Church Street, Suite 203
The Guaranty Building
Buffalo, NY 14202

Dear Senator Moynihan:

This is in response to your letter dated May 22, 1991, regarding
your constituent, Gary L. Koniz.

Mr. Koniz has written to the Civil Aviation Security Division of
the Eastern Region Federal Aviation Administration (FAA), over the
past several months. In his letters, Mr. Koniz has expressed his
concerns regarding drug trafficking as well as the use of illegal
substances and chemicals and their effects on aviation safety and
the environment. He has also indicated that on May 09, 1991, he
corresponded with the Central Intelligence Agency concerning this
issue.

The FAA's Drug Interdiction Support Program conducts comprehensive
investigations into aviation related drug activities relevant to
civil aviation. The program provides technical expertise to
federal, state, and local law enforcement agencies involved in
national anti-drug efforts and serves as a focal point for the
conduct of joint investigations including military units. A
Special Agent assigned to the Drug Interdiction Support Program in
the Eastern Region, has been apprised of Mr. Koniz' concerns and
will coordinate and monitor interagency activities.

We hope the information provided will assist you in replying to
your constituent. We appreciate and share the concerns expressed
for the safety of the aviation community.

Sincerely,

Daniel J. Peterson
Regional Administrator

Enclosure
Transmitted Correspondence

cc: Washington Office

"ONE POWERFUL VOICE"

UNITED STATES MISSION TO THE UNITED NATIONS

November 16, 2006

140 EAST 45 STREET
NEW YORK, N.Y. 10017

Mr. Gary Koniz, Journalist/Correspondent
9480 Princeton Square Blvd. S., #815
Jacksonville, FL 32256

Dear Mr. Koniz:

I received your letter of November 5 expressing your concerns about international drug trafficking. As I have mentioned many times before, the U.S. Mission does not initiate action or policy at the UN. The Ambassador and the U.S. Mission carry out the policies of the Administration. Therefore, it is impossible for me to ask the Ambassador to present issues before the United Nations, as all issues must be approved first by the Department of State.

The issue of international crime and drugs, however, is brought up at the United Nations. Last month, the Deputy Assistant Secretary for the Bureau of International Narcotics and Law Enforcement Affairs of the Department of State gave the U.S. statement in the Third Committee on crime and drugs. For your reference, I am enclosing a copy of this statement given on October 4, 2006. I am also enclosing information on the Department's Bureau.

The United Nations has an Office on Drugs and Crime and I am enclosing from the web site information on their work. On the home front there is a Drug Enforcement Administration and in the White House, there is the Office of National Drug Control Policy. This is a very important and active issue. Perhaps you should start at your local level to become involved in this issue as there are many nongovernmental agencies that fight drug abuse in communities.

I took a few weeks off during the holidays last year and did not receive your Christmas card and request. However, I would not have been able to assist you with information on civilian employment in Afghanistan or Iraq as we do not hire individuals for work overseas, but the U.S. Agency for International Development and the Department of Defense employ civilians in these regions.

Sincerely,

Patricia Kuffler
Public Affairs Officer

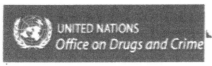

Home   Site Map   Links   Contact Us   Regional Websites select the site ▼

Login

Search

Home \ News and Publications \ Press Releases

Saturday, 2 December 2006Saturday, 2 December 2006

News and Publications

Press Releases

Speeches

Events

Newsletters

Multimedia

Publications

Promotional Material

Drug Abuse & Demand Reduction

Drug Supply Reduction

Terrorism, Corruption & Human Trafficking

Treaty & Legal Affairs

Research, Analysis, Statistics & Scientific Support

About Us

Employment Opportunities

United Nations Crime and Drug Conventions

Crime Commission (CCPCJ)

Commission on Narcotic Drugs (CND)

Global Youth Network

Information Services for Member States

UNOV/UNODC Online Services for Staff

UN drugs chief warns European mayors about risk of overdoses from bumper Afghan opium crop

VIENNA, 22 November 2006 (UNODC) - Europe's cities face the risk of a significant increase in the number of deaths from heroin overdoses because of the record opium crop in Afghanistan this year, the Executive Director of the United Nations *Office on Drugs and Crime*, Antonio Maria Costa, said on Wednesday.

In a letter to 63 mayors of European cities, he repeated the warning he has made to the world's national health authorities that a sharp rise in the supply of heroin tended in the past to lead to an increase in the purity of the end product rather than lower street prices.

"I strongly encourage the mayors of Europe's cities and the community drug treatment centres in your country to take every possible measure in the period ahead and to alert practitioners to the possible risk increase," Mr Costa said in the letter.

At a meeting on Wednesday with Tomas Hallberg, Director of European Cities Against Drugs (ECAD), the UNODC chief discussed efforts by cities and municipalities to combat drug abuse more effectively.

"I welcome ECAD's efforts to get European cities united around the goal of reducing drug addiction," Mr Costa said. "Some cities take the problem more seriously than others. Illicit drugs are a serious threat to our young people and the very future of our societies. We need a robust and consistent response."

Mr Hallberg urged European politicians "to take responsibility for what is happening in their own backyards." "They cannot simply sit back and wait in the hope that their drug problem will disappear by itself or be solved by others," he said.

The two men agreed that rising cocaine use in Europe, especially in Italy, Spain and the United Kingdom, was a cause for serious concern.

ECAD is the leading organization for promoting a drug-free Europe. Representing millions of European citizens, ECAD member cities work to develop initiatives against drug abuse and in support of the United Nations conventions to strengthen the international drug control system.

***

For further information, please contact:

Richard Murphy
UNODC Spokesman
Tel +43 1 26060 5761
Mobile +43 699 1459 5761
richard.murphy@unodc.org

"ONE POWERFUL VOICE"

Woodstock 1969

"ONE POWERFUL VOICE"

ORIENTATION

Better to light a candle, as the saying goes, than to curse the darkness. "The Darkness," being not knowing God, and the pang of fear of the unknown that we experience in having to live our lives in the great doubt and uncertainty of the shadow of death and nonexistence, and with being confronted by all manner of ill-inducing evils and bad habits that in turn induce all manner of self-destructive behavior and undermines the very character of a successful life, in the meaning of being virtuous and proud of one's self.

This is a report about The Drug War as it was occurring then in the mid-to late 1980s, in the mid-Hudson Valley Region of New York State, of Poughkeepsie, NY, and the Immigrant Stronghold of The Italian Mafia; and concerning the Gulag Archipelago, of the Nation's Mental Health Psychiatric Facility System, that was set up in their design to be The Active Arm of their brand of Communism known as American Fascism; using methods of involving and entrapping the population into conspiracy with Drug Addiction and Drug Trafficking and Pornographic Criminalizing, and by the means of Black Hand, Black Mail, and Coercion, to perpetrate Drug Chemical Warfare upon the population; a condition in which the entire indigenous population of the Region, on both sides of the Hudson River, was being mercilessly attacked by in a relentless siege perpetration of Drug Chemical Warfare, the victims of which who were then made into Mental Patients and taken into Psychiatric Detention, where they were then assaulted by Legal Means of Forced Treatment with deadly Drug Chemicals designed to maim and to disable them, the victims of this Type of War, by Pharmacy touted to be beneficially necessary medications for the treatment of the Induced Mental Illness Disorders; and only to destroy them. And which, for point of fact, do themselves, as to these medications, Induce the Disorders they are advertised to cure. Which was then being allowed to Stage Itself without Intervention from the Established Authorities, and without Legal Due Process of The Constitution in Place to Protect The Rights of the Psychiatric Accused To Fair and Equal Justice.

This Clandestine War was also surreptitiously being waged by Corrupt Alliances to the Italian Heroin and Cocaine and Pornography Drug Mafia Business, by Jewish Zionist Mafia Gangs bent on the aggrandizement of The United States for their own kind as to their motives being to deal drugs, and by other Racial and Ethnic designs of Domination and fueled by Black Heroin Mafia Demagogic Hatred, and Enemies All of The United States, in the same sense as other Terrorist Organizations such as Al Qaeda are to be conceived. And which War was also being waged relentlessly for Personal Motives such as Homosexuality and Women's War Agendas, and for Seditious Purposes such as Drug Dealing, Monetary Corruptions, and Pornography, joining together in Warfaring Fronts.

And in the Criminal Political Meaning also being taken Liberal Advantage as a Voting Constituency, in Gerrymander of The Mafia Populations, for Political Advantage; also being Co-Conspired to for Profit by the Corruptions of the Medical, Pharmaceutical, Administrative, and Judicial, and Law Enforcement, Legal, and Legislative Malfeasances of the Bureaucracy, in the Nature of Treason, to the detriment and destruction of The American People, and as a State Of War occurring Against The United States itself. And of this war which was then, and that still is now, especially targeting American Combat Veterans, returned from the ongoing and relentless

"ONE POWERFUL VOICE"

Wars Abroad, "To Eliminate," as who represent America's First Line of Defenses Against All Forms of Enemy Insurgency Aggressions of be they Foreign Enemy, Enemy Terrorist, or Domestic Criminal in nature.

War Is The Chosen Hell Of Our Own Making to what theme that This book is about concerning our life and death struggles of sacrifices engaged in the Military Service of our Nation here on the planet Earth; and about The Creator of All Things and the Nature of Good versus Evil present that has been written into it under The Creator's Hand of direction, this knowledge of Good and Evil, and to HIS Own logic in discerning Eternal Wisdom, as To Why that the subject of the Evil of War continues to exists unto Us of the Human Form to have to deal with, of HIS, The Creator's thoughts on the subject; concerning this Duality of Good versus Evil. To what that I am the sole Medium To in eternity of the event of this discussion. And humbly stated as that is; that I am certainly most appreciative to The Heavenly Father for HIS courtesy to have taken me into HIS Heart for the job and for the opportunity of Enlightening You, to serve in the cause of bringing about a solution to the problem of the Eternal Error, and of the Eternal Horror, OF WAR, that left unresolved will certainly result in THE ETERNAL PERDITION of Mankind in our own making; which The Creator has to suffer and along with everyone else of humanity being dragged into It, THE HELL Of Our Making. And, as The Creator Is Everything There Is, to be conceived of "As All One Thing," as "EVERYTHING" Exists in the Creator's Thought and to HIS the Will of HIS Imagination of the perceived life and circumstances of its existence, be they; male, female, or inanimate, Who are all The Mind Substance of The Creator, and the exact same Substance As The Creator, and WHO is not a Human Form, but Unfathomable.

The rendition of events of this book is set in the time period of the early 1980's. It was then as a period of Anarchy in American History, coined in hip phrase as Helter-Skelter, in the height The Drug War Epidemic sweeping across the Nation of The United States of America, of the American Version of it, Coast to Coast, involving us in a Drug-Chemical-Poison Warfare, and in particular at that time with the deadly drug-chemicals known as LSD, or Acid, and PCP Angel Dust, in the height of the Cold War with The Soviet Union and amid the combined turmoil of; a Class War, a Race War, various Ethnic Denominational Wars vying for their ascendency on American Soil, and a Social Consciousness Revolution involving Environmental Issues and for other Causes of Humanity of Social Equality, involving Trans Gender Identity Rights, Pornographic Immorality, and Women's Rights of Upheaval; and each using the Hue and Cry of their particular bent on warfare upon the Traditional America as justification for their Illegal Use of Drugs, Drug Dealing, Monetary and Political Corruption, Drug/Chemical Sabotage, Murder/Mayhem, and otherwise Foul Play Activities upon American Life that was just awakening from a Dark Age of an intractable Ignorant Obtuseness set in its ways of error being swept along in the Light of an Activism to do something about it, to right the wrongs of past social errors and oppressions, that was simultaneously being swept away by a lower nature depravity of Homosexuality and Immoral Sexual Pastime overall being induced by the Drug Heroin and other Drugs in Antithetical Arrangement to the Mainstream, either in direct use of or as a result of the effects of the

"ONE POWERFUL VOICE"

Heroin/Opium due to sabotage or from the outright contamination of the air supply around the users of the drug from nasal snorting termed Contact Effect; and otherwise of Its negative social influence upon society of such induced aberrant behavior becoming the norm to being taken up with by Peer Pressure. Most notably of these wars to express on and the most hapless to defend against was the War of The White Females who had allied with the cause of Negro Mulatto Males, the militant and hostile Half-Breeds of the society Underground Railroad style in their Use of Drugs and Drug Warfare in the Kitchen Against the unsuspecting White Males.

It was also a time of a Depressed Economy in the U.S., locally and nationally, and particularly in the aftermath of the Vietnam War with little work for the hapless citizenry except to work that lent power to the underworld sources of income; of Prostitution, Pornography, and Drug Dealing, that had moved-in and indeed that had always been there feeding the seedy underworld activities, of the underworld incomes to be derived there from drug dealing, prostitution, and pornography, that were being organized and taken advantage of be a certain Mafia and with its graft and corruption politically with Police Protection unto itself to protect itself.

And in total, truth be known, that this sort of thing as going on Region by Region upon the Nation of The United States in general that was already undermined and sapped of its strength to struggle by the Vietnam War. It was an age when the rebel Draft Dodger Hippies, the Counter-Culture Americans, and the arising Mafia Third World Populations Enemy At The Gate consisting of Drug Dealers and their Third World Drug Trafficking Suppliers holding the Power over the White Population who they supplied with their Illicit Drugs, and all together combined with the Pornographic Industry, held the sway here and occupied our America in surrender to the Third World Civil Rights Activist Drug Army whose alliances included along with its White American Partisan Sympathizers certain Ethnic American Groups vying for the Ascendency and Hegemony of the Elected Politics, and other Mafia Nationals from abroad in collusion to it and in forthright Take-Over of sadistic preying over the lives of the legitimate population, who were not safe anywhere from this Contract Style Warfare with its Region by Region Reciprocity, of being able to put the word out and to murder anyone simply by contacting their counterparts in a different region where there was a Drug and Porno Outlet in Operation; about these Immoral Degenerates of The Liberal Society who were Waging War Against the Legitimate Traditional Americans by means of Drug-Chemical Warfare and Economic Style Warfare fashion of intrigues; and of the Drug-Chemicals being perpetrated to make people feel that they are sick and mentally ill from naturally occurring causes, but which in fact were really being induced by the Drug-Chemical-Poison Methods of the Warfare; and to what that no one could, or still can in the present tense, complain of, due to The State Imposed Psychiatric Penalty, to Forced Commitment Without Due Process of Law in Psychiatric Facilities for the complaining, and to pharmacy induced disablement and unto death by Forced Treatment with Psychiatric Chemicals, for the mention of, or resulting from the outright effect of, the drug chemical warfare being perpetrated.

There was also a corrupt psychological domination over the legitimate population occurring, in moral sapping of the nation's energy, by forcing the acceptance of the pornographic rape and

"ONE POWERFUL VOICE"

plunder of the horrified population. Who were named, the combination of forces that had taken us over at the time, to be called "The New Regime;" which is another term for Fascism; and who that you were either involved with under domination of and to your death of peril, or an outsider to, and to your death of peril, either way, of exposure from harm of retaliation, as to the way of things as they really do exist in that reality.

At that time we were all that The Creator, Our Heavenly Father, and our Nation of The United States of America had against this onslaught of immoral anarchy and injustice, just the band of us Vietnam Veterans and depending upon who showed up on any particular day to count, more or less, give or take, who met each day at a Diners across America to converse and to plan out our agendas with no specific goals in mind other than for the love of just being together in the presence of The Holy Spirit that each of us felt with a fervor to do the bidding of regarding the required actions that were necessary to take in reaction to the events that were occurring then at a time in our American History when our prevailing homelessness allowed Life such Freedom of Idle Time to work on esoteric projects in the Holy Mission to look after the people, to care about them personally, and to heal their suffering; physically, mentally, and spiritually/emotionally, and to socially challenge the way that people think in their hatred, bigotry, and miss-treatment of others, on personal levels, and socially/economically of the larger issue involved, or the politics of the idea; and to offer consolation and advice to anyone who would take the time to listen; to either adapt gracefully to their travails and hardships that had befallen them in dignity, and/or, depending upon circumstances to help others to survive when in need of such assistance; and overall to make the necessary changes here on the Earth by changing the attitude of the people, for us to redeem the stature of humanity by and to survive here in the Good Grace of The Creator's Eyes to HIS terms of Dignity and Respect and Reverence and Cherishment for The Life we possess as Human Beings; to what end and purpose that this book is wholly devoted to accomplish; with sincerely and with all due respect, to have a Purpose Driven Life for our Nation Under God, Indivisible, with Liberty and Justice for all.

My position with you here is always that of a surviving Vietnam Veteran in Task Force Attachment to The Drug War and for the survival of our beleaguered Nation in approach. What you need to understand about The Drug War, and about the concept of Mafia Pornography coinciding to it, that is being allowed and even encourage to flourish here on both accounts; is that it involves us, the citizenry, in a Real War, attacking us with the condition of Drug Warfare, at close range involving our "Loved Ones" and "Family Members," and to the Physical and Mental Maladies that such a Warfare induces, and for the Psychiatric Intake of the population of that regard, to be finished off by, legally to their demise with Lethal Psychiatric Style Pharmacy while the Legal Authorities motivate the Afflicted Population into its Intake and "Look-On;" that, for the sake of our lives and the lives of our loved ones at stake, that needs to be intervened to properly and in a life-saving timely way; that we, as civilians, are unable to intervene to ourselves on our own to defend our lives about. And who therefore have to complain directly to the authorities, who in certain instances may be themselves involved with the criminal conspiracy.

And not only do we have to contend with the issue of Drugs and Pornography in their raw motives of viciousness of foul play occurring to us, but also which involves certain Ethnic and Racial

"ONE POWERFUL VOICE"

Motives For War using the corruptions and addictions of Drugs and Pornography as a War Machine against the innocent population, "to whittle us down," inch by inch, in a sustained and dramatically forcible Attack taking place at a glacier speed in slow motion over centuries, and against the larger mass of an unsuspecting host population in objective to defeat it by being systematically replacing it and which goes on barely perceptibly. That involves "The Intake" and "Initiation" of the population into the use of Hard Drugs and Pornography, (to what they have to prove "Their Loyalty To," by murdering a family member or friend, or loved one, by Drug Warfare, to obtain their drug supply, and otherwise to be blackmailed and coerced in extortion to the behest of their Drug Suppliers to do their bidding, whatever that may be, (as to indicate as to whoever is supplying their addicting drugs to someone, having The Power over the craving of their addictions, to involve them with The Active Warfare Arm of their Enemy Aggressions.

And on the topic of The Pornography Mafia that once they have anyone in their grip, (and they begin very young with the homosexuals on the young boys beginning at the age of puberty, and with the young girls too that way who their addict mothers initiate into child pornography,) to what that they become "The Property" of the Pornography Ring for all time to come after that and from what they can never escape from. So that, The Pornography Ring, (and who all know who each other are to themselves, but not so the "outsiders" to,) can essentially "gang-up" on anybody and do them in with foul play, and that is especially sinister and lethal to the households; the parents, relatives, and the siblings, involved with these individuals, to able to "Hit" with Drugs and Chemicals and Poisons, for the sake of the Ethnic or Racial Motives of the advancing Army. And that is particularly heart-felt regarding the plight of the young girls who are inducted and who become the prisoners of a Pornography Mafia when it comes time for them to fall in love and get married, who then have to "bump-off" their boyfriends or husbands at the behest.

And let us here have The Reasoning Right about The Miscegenation of the Black Heroin Mafia and concerning their sense of Inter-Racial Marriage being used as a means to Wage War By Assimilation of The White Race to create The Race of Mulattoes in The Islamic Design of Conquest, by coercive means of forcible aggressions against the White Females, involving their entrapment to the use of Heroin and Cocaine, and other means of White Slavery Prostitution, to attack the White Males by with Drugs and Poisons.

We are now entering an age where Pagan Idolatry has sway and we need presently to do something about it promptly before it ruins the youth of our era, in the meaning of its being a corruptive and perilous influence, any more than it has already. For, if humanity is to survive, it needs to be proud of itself to do so. And in being corrupt, as to say; depraved and immoral, indecent, and dishonest in our dealing, hurtful of others, and indifferent of stature in failing to combat these issues and prevent their harm to our society and our civilization Unto God The Creator, then we are doomed to failure.

Let us therefore, band together at this, those of us who are still willing to do so, for the good of our society, and for God our Creator to redeem HIS Heart, for the Love of Humanity in our doing, To Do Something About The Evils here as they present themselves to take our place beside The Creator proudly in eternity without begging forgiveness and without shame.

"ONE POWERFUL VOICE"

United States Constitution

Article. IV.

Section. 4. The United States shall guarantee to every State in the Union a Republican Form of Government, and shall protect each of them against Invasion; and on Application of the Legislature, or of the Executive (when the Legislature cannot be convened), against domestic Violence.

Amendment IV

The right of the people to be secure in their persons, houses, papers, and effects, against unreasonable searches and seizures, shall not be violated, and no Warrants shall issue, but upon probable cause, supported by Oath or affirmation, and particularly describing the place to be searched, and the persons or things to be seized.

Amendment V

No person shall be held to answer for a capital, or otherwise infamous crime, unless on a presentment or indictment of a Grand Jury, except in cases arising in the land or naval forces, or in the Militia, when in actual service in time of War or public danger; nor shall any person be subject of the same offence to be twice put in jeopardy of life or limb; nor shall be compelled in any criminal case to be a witness against himself, nor be deprived of life, liberty, or property, without due process of law; nor shall private property be taken for public use, without just compensation.

Amendment VI

In all criminal prosecutions, the accused shall enjoy the right to a speedy and public trial, by an impartial jury of the State and district wherein the crime shall have been committed, which district shall have been previously ascertained by law, and to be informed of the nature and cause against him; to have compulsory process for obtaining witnesses in his favor, and to have the Assistance of Counsel for his defense.

Amendment IX

The enumeration in the Constitution, of certain rights, shall not be construed to deny or disparage others retained by the people.

Amendment XIV

Section. 1. All persons born or naturalized in the United States, and subject to the jurisdiction thereof, are citizens of the United States and of the State wherein they reside. No State shall make of enforce any law which shall abridge the privileges or immunities of citizens of the United States; nor shall any State deprive any person of life, liberty, or property, without due process of law; nor deny to any person within its jurisdiction the equal protection of the laws.

"ONE POWERFUL VOICE"

(g) Veterans Administration *Special Consent Situations*: In addition to the other section requirements, additional protections are required in the following situations.

(1) No patient will undergo any unusual or extremely hazardous treatment or procedure, *e.g.,* that which might result in irreversible brain damage or sterilization, except as provided in this paragraph (g). Before treatment is initiated, the patient or surrogate must be given adequate opportunity to consult with independent specialists, legal counsel or other interested parties of his or her choosing. The patient's or surrogate's signature on a VA authorized consent form must be witnessed by someone who is not affiliated with the VA health-care facility, *e.g.,* spouse, legal guardian, or patient advocate. If a surrogate makes the treatment decision, a multi-disciplinary committee, appointed by the facility Director, must review that decision to ensure it is consistent with the patient's wishes or in his or her best interest. The committee functions as the patient's advocate and may not include members of the treatment team. The committee must submit its findings and recommendations in a written report to the facility Director. The Director may authorize treatment consistent with the surrogate's decision or request that a special guardian for health care be appointed to make the treatment decision.

(2) Administration of psychotropic medication to an involuntarily committed patient against his or her will must meet the following requirements. The patient or surrogate must be allowed to consult with independent specialists, legal counsel or other interested parties concerning the treatment with psychotropic medication. Any recommendation to administer or continue medication against the patient's or surrogate's will must be reviewed by a multi-disciplinary committee appointed by the facility Director for this purpose. This committee must include a psychiatrist or a physician who has psychopharmacology privileges. The facility Director must concur with the committee's recommendation to administer psychotropic medications contrary to the patient's or surrogate's wishes. Continued therapy with psychotropic medication must be reviewed every 30 days. The patient (or a representative on the patient's behalf) may appeal the treatment decision to a court of appropriate jurisdiction.

(3) If a proposed course of treatment or procedure involves approved medical research in whole or in part, the patient or representative shall be advised of this. Informed consent shall be obtained specifically for the administration or performance of that aspect of the treatment or procedure that involves research. Such consent shall be in addition to that obtained for the administration or performance of the non-research aspect of the treatment or procedure and must meet the requirements for informed consent set forth in 38 CFR Part 16, *Protection of Human Subjects.*

(4) Testing for Human Immunodeficiency Virus (HIV) must be voluntary and must be conducted only with the prior informed and (written) signature consent of the patient or surrogate. Patients who consent to testing for HIV must sign VA form 10–012, "Consent for HIV Antibody Testing." This form must be filed in the patient's medical record. Testing must be accompanied by pre-test and post-test counseling.

"ONE POWERFUL VOICE"

New York State Mental Hygiene Law

§ 9.07 Notice to all patients of their rights and of the availability of the mental hygiene legal service.

(a) Immediately upon the admission of any patient to a hospital or upon his conversion to a different status, the director shall inform the patient in writing of his status, including the section of this chapter under which he is hospitalized, and of his rights under this article, including the availability of the mental hygiene legal service. At any time thereafter, upon the request of the patient or of anyone on the patient's behalf, the patient shall be permitted to communicate with the mental hygiene legal service and avail himself of the facilities thereof.

(b) The director of every hospital shall post copies of a notice, in a form and manner to be determined by the commissioner, at places throughout the hospital where such notice will be conspicuous and visible to all patients, stating the following:

1. the availability of the mental hygiene legal service.

2. a general statement of the rights of patients under the various admission or retention provisions of this article.

3. the right of the patient to communicate with the director, the board of visitors, the commissioner of mental health, and the mental hygiene legal service.

§ 9.31 Involuntary admission on medical certification; patient's right to a hearing.

(a) If, at any time prior to the expiration of sixty days from the date of involuntary admission of a patient on an application supported by medical certification, he or any relative or friend or the mental hygiene legal service gives notice in writing to the director of request for hearing on the question of need for involuntary care and treatment, a hearing shall be held as herein provided. The patient or person requesting a hearing on behalf of the patient may designate the county where the hearing shall be held, which shall be either in the county where the hospital is located, the county of the patient's residence, or the county in which the hospital to which the patient was first admitted is located. Such hearing shall be held in the county so designated, subject to application by any interested party, including the director, for change of venue to any other county because of the convenience of parties or witnesses or the condition of the patient upon notice to the persons required to be served with notice of the patient's initial admission.

(b) It shall be the duty of the director upon receiving notice of such request for hearing to forward forthwith a copy of such notice with a record of the patient to the supreme court or the county court in the county designated by the applicant, if one be designated, or if no designation be made, then to the supreme court or the county court in the county where such hospital is located. A copy of such notice and record shall also be given the mental hygiene legal service.

(c) The court which receives such notice shall fix the date of such hearing at a time not later than five days from the date such notice is received by the court and cause the patient, any other person requesting the hearing, the director, the mental hygiene legal service, and such other persons as the court may determine to be advised of such date. Upon such date, or upon such other date to which the proceeding may be adjourned, the court shall hear testimony and examine the person alleged to be mentally ill, if it be deemed advisable in or out of court. If it be determined that the patient is in need of retention, the court shall deny the application for the patient's release. If the patient is in a psychiatric hospital maintained by a political subdivision of the state or in a general hospital the court, upon notice to the patient and the mental hygiene legal service and an opportunity to be heard, may order the patient transferred to the jurisdiction of the department for retention in a hospital operated by the state designated by the commissioner or to a private facility having an appropriate operating certificate for retention therein for the balance of the period for which the hospital is authorized to retain the patient. If it appears, however, that the relatives of the patient or a committee of his person are willing and able properly to care for him at some place other than a hospital, then, upon their written consent, the court may order the transfer of the patient to the care and custody of such relatives or such committee. If it be determined that the patient is not mentally ill or not in need of retention, the court shall order the release of the
patient.

(d) If the court shall order the release of the patient, such patient shall forthwith be released.

(e) The department or the director of the hospital authorized to retain or receive and retain such patient, as the case may be, shall be immediately furnished with a copy of the order of the court and, if a transfer is ordered, shall immediately make provisions for the transfer
 of such patient.

(f) The papers in any proceeding under this article which are filed with the county clerk shall be sealed and shall be exhibited only to the parties to the proceeding or someone properly interested, upon order of the court.

§ 9.39 Emergency admissions for immediate observation, care, and treatment.

(a) The director of any hospital maintaining adequate staff and facilities for the observation, examination, care, and treatment of persons alleged to be mentally ill and approved by the commissioner to receive and retain patients pursuant to this section may receive and retain therein as a patient for a period of fifteen days any person alleged to have a mental illness for which immediate observation, care, and treatment in a hospital is appropriate and which is likely to result in serious harm to himself or others. "Likelihood to result in serious harm" as used in this article shall mean:

1. substantial risk of physical harm to himself as manifested by threats of or attempts at suicide or serious bodily harm or other conduct demonstrating that he is dangerous to himself, or

2. a substantial risk of physical harm to other persons as manifested by homicidal or other violent behavior by which others are placed in reasonable fear of serious physical harm.

The director shall cause to be entered upon the hospital records the name of the person or persons, if any, who have brought such person to the hospital and the details of the circumstances leading to the hospitalization of such person.

The director shall admit such person pursuant to the provisions of this section only if a staff physician of the hospital upon examination of such person finds that such person qualifies under the requirements of this section. **Such person shall not be retained for a period of more than forty-eight hours unless within such period such finding is confirmed after examination by another physician who shall be a member of the psychiatric staff of the hospital.** Such person shall be served, at the time of admission, with written notice of his status and rights as a patient under this section. Such notice shall contain the patient's name. At the same time, such notice shall also be given to the mental hygiene legal service and personally or by mail to such person or persons, not to exceed three in number, as may be designated in writing to receive such notice by the person alleged to be mentally ill. **If at any time after admission, the patient, any relative, friend, or the mental hygiene legal service gives notice to the director in writing of request for court hearing on the question of need for immediate observation, care, and treatment, a hearing shall be held as herein provided as soon as practicable but in any event not more than five days after such request is received, except that the commencement of such hearing may be adjourned at the request of the patient.** It shall be the duty of the director upon receiving notice of such request for hearing to forward forthwith a copy of such notice with a record of the patient to the Supreme Court or county court in the county where such hospital is located. A copy of such notice and record shall also be given the mental hygiene legal service. The court which receives such notice shall fix the date of such hearing and cause the patient or other person requesting the hearing, the director, the mental hygiene legal service and such other persons as the court may determine to be advised of such date. Upon such date, or upon such other date to which the proceeding may be adjourned, the court shall hear testimony and examine the person alleged to be mentally ill, if it be deemed advisable in or out of court, and shall render a decision in writing that there is reasonable cause to believe that the patient has a mental illness for which immediate inpatient care and treatment in a hospital is appropriate and which is likely to result in serious harm to himself or others. If it be determined that there is such reasonable cause, the court shall forthwith issue an order authorizing the retention of such patient for any such purpose or purposes in the hospital for a period not to exceed fifteen days from the date of admission. Any such order entered by the court shall not be deemed to be an adjudication that the patient is mentally ill, but only a determination that there is reasonable cause to retain the patient for the purposes of this section.

(a), the filing of an application for involuntary admission on medical certification shall not delay or prevent the holding of the hearing.
(b) Within fifteen days of arrival at the hospital, if a determination is made that the person is not in need of involuntary care and treatment, he shall be discharged unless he agrees to remain as a voluntary or informal patient. If he is in need of involuntary care and treatment and does not agree to remain as a voluntary or informal patient, he may be retained beyond such fifteen day period only by admission to such hospital or another

appropriate hospital pursuant to the provisions governing involuntary admission on application supported by medical certification and subject to the provisions for notice, hearing, review, and judicial approval of retention or transfer and retention governing such admissions, provided that, for the purposes of such provisions, the date of admission of the patient shall be deemed to be the date when the patient was first received under this section. If a hearing has been requested pursuant to the provisions of subdivision

(c) If a person is examined and determined to be mentally ill the fact that such person suffers from alcohol or substance abuse shall not preclude commitment under this section.

§ 33.13 Clinical records; confidentiality.

(f) Any disclosure made pursuant to this section shall be limited to that information necessary in light of the reason for disclosure. Information so disclosed shall be kept confidential by the party receiving such information and the limitations on disclosure in this section shall apply to such party. **Except for disclosures made to the mental hygiene legal service, to persons reviewing information or records in the ordinary course of insuring that a facility is in compliance with applicable quality of care standards,** or to governmental agents requiring information necessary for payments to be made to or on behalf of patients or clients pursuant to contract or in accordance with law, a notation of all such disclosures shall be placed in the clinical record of that individual who shall be informed of all such disclosures upon request; provided, however, that for disclosures made to insurance companies licensed pursuant to the insurance law, such a notation need only be entered at the time the disclosure is first made.

§ 33.16 Access to clinical records.

(g) Challenges to accuracy. A qualified person may challenge the accuracy of information maintained in the clinical record and may require that a brief written statement prepared by him/her concerning the challenged information be inserted into the clinical record. This statement shall become a permanent part of the record and shall be released whenever the clinical record at issue is released. This subdivision shall apply only to factual statements and shall not include a provider's observations, inferences or conclusions. A facility may place reasonable restrictions on the time and frequency of any challenges to accuracy.

(h) Waivers void. Any agreement by an individual to waive any right to inspect, copy or seek correction of the clinical record as provided for in this section shall be deemed to be void as against public policy and wholly unenforceable.

(i) Disclosure. Nothing contained in this section shall restrict, expand or in any way limit the disclosure of any information pursuant to articles twenty-three, thirty-one and forty-five of the civil practice law and rules or section six hundred seventy-seven of the county law.

(j) Proceedings. No proceeding shall be brought or penalty assessed, except as provided for in this section, against a facility, which in good faith, denies access to a clinical record.

(k) Immunity from liability. No facility, practitioner, treating practitioner, mental health practitioner or clinical records access review committee member shall be subjected to civil liability arising solely from granting or providing access to any clinical record in accordance with this section.

9480 Princeton Square Blvd. S., #815
Jacksonville, FL 32256
February 14, 2009

Ira Katz, MD, PhD
Deputy Chief Patient Care Services
Officer for Mental Health
Veterans Health Administration
810 Vermont Avenue, N.W.
Washington, D.C. 20420

Dear Doctor Katz,

Thank you in deepest gratitude for your most encouraging letter of February 6, 2009 in reply to my inquiries of Psychiatric Revue to the former Secretary of Veterans Affairs Doctor James B. Peake concerning the conduct of care and treatment for our returning home from combat American Veterans, present and past, as it relates to the harmful and damaging effects of Anti-Psychotic Medications, and for the easing of the prevailing Stigma associated to the Diagnosis and Treatment of Mental Disorders; to its being legally clarified; particularly as to what constitutes a Legal Diagnosis and concerning a person's Right To Refuse Treatment, and with appropriate protection of Legal Counsel to be provided for by The Veterans Administration, as to The Rights of our Veterans to be covered under the Ninth and Fourteenth Amendments by Legal Due Process in the event of their being Psychiatrically Accused, and to their Safeguard of Beneficial Treatment.

I was personally, and expressing for the behalf of the entirety of the remaining Veterans of The Vietnam War Organization, (68,000 of whom have committed suicide, of the over 1,000,000 of whom who were made into psychiatrics, in their own eyes, and in the eyes of society,) and for all Veterans, as a body of men collectively, very impressed with your detailed and clarifying letter in heartfelt sincerity for the burden of your position relating to your duties of responsibility in care to the lives, and livelihoods, and families involved, of our Veterans at issue for the present status of care and treatment of; Post Traumatic Stress Disorder (PTSD), Traumatic Brain Injury (TBI), Major Depression, types of Mental Disorders such as Schizophrenia and Bipolar Illness, Mood and Anxiety Disorders, and for other forms of Stress Related Conditions as they manifest in the Addictive Disorders of Substance Abuse; to thank you for your personal time and assistance in assurances to us that our Veterans will be receiving the very best Health Care possible throughout our Nation's Veterans Administration Health Care Facilities, and as you stated for so nobly for in your own words in closing to us, to: "Be assured that VA health care providers share your concerns about the stigma that has been associated with mental disorders and the importance of eliminating that stigma. Also be assured that VA providers take every care to prescribe only those medications that are necessary for improvement of the patient and only for so long as those medications are needed."

We do know the very difficult position you face with these issues, the hardest part being to try and change the current errors involving psychiatric stemming from the past which the government doesn't want to admit to having errors with, (in face saving and involving litigation,) and so which continue on about themselves in that vein of being made excuses for remaining uncorrected. But it occurs to me that we are suffering here to our end from a misunderstanding of the terms in our purpose of objectives in not being able to get through to an appropriate response from The Veterans Administration about.

"ONE POWERFUL VOICE"

This is a very old case concerning the destructive treatment of our Veterans with Anti-Psychotic Drugs, and for the removal, or easing of, the tortured stigma associated with the idea of being Mental Ill. Everyone knows that the genuine issue of insanity does exist in the society, of those who portray irrational and oftentimes violent behavior to be severely dealt with; and of necessity, who are therefore deemed to be that way by the Courts and placed in the protective custody of the State confined to Mental Asylums. And which involves also of those as well, who are mentally defective, mentally deficient, brain damaged, and retarded, to be cared for by the State, under the wording of Parens Patriae, or Wards of the State. As into what generalized setting, termed "Mental Health," in the eyes of society, and in terms of their own Self-Esteem, are placed the precious lives of our Veterans who have survived mortal combat in the service of their country, in the supreme offering of their lives, to return here with Service Connected and Combat Stress Related Emotional Problems and Disorders to be treated for and assisted to recover from, and only to their being placed in with and alongside of these truly mentally ill, mentally defective persons, who then that the public presumes our Veterans to be, and to our Veterans then being treated as presumed to be insane, who are otherwise normal and only needing temporary assistance to recover, and to their being undifferentiated by treatment with the Neuroleptic, Anti-Psychotic, Strong Tranquillizers, and to their utter ruination.

And with that being said, the problem is and still remains; that there is more to this issue of Mental Health Psychiatric, (on the corrupt and dirty maniacal business side of the Medical/Pharmaceutical Psychiatric Industry, (that has a Captive Market in which a person perversely has NO Rights whatsoever over their Diagnosis, Commitment, and Treatment to occur under the heading of Mental Hygiene Law, and having also to do with social fears, biases, and ignorance,) some of it involving the VA to correct, and some of it lying beyond the scope of The VA in the civilian sector pertaining for the Courts, local Mental Health Centers, local Hospitals, and State Psychiatric Facilities, incumbent up to the already beleaguered and overworked staffing of the VA to oversight and contain.

That we specifically requested from Secretary Peake to elaborate on as to whether or not that he personally approved of the Anit-Psychotic, Neuropleptice, Psychotropic, Strong Tranquillizer type pharmacy chemicals being given for treatment to our Veterans, whether voluntarily to be taken under advisement of physician and regardless of their being administered with informed consent, or otherwise of the "Forced Treatment" issue, as to any of these prevailing drugs being declared to be Safe and Beneficial for our Veterans to take, or otherwise to be a harmful nature? As I previously named for Dr. Peake: such as; Thorazine, Prolixin, Navane, Trilifon, Lithuim, Loxitane, *Congentin, (which is used to control the Tremors, or Parkinson-like symptom, of the other Anti-Psychotic drugs being listed,) and others of that Classification; for what you stated for in your letter in your response to us; "that no medication is without potential Side-Effects."

But we are not talking here about "dry mouth," or "constipation," with being carefully weighed of their side effects over in "Informed Consent" by the patient to take, but for the catastrophic ruination of a person's whole and complete physiognomy, physically, mentally, emotionally, and spiritually to the gloom of suicide. To what that there is no one naïve about this situation is there, in consultation with The Physicians' Desk Reference (PDR), and concerning the personal testimony of persons who have experienced these drugs, (which you term as "Clinical Trails," which translates over to direct Experimentation with Human Subjects as Guinea Pigs, to where you derived your wordings of Effects, Side-Effects, Adverse Effects, and Contra-indications to be used in your Clinical Practice Guidelines;) which besides of what, that these drugs, and all of them, are "excruciatingly painful to endure," what the PDR refers to as "Uncomfortable States of Being," and which also cause; many other torturous disabling Adverse Effects.

"ONE POWERFUL VOICE"

Which brings me to the other point in matter of Mis-Communication with you that you don't really understand these drugs other than for their description in the PDR and Clinical Practice Guidelines and need to experience the actual effects yourself, as the Veterans have, to have a real and honest evaluation of what they are really experiencing, starting with 200 mg of Thorazine over an extended length in period of time for at least a month or two, as our Veterans are being "Treated With," and have "Suffered," in the past to be returned to society on to commit suicide from the effects of, to really evaluate and understand our denunciation of them. Which I know you are not going to do, because in your intelligent mind you know that these drugs, as you term to be "Medications," would cause you severe harm and disable you. These are not "feel good" types of drugs. The primary purpose of these drugs; which are used in the treatment of so called Mental Disorders, is to "restrain and destroy people;" and which renders them unable and unfit to assume their normal functions in society. Which in a matter of concurrence to you and involving to the hopelessly insane, as you indicated for about in your letter, that these drugs would indeed prove to be of beneficial value to, if a person is screaming lunatic, but these drugs will destroy the normal person and that they are Not To Be Approved For our Veterans to take for temporary Stress and Emotional Disorders and for other mental disturbances associated with combat; which need to be taken care of with; Best Rest Convalescence, Counseling, Therapy, and Sound Nutrition, in a quite setting to be called "Seclusion/Recovery," no longer the Psyche Ward. Mental Health as well, with its stigma of inferior irrationality presumed, needs to be renamed to, "Professional Services;" which would include for Guidance Counseling and Therapy in a Benign and Beneficial Setting.

Furthermore, it is not true and you cannot lawfully and ethically tell patients that they have to take Anti-Psychotic Drugs for the rest of their lives to replace missing enzymes secretions or a genetic deficiency, the lack of which is causing a person's mental illness, in similarity as to how; Thyroidism, Diabetes, and Hypertension are perceived, as according to the PDR Manual there is no evidence to support this claim. Also you legally and ethically cannot "hold the threat" of indefinite commitment confinement over someone, allowed for under Mental Hygiene Law, unless they agree to voluntarily comply with their treatment plan to take the Anti-Psychotic Drugs prescribed for them by the medical industry. And unfortunately however that "Forced Treatment" is "at all times" the way of psychiatric warehousing; which you state in your letter only occurs; "in the rare instance in an emergency situation when a patient is presenting an active danger to themselves or others," that is not true. To what matter of Forced Treatment with deadly drugs that our Veterans need Legal Clarification from the VA to protect themselves from.

Most Sincerely,
Gary L. Koniz
Veterans of the Vietnam War

"ONE POWERFUL VOICE"

9480 Princeton Square Blvd. S., #815
Jacksonville, FL 32256
December 11, 2008

Robert S. Mueller, III - Director
Federal Bureau Of Investigation
935 Pennsylvania Avenue, N.W.
Washington, D.C. 20535-0001

Dear Director Mueller:

   This case needs resolution, as it Involves the returning Combat Veterans from the Nation's Wars presently being fought in Afghanistan, and Iraq, (who are being ill-advised in massive numbers of psychiatric intake,) and stemming through to the duration of the returning Veterans of The Vietnam War that way, (as well also in massive numbers,) and to their aggressive intake into The V.A.'s Psychiatric System by intensive outreach into the population on the part of The Veterans Administration to bring as many Veterans in as possible, (in feigned paternal approach,) in Conspiratorial Evaluation to be "Screened" and "Diagnosed" for Psychiatric Conditions, and thereunto to be "Treated," (across the board in huge numbers,) with Deadly Drug Chemical Agents known as Anti-Psychotic "Psychotropic Pharmacy;" being "Prescribed" under the guise of "Beneficial Treatment," or to the outright Forcing of Treatment with these Chemicals, being perpetrated under the fraudulently Misleading Captioning of Medication, and to the nature of **War Crimes in Criminal Malfeasance**, without any "Due Process," and without "Genuine Informed Consent." And to the American Public being misled (who are told that the Veterans need their Medication in order to live safely in society; what is a deception and not the case.)

   And who society holds therefore, the Veterans, in the judgment of society thereafter to be unaccepted as Psychiatrically Defective, in psychologically maiming judgment for the labeling of them in that way, of their being thought of as, non-compos-mentis, "Trained Killers," who are unpredictable and unsafe to be around, of an extremely violent nature to be feared; being fed by Media Propaganda in the nature of the public's mass hysteria over the subject of war; and made worse in the instances of these Veterans, to being thought of as irrational in their derangement to be disposed of with Thorazine Treatment and/or with similar chemicals of a maiming nature in the name of Treatment; and whose only basis is, not to cure in a therapeutic sense, but to cripple and to maim and to render incapacitated; to be left unable to be of a threat in the vegetative state; to drool, and to suffer cramps and tremors of the extremities, with gnarled hands and feet, sexually impotent, incontinent of bladder and bowel, and depressed, **in that meaning of medication**; that is not treatment at all, but the **foul murder of our Veterans**; who the V.A. maintains they are treating for rehabilitation and recovery, but who are not returned back to society as normal healthy human beings in a beneficial transition; but who The V.A. routinely disables to abandon to social alienation, joblessness, homelessness, and ultimately to their deaths by suicide. And to point-out to you also, that there are numerous "Subversive Forces" who are making use of The Psychiatric Intake of our Veterans to ensure their removal as a threat to them. Pornography and Drug Mafia Motives and Ethnic/Racial Wars would constitute such Forces,

Most Respectfully,
Gary L. Koniz - Corresponding
Veterans Of The Vietnam War

"ONE POWERFUL VOICE"

9480 Princeton Square Blvd. S., #815
Jacksonville, FL 32256
June 8, 2013

Dr. Dillie Warren, Ph.D
V.A. Staff Psychologist
V.A. Compensation & Pension Clinic
5415 SW 64th Street
Gainesville, FL 32608

Dear Dr. Warren:

I am writing cover some issues with you involving the denial of my claim for Compensation Damages under 38 U.S.C. 1151, in V.A. Liability for Inappropriate Diagnosis and Thorazine Treatment resulting in very serious Debilitating Conditions occurring to me. And as I went over the substances of my claim with you on V.A. Negligence I am hoping that you will be able to redress these matters before the Court of Appeals for Veterans Claims convenes to hear the case.

(1.) That I Was Not Complaining about any "On-Going" Condition of PTSD or other Disability; (which the Examiner seems to think I was;) but rather that my claim was for Damages Suffered during the time-frame of my injury at the V.A. Hospital in Albany, NY in 1982, and for the years afterwards; and that I was suffering from PTSD at that time and was improperly and illegally diagnosed with the stigma of Paranoid Schizophrenia and did not receive the proper professional care and treatment from the V.A. that was entitled to which resulted in my suffering severe and grievous metabolic damages from the Chemical Thorazine, (to be proved about in an elaborate brief,) that I was Force Ordered To Take on the day of my arrival at the V.A. without sufficient assessment of my condition; that caused me to suffer the gainful loss of my Professional Income, and that left me below the Economic Threshold to survive, disabled and homeless, dependent on the charity of friends and family, unable to work; to have money for rent, transportation, food, clothing, and necessities. To point-out; that is really Does Matter if the Thorazine caused me to suffer the "Unemployability" I am claiming and to lose my way in life even if it was for the duration of months into years of being "Unable To Work," having long-term Effects; of it being Impossible To Negotiate from "Beneath A Functioning Economic Threshold," even if recovered.

(2.) That the anonymous "Examiner" who denied my claim, did so without my being able "To Confront" the Negative and Erroneous Testimony about me; which I specifically told you about and asked for Due Process to be able to Review My Records in the presence of Legal Counsel in order to Correct the Gross Errors of Malicious Hearsay Testimony and Malpractice Fabrications.

Most Sincerely,
Gary. L. Koniz
Veterans of the Vietnam War

"ONE POWERFUL VOICE"

9480 Princeton Square Blvd. S., #815
Jacksonville, FL 32256
April 19, 2013

Re: VA File No. 115365132 / 24 891 327

Department Of Veterans Affair
Special Ops
PO Box 465
St. Petersburg, FL 33744

Dear Department of Veterans Affairs,

Respectfully. I am sorry to concern you with the misunderstanding here regarding the VA information letter, dated April 12, 2013, soliciting information from my current employer, DeerCreek Country Club, regarding my urinary incontinence condition in continuance of the disability incurred from the effect of the Thorazine Treatment that I was forced to undergo while in the care of the VA Treatment Facility in Albany, NY on the dates from April through May of 1982. I know that you are overloaded with work and have many more worthy cases than my own to attend to. However I am therefore most grateful for your understanding in this matter.

The point with my case is, (to which I am under a doctor' care for and taking an expensive prescribed medication called Rappaflow what helps a great deal;) but as I told you in my last correspondence on the matter that I have to continually go to the bathroom every thirty minutes or so with my condition but that I am able to get away with it, on the QT, by stepping into the woods discretely while working out on the golf course if no one is watching, and otherwise to have to use the restroom facilities in that regard. I have been told not to urinate in the woods as a condition of continuing employment there but I have to urinate in the woods anyway, as there are only two restrooms out on the course and they are often a long ways off from the site where I am having to work. When I feel that I have to go, I have five minutes to get to a place, either in the woods, or at a facility, before it becomes very painful to hold and starts on its own to come out to wet my pants. This is not something that I would otherwise want to bring to the attention of my employer, (in the manner of asking them to fill out your questionnaire, which does not apply to me anyway, as I am still in their employ,) about the number of times that "I Have To" go to the bathroom, which would put my current position, (and a blessed paying job for me,) in jeopardy.

So I am returning the form you sent as "Non Applicable" in this current setting. However, there are many jobs which I would not be able to do with this condition of having to endure prolonged periods of time without benefit of being able to go the bathroom, (as I stated in my initial correspondence,) as the urine becomes extremely painful to hold and starts to come out, and if I try to hold it past that painful point, when I do get to go it won't come out at all. I have to center my life around the urgent availability of a bathroom, and I am up at frequent intervals during the night to go. And so that although I am able to work with the disability (somewhat

"ONE POWERFUL VOICE"

carefully worded on the QT) in my present setting of employment, close to relief in the woods, it is not otherwise the case, in situations of driving on the road, flying in a light aircraft, working in a factory or on an assembly line, waiting on customers doing retail, and so on involving many other jobs, where urinary relief is not available; that it is my disability (directly resulting from VA Thorazine Treatment.) Here I will cite from The Physicians' Desk Reference on the subject.

For VA Healthcare Professionals and Legal Counsel Review

Applies to chlorpromazine: compounding powder, injectable solution, oral capsule extended release, oral concentrate, oral syrup, oral tablet, rectal suppository.

- twitching or uncontrollable movements of your eyes, lips, tongue, face, arms, or legs;
- **<u>Memory loss</u> and <u>amnesia</u> have also been reported.**
- tremor (uncontrolled shaking), drooling, trouble swallowing, problems with balance or walking;
- feeling restless, jittery, or agitated;
- feeling like you might pass out;
- seizure (black-out or convulsions);
- nausea upper stomach pain, itching, and jaundice (yellowing of the skin or eyes);
- pale skin, easy bruising or bleeding, fever, sore throat, flu symptoms;
- high fever, stiff muscles, confusion, sweating, fast or uneven heartbeats, rapid breathing;
- unusual thoughts or behavior;
- decreased night vision, tunnel vision, watery eyes, increased sensitivity to light;
- **prostatism, frequent urination, urinating less than usual or not at all;**
- enlarged testicles in males, joint pain or swelling with fever, swollen glands, muscle aches, chest pain, vomiting, and patchy skin color; or
- slow heart rate, weak pulse, fainting, slow breathing (breathing may stop).

Less serious side effects of chlorpromazine may include:

- dizziness, drowsiness, anxiety, sleep problems (insomnia);
- breast swelling or discharge;
- changes in menstrual periods;
- weight gain, swelling in your hands or feet;
- dry mouth or stuffy nose, blurred vision;
- constipation; or
- impotence, trouble having an orgasm.

This is not a complete list of side effects and others may occur. Call your doctor for medical advice about side effects.

General

General side effects have included cases of muscle necrosis after repeated injections of chlorpromazine (the active ingredient contained in Thorazine) The low pH of parenteral chlorpromazine solutions may be responsible for the necrosis. Subcutaneous injections should be avoided.

Nervous system

Nervous system side effects are common and include sedation, drowsiness and rarely seizures. Tardive dyskinesia, dystonia, pseudoparkinsonism, increased neuromuscular excitability, and the neuroleptic malignant syndrome have also been reported.

The drowsiness associated with chlorpromazine therapy may resolve after several doses.

Tardive dyskinesia involves involuntary, dyskinetic, repetitive movements and may be more common in elderly women receiving chlorpromazine. Tardive dyskinesia may be irreversible and is related to both the duration of therapy and the total amount of drug consumed. Frequent discontinuation and resumption of therapy may predispose patients to the development of tardive dyskinesia.

Dystonias frequently involve tongue protrusions, muscle rigidity, torticollis, and opisthotonos. Dystonias usually resolve after neuroleptic discontinuation, but may require antihistamine and antiparkinsonian therapy if symptoms are severe or if respiration is compromised. Treatment of dystonic reactions and extrapyramidal effects, in addition to general supportive measures, may include judicious use of one or more of the following: benztropine, trihexyphenidyl, biperiden or diphenhydramine.

Pseudoparkinsonism involves flat facies, pill-rolling tremor, shuffling gait, and cogwheel rigidity. Pseudoparkinsonism symptoms may respond to judicious use of one or more of the following: benztropine, trihexyphenidyl, biperiden or diphenhydramine.

Fever, altered consciousness, autonomic dysfunction and muscle rigidity are the hallmarks of the neuroleptic malignant syndrome. The neuroleptic malignant syndrome is associated with a case fatality rate of about 20%. Immediate discontinuation of neuroleptic therapy and intensive monitoring and supportive care are indicated.

Seizures associated with chlorpromazine have been reported, but many of the reports involve patients with a history of seizures or underlying organic brain disease.

Psychiatric

Psychiatric side effects including psychotic symptoms, excitability, and reversible catatonic states have been reported. There may also be rare paradoxical psychiatric effects with chlorpromazine (the active ingredient contained in Thorazine) therapy.

Hematologic

"ONE POWERFUL VOICE"

Hematologic side effects have included reversible agranulocytosis (which occurs in about one out of 10,000 patients). Hemolytic anemia, thrombocytopenia, and eosinophilia have also been reported.

A 40% decrease in platelet counts was observed in 21% of patients on chlorpromazine in one study. The thrombocytopenia persisted for up to 6 months after discontinuation of chlorpromazine.

Some clinicians have suggested that any sign or symptom of infection in patients on chlorpromazine therapy should be evaluated with a complete blood count and differential.

Cardiovascular

Cases of cardiopulmonary arrest in otherwise healthy young patients have been reported rarely. Edema in association with chlorpromazine (the active ingredient contained in Thorazine) therapy has also been reported rarely.

Hypotension is more likely in patients with intravenous administration.

Cardiovascular side effects have included profound orthostatic hypotension and reflex tachycardia. These effects may subside after several doses. Chlorpromazine has mild negative inotropic properties, which may be important in some patients with a history of congestive heart failure. ECG changes include prolongation of the PR interval, prolongation of QTc segments, diffuse T-wave flattening, and ST segment depression.

Hypersensitivity

Rare cases of anaphylaxis, toxic epidermal necrolysis, and angioedema have been reported. A case of contact dermatitis associated with crushed chlorpromazine (the active ingredient contained in Thorazine) tablets has been reported.

Hypersensitivity side effects to chlorpromazine are usually mild and presents as an urticarial rash. Pustular eruptions, severe anaphylaxis and angioedema have been reported rarely.

Hepatic

Chlorpromazine- induced cholestatic jaundice usually resolves without sequelae 2 to 8 weeks after discontinuation of the drug. However, severe and prolonged jaundice, resembling primary biliary cirrhosis, has been reported in a minority of cases. The prognosis of this condition is generally favorable. However, progression to biliary cirrhosis has been reported.

A case of chronic active hepatitis associated with chlorpromazine (the active ingredient contained in Thorazine) has been reported. A Danish study has reported 5 cases of fatal hepatitis associated with chlorpromazine. A recent study of 10,502 users of chlorpromazine has reported 14 illnesses which were considered to be compatible with drug induced liver disease. The frequency of drug induced liver disease in that group was 1.3 per 1,000 users of chlorpromazine.

"ONE POWERFUL VOICE"

Monitoring of liver function tests during chlorpromazine therapy may be helpful in patients with liver disease.

Hepatic side effects including mild reversible elevations of liver function tests have been reported. Cholestatic jaundice has been reported in as many as 1% of patients taking chlorpromazine, however many clinicians believe that the reported frequency of cholestatic jaundice may be referable to impurities in early formulations of the drug. Severe hepatitis has also been reported.

Immunologic

In one study 35% of patients on chlorpromazine (the active ingredient contained in Thorazine) tested positive for the lupus anticoagulant. In another study of 64 patients on chlorpromazine, 45% tested positive for the lupus anticoagulant, 39% for positive ANA titers, 34% for the anticardiolipin antibody, 50% for rheumatoid factor, and 27% for an elevation in IgM.

A case of Henoch-Schonlein purpura has been associated with chlorpromazine.

Chlorpromazine- induced antiphospholipid antibody syndrome developed in a patient after taking chlorpromazine 100 mg daily for a year. Symptoms included encephalopathy, seizures (i.e., generalized tonic-clonic, status epilepticus), confusion, and drowsiness. All symptoms resolved following discontinuation of chlorpromazine.

Immunologic side effects have included a variety of adverse immunologic effects including antiphospholipid antibody syndrome which appear to be related to the total dose consumed.

Gastrointestinal

Gastrointestinal side effects including dry mouth, constipation, and less commonly, diarrhea have been reported.

The gastrointestinal side effects may result from the anticholinergic properties of chlorpromazine.

Endocrine

Endocrine side effects including hyperglycemia, hyperprolactinemia, galactorrhea, amenorrhea, and the syndrome of inappropriate secretion of antidiuretic hormone have been reported.

Dermatologic

Dermatologic side effects including skin hyperpigmentation has been reported in patients after long-term chlorpromazine (the active ingredient contained in Thorazine) therapy (doses of 500 to 1,500 mg over 2 to 3 years). The hyperpigmentation commonly presents as a gray- blue discoloration in exposed areas, including the eyelids.

The hyperpigmentation associated with chlorpromazine therapy appears to be reversible in some patients after discontinuation of chlorpromazine and initiation of alternative neuroleptic therapy.

"ONE POWERFUL VOICE"

Contact dermatitis has been reported in a person who crushed chlorpromazine tablets for a patient. Leukocytoclastic vasculitis associated with Henoch-Schonlein purpura has been reported during chlorpromazine use.

Genitourinary

Genitourinary side effects including enlargement of the prostate gland, urinary retention, impotence and priapism have been associated with chlorpromazine (the active ingredient contained in Thorazine) therapy.

Ocular

Chlorpromazine may induce lens and corneal pigmentary changes which have produced visual impairment such as halos around lights, hazy vision, photophobia, and watering eyes. One case of orbital cellulitis has been reported following the retrobulbar injection of chlorpromazine (the active ingredient contained in Thorazine) for intractable pain in a patient with irreversible blindness.

Ocular side effects have been reported primarily in patients receiving chlorpromazine for two or more years in dosages of 300 mg daily or more. Ocular changes are characterized by deposition of fine particulate matter in the lens and cornea. In more advanced cases, star- shaped opacities have also been reported in the anterior portion of the lens. The nature of the deposits has not been reported. Anterior capsular cataracts have also been reported. Some visual impairment has been reported in a small number of patients with more severe ocular changes. Epithelial keratopathy and pigmentary retinopathy have also been reported. Reports suggest that the eye lesions may regress after withdrawal of the drug.

My case with the VA is, to reiterate; (and I know that there are many more serious cases than mine to feel for;) but I lost twenty years (20 years,) of my life due to the **ruinous effects** of the Thorazine Treatment that I improperly received, and from the **stigma of Psychiatric Labeling**, that robbed me of my life's vigor and positive self-image of personal identity to be able to function effectively in society. It is only by the Grace of God and the love a kind woman, my wife, that I survived, where many of our comrades in arms did not, dying untimely deaths or committing suicide. I am 67 years old now and cannot be expected to do the heavy physical labor that I do each and every day forever. Social Security pays me $1,015 a month after taxes which is not enough for me to live on. I am asking the VA for polite recognition of my current condition of incontinence, and for Legitimate Legal Compensation for my injuries suffered (which robbed me of the time I needed to be working and saving money for my retirement,) as a direct result of the Thorazine Treatment that was Force Administered to myself and many others.

Most Sincerely,

Gary L. Koniz
Veterans Of The Vietnam War

"ONE POWERFUL VOICE"

NEW YORK, Nov. 13, 2007

Suicide Epidemic Among Veterans

A CBS News Investigation Uncovers A Suicide Rate For Veterans
Twice That Of Other Americans

By Armen Keteyian

(CBS) They are the casualties of wars you don't often hear about - soldiers who die of self-inflicted wounds. Little is known about the true scope of suicides among those who have served in the military. After witnessing the carnage and bloodshed of war, many veterans return home with mental problems that place them at high risk of suicide. The No. 1 problem facing vets of Afghanistan and Iraq will be mental health. Soldiers returning from war are at risk of suicide linked to post-traumatic stress disorder.

But a five-month CBS News investigation discovered data that shows a startling rate of suicide, what some call a hidden epidemic, Chief Investigative Reporter Armen Keteyian reports exclusively.

Keteyian spoke with the families of five former soldiers who each served in Iraq - only to die battling an enemy they could not conquer. Their loved ones are now speaking out in their names. They survived the hell that's Iraq and then they come home only to lose their life.

Beyond the individual loss, it turns out little information exists about how widespread suicides are among these who have served in the military. There have been some studies, but no one has ever counted the numbers nationwide.

Sen. Patty Murray, D-Wash., is a member of the <u>Veterans Affairs Committee</u>.

"Nobody wants to tally it up in the form of a government total, because they don't want the true numbers of casualties to really be known. If you're just looking at the overall number of veterans themselves who've committed suicide, we have not been able to get the numbers," Murray said.

CBS News' investigative unit wanted the numbers, so it submitted a Freedom of Information Act request to the Department of Defense asking for the numbers of suicides among all service members for the past 12 years.

Four months later, they sent CBS News a document, showing that between 1995 and 2007, there were almost 2,200 suicides. That's 188 last year alone. But these numbers included only "active duty" soldiers.

CBS News went to the <u>Department of Veterans Affairs</u>, where Dr. Ira Katz is head of mental health.

"There is no epidemic in suicide in the VA, but suicide is a major problem," he said.

"ONE POWERFUL VOICE"

Why hasn't the VA done a national study seeking national data on how many veterans have committed suicide in this country?

"That research is ongoing," he said.

So CBS News did an investigation - asking all 50 states for their suicide data, based on death records, for veterans and non-veterans, dating back to 1995. Forty-five states sent what turned out to be a mountain of information. And what it revealed was stunning.

In 2005, for example, in just those 45 states, there were at least 6,256 suicides among those who served in the armed forces. That's 120 each and every week, in just one year.

Dr. Steve Rathbun is the acting head of the Epidemiology and Biostatistics Department at the University of Georgia. CBS News asked him to run a detailed analysis of the raw numbers that we obtained from state authorities for 2004 and 2005.

It found that veterans were more than twice as likely to commit suicide in 2005 than non-vets. (Veterans committed suicide at the rate of between 18.7 to 20.8 per 100,000, compared to other Americans, who did so at the rate of 8.9 per 100,000.)

One age group stood out. Veterans aged 20 through 24, those who have served during the war on terror. They had the highest suicide rate among all veterans, estimated between two and four times higher than civilians the same age. (The suicide rate for non-veterans is 8.3 per 100,000, while the rate for veterans was found to be between 22.9 and 31.9 per 100,000.)

"Wow! Those are devastating," said Paul Sullivan, a former VA analyst who is now an advocate for veterans rights from the group Veterans For Common Sense.

"Those numbers clearly show an epidemic of mental health problems," he said.

"We are determined to decrease veteran suicides," Dr. Katz said.

"One hundred and twenty a week. Is that a problem?" Keteyian asked.

"You bet it's a problem," he said.

"Is it an epidemic?"

"Suicide in America is an epidemic, and that includes veterans," Katz said.

Sen. Murray said the numbers CBS News uncovered are significant:
"These statistics tell me we've really failed people that served our country."

Do these numbers serve as a wake-up call for this country?

"ONE POWERFUL VOICE"

"If these numbers don't wake up this country, nothing will," she said. "We each have a responsibility to the men and women who serve us aren't lost when they come home."

An update: The chairman of the Senate Veterans' Affairs Committee, Sen. Daniel Akaka, D-Hawaii, responded to the CBS News story Tuesday.

"The report that the rate of suicide among veterans is double that of the general population is deeply troubling and simply unacceptable. I am especially concerned that so many young veterans appear to be taking their own lives. For too many veterans, returning home from battle does not bring an end to conflict. There is no question that action is needed."

When CBS News began looking into veteran suicide, we found that no federal organization or agency tracks the number of veteran suicides nationally. To our knowledge, no one is keeping count. We wanted to know how many veterans are committing suicide nationwide and how the rate of suicide for veterans compares to non-veterans.

Looking for Data

CBS News first approached the Department of Defense (DoD), the Department of Veterans Affairs (VA), the National Center for Health Statistics (NCHS) and the Centers for Disease Control and Prevention (CDC) in June and July asking for suicide data for those who have served in the military.

We were told the DoD only tracks suicides committed by military personnel who are on active duty. The VA said they had no suicide data on file at the time. The NCHS (which is the federal organization responsible for maintaining most of the nation's health statistics and is a center within the CDC) does not monitor the military status of those who have committed suicide. Finally, the CDC's Injury Center (also known as the National Center for Injury Prevention and Control) started a program in 2003 called the National Violent Death Reporting System which has collected some veteran suicide data from state death records but does not currently have nationwide counts. The CDC told CBS News that the information they have about veteran suicides "cannot be generalized to draw conclusions about the entire country."

Finding the Numbers

CBS News learned that state vital statistics departments keep count of suicides based on information obtained from death records which can be separated by military status.

Therefore, over the course of five months, we contacted all 50 states asking them to provide us with their suicide data. Most of the states were able to tally the counts from their databases while some states had to go through death records counting suicides by hand.

Some states charged us a fee for the time and labor involved in gathering the data. In total, CBS News paid about $3,000 in processing fees to the states.

"ONE POWERFUL VOICE"

Privacy Issues

Obtaining suicide data from the states involved more than just a basic public records request.

Initially, several states refused to provide the data to CBS News for privacy concerns. Here's why: the suicide numbers in some categories are small enough that individuals could be identified, violating state privacy policies. For example, one state could have two non-white females between the ages of 30-34 committing suicide in 2004 who had served in the armed forces. Because of the small number in that category, those individuals could be identified and the cause of their death would then be made public.

Therefore, in order to get the data, CBS News had to give assurance to the states that we would keep the raw data confidential. Some states insisted upon written agreements to this effect. The data, however, can be obtained upon request from the files of each individual state.

Gathering Data - Stage 1

CBS News collected the data in two stages over the course of several months.

First, we asked all 50 states to provide us with veteran and non-veteran suicide counts from 1995 to 2005 broken down by year, age, race, gender and manner of suicide. (Note: The most recent year most states have suicide data available is for the year 2005.)

Forty-five states responded to this initial request which resulted in a massive amount of varied raw information.

Five states did not provide us with raw data and total counts for suicides because they said it was not available. Those states were Georgia, Kentucky, Nebraska (only had 2004 data), Nevada and North Carolina.

In looking at the 2005 suicide counts, among 45 states that shared data, there were a total of 6256 suicides by those who served in the military for both men and women of all ages and races.

Forced Psychiatric Treatment is Torture, Says United Nations

By Andrea Shettle, MSW | January 6, 2009

[**Note:** *The following press release from the Center for the Human Rights of Users and Survivors of Psychiatry refers to a recent Interim Report from the United Nations Special Rapporteur on Torture. and also go to* http://www2.ohchr.org/english/issues/disability/index.htm.]

Date: September 24, 2008

The Center for the Human Rights of Users and Survivors of Psychiatry welcomes the Interim Report by the United Nations Special Rapporteur on Torture
The Center for the Human Rights of Users and Survivors of Psychiatry (CHRUSP) welcomes the Interim Report by UN Special Rapporteur on Torture Manfred Nowak, which signals an end to impunity for psychiatric torture and ill treatment. The report focuses attention on torture and persons with disabilities, applying the Convention on the Rights of Persons with Disabilities (CRPD) to the obligations of states to prevent and punish torture.

The Special Rapporteur names forced psychiatric interventions (such as psychosurgery, electroshock and administration of mind-altering drugs including neuroleptics) among practices that may constitute torture or ill treatment. Other medical practices that may constitute torture or ill treatment are restraint and seclusion, forced abortion or sterilization and involuntary commitment to psychiatric institutions. The medical context itself is one where "serious violations and discrimination against persons with disabilities may be masked as 'good intentions' on the part of health care professionals."

In his conclusions, the Special Rapporteur calls on states to ratify and implement the Convention and its Optional Protocol, to legislate recognition of the legal capacity of persons with disabilities and ensure that support in decision-making is provided where needed, and to issue guidelines on free and informed consent in line with the Convention. He calls for independent human rights monitoring of institutions where persons with disabilities may reside, and for UN and regional human rights mechanisms to take account of the Convention and integrate its standards into their work.

"This development is significant for several reasons," said Tina Minkowitz, founder of CHRUSP. "It makes explicit what the Convention had left implicit: that forced psychiatric treatment is a serious violation of human rights, even when done with the best intentions. States that do not make the necessary reforms to eliminate forced treatment and institutionalization and to respect the legal capacity of persons with disabilities may run afoul of their obligations to effectively stop torture and ill treatment. The report gives us new tools for legal advocacy and redress of violations, in states that have ratified the CRPD and in those that have not yet ratified."

**** END ****

About the Center for Human Rights of Users and Survivors of Psychiatry (CHRUSP):
The purpose of the organization is to work for full legal capacity, an end to forced psychiatric treatment, and equality and advancement for users and survivors of psychiatry within a human

"ONE POWERFUL VOICE"

rights framework.

The aims of the organization are to:

• Advocate for the advancement of the human rights of users and survivors of psychiatry.

• Provide international consultation to influence key decision-makers regarding matters that affect users and survivors.

• Develop model legislation focusing on legal capacity and free and informed consent.

• Facilitate sharing of information and knowledge among user / survivor organizations around the world

• Monitor progress on human rights instruments including the United Nations Convention on the Rights of Persons with Disabilities with respect to issues affecting users and survivors of psychiatry

And it is to this sentiment of Human Rights, that we in The United States have to address, particularly for each of our Armed Forces Veterans and for the public as a whole, that "America Stands For Something" beyond the basic premise of The Right To Live Here; and which is The Right To Be Free Here and To Remain Unmolested here, and to Have Basic Civil Rights Not To Be Discriminated Against, and Fundamental Civil Liberties To A Fair And Impartial Justice System Accorded To Everyone; which Cannot Be Violated! In This Nation, and not while the people who are elected overhead and appointed to us overhead are in power and charged with their sacred oaths of office to uphold The Constitution and to Protect and Defend The Lives of The People in their obligation, and have the power vested in them to do so. That is not a political game about it, to be flaunting of these rights in the face of a suffering humanity, which men have fought hard for and suffered for and died for, to be so flagrantly profaned in such a scurrilous manner of allowing a certain Special Interest Bloc of Criminals, To Replace The Rights of The Sacred Constitution, with a term labeled to be Mental Health, in which an individual has No Rights At All, and in further infamy for everyone to be allowed over to be tortured and ruined of their lives with drug chemicals, without any Due Process of Law or Human Rights Intervention. That ultimately falls into the burden of your lap locally to resolve.

Nobody is defending The United States of the established White European Americans, termed The American People, because its not their Country any longer in the aftermath of The Civil Rights War to care about, and with being daily invaded by foreigners as we speak, in a passionate meaning of Patriotism, To Defend. That in the end will surely all result in a Real Bloodshed War for The United States and its Territory, after they have bankrupted us, and turned the population into Forced Chemical Psychiatrics without Due Process. But first it has to defeat those of US who are still functioning. We're still here.

"ONE POWERFUL VOICE"

SUICIDE STATISTICS

According to a study by Tim A. Bullman and Han K. Yang in the Federal Practitioner 12 (3) : 9-13 (March 1995), "...no more than 20,000 Vietnam Veterans died of suicide from the time of discharge through the end of 1993". However there are others that claim that many more veterans have died of suicide since the Vietnam War.

In Chuck Deans' book, *Nam Vet.*, printed in 1990 by Multnomah Press, Portland, Oregon, 97226, the author states that "Fifty-eight thousand plus died in the Vietnam War. Over 150,000 have committed suicide since the war ended". According to this book, Chuck Dean is a Vietnam Veteran who served in the 173rd Airborne, arriving in Vietnam in 1965. At the time the book was written, Mr. Dean was the executive director of Point Man International, a Seattle based, non-profit support organization dedicated to healing the war wounds of Vietnam Veterans.

While doing research for his novel, *Suicide Wall*, Alexander Paul contacted Point Man International and was given the name of a retired VA doctor, and conducted a phone interview with him. In that interview, the doctor related that his estimate of the number of Vietnam Veteran suicides was 200,000 men, and that the reason the official suicide statistics were so much lower was that in many cases the suicides were documented as accidents, primarily single-car drunk driving accidents and self inflicted gunshot wounds that were not accompanied by a suicide note or statement.
According to the doctor, the under reporting of suicides was primarily an act of kindness to the surviving relatives.

If the estimate of over 150,000 veterans of the Vietnam War having committed suicide since returning home is true, the figure would be almost three times the number killed in the war. When these deaths are added to the 50,000 plus Vietnam War casualties, the number approaches the 292,000 American casualties of World War II.
The Suicide Wall web site is an attempt to determine how many Vietnam Veterans have actually taken their own lives, as well as a place to memorialize and honor those who served their country, and finally a place which may serve to help prevent suicides in the future. The desire to commit suicide is a temporary, passing emotion, and if it can be prevented, the suicidal person can receive counseling and treatment to prevent the reoccurrence of such feelings.

One Vietnam Veteran, who had been suicidal and wishes to remain anonymous, said, "After reading *Suicide Wall,* I am determined never to have my name on such a memorial." It is the hope of PakDonald Publishing and Alexander Paul, that this web site might help others in time of distress

"ONE POWERFUL VOICE"

9480 Princeton Square Blvd. S., #815
Jacksonville, FL 32256
October 24, 2008

Superintendent Franklin L. Hagenbeck,
Lieutenant General, US Army
United States Military Academy
West Point, NY 10996

Dear General Hagenbeck,

As always, to thank you so very much for your personal attention to these matters of discussion here presented on the topic of Drug-Chemical Warfare Subversion leading to Psychiatric Intake, (and for the genuine substance issues also of TBI, Traumatic Brain Injury, PTSD, Post Traumatic Stress Disorder, and Clinical Deep Depression,) requiring our urgent attention, as it is occurring to our incoming Combat Service Personnel presently from Afghanistan and Iraq, and also as it affected and still affects the prior Combat Theaters to us of our nation's wars, and most specifically regarding The Vietnam War incident where over 1,000,000 of our Veterans who served this Nation in Vietnam were made into psychiatrics, and of these, of the 68,000 who committed suicide as a result from such psychiatric treatment to date, and 10,000 more than who died in combat outright in Vietnam, and not to overlook the soldiers from The Gulf War and The Bosnian War in alert. And which to us is a life threatening setting requiring the direct and unmitigated intervention in our behalf by our established Military Commanders.

As you see here from my detailed analysis in pertinent synopsis of The Defense Forum Washington Conference of September 17, 2008, (provided by The Military Officers Association Of America, at: moaa.org/serv_prof_forum_transcript.htm,) entitled, Keeping Faith with Wounded Warriors and Their Families, (featuring Senator Carl Levin, Michigan, Chairman, Senate Committee on Armed Services, and The Honorable James B. Peake, U.S. Secretary of Veterans Affairs, 12/20/07;) that not anything was mentioned about The Drug Condition being allowed to proliferate here in our United States in targeting of these returning Veterans, and nor to The V.A. and Civilian Mental Health Facilities use of Ruinous Labeling, and Catastrophically Lethal Psychiatric Pharmacy, described as, The Strong Tranquillizer Class, Neuroleptic and Psychotropic Pharmacy Chemicals, that such have been "Approved" for use, (and against the sound medical judgment of evidential research,) by The Nation's Food and Drug Administration, and by The Veterans Administration itself, against our Nation's Veterans seeking the assistance of The Veterans Administration for their traumas of war and otherwise as the victims of social prejudice, and in harm's way concerning the drug war peril in this regard, that may or may not include the spouses on Heroin of these returning Veterans, and else-ways of family members and social contacts, as victims of sabotage.

In point of contention to what, that it matters not to appropriate more money to expand the vet centers and put on addition personnel, if they murder our Veterans with pharmacy.

Gary L. Koniz
Veterans of The Vietnam War

"ONE POWERFUL VOICE"

9480 Princeton Square Blvd. S., #815
Jacksonville, FL 32256
March 3, 2009

Warren S. Lacy - Editor in Chief
Colonel, U.S. Army (Ret.)
Military Officer Magazine
201 North Washington Street
Alexandria, VA 22314-2539

Dear Colonel Lacy:

In final summation to the Veterans Psychiatric Case, (and for which we should not be having to argue; but in having to,) to thank you for your support to set things right about the matter and for your determination in assistance to us without which, in peer oversight, that we would not be as far along with the case, as we are progressing in opportunity now of correcting the enormous errors of the past with the healthy change in Administrations for our Veterans Mental Health Issues being presented regarding our Nation's Honor, concerning their Diagnostic Labeling and Treatment for the matter of psychiatric intake following their separation from service, as we have been conveying to The Military Officers Association of America, that the V.A. and the Psychiatric Industry overall have been mis-labeling, mis-handling, and mis-treating our Combat Soldiers with disabling chemical pharmacy such as Thorazine, and other deadly Neoroleptic Drugs and causing them very grave and serious harm to the point of mass suicide to date. Which matter needs to be urgently redressed, as to the substance for the grievances themselves being corrected, (and for just disability compensation to be provided to those aggrieved for their damages to ease their inflicted burden.) And in all that we have been in the need for a Supreme Court Ruling On, (presently lacking finances to formally appeal,) on the safety of Psychiatric Drugs and for the Legal Rights of The Psychiatrically Accused to ensure their Civil Rights Protection to Diagnosis Labeling, Commitment, and Forced Treatment.

We started working on this project together as an MOAA agenda in National Alarms several years ago; with The Veterans Administration, The U.S. Military, The Federal Government, and The F.B.I., in the need for dramatic intervention; and coinciding to the urgent Removal of the Heroin and other Dangerous Drugs from our society, and for the resulting Drug Warfare occurring in peril causing psychiatric conditions to the population particularly to our returning from war Veterans, and our first line of homeland defense to be eliminated; and to our suffering the loss of our American Nation over it, the trafficking in drugs, (of the American United States of the WWII generations,) for the aggressions of the many ways of wars having been allowed to overtake us; of corrupt, irrational, and immoral ideologies, and for the allowing of decidedly foreign peoples to politically and economically overrun us here, in the malaise of a drugged and corrupt society, to be left defenseless against. That we do at this time need to be intervening to the War Crimes involved with psychiatric coinciding to the Opium/Heroin Trafficking from Afghanistan.

Gary L. Koniz – Secretary Correspondent
Veterans Of The Vietnam War

"ONE POWERFUL VOICE"

9480 Princeton Square Blvd. S., #815
Jacksonville, FL 32256
August 2, 2009

The Honorable Eric K. Shinseki
Secretary of Veterans Affairs
Department of Veterans Affairs
811 Vermont Avenue, N.W.
Washington, D.C. 20420

Dear Secretary Shinseki:

We do need to Officially Challenge the rules of conduct to be changed by Formality of
Congressional Oversight Committee to accommodate the case matter of Psychiatric Malfeasance;
that we are no longer appealing politely in good order about in formality of bureaucratic protocol,
but in the straightforward language of good Common Military Justice Sense in Direct Order, to do
what we have detailed for you to do thus far to the Veterans Administration in your charge to carry
out the necessary reforms in protection and safeguard of our Veterans. Regarding in first sense of
meaning to the altering of the stigmatizing nomenclature of the "Psychiatric," Mental Wards, to
the benign setting of; "Bed Rest, Convalescence, Counseling, and Therapy," in Wards to be
named, "Seclusion Recovery;" that is furthermore to be protected by a strict protocol of "Safe
Treatment," to be conducted, stressing Rest and Medical Nutrition and to the discontinued routine
use of Disabling and Proven Harmful Anti-Psychotic Chemo-Treatment. And for you to do the
job promptly as we have detailed concerning these reforms, or to face the awkward circumstances
of disavowing your Country, as this is not a "Cover-Up" matter to be tolerated, but a Corrections
Issue; involving the safety and lives of our fellow Veterans.

The Psychiatric Medical/Pharmacy Industry no longer has "the power" to diagnose and to treat-
destroy anyone they personally choose to with any drug chemical, surgery, or electro-insulin shock
treatment they arbitrarily determine, and with Sovereign Immunity from civil and criminal
prosecution as is currently built in to their present practices. And that they no longer have the
tyrannical personal power over the freedom and the lives of our Veterans, (in Captive Market
arrangement,) to imprison-detain anyone they choose indefinitely and to set the terms of their
release, and to do with whatever they want to under the current terms of Mental Hygiene Law
regarding Commitment "to the terms of treatment," without any Substantive Due Process of Law
and in the name of Medicine. As is being carried out and conducted now, Communist-Bloc Style,
in Rights Violations.

Which for the record to add also, that there are all too many numerous cases to cite; of medical
malpractice, medical fraud, kickback complicity with the pharmaceutical companies, and medical
monetary corruption involving political, pornographic, and drug conspiracies, to organized crime.
The Constitutional Rights to Due Process cannot be allowed abridged in the face of such
subversion and corruption just because the legal rendering of Mental Hygiene happens to fall
under Medical Non-Criminal Civil Law.

Gary L. Koniz – Corresponding
Veterans Of The Vietnam War

9480 Princeton Square Blvd. S., #815
Jacksonville, FL 32256
October 18, 2009

The Honorable Eric H. Holder
Attorney General of The United States
U.S. Department of Justice
950 Pennsylvania Avenue, N.W.
Washington, D.C. 20530-0001

Dear U.S. Attorney General Holder:

I need you, respectfully, to take an interest in this case of ours, for presentation to The U.S. Supreme Court for decision, pertaining for The Legal Rights of Psychiatric Due Process to be clearly defined, and that No One in this Nation of any responsible authority seems inclined to do anything about. Which, to date, they have not been. And which, and furthermore to date, are being side-stepped with in evasive tactics by The Veterans Administration, The Congress, The Supreme Court, The U.S. Attorneys Offices, The State's Attorney Generals, and other Agencies of the Government who we have appealed to concerning this issue in the need for justice in clarification. Specifically to the case:

(1.) As to what precisely in legal definition constitutes for a "Valid Grounds for a Psychiatric Diagnosis," to be place administratively to someone's person, such as; "Schizophrenia," "Manic-Depression," "Dementia," and other matters of such nature.

(2.) As to what precisely in legal grounds, can anyone be "Force Treated" with an Anti-Psychotic Chemical Agent, or with other types of disabling treatment, against their will.

(3.) What are the legal grounds that a person can be "Committed" to a Psychiatric Facility, and what are the terms of Informed Consent for Voluntary Commitment.

(4.) And, most importantly, what exactly are a person's legal rights to Due Process concerning; the 4th, 5th, and 6th 9th, and 14th, Amendments of The Bill of Rights; and to Safe Treatment, pertaining for the disabling and maiming effects of the Anti-Psychotic, Psychotropic and Neuroleptic, Strong Tranquillizer Class Chemical Drugs in prevailing trend of modern use; to be named in part such as: Thorazine, Prolixin, Navane, Trilifon, Haldol, Lithium, Loxitane, and others; and in the wording of Voluntary Consent as for the harmful consequences of taking such chemicals termed erroneously as "Medications;" including for the permanent or temporary mental and psychological implications, as well as for the physical; side effects, adverse effects, contraindications, (reactions with other drugs,) and paradoxical reactions, (as inducing the same effects being touted to alleviate.)

Most Respectully,

Gary L. Koniz - Secretary
Veterans of The Vietnam War

"ONE POWERFUL VOICE"

9480 Princeton Square Blvd. S., #815
Jacksonville, FL 32256
April 11, 2010

The Honorable Eric H. Holder
Attorney General of The United States
U.S. Department of Justice
950 Pennsylvania Avenue, N.W.
Washington, D.C. 20530-0001

Dear U.S. Attorney General Holder:

We need to achieve a consensus with the argument that our society cannot endure to continue on with "Two Systems of Law;" the one in guarantee of Due Process under The Constitution, and the other that is devoid of All Rights on Medical Certificate, that is my case in Motion For Summary Judgment with Hudson River Psychiatric on grounds that:

1. They have not proved their case against me in a Court of Law, and that I was denied my Constitutional Rights to Due Process and for a Fair Judicial Hearing under The Law concerning my Commitments there for two nearly consecutive sixty day periods of detention on Medical Certificate at the behest of Local Law Enforcement; that has to do in rebuttal with a Common Defense of our United States Constitution from Criminal and Police Conspiracies using Psychiatric as a means to cover-up their involvement with the local Heroin Drug Trafficking and Pornography; of which case I was working on as an Investigative Reporter with The New York State Police and The Poughkeepsie Journal.

2. That I was deliberately falsely accused, in outright and criminal slander allegations of fabricated lies and distorted exaggerations of the truth and Falsely Imprisoned in direct Violation of my Civil Rights; and Falsely Labeled, (based to the false and misleading testimony presented against me,) with a Mental Illness of Paranoid Schizophrenia, in grave consequence to myself and my career, and of which that I was not guilty of having.

3. That I was Assaulted, Force Treated, and Gravely Damaged, (in violation of the legal stipulations of the law for such treatment,) with a Life Threatening and very Painful to Endure Drug Chemical called Navane, (the full description for its ill-effects attached.)

4. And to what that I am hereby seeking the Summary Judgment to as the Plaintiff; to have the record of any alleged Psychiatric History, and any alleged Mental Disorder Condition, permanently expunged and exonerated; for what that I am also pressing for Substantive Damages amounting to $1,000 a day for day of False Imprisonment, and for Punitive Damages in an undermined amount to be evaluated by the Court, for the severe and serious damages suffered to my reputation, professional career, and upon my person.

Most Sincerely,
Gary Koniz - Corresponent
Veterans of the Vietnam War

"ONE POWERFUL VOICE"

9480 Princeton Square Blvd. S., #815
Jacksonville, FL 32256
October 17, 2010

Robert S. Mueller, III - Director
Federal Bureau Of Investigation
935 Pennsylvania Avenue, N.W.
Washington, D.C. 20535-0001

Dear Director Mueller:

I am petitioning you this day in an attempt to resolve an era of sinister quagmire in our American History together: of The Injustice termed Psychiatric Venue, replacing The U.S. Bill of Rights of The American Constitution and The Miranda Legislation in safeguard of our Civil Liberty; that not only has the power to detain anyone to a virtually indefinite period of time, but to Socially Disgrace them, and to Dispose of them as well with deadly Chemical Pharmacy, Surgery, and Insulin/Electro-Shock Treatment, on the inviolable "say-so" of Medical Diagnosis/Opinion, without The Psychiatrically Accused having the ability in legal recourse to challenge the grounds of such determinations.

That, No One, (including; The Congress, The U.S. Supreme Court, The U.S. Attorney General, The State Attorney Generals, and The Federal Authorities, to date,) is ever attempting to come to conclusive terms with, as far as discerning the <u>Specific Terms</u> of the <u>Due Process Rights</u> regarding the Legal Grounds; for Diagnosis, Commitment, and Forced Treatment; to do anything about. To make matter worse, what The Local Court Justices have been making use of To Channel persons into Psychiatric Custody by the dangerous ground of Court Ordering Psychiatric Evaluations to dispose of them in that way, to Mental Health, in expediency to avoid the length and cost of Court Proceedings.

To what I am asking you for your personal assistance of involvement to my specific case in reasoning it out, (and even though which is 24 years old, which is still active in the manner of its "History" and "Stigma" needing permanent resolution in justice's name, as to the determination of my Innocence, (and the Innocent Victim of Crimes against me,) and still active in its criminal setting; in that I was Falsely Accused, Held Captive for a total period of 120 days without benefit of Court Proceedings, and Forcibly Tortured with Repeated Injections of large doses of a lethal drug, Navane, (tantamount to my having been Kidnapped, by persons acting in the interests of, "The State," and Most Grievously Assaulted with a Disabling Chemical, which fact can be verified, and for which there is no Statute of Limitations, and which is further Tolled by Late Discovery.) That is very important to me, and that has been all along these many years gone by, to my exhaustive appeals being blatantly ignored by the Authorities, as they have been all along, for you to intervene to, to assist the necessary resolution of, which would benefit me, in freeing me from the stigma and disgrace of having a False Psychiatric History which was Criminally Attributed to me, and which is Criminally Being Conspired To in the aftereffects, to be covered-up. That if resolved, would free the entire system thereafter to function properly.

Most Respectfully Regarding,
Gary L. Koniz - Correspondent
Veterans of the Vietnam War

"ONE POWERFUL VOICE"

FAA Medical Standards, Protocols and Forms

Synopsis of Medical Standards, AME Guide - Revised April 3, 2006

Certificate Class Pilot Type	First-Class Airline Transport	Second-Class Commercial	Third-Class Private
DISTANT VISION	20/20 or better in each eye separately, with or without correction.		20/40 or better in each eye separately, with or without correction.
NEAR VISION	20/40 or better in each eye separately (Snellen equivalent), with or without correction, as measured at 16 inches.		
INTERMEDIATE VISION	20/40 or better in each eye separately (Snellen equivalent), with or without correction at age 50 and over, as measured at 32 inches.	No requirement.	
COLOR VISION	Ability to perceive those colors necessary for safe performance of airmen duties.		
HEARING	Demonstrate hearing of an average conversational voice in a quiet room, using both ears at 6 feet, with the back turned to the examiner OR pass one of the audiometric tests below or:		
PULSE	Not disqualifying per se. Used to determine cardiac system status and responsiveness.		
BLOOD PRESSURE	No specified values stated in the standards. Current guideline maximum is 155/95.		
AUDIOLOGY	Audiometric speech discrimination test: (Score at least 70% discrimination in one ear) or: Pure tone audiometric test: Unaided, with thresholds no worse than: 500Hz 1,000Hz 2,000Hz 3,000Hz Better Ear 35Db 30Db 30Db 40Db Worst Ear 35Db 50Db 50Db 60Db		
EAR, NOSE, THROAT	No ear disease or condition manifested by, or that may reasonably be expected to be manifested by, vertigo or a disturbance of speech or equilibrium.		
ELECTRO-CARDIOGRAM	At age 35 & annually after age 40.	Not routinely required.	
MENTAL	No diagnosis of psychosis, or bipolar disorder, or severe personality disorders.		
SUBSTANCE DEPENDENCE & SUBSTANCE ABUSE	A diagnosis or medical history of substance dependence is disqualifying unless there is established clinical evidence, satisfactory to the Federal Air Surgeon, of recovery, including sustained total abstinence from the substance(s) for not less than the preceding 2 years. A history of substance abuse within the preceding 2 years is disqualifying. Substance includes alcohol and other drugs (i.e., PCP, sedatives and hynoptics, anxiolytics, marijuana, cocaine, opioids, amphetamines, hallucinogens, and other psychoactive drugs or chemicals).		
DISQUALIFYING CONDITIONS Airman with these conditions may still be eligible for "Special Issuance" of a medical certificate.	Unless otherwise directed by the FAA, the Examiner must deny or defer if the applicant has a history of: (1) Diabetes mellitus requiring hypoglycemic medication; (2) Angina pectoris; (3) Coronary heart disease that has been treated or, if untreated, that has been symptomatic or clinically significant; (4) Myocardial infarction; (5) Cardiac valve replacement; (6) Permanent cardiac pacemaker; (7) Heart replacement; (8) Psychosis; (9) Bipolar disorder; (10) Personality disorder that is severe enough to have repeatedly manifested itself by overt acts; (11) Substance dependence; (12) Substance abuse; (13) Epilepsy; (14) Disturbance of consciousness and without satisfactory explanation of cause, and (15) Transient loss of control of nervous system function(s) without satisfactory explanation of cause.		

"ONE POWERFUL VOICE"

DEPARTMENT OF TRANSPORTATION
FEDERAL AVIATION ADMINISTRATION
SPECIFICATIONS FOR PSYCHIATRIC AND PSYCHOLOGICAL EVALUATIONS

I.   RECORDS: Provide all records covering prior psychiatric hospitalizations and/or other periods of observation or treatment, which have not been previously submitted. These records must be in sufficient detail to permit a clear evaluation of the nature and extent of any previous mental disorders.

II.   PSYCHIATRY: A report by a qualified psychiatrist is required. Preferably, the psychiatrist will be Board Certified by the American Board of Psychiatry and Neurology, or have the training and experience equivalent to that required for Board Eligibility. A personal physician is often a good source for a referral.

The examination must be of recent date, and the report should be in sufficient detail and depth to permit an accurate evaluation of the examinee's interval history and current psychiatric status. The usual elements of an evaluation such as past history, family history, and current mental status should be included.

III. PSYCHOLOGY: A report by a qualified clinical psychologist is required. The psychologist must be experienced in administering and evaluating tests such as those described below. Preferably the psychologist will meet the requirements for state licensure or certification, and have a Doctorate in Psychology. A local psychological society or mental health organization may be a referral source for a psychologist.

The psychological evaluation and report (including a copy of the test protocols) should be complete and comprehensive, and should be based on a detailed examination using a battery of psychological tests including -

    1. The complete Wechsler Adult Intelligence Scale - Revised (WAIS-R)
    2. The Minnesota Multiphasic Personality Inventory (MWI-2/MMPI)
    3. Any three or more of the following tests or their equivalents
        a. A cognitive function screening including such tests as -
            1. The Trails Making Test
            2. The Category Test, Booklet or Machine
            3. A memory scale such as -
                a. The Wechsler Memory Scale
                b. The California Verbal Learning Test
                c. The Rey Auditory Verbal Learning Test
        b. A projective test such as the Rorschach or Sentence Completion
        c. A personality inventory test such as -
            1. The NEO-R
            2. The Personality Assessment Inventory
            3. The Millon Clinical Multiaxial Inventory (MCMI)
        d. A symptom screening test such as -
            1. The Beck or Hamilton for depression
            2. The MAST test for alcoholism

The evaluating psychologist should select the particular tests based upon his or her experience, considering the particular issues involved.

Updated Jun 05 2000, AGL-300

"ONE POWERFUL VOICE"

38 USC § 1151 - Benefits for persons disabled by treatment or vocational rehabilitation

Title 38 U.S.C. Section 1151 allows VA to pay compensation for death or disability "as if service-connected." Don't be confused with this subtle difference. The disability is not considered service-connected. Under Section 1151, benefits may be paid for:

- Injuries incurred or aggravated while receiving VA-sponsored medical treatment.
- Injuries incurred or aggravated while pursuing a course of vocational rehabilitation under 38 U.S.C. Chapter 31 or participating in compensated work therapy under 38 U.S.C. 1718.

If eligibility is established under Section 1151, the disability is considered service-connected for payment purposes ONLY.

Eligibility Requirements

- You must be a Veteran
- You must have a disabling condition that is the result of or has been aggravated due to VA sponsored medical treatment or training

Evidence Requirements

As a result of VA hospitalization, medical or surgical treatment, examination, or training, the evidence must show you have:

- An additional disability or disabilities, **OR**
- An aggravation of an existing injury or disease, **AND**

The disability was:

- The direct result of VA fault such as carelessness, negligence, lack of proper skill, or error in judgment, **OR**
- Not a reasonably expected result or complication of the VA care or treatment **OR**
- The direct result of participation in a VA Vocational Rehabilitation and Employment or compensated work therapy program.

Example

A Veteran was pursuing training under VA's Chapter 31 Vocational Rehabilitation and Employment program. He was receiving on-the-job training as a car mechanic. During training, a jack slipped from a car and crushed his left foot. Disability compensation may be paid for his foot injury because the injury occurred while the Veteran was pursuing training under a VA Vocational Rehabilitation and Employment program.

DEPARTMENT OF VETERANS AFFAIRS
Veterans Health Administration
Washington DC 20420

MAY 2 2 2009

Mr. Gary L. Koniz   In Reply Refer To:
Veterans of the Vietnam War
9480 Princeton Square Blvd. S., #815
Jacksonville, FL 32256

Dear Mr. Koniz:

Your message to the Honorable Eric Shinseki, Secretary of Veterans Affairs was referred to my office for reply. In your expressed concerns over the potentially harmful effects of neuroleptic drugs such as Thorazine (also called chlorpromazine); circumstances under which patients could be "force treated" with such drugs, and legal recourse for Veterans to challenge diagnoses and commitment procedures.

All medications have potential side effects as well as therapeutic effects and chlorpromazine is no exception. Neuroleptic or antipsychotic medications have been proven effective and even life saving over decades of research and practice for thousands, if not millions, of persons suffering from psychotic disorders. With proper medications and other psychosocial supports people who in previous eras might have spent their lives in mental institutions are now able to live successful and satisfying lives in the community. Chlorpromazine is not much used in VA currently, (only 0.1% of Veterans received this medication in FY 2008), while other medications with fewer side effects are in more common use.

Patients have the right to accept or refuse any medical treatment or procedure recommended to them. The decision to employ a treatment is the joint decision of the patient and the clinician treating them, with the potential gains and risks of accepting or rejecting treatment made clear. The only situation in which a patient might be compelled to accept a medication, such as an antipsychotic medication, is if there is clear evidence that not doing so would endanger the patient or others. An involuntary commitment procedure would be required for this and there is a statutorily prescribed process that must be followed which is established in 38 C.F.R.17.32(g) (2) along with procedures set forth in VHA Handbook 1004.1 Informed Consent for Clinical Treatments and Procedures. Commitment procedures are regulated by State law and adjudicated by the courts. Involuntary commitment status must be reviewed on a regular basis: once conditions for commitment no longer apply, the involuntary commitment is terminated.

"ONE POWERFUL VOICE"

THE LOST WAR   62

Page 2

Mr. Gary L. Koniz

Your concern with the rights of America's Veterans suffering from mental disorders is appreciated, and shared by the Department of Veterans Affairs.

Sincerely,

Ira Katz, MD
Deputy Chief Patient Care Services
Officer for Mental Health

"ONE POWERFUL VOICE"

U. S. Department of Justice

Civil Rights Division

TW: DG
DJ 144-17M-0

Washington, D.C. 20530

May 26, 2010

Mr. Gary L. Koniz
9480 Princeton Square Boulevard
Suite #815
Jacksonville, Florida 32256

Dear Mr. Koniz:

This is in reply to your correspondence. We apologize for the delay of this response.

The matter with which you are concerned is one within the jurisdiction of the Department of Veterans Affairs. This Department is, therefore, without authority to take any action.

We have forwarded your letter to The Honorable Eric Ken Shinseki. We are sure it will receive careful consideration.

Any inquiries you have concerning this same matter in the future should be sent directly to:

Honorable Eric Ken Shinseki
Secretary
Department of Veterans Affairs
810 Vermont Avenue NW
Washington,DC20420

Sincerely,

Theresa Weathers
Civil Rights Division

"ONE POWERFUL VOICE"

Military Officers Association of America

November 4, 2008

Gary L. Koniz
9480 Princeton Square Blvd S, #815
Jacksonville, FL 32256

Dear Mr. Koniz:

I am writing in response to your October 26, 2008, letter discussing the
MOAA/USNI forum, "Keeping Faith with Wounded Warriors and Their
Families."

I've passed your letter to MOAA's professionalism section, which managed the
event, and MOAA's Government Relations Department, which follows legislation
and activities having to do with military health care. They are the experts in these
matters and will consider your comments. As the magazine editor, I am not an
operator in this field, and I cannot address your concerns.

Again, thanks for contributing your thoughts, and thanks for all your work in this
area.

Best wishes,

Warren S. Lacy
Colonel, U.S. Army (Ret.)
Editor in Chief
Military Officer magazine

201 N. Washington Street
Alexandria, VA 22314-2539
800.234.6622 phone
www.moaa.org

One Powerful Voice.

"ONE POWERFUL VOICE"

Department of Veterans Affairs
Office of the General Counsel
Washington, DC 20420

January 12, 2010

Mr. Gary L. Koniz
9480 Princeton Square Blvd S. #815
Jacksonville, FL 32256   In Reply Refer To: FOIA Request 10-003

Dear Mr. Koniz:

I respond to your letter dated October 12, 2009, which I received on
October 20, 2009. In your letter, you renew your request for an "overall
statement of the safety of 'Anti-Psychotic' drugs."

A FOIA request must contain descriptions of the records sought that would
enable a professional agency employee familiar with the subject area to locate
the record with a reasonable amount of effort. I have provided you two prior
letters in response to your requests. In my July 27, 2009 letter, I sent you
responsive material provided by the Veterans Health Administration (VHA) and
referred you to VHA for further information. In my October 5, 2009 letter, I
indicated to you that OGC does not have any records responsive to your request.

I have reviewed your letter and have determined you still have not made a
definitive request for information under FOIA. OGC does not have any records
responsive to your request. Therefore, this office is closing this matter.

Sincerely yours,

David M. Donahue

David N. Donahue
FOIA Officer
Office of the General Counsel

Notice of Appeal Rights: If you consider this response to be a denial of any part of your request, you may
appeal by writing to the Assistant General Counsel (024), Department of Veterans Affairs, 810 Vermont
Avenue, N.W., Washington, DC 20420. Please include your case number in any appeal. If you wish to
request additional records or clarification, please write directly to the person signing this letter. Doing this will
not change your appeal rights.

"ONE POWERFUL VOICE"

United States Senate
WASHINGTON, DC 20510-0905

January 19, 2010

BILL NELSON
FLORIDA

Mr. Gary Koniz
Secretary Correspondent
United Labor
9480 Princeton Square Boulevard, South
Apartment 815
Jacksonville, Florida 32256

Dear Mr. Koniz:

Thank you for contacting me regarding the health care reform process as it relates to America's veterans.

For the past few years, some in Washington have advocated either increasing TRICARE fees, reducing coverage, or reducing the overall budget for the Department of Veterans Affairs as a means of controlling the deficit. I have opposed these ideas at every turn, because they represent a failure of the government to meet its commitment to American veterans.

Among my priorities for health care reform are emphasizing wellness and prevention, reducing the cost of prescription drugs especially for Medicare patients, providing universal access to quality health insurance, and strengthening our health care workforce. Rest assured that I will not support any proposal that would compromise our veterans' access to affordable health care.

The task before us is immense, but Americans will rise to the challenge. I will be sure to take your views into consideration as the debate progresses. Please do not hesitate to contact me in the future.

Sincerely,

Bill Nelson

P.S. From time to time, I compile electronic news briefs highlighting key issues and hot topics of particular importance to Floridians. If you'd like to receive these e-briefs, visit my Web site and sign up for them at http://billnelson.senate.gov/news/ebriefs.cfm

"ONE POWERFUL VOICE"

DEPARTMENT OF VETERANS AFFAIRS

St. Petersburg Regional Office
P.O. BOX 1437
St. Petersburg FL 33731

MAY 2 1 2013

GARY L KONIZ
9480 PRINCETON SQUARE
BLVD S   APT 815
JACKSONVILLE, FL 32256

In Reply Refer To: 317/VSC/SPOPS/LJD
C 24 891 327
KONIZ, Gary Lee

Dear Mr. Koniz:

We made a decision on your claim for service connected compensation received on
April 1, 2011.

This letter constitutes our decision based on all issues we understood to be specifically made,
implied, or inferred in that claim.

This letter tells you about what we decided. It includes the evidence used and reasons for our
decision. We have also included information about what to do if you disagree with our decision,
and who to contact if you have questions or need assistance.

What We Decided

> *Please see the enclosure for more information regarding the evidence considered.*

We determined that the following conditions were not related to your military service, so
service connection couldn't be granted:

Service connection for posttraumatic stress disorder (PTSD) is denied.

Entitlement to compensation under 38 U.S.C. 1151 for crippled nervous system is denied.

Entitlement to compensation under 38 U.S.C. 1151 for amnesia is denied.

Entitlement to compensation under 38 U.S.C. 1151 for impotency is denied.

Entitlement to compensation under 38 U.S.C. 1151 for crippled muscular system is denied.

Entitlement to compensation under 38 U.S.C. 1151 for incontinence is denied.

Entitlement to individual unemployability is denied.

"ONE POWERFUL VOICE"

GARY L. KONIZ
24 891 327
Page 4

Department in furnishing the hospital care, medical or surgical treatment, or examination must be shown; or the proximate cause of disability must be an event not reasonably foreseeable. For training and rehabilitation services or compensated work therapy program, it must be shown that the veteran's participation in an essential activity or function of the training, services, or CWT program provided or authorized by VA proximately caused the disability. Merely showing that a veteran has additional disability is not sufficient to establish causation.

Service connection may be granted for a disability which began in military service or was caused by some event or experience in service.

Service Treatment Records from August 14, 1964 through August 11, 1967 noted no diagnosis, treatment or complaint of nervous system disorder.

Treatment reports from VA Medical Center Albany, NY from April 19, 1982 through June 3, 1988 noted that you were treated with thorazine for paranoid schizophrenia from April 19, 1982 to May 3, 1982. The only side effect of the drug noted while under treatment was orthostatic hypotension.

Private medical record from Dr. Charles Cobb of Jacksonville, FL dated May 14, 2012 noted no dizziness, tremor or numbness/tingling in your extremities.

VA examination results from VA Medical Center Bay Pines, FL dated May 13, 2013 noted a complete review of you claims file to include all available records from VA medical Center Albany, NY. The examiner opined that it is more likely that the your crippled nervous system IS UNRELATED, caused, by or aggravated by medical treatment, rehab program, or participation in a compensated work therapy program activity at VA Medical Center Albany, NY. The examiner reasoned that you wer admitted for the treatment of an acute exacerbation of your paranoid schizophrenia on April 19, 1982 manifested by auditory and visual hallucinations. You were prescribed Thorazine which is an accepted and a necessary treatment for this condition. Alternative agents like Loxitane and Cogentin were not used due to the side effects experienced by you. The hospital discharge continues that you were prescribed Thorazine for from 4/19/1982 to May 3, 1982. The dose given to you was a therapeutic one for your condition. However it was discontinued due to problems with orthostatic hypotension that you developed. No other issues such as the amnesia, crippled nervous system, impotence, incontinence, and enlarged prostate were mentioned during that hospitalization alone or arising from the use of the Thorazine medication. The evidence in your current claims file makes no references to any of the above issues that you have which have been evaluated, diagnosed and treated. As such there may be many reasons why you have your conditions if they do indeed exist aside from the short term use of the Thorazine some thirty years ago. Additionally while it has been mentioned that Thorazine in the medical literature may result in impotence and urinary retention, this would be true only during the time that an individual would be taking this agent. Such conditions would resolve with the cessation of the Thorazine. As far as the enlarged prostate, crippled nervous system, crippled muscle system, and amnesia, no long term effects or complications have been noted to arise either during the use of Thorazine or after it has been discontinued.

U.S. Court of Appeals for Veterans Claims

Gary L. Koniz   The Honorable Eric K. Shinseki
317/VSC/SPOPS/LJD   Secretary of Veterans Affairs
C 24 891 327 – 05/27/13,

     v   The Honorable Eric H. Holder
Department of Veterans Affairs   Attorney General of The United States
St. Petersburg Regional Office,

Notice Of Disagreement

On the grounds of <u>Incompetent Medical Authority</u> I have disagreement with the decision to Deny my Claim for just Compensation Damages; (as to the V.A.'s denial, dated May 21, 2013,) for a Crippled Nervous System, (Mental and Emotional Debility, Dyskinesia, Vision Problems, and Severe Cramping,) Amnesia, (loss of personality,) Crippled Muscular System, (Flat Affect Impotency, Lethargy, and Chronic Fatigue,) Incontinence, (from resulting enlarged prostate,) Chronic Depression, and overall un-employability, that I suffered (from the Effects of Thorazine Treatment;) in the time frame of those years following my treatment by the V.A., (exacerbated by the stigma of Psychiatric Labeling, PTSD, and homelessness below the Economic Threshold to function;) resulting in the loss of my Professional Income. My claim was submitted to the St. Petersburg Regional Office of Veterans Affairs on April 1, 2011, over two years ago; for an entitled compensation claim under 38 U.S.C. 1151 <u>for Unlawful Psychiatric Labeling and Forced Thorazine Treatment</u> in Malpractice/Malfeasance Issue while I was in the care of the Albany, NY VA Medical Center (from 4/19/82 to 5/13/82.) I had reported there for a Service Connected Post Traumatic Stress Disorder (PTSD) and severe Withdrawal Complications arising from a recent Forced Commitment and subsequent Forced Disabling Chemo-Treatment with Loxitane and Cogentin that I was subjected to for Alleged Paranoid Schizophrenia, while at the G. Werber Bryan Psychiatric Hospital In Columbia, SC; resulting in deadly Contraindication Effects, (both long and short term,) of the Thorazine Treatment that I was Subjected To by the V.A. (on illegal grounds,) in combination with the Loxitane/Cogentin. For what that I am seeking compensatory damages for, of a fair and just amount, (as I was discharged from the V.A. listed as "Disabled.")

And to note here for <u>Due Process</u>, that I do express alarm for the <u>Contemptuous Nature</u> of the denial of my claim; for the Examiner's snide remark; "**if indeed they to exist**;" pertaining to my claim for damages from the deadly effects of the Drug Thorazine that I suffered; which induce the devastation that that drug does regardless of whether these Effects were ever Documented by an Incompetent Physician to be able to prove. I have sent the V.A. detailed documentation and personal testimony of what occurred to myself; and regarding the disputation of the Psychiatric Charges and the Hearsay Allegations made about me; None Of Which were ever noted and referred to in the Denial of my claim; and much of what was deliberately Mis-conveyed in bias to side with the V.A. Health Administration, the Physicians, and the Pharmaceutical Industry.

"ONE POWERFUL VOICE"

U.S. Court of Appeals for Veterans Claims

Gary L. Koniz
317/VSC/SPOPS/LJD
C 24 891 327 – 05/27/13,
v
Department of Veterans Affairs
St. Petersburg Regional Office,

The Honorable Eric K. Shinseki
Secretary of Veterans Affairs

The Honorable Eric H. Holder
Attorney General of The United States

Complaint

It is to be reasoned for here, that I was, and am, considered to be an Intelligent and Thoroughly Competent Above Board Professional Person; that I served bravely throughout my tour of duty in the Vietnam War; and that I worked extremely hard to qualify for and to obtain a career as an Operator with The Operating Engineers Union after separation, and that I also worked extremely hard at considerable personal time and expense to attend and graduate Summa Cum Laude from the State University under the G.I. Bill, and to earn my Wings as a Commercial Aviation Pilot.

To what madness then to be cut-down with the Drug Thorazine in the prime of one's life by V.A Warehousing Policy allowing Incompetent Physicians the Diagnostic Power of Life and Death over their trusting patients, the lives of our brave Veterans and Service Members; to suffer brain damage, and neuro-muscular damage, and psychological devastation, unto lingering ill-health and to suicide death and otherwise occurring, by the forced-used of Strong Neuroleptic (Anti-Psychotic) Pharmacy; to what I Am The Victim Of, to state. And concerning what, as a Prime Witness To, that I Am Delivering My "Credible Expert Testimony" About here at this time; and "Expert" in the reasoning of my being a trained Mental Health Medical Professional myself, and in conjunction with Para-Legal Certification to be qualified To Testify on Competent Authority.

My own room-mate at the V.A. Medical Center in Albany, NY killed himself while I was there in April and May of 1982 (and with whom, as with the whole ward of 20 patients that I spent the weeks with hooked up to Blood Pressure Machines in the early morning a.m. shortly after wake-up at 5:30 a.m. to sit there in the day room of the 10th floor of the V.A. to have our low blood-pressure monitored, in a Clinical Trial and the issue of this case, before reporting to the window to get our morning doses of Thorazine under the Doctor's Orders of Dr. Byung Kim, M.D. Staff Psychiatric.) And who, (my roommate,) had become a close companion friend to me in our days and nights there, who went home on a weekend pass several weeks into the program and killed himself by shooting himself in the head with a 22 rifle, after appearing in the doorway of our room before his departure, with the most gloomy and ashen crest-fallen face as one could ever suffer empathically to bear witness and relate to; and stated, as I will always remember his exact words that still haunt me to this day, poor fellow, "Perhaps I can get a job in a Sheltered Work-Shop somewhere." If you would like to know what that drug Thorazine is like and can do to you.

"ONE POWERFUL VOICE"

On the Monday morning following my roommates suicide, while at our regularly scheduled weekday morning group meeting and seated at the tables in the break-room at 10:00 a.m., the group of us of twenty or so Veterans who were in the Psych Ward being subjected to Thorazine Trials together during the time, that Dr. Byung Kim came in and announced the suicide death of my friend and fellow patient, and asked us, "what we thought about it?" That night, I had a dream, one of those bizarre vivid nightmare dreams that seem to be real which occur nightly with the use of Psychotropic Chemical Pharmacy, (that I do not label as Medicine;) in which (about this particular nightmare,) that I was walking down an enclosed tile corridor that was the color of wheat, like the tile walls in an enclosed gym shower room would look to be described, only more narrow and confined, that turned a corner left at right angles and then at right angles again where the angle of the floor then changed and began to descend as I continued walking to get steeper and steeper and more slick to the feel of my bare feet, to discover, with a sinking feeling in my heart, that it dropped away into a dark abyss. Realizing; I halted and carefully retraced my way, using my hands as friction to work myself back onto the level part again. And so it is with Thorazine, you can't sleep, and you can't stay awake; you can't sit still, and you can't sit down. The next morning I told Dr. Kim about the dream and began to process myself out of the V.A..

The particulars then of my complaint concerning Incompetent Medical Authority are as follows:

1. That the person, or individuals, who reviewed my case and issued their denials, did not identify themself, or themselves. And to whom then, other than General Administration, that I have no way of challenging directly their Incompetent Renderings (and here I say of a criminal conspiracy nature, conspiring to deprive the petitioning veterans having legitimate claims to their Benefits, to preserve and protect the medical status-quo; and given to the severity of the <u>defense issues</u> being discussed, which are the health and safety and well-being of our Nation's Veterans, <u>a matter of treason</u>;) as to who exactly is denying them, and for what reasons. That perhaps, and as being mis-appropriately attributed to me, that these persons have the Paranoid Schizophrenia about, of being fearful that those who they deny their benefits to will be "out to get them," (if they provide their names.) And to my point being; that just because a person fears that people are out to get them, does not mean that they aren't. And referring to my specify case concerning Hippie Mafia Drug Use and Trafficking in my family (occurring at the time-frame of the incident in question;) and regarding my work as an Embedded Journalist covering the Drug War and working closely with; Law Enforcement, the Military, and Government Agencies and Officials; for you perhaps to concede that there may have been people "out to get me" and particularly regarding certain Mafia Elements concerning the information being supplied against themselves.

2. On the subject of Reasons for Decision: **Service Connection for Posttraumatic Stress Disorder (PTSD): Denied**. And **Entitlement to Compensation under 38 U.S.C. 1151** on each of the six counts **related to the Administration of the Drug Thorazine**; for Crippled Nervous and Muscular System, Amnesia, Impotency, Incontinence, and Unemployability: **Denied**; one only has to review and to digest **the damning information on this Drug** being supplied by Competent Patient/Victim Testimony and by Competent Professional Authority; pertaining to The Federal Food and Drug Administration, The Physicians' Desk Reference, (PDR;) and by Professional Trade Journals, News Articles, and the Testimony of The Medical Profession; to understand that the Reviewer(s) who issued the Denial to my claim, are Programmed To Deny, and <u>clearly they do not know what they are talking about</u> and are <u>Not Competent To Evaluate</u>.

"ONE POWERFUL VOICE"

U.S. Court of Appeals for Veterans Claims

Gary L. Koniz
317/VSC/SPOPS/LJD
C 24 891 327 – 05/27/13,

v

Department of Veterans Affairs
St. Petersburg Regional Office,

The Honorable Eric K. Shinseki
Secretary of Veterans Affairs

The Honorable Eric H. Holder
Attorney General of The United States

Answer

This is a **Latches Case**, in that it is in need of a Fair and Equitable Judgment where no Legal Mental Hygiene Legislation of Due Process Exists to base a rightful decision upon. And so that, we are clear on the matter of Mental Hygiene Law being without guarantee and individual safety of protection of the U.S. Constitution of Law as it is understood in the terms of The Fourteenth Amendment: that, "No person shall be denied their sacred and inherent right to Life, Liberty, and Property without Due Process of Law; which Mental Hygiene Law (which law there is of it,) has been written to serve the interests of the State and the Medical Industry, (**who have the power to deprive liberty and to destroy body and mind** without benefit of legal counsel and court processing;) over the rights and well-being of the individual; regarding of the "**allegation**" of my having the serious condition of Paranoid Schizophrenia impugned upon my good name, and being based upon Unfounded Legal Medical Evidence as per the criteria of the DSM-IV established for that condition to exist, (of my having a distorted view of the real world, greatly reduced ability to fulfill daily routines, and by abnormal ways of thinking, feeling, and behaving, over an extended six month period of time;) that was charged against me from Unknown Sources of Hearsay Information with no right to confront and challenge such testimony in court; and thereby to being Force Treated with the dosing of Strong Anti-Psychotic Tranquilizer Thorazine; that was, and is, Unconstitutional without being provided with the Rights to Defend Oneself.

This is also an **Estoppel Case**, in that The Veterans Health Administration, based its diagnosis (in Medical Incompetency Malpractice,) on "the Adverse Effects" of the Strong Tranquillers, (Loxitane and Cogentin,) that I was "Force Treated" with while in the custody of G. Weber Bryan Psychiatric Hospital where I was taken in handcuffs from General Hospital in Columbia, SC by two Sheriff's men who asked me if I was a Vietnam Veteran, (with the wording, "We're not taking any chances,") after complaining to the Medical Authorities, of a Drug Assault at the time. And along with the lingering Adverse Effects of the 28 days of Loxitane and Cogentin that I suffered from the Force Treatment of, and after several days of resulting insomnia from too rapid a withdrawal; of temporarily feeling dizzy and seeing red spots drifting before my eyes in the morning, (**Of The Spots That I Complained About**,) and hearing my sister's voice with her young children talking to me from outside of my bedroom door at my parent's house, where I had taken refuge after my release from G. Werber Bryan, urging me **to go to the V.A. To Seek Help**; (**which were the Voices that I mentioned to Dr. Kim**;) who in Negligent Incompetence, attributed the condition of Paranoid Schizophrenia to me over and utilized the effects of the drugs; of flat-affect and unresponsiveness, as grounds to fabricate his medical testimony and to cause great damage to myself by his Doctor's Order for Thorazine; on seven (6) separate counts.

"ONE POWERFUL VOICE"

1. On the specified issues: **Service connection for posttraumatic stress disorder is denied**.

My case **was never stated to be in the present** and was always presented to the V.A. as being Retroactive in the era of late 1970'2 and early 1980's, and refers to my "Original Claim" to the V.A. in 1986 that was denied Without Proper Legal Counsel and Due Process and based to fraudulent information that I was never made privy to at the time regarding my Medical Records. But what was In Connection To the Undocumented-Unsubstantiated Rubber-Stamped Diagnoses for Paranoid Schizophrenia (in my case,) having no justification for such labeling per DSM-IV (Diagnostic and Statistical Manual of Mental Disorders, IV Edition,) Criteria for the Diagnoses; that were thereby used in basis for Denial of my Claim, and that I received proper treatment, for this Diagnosis that was taken to be valid without examination. Also, and here being that I have been wrongfully accused, here, by the Examiners Review that: **"records noted that in 1972-1973 I abused marijuana heavily as well as other drugs including LSD,"** that was made by an informant, probably a family member," (and here referring to my Hippie younger brother.) That in all regards **Is Not True! and IS DENIED!** And what is thereby being based on Malicious Testimony, WITHOUT DUE PROCESS OF LAW, and is an Illegal Breach of Medical Ethics.

2. Entitlement to compensation under 38 U.S.C. 1151 for crippled nervous system is denied.

The Examiner here reasons I was were admitted to the V.A. Medical Center Albany, NY on April 19, 1982 for treatment of acute exacerbation of your Paranoid Schizophrenia manifested by auditory and visual hallucinations. "You were prescribed Thoarazine which is **an accepted and a necessary treatment for this condition**," (the examiners own words.) And that "**the dose given you (100 mg. daily X3,) was a therapeutic one for your condition**," (and once again to indicate here that the diagnosis WAS NOT LEGALLY VALID based to the DSM-IS criteria for the stated condition, and thereby an issue of Malpractice to be Force Ordered on Thorazine for it; which the Examiner states was "Therapeutic.") Also it says here, as noted by the Examiner, that the only reported problem noted from the Adverse Effects of the Thorazine was Orthostatic Hypotension (and stated as if that was "of no consequence.) **Orthostatic Hypotension is a Very Serious Condition** involving; Loss of Mental Acuity, and causing Major Suicidal Depression from "the loss of blood flow" to the brain and other body organs, (which in themselves begin to deteriorate.) The fact that No Other Thorazine Related Adverse Effects were named at the time of the V.A. Hospitalization, such as: the Amnesia, Crippled Nervous System, Crippled Muscular System Impotence, Incontinence, and Enlarged Prostate, **is of No Significance**; since each of these condition is self-evidently to be experienced as a result of taking this drug (and I do not use the word medication,) that were experienced by myself in the time of their occurring; either while at the V.A. during my stay (as expressed to the Incompetent Physician Dr. Byung Kim and not recorded,) or having been debilitated by in the aftermath of my release to be experienced; which I would in no-wise have the opportunity, or motive, or financial wherewithal of resources "to technically consult" a physician about on the grounds that this "recorded information" would be needed by the V.A. in order for me "to prove" my claim that I was debilitated by the Forced Administration of the Drug Chemical Thorazine; which I AM Delivering my Testimony to now. And again here to stress, that it does not matter whether I was disabled by this drug during the time of Treatment, or for months to years afterwards; the fact being **that I WAS Disabled by It**.

"ONE POWERFUL VOICE"

This section also makes note of two related Illegal Commitment Incarcerations, (6/22/85 and 12/11/85) at the Hudson River State Psychiatric Hospital for the Insane, where I was summarily taken without Rights as a Vietnam Veteran with "Prior V.A. History;" for being the **innocent victim** of an altercation with my brother and my father on the first incident, and following a mugging robbery on the second; both of which were rendered against me without Due Process and I was Forced into Destructive Treatment with the drug Navane, (which is another deadly Chemical classified under the Anti-Psychotic Psychotropic Phenothiazine Class, and unbearable to endure.) And during which interval of time, between the first and the second commitment, that I had the good fortune to be hired as a Freight Processor Trainee as "Temporary Help" for six months at Minimum Wage. Which employment was "cut short" three months into the program by the mugging robbery that I was the victim of and subsequent second commitment. That is being used here by the Examiner with the wording that "I went off my meds," and had to be "admitted once more for treatment" of my Chronic Paranoid Schizophrenia (which was not the case.) The true of the fact being, that I was "railroaded" into Hudson River Psychiatric for being a Vietnam Veteran with a V.A. history of Mental Disorder, (and to be destroyed without Due Process.) The Examiner goes on to note: that there was no compromise of my neurological or musculoskeletal systems since I was able to do Ad Lib endeavors (whatever that is,) and being gainfully employed. (And here to say "gainfully employed" at what? a high paying professional career job? or doing low level perfunctory task work for the minimum wage and at lowered level of alertness and mental competency being able "to get by at.") The Examiner here is either being "naïve" or is "manipulative and corrupt," not to realize the **Professional Issue at stake here**.

3. Entitlement to compensation under 38 U.S.C. 1151 for amnesia is denied.

Let it here be noted that according to all "Pharmaceutical Evidence," **the drug Thorazine** acts as a **"Chemical Lobatomy,"** on a person's brain functions, "Effaces" a person's "Sense of Self" in "Dissociative Disability" and causes that person "To Forget" their accomplishments and who they are as person and to the loss of their Self-Esteem and Personality. This Drug also destroys a person's aggressiveness and ambition drive and renders them "inert" flat-affect and zombie-like, making them unable to compete. Are you really feigning such ignorance as not to realize this?

4. Entitlement to compensation under 38 U.S.C. 1151 for impotency is denied.

And here it is **"Opined" by the Examiner** that my impotency IS UNRELATED (capital letters supplied by the reviewer.) And in which the Examiner goes on to make a **Snide-Remark**. "That the evidence in your current claims file makes not references to the above conditions that you have that have been evaluated, diagnosed, and treated for. AS such there may be many reasons why you have your conditions, (**if they do indeed exist,**) aside from the short-term use of Thorazine some thirty years ago;" and that: "Such conditions, such as Impotency and Enlarged Prostate would resolve with the cessation of the Thorazine." REALLY? Are you really stating this as Medically Sound Fact? When I can easily prove otherwise. Are you forgetting medically noted, that I was also on Loxitane and Cogentin for 28 days preceding the Forced Thorazine Treatment ordered for by the V.A. in combined effect of Contraindication in lingering Adverse Reactions. And here once again to add, that my case was never "stated to be in the present" and was only being presented for damages suffered for an "untenable `mount of time" following my mis-treatment by the V.A. in 1982, and for my suffering and lost income during this interval.

5. Entitlement to compensation under 38 U.S.C. 1151 for crippled muscular system denied.

"ONE POWERFUL VOICE"

And here, the Examiner has nothing further to add but only makes further re-utterance of the V.A.'s generic denial, that: "no long term effects or complications have been noted to arise either during the use of Thorazine or after it has been discontinued." And again pinning the issue on the Patient/Victim's ability in financial resources, willingness, or necessity, to further consult with a Qualified Physician about what is truly ailing them; (and I would here say under the term, "willingness" of a Veteran's willingness "to trust" any of the doctors of the so called Psychiatric Industry with their lives, and after "escaping their clutches," (of being turned into a life-long mental patient,) to experiment with people and cause them grave harm unto death by suicide.

Here are some serious **WARNINGS/PRECAUTIONS and ADVERSE REACTIONS** associated with the drug chemical Thorazine: **Extrapyramidal symptoms,** akinesia (inability to initiate movement) and akathisia (inability to remain motionless), **tardive dyskinesia** (TD), **Neuroleptic malignant syndrome** (NMS); **impaired mental/physical abilities, Drowsiness, jaundice, agranulocytosis,** (lowered white blood cell count) **hypotensive effects, ECG changes, dystonia,** (a neurological movement disorder,) **motor restlessness, pseudo-parkinsonism, anticholinergic effects,** (decreasing saliva production,) **NMS,** (a life-threatening neurological disorder most often caused by an adverse reaction to neuroleptic or antipsychotic drugs, manifesting in muscle rigidity, fever, and autonomic instability,) **ocular changes.**

Are you kidding? **These doctors need to take the Thorazine themselves** to evaluate its effects, to think of us as being of no consequence to fall for their heinous version of Thorazine as being a beneficial drug necessary to the treatment of Alleged Mental Illnesses, having no lingering Adverse Effects after cessation of treatment, and Denying us our Integrity of Credible Testimony to the contrary. This is **a criminal matter** regarding the staggering and heartfelt numbers of Veterans Suicides coinciding to the Forced Use of this Drug for the V.A. to be responsible for.

6. **Entitlement to compensation under 38 U.S.C. 1151 for incontinence is denied.**
7. **Entitlement to individual unemployability is denied.** (As having been already discussed.)

WHEREAS: the aforementioned Disabilities **have been proved to be the result of Thorazine Treatment** and **the actual fault of V.A.'s Carelessness, Negligence, Lack of Proper Skill, and Error In Judgment**; and with similar instances of Fault Occurring at the hands of the two State Psychiatric Facilities previously named, pertaining to their Unsupported Psychiatric Diagnoses, and Inappropriate Treatment, in failing to furnish proper and accepted levels of medical care and in violations all of their professional oaths and duties in the matter of the Hippocratic Oath and Safeguard of the Human Rights of Accused, to be treating their charges as gullible victims with the Power of Life and Death over them, having Indefinite and Undefined powers of confinement, and to their whim of Unscrupulous Treatment with any; drug, surgery, or experiment they would chose to inflict, and without any safeguards of Due Process Rights legality to protect the hapless Psychiatrically Accused that I am pressing judgment to and for you to side with my case here for Compensation. Failing to do so is clearly a Co-Conspiracy with the issue of Medical Corruption.

"ONE POWERFUL VOICE"

Approved exception to SF 502

PATIENT'S NAME	AGE	SEX	RACE	SOCIAL SECURITY NO.	CLAIM NO.	NAME OF HOSPITAL
KONIZ, Gary	35	M	W	115 36 5132	c- *unknown*	AVAMC 500 Albany,

DIAGNOSES (List in numerical order; first, the established clinical diagnosis responsible for the major part of patient's stay; then, in order of clinical importance, other established diagnoses for which treatment was given. Place letter "N" before diagnoses (es) responsible for Nursing Care placement. List Problem numbers after diagnoses.)

			ICDA CODE
1.	Axis I:	Chronic paranoid schizophrenia: acute exacerbation	295.34
2.	Axis II:	No diagnosis	V71.09
3.	Axis III:	No diagnosis	
4.	Axis IV:	Unspecified	
5.	Axis V:	Very poor	

PERTINENT CLINICAL DIAGNOSES NOTED BUT NOT TREATED (Include autopsy diagnoses not listed as clinical above)

OPERATIONS/PROCEDURES PERFORMED AT THIS HOSPITAL DURING CURRENT ADMISSION	DATE	
Audiometry	4-19-82	95.41

SUMMARY (Brief statement should include, if applicable, history; pertinent physical findings; course in hospital; treatment given; condition at release; date patient is capable of returning to full employment; period of convalescence, if required; recommendations for follow-up treatment; medications furnished at release; competency opinion when required; rehabilitation potential; and name of Nursing Home, if known.)

The patient is a 35 year old, white, divorced twice, unemployed, male veteran living with his parents in Poughkeepsie, NY. He admitted himself to 10B complaining of auditory and visual hallucinations - he was seeing red dots and hearing voices of children telling him to do or not to do things, and sometimes hearing voices talking to one another about the patient. Also he complained of his feeling that people were trying to get him. The patient states he had his first psychiatric hospitalization for approximately a week at St. Francis Hospital, Poughkeepsie, NY, in 1977 for auditory and visual hallucinations, and paranoid ideations, but the details regarding this experience were unclear from the patient. Since then he states he has been having these experiences on and off, but he has never sought psychiatric help up until several weeks ago when he voluntarily admitted himself to a hospital in South Carolina while he was traveling the southern states. However, the information from his parents later during the hospitalization revealed a somewhat different story. They indicated that the patient has been grossly psychotic with hostile behavior and delusions at least for the last year. They reported that the patient had sent a letter to a local police department accusing his family of dealing illegal drugs. Also, he felt his family was poisoning his food. There was one time that he believed his girlfriend was also involved in this illegal act with his own family. His family seemed to have made many efforts to persuade the patient to receive psychiatric help without success up until this time. The patient signed himself out of the hospital in South Carolina a few weeks ago, and returned to the Poughkeepsie area. Since then he didn't take medications: Loxitane and Cogentin because

Byung Ock Kim, M.

ADMISSION DATE	DISCHARGE DATE	TYPE OF RELEASE	INPATIENT DAYS	ABSENCE DAYS	WARD NO.	SIGNATURE OF PHYSICIAN
4/19/82	5/13/82	Regular	23	0	10B	BYUNG KIM, M.D. Staff Psychiatrist

VA FORM 10-1000 MAR 1972   EXISTING STOCKS OF VA FORM 10-1000, JAN 1971 WILL BE USED.   **HOSPITAL SUMMARY**

MEDICAL RECORDS SECTION   INITIALS *BL* DATE *6-11-82*   D-5/14/82 T-5/21/82 jed   *BL*

☆ U.S. GOVERNMENT PRINTING OFFICE: 1981— 361-488-5244

"ONE POWERFUL VOICE"

of "shakiness of his legs". He complains that since he has stopped medication he has been having increasing auditory and visual hallucinations and paranoid ideations.

The patient is the eldest of 5 children in the family. His father works as a chemist, and mother is a dietician at a local hospital. All the siblings are either college graduates or college students, and all of them seem to be successful. The patient also had 4 years of college education. He was in the Army in 1964 - 1967, highest rank was E4, worked as a heavy equipment operator. He spent 7 months in Vietnam, but was never involved in combat experiences. He worked as a heavy equipment operator between 1967 - 1977 as a civilian, and since then he has been working sporadically in various jobs including a landscaper, a mountain ranger, and mental health nurse's aide, etc. He hasn't been employed for the last year since he was laid off of his job as a mental health nurse's aide. He married twice; first marriage was from 1970 - 1972, and the second one lasted only 6 months in 1976. The details about his marital relationships were unclear at this time. The patient seems to have been living a quite seclusive and withdrawn life for the last year or so, as he claims that he takes "a long walk" by himself, and occasionally he does things around his house. There is no family history of psychiatric illness. He occasionally smokes marijuana, but denied other drugs or alcohol abuse.

Mental status examination found him to be alert, fully oriented, reasonably clean, generally cooperative, but at times he appeared to be guarded and frequently inattentive to the interviewer. Auditory and visual hallucinations were described previously. Paranoid ideation and delusions were also evident. His mood was neutral. Affect was flat. He denied suicidal or homicidal ideations. His association was tight based on his relatively short reply to the questions during the interview. Memory was intact. Insight was fair to limited.

Medical history was not significant.

Physical examination was not significant.

Laboratory tests were not significant. EKG was normal. Chest x-ray was negative.

Hospital course: The patient was started on Thorazine 100 mg. po tid, and dosage was raised up to 200 mg. po hs, and 100 mg. po tid, but he developed orthostatic hypotension. Thorazine was changed to Trilafon which dosage was gradually increased to 8 mg. po tid, and the patient tolerated this dosage well without any significant side effects. The patient seemed to be responding fairly well to this medication, as his hallucinations and delusions subsided, and his behavior appeared to be appropriate. However, the patient remained withdrawn, seclusive, preoccupied, and showed little interaction with other patients on the ward throughout the hospitalization. Many efforts were made to get him involved in various therapeutic activities, but his involvement

Standard Form 507   o4S--15--51472p-3   spo

CLINICAL RECORD	Report on ___ DISCHARGE SUMMARY
	or
	Continuation of S. F. ___ 10-1000
	(Strike out one line) (Specify type of examination or data)

(Sign and date)

with these activities was quite marginal, ~~and he complained his problems were so dull~~.

The patient was discharged on 5/13/82 with 1 week supply of Trilafon 8 mg. po qid, with recommendation that he should be followed by a daily program from local mental health facilities on a long term basis.

He is felt to be competent to handle his funds, but considered *disabled* for an undetermined period. Diet-regular diet. *Condition on discharge is improved.*

BYUNG KIM, M.D.
Staff Psychiatrist

(Continue on reverse side)

PATIENT'S IDENTIFICATION *(For typed or written entries give: Name--last, first, middle; grade; date; hospital or medical facility)*   REGISTER NO. 36 5132   WARD NO.

KONIZ, Gary
AVAMC #500 ALBANY, NY
D-5/14/82 T-5/21/82 jed

REPORT ON ___ or CONTINUATION OF ___
STANDARD FORM 507
General Services Administration and
Interagency Committee on Medical Records
FPMR 101-11.80 6-8
October 1975 507-106
☆U.S. Government Printing Office: 1981-341-488/6638

"ONE POWERFUL VOICE"

| MEDICAL RECORD | DOCTOR'S ORDERS |

NOTE: Physician's signature must accompany each entry including standing orders. Date and time for instituting and discontinuing the orders must be recorded.

DATE AND TIME	PROB. NO.	ORDERS *(Another brand, equal in quality, of the same basic drug may be dispensed, UNLESS checked.)*	✓	NURSE'S SIGNATURE
4/19/82		admit to 18B	✓	
		group 1	✓	
		regular diet	✓	
		CBC, urinalysis, VDRL, profile 1	✓	
		chest x-ray	✓	
		EKG	✓	
		Thorazine 100mg p.o. t.i.d		
		Thorazine 50mg q.h. or 100mg p.o. q 2h prn up to 400 mg		
4/19/82		check B.P. before administer Thorazine. Kim, M.D.		
4/19/82 6 PM		Tylenol 650 mg po q 4h prn. Phone order Dr Ryder Kim, M.D.		
4/21/82		↑ Thorazine 100 mg p.o. t.i.d during day & 200mg p.o. HS. Group 2 Kim, M.D.		

Enter in space below: PATIENT IDENTIFICATION – TREATING FACILITY – WARD NO. – DATE

MEDICAL RECORD
DOCTOR'S ORDERS

VA FORM OCT 1975 10-1158

EXISTING STOCK OF VA FORM 10-1158 MAY 1973 AND VA FORM 10-1158c, NOV. 1972, WILL BE USED.

"ONE POWERFUL VOICE"

| MEDICAL RECORD | | DOCTOR'S ORDERS |

NOTE: Physician's signature must accompany each entry including standing orders. Date and time for instituting and discontinuing the orders must recorded.

DATE AND TIME	PROB NO.	ORDERS (Another brand, equal in quality, of the same basic drug may be dispensed, UNLESS checked.)	▶	✓	NURSE'S SIGNATURI
4-22-82		Repeat CBC c̄ diff. in AM			
	4/ 27/82	WARD PHYSICIAN: PLEASE FILL OUT AND SIGN SECTION #1, 2, PART VI OF THE ORAL-MAXILLOFACIAL INITIAL ASSESSMENT AND PLANS.			
		DR. D. DIGIACOMO			
4/28/82		Group 3 Kim, M.D.			
4/30/82		✓ Thorazine 100mg p.o. tid			
4/30/82		Trilafon 4mg p.o. qid ✓ Thorazine 100mg p.o. tid only Day pass prn over the weekend Kim, M.D.			
5/3-82		D/C Thorazine ↑ Trilafon 8mg p.o. tid cogentin 2mg p.o. qid BID Kim, M.D.			5/3/82

MEDICAL RECORD

DOCTOR'S ORDERS

Exception to Standard Form 50:
Approved by OMI

| MEDICAL RECORD | | DOCTOR'S ORDERS | | |

NOTE: Physician's signature must accompany each entry including standing orders. Date and time for instituting and discontinuing the orders must be recorded.

DATE AND TIME	PROB. NO.	ORDERS (Another brand, equal in quality, of the same basic drug may be dispensed, UNLESS checked.)		✓	NURSE'S SIGNATURE
5/6/-82		T Trilafon 8mg p.o. qid			ARM
5/6/-82		Weekend pass Fri - Sun			
5/11-82		Discharge regular			

Enter in space below: PATIENT IDENTIFICATION – TREATING FACILITY – WARD NO. – DATE

MEDICAL RECORD
DOCTOR'S ORDERS

EXISTING STOCK OF VA FORM 10-1158 MAY 1973 AND VA FORM 10-1158c, NOV. 1973 WILL BE USED.
VA FORM OCT. 1975 10-1158

Thorazine Treatment

If my blood pressure stays around 85/55, do I have a health problem?

As long as you are not experiencing symptoms of low blood pressure, there is no need for concern. Most doctors consider chronically low blood pressure dangerous only if it causes noticeable signs and symptoms, such as:

- **Dizziness or lightheadedness**
- **Fainting (called <u>syncope</u>)**
- **Dehydration and unusual thirst**
  Lack of concentration
- **Blurred vision**
- **Nausea**
- **Cold, clammy, pale skin**
- **Rapid, shallow breathing**
- **Fatigue**
- **Depression**

Low blood pressure can occur with:

Certain medications
A number of drugs can cause low blood pressure, including diuretics and other drugs that treat hypertension; heart medications such as beta blockers; drugs for Parkinson's disease; tricyclic antidepressants; erectile dysfunction drugs, particularly in combination with nitroglycerine; narcotics and alcohol. Other prescription and over-the-counter drugs may cause low blood pressure when taken in combination with HBP medications.

With very low blood pressure, the <u>brain</u>, heart, and other vital organs may not receive enough blood. Ultimately, this can cause these organs to fail to function properly and even to become permanently damaged. The lack of <u>oxygen</u> can also cause a person to experience blackouts, particularly when standing up or sitting up too quickly after lying down. This type is generally referred to as *orthostatic hypotension*.

Peter Breggin, M.D., psychiatrist, points out clearly that the purpose of Thorazine is to alter and disable normal brain functions. It is actually the HARM caused by the drug which produces the effect.

"The brain-disabling principle applies to all of the most potent psychiatric interventions - neuroleptics, antidepressants, lithium, electroshock, and psychosurgery. . . the major psychiatric treatments exert their primary or intended effect by disabling normal brain function. Neuroleptic lobotomy, for example, is not a side effect, but the sought-after clinical effect. Conversely, none of the major psychiatric interventions correct or improve existing brain dysfunction, such as any presumed biochemical imbalance. If the patient happens to suffer from brain dysfunction, then the psychiatric drug, electroshock, or psychosurgery will worsen or compound it."

"ONE POWERFUL VOICE"

Chlorpromazine
Chlorpromazine Hydrochloride Tablets

THERAPEUTIC CLASS

Phenothiazine

INDICATIONS

Treatment of schizophrenia. Control of N/V. Relief of restlessness and apprehension before surgery. Acute intermittent porphyria. Adjunct in the treatment of tetanus. To control the manifestations of the manic type of manic-depressive illness. Relief of intractable hiccups. Treatment of severe behavioral problems in children (1-12 yrs). Short-term treatment of hyperactivity in children. (Tab) Management of manifestations of psychotic disorders.

ADULT DOSAGE

Adults: Inpatient: **Acute Schizophrenic/Manic State**: Initial: (IM) 25mg, then 25-50mg in 1 hr PRN. Titrate: Increase gradually over several days up to 400mg q4-6h until controlled, then switch to PO. (PO) Usual: 500mg/day. Gradual increases to 2000mg/day or more may be necessary. Less Acutely Disturbed: (PO) 25mg tid. Titrate: Increase gradually to effective dose. Usual: 400mg/day. Outpatient: (PO) 10mg tid-qid or 25mg bid-tid. More Severe Cases: (PO) 25mg tid. Titrate: After 1-2 days, may increase by 20-50mg semi-weekly until calm and cooperative. Prompt Control of Severe Symptoms: Initial: (IM) 25mg, may repeat in 1 hr. Subsequent Doses: (PO) 25-50mg tid. N/V: Usual: (PO) 10-25mg q4-6h PRN; (IM) 25mg, subsequently 25-50mg q3-4h PRN until vomiting stops if no hypotension, then switch to PO. During Surgery: (IM) 12.5mg, may repeat in 1/2 hr if no hypotension and PRN; (IV) 2mg per fractional inj at 2-min intervals. Max: 25mg. Presurgical Apprehension: (PO) 25-50mg 2-3 hrs, or (IM) 12.5-25mg 1-2 hrs, before operation. Intractable Hiccups: Initial: (PO) 25-50mg tid-qid. May give IM 25-50mg if symptoms persist after 2-3 days; if symptoms still persist, IV 25-50mg slow infusion with patient flat in bed. Porphyria: (PO) 25-50mg tid-qid; (IM) 25mg tid-qid until patient can take PO therapy. Tetanus: (IM) 25-50mg tid-qid; (IV) 25-50mg. Elderly/Debilitated/Emaciated: Start at lower end of dosing range, increase gradually, monitor closely.

CONTRAINDICATIONS

Comatose states or the presence of large amounts of CNS depressants (eg, alcohol, barbiturates, narcotics, etc).

WARNINGS/PRECAUTIONS

Extrapyramidal symptoms may be confused with CNS signs of undiagnosed primary disease responsible for vomiting; avoid in children/adolescents with signs of Reye's syndrome. Risk of **tardive dyskinesia** (TD), especially in elderly; consider d/c if signs/symptoms appear. **Neuroleptic malignant syndrome** (NMS) reported; d/c therapy and carefully monitor for recurrences if therapy is reintroduced. **May impair mental/physical abilities**. Neonates exposed during 3rd trimester of pregnancy are at risk

"ONE POWERFUL VOICE"

for extrapyramidal and/or withdrawal symptoms. Leukopenia, neutropenia, and agranulocytosis reported. Monitor for fever or infection with neutropenia; d/c in patients with severe neutropenia (absolute neutrophil count <1000/mm^3). Caution with chronic respiratory disorders, acute respiratory infections (especially in children), glaucoma, cardiovascular, hepatic, or renal disease. May suppress cough reflex; aspiration of vomitus possible. Caution if exposed to extreme heat. May elevate prolactin levels. May produce α-adrenergic blockade. May mask signs and symptoms of overdosage of other drugs and obscure diagnosis and treatment of other conditions (eg, intestinal obstruction, brain tumor, Reye's syndrome). **Avoid abrupt withdrawal of high-dose therapy**. Evaluate patients with a history of long-term therapy on whether the maintenance dose could be lowered or d/c therapy to lessen likelihood of adverse reactions related to cumulative drug effect. May produce false-(+) phenylketonuria test results. (Inj) Contains sulfites.

ADVERSE REACTIONS

Drowsiness, jaundice, agranulocytosis, (lowered <u>white blood cell</u> count) **hypotensive effects, ECG changes, dystonia, motor restlessness, pseudo-parkinsonism, TD, anticholinergic effects, NMS, ocular changes, skin pigmentation, allergic reactions.**

DRUG INTERACTIONS

See Contraindications. Monitor for neurological toxicity with lithium; d/c if signs occur. Prolongs and intensifies action of CNS depressants (eg, anesthetics, barbiturates, narcotics); administer about 1/4 to 1/2 the usual dose of such agents when used concomitantly. Caution with organophosphorus insecticides, atropine or related drugs. Avoid use of alcohol due to possible additive effects and hypotension. May counteract the antihypertensive effect of guanethidine and related compounds. Diminished effect of oral anticoagulants reported. May lower convulsive threshold; anticonvulsant dose adjustment may be needed. May interfere with phenytoin metabolism and precipitate phenytoin toxicity. Increased plasma levels of both agents with propranolol. Thiazide diuretics may potentiate orthostatic hypotension. Do not use with metrizamide; d/c at least 48 hrs before myelography and should not be resumed for at least 24 hrs after; do not administer for control of N/V prior to or after procedure with metrizamide. May obscure vomiting as a sign of toxicity of chemotherapeutic drugs. Certain pressor agents, such as epinephrine, may cause paradoxical further lowering of BP; do not use to control hypotension.

PREGNANCY

Safety not known in pregnancy, not for use in nursing. Found in breast milk

MECHANISM OF ACTION

Phenothiazine; not established. Suspected to act at all levels of CNS, primarily at subcortical levels as well as on multiple organ systems.

"ONE POWERFUL VOICE"

The P-I-E-N-O Parkinson's List Drug Database
loxapine /Loxitane^{TM}
__ANTIPSYCHOTIC__
HIGH RISK

Description: Loxapine is a typical antipsychotic drug that is structurally similar to the antidepressant amoxapine. Loxapine is used in the treatment of psychotic disorders and schizophrenia. It most often is used in patients who have not responded to other antipsychotic drugs. A 10 mg loxapine dose would be equivalent to 100 mg chlorpromazine, the prototype antipsychotic. Loxapine was approved by the FDA in 1975.

Mechanism of Action: Loxapine blocks postsynaptic dopamine receptors in the mesolimbic system and increases dopamine turnover by blockade of the DA somatodendritic autoreceptor. After approximately 12 weeks of chronic therapy, depolarization blockade of dopamine tracts occurs. The decrease in dopamine neurotransmission has been found to correlate with the antipsychotic effects. DA-receptor blockade is also responsible for the potent extrapyramidal effects observed with this drug. Dopamine blockade in the chemoreceptor trigger zone accounts for the antiemetic effects. Loxapine possesses moderate anticholinergic and strong ›-adrenergic receptor blocking effects. Blockade of ›A-adrenergic receptors produces sedation; muscle relaxation; and cardiovascular effects such as hypotension, reflex tachycardia, and minor changes in ECG patterns. Pharmacokinetics: Following oral administration, loxapine is rapidly and completely absorbed from the GI tract. Intramuscular administration, used for agitated patients or patients unable to take oral preparations, is also rapidly absorbed. First-pass hepatic metabolism reduces bioavailability to roughly 30% compared with intramuscular doses. Peak serum concentrations are attained more slowly following IM administration but are similar at steady state to those attained after oral administration. After oral doses, sedative effects are seen in about 20-30 minutes, with peak effects in about 1.5-3 hours and a duration of about 12 hours. Several days of therapy are required to produce steady-state serum levels, and maximum antipsychotic effect may require weeks.

There is wide distribution of loxapine, mainly into brain, lungs, heart, liver, and pancreas. The drug appears in the CSF, crosses the placenta, and is distributed into breast milk. Half-life of loxapine depends on the route of administration. Half-life is roughly 4 hours after oral administration and about 12 hours after IM administration, possibly due to slow absorption from muscle tissue. Metabolism is extensive. Loxapine has several active metabolites, 8-hydroxyloxapine, 7-hydroxyloxapine, and undergoes demethylation to amoxapine and its hydroxy metabolites. Insignificant amounts of unchanged drug are found in the urine and feces; most excretion of metabolites is as glucuronide or sulfate conjugates. About 50% of an oral dose is excreted in urine and feces within 24 hours.

CONTRAINDICATIONS/PRECAUTIONS: Loxapine should be used with extreme caution in patients with thyroid disease such as thyrotoxicosis or hyperthyroidism. Antipsychotic agents can cause extremely severe extrapyramidal symptoms such as dystonias or rigidity. Laryngospasm can prevent breathing and could be life-threatening.

Patients with hypocalcemia may be at an increased risk for having dystonic reactions, so loxapine should be used with caution in this patient population.

Severe adverse CNS reactions induced by loxapine may appear similar to neurologic symptoms of CNS disorders such as encephalitis, Reye's syndrome, encephalopathy, meningitis, and tetanus. In addition, loxapine can suppress the symptoms of these disorders, if they are present. Loxapine is

"ONE POWERFUL VOICE"

contraindicated in patients who are in a coma, who have a brain tumor, or who exhibit severe toxic CNS depression.

Loxapine also should be used with caution in patients with cardiovascular disorders or cardiac disease. Severe hypotension, myocardial depression, arrhythmias, and changes in ECG patterns occur. While these effects are generally reversible, they can lead to cardiac arrest.

Patients receiving anticonvulsant agents or who have a history of a seizure disorder, epilepsy, or EEG abnormalities should be carefully monitored during therapy with loxapine due to its potent lowering of seizure threshold, particularly at very high doses. Adequate anticonvulsant therapy should prevent an increase in seizure frequency during treatment with loxapine. High doses and large changes in loxapine doses should be avoided in patients with a known history of seizures.

Loxapine should be used with caution in patients with hepatic disease because the drug's metabolism can be decreased, increasing toxicity.

Loxapine should be used with caution in patients with renal impairment, or in elderly or debilitated patients. Reduction in dosage may be required.

Loxapine should be used with caution in patients with glaucoma. Other antipsychotics have caused lenticular opacity, resulting in visual impairment.

ADVERSE REACTIONS: Extrapyramidal symptoms (EPS) occur occasionally during treatment with loxapine and appear to be the result of blockade of the DAreceptor. These symptoms occur with greater severity and frequency during high-dose therapy. Extrapyramidal symptoms are categorized as dystonia, akathisia (subjective and objective motor restlessness), and parkinsonism. Parkinsonian symptoms are more common in the elderly, whereas children most often develop dystonic reactions, which can be worsened by acute infections or severe dehydration. Dystonic reactions are seen during the first week of treatment. Akathisia and parkinsonian symptoms usually develop several days to weeks into therapy. Dystonia and pseudoparkinsonism usually are easily treated with concomitant benztropine, diphenhydramine, lorazepam, or amantadine. Akathisia can respond to dosage reduction or concomitant administration of a benzodiazepine (usually lorazepam) or propranolol. However, patients should be monitored carefully for excessive sedation and respiratory depression (see Drug Interactions). Loxapine is less likely to cause EPS than are high-potency antipsychotics such as haloperidol. Neuroleptic malignant syndrome (NMS) can occur in patients receiving loxapine. NMS is characterized by hyperthermia, severe extrapyramidal dysfunction, alterations in consciousness, altered mental status, and autonomic instability. Increased serum creatine phosphokinase (CPK), acute renal failure, and leukocytosis also have occurred. NMS does not appear to be doserelated. Severe cases have resulted in death occurring 3-30 days after onset of the syndrome. Several predisposing factors can contribute to the development of NMS, including heat stress, physical exhaustion, dehydration, and organic brain disease. NMS occurs more frequently in young men. Loxapine should be immediately discontinued and appropriate supportive therapy initiated as soon as symptoms of NMS are discovered.

Tardive dyskinesia (TD) is characterized by involuntary movements of the perioral region (tongue, mouth, jaw, eyelids, or face) or choreoathetoid movements in the extremities. It can develop during long-term therapy or following discontinuation of loxapine, and it occurs more frequently in elderly women. The incidence may be higher in patients with bipolar disorder than with schizophrenia. Some cases can be irreversible. While contradictory evidence exists, it has been suggested that the likelihood of developing TD increases with prolonged treatment and cumulative doses. Although this complication often occurs following prolonged treatment or with administration of high dosages, it also has been reported to occur after short periods of time and with low dosages. Routine monitoring (at 3to 6month intervals) of movement disorders is

"ONE POWERFUL VOICE"

considered the standard practice when using loxapine. If signs or symptoms of TD develop, loxapine use should be reevaluated and possibly discontinued.

Drowsiness is a CNS effect that frequently occurs during initial treatment with loxapine. Tolerance usually develops with continued therapy. Other CNS effects reported less frequently include restlessness, insomnia, depression, headache, and cerebral edema. Seizures can occur and are of special significance in patients who have preexisting seizure disorders or EEG abnormalities.

Anticholinergic effects related to loxapine administration include blurred vision, mydriasis, nausea, adynamic ileus, urinary retention, impotence, sinus tachycardia, and constipation. These effects can be enhanced by the concomitant administration of anticholinergic antiparkinsonian drugs, antidepressants, or other anticholinergic agents.
Cardiac arrhythmias, such as sinus tachycardia, can occur during therapy with loxapine. More serious ventricular arrhythmias, (eg. ventricular tachycardia) including those that can produce hypotension, can occur but are relatively rare unless large doses are used.

Hypothermia and hyperthermia have been reported and may result from loxapine's effect on the hypothalamic control of temperature regulation. Hyperpyrexia and heat stroke unrelated to NMS also have occurred.

Hematologic disturbances that have been reported following loxapine administration include leukopenia, leukocytosis, thrombocytopenia, pancytopenia, aplastic anemia, and anemia. Agranulocytosis has occurred rarely and has been associated with combination treatment with other agents.

Skin hyperpigmentation secondary to loxapine administration is more likely to occur following prolonged therapy. Changes in skin pigmentation generally are restricted to areas of the body exposed to sunlight. Severe photosensitivity can result, so patients should be warned either to keep out of the sun or to use effective sunscreens (SPF 15+) on exposed areas of the body. Withdrawal of the drug can reverse the effects, and the clinician must decide whether therapy should be continued if pigmentary changes occur. Contact dermatitis has occurred when some antipsychotic liquids remain on the skin. Precautions to avoid contact should be taken, and any inadvertent spillage should be washed off immediately.

Pigmentary retinopathy due to loxapine can occur with or without pigmentary changes in the skin. Symptoms of blurred vision, difficulty with nighttime vision, or defective color vision should be investigated promptly. Wearing protective dark glasses can reduce the possibility of developing this reaction. The drug has been associated with frequent ocular changes including deposition of fine particles in the lens and cornea, which can cause visual impairment.

Medication : Navane - (Thiothixene)

Possible side effects, warnings and cautions associated with this medication are listed below. This is not an all inclusive list but is representative of Items of potential clinical significance to you. For more information on this medication, you may consult further with your physician or refer to a standard text such as the PDR or the United States Pharmacopoeia Dispensing Information (USPDI). As part of
monitoring some of these potential side effects, your physician may order laboratory or other tests. The treatment team will closely monitor individuals who are unable to readily communicate side effects in order to enhance care and treatment.

Possible side effects warnings and cautions associated with this medication. The most common side effects include: Constipation: decreased sweating: dizziness, lightheadedness, or fainting: drowsiness {mild}: dryness of mouth: increased appetite and weight: increased sensitivity of skin to sunlight (skin rash, itching, redness or other discoloration of skin, or severe sunburn): stuffy nose. Check with your doctor as soon as possible if any of the following side effects occur: difficulty in talking or swallowing: inability to move eyes: lip smacking or puckering: loss of balance control: mask-like face: muscle spasms, especially of the neck and back: puffing of cheeks, rapid or worm-like movements of tongue: restlessness or need to keep moving (severe): shuffling walk: stiffness of arms and legs: trembling and shaking of fingers and hands: twisting movements of body: uncontrolled chewing movements: uncontrolled movements of the arms and legs

Less common side effects include: Changes in menstrual period, decreased sexual ability: swelling of breasts (in males and females): unusual secretion of milk. Check with your doctor as soon as possible if any of the following side effects occur: Blurred vision or other eye problems: difficult urination: fainting: skin discoloration: skin rash. Check with your doctor as soon as possible if any of the following rare side effects occur: Hot, dry skin or lack of sweating: increased blinking or spasms of eyelid: muscle weakness: sore throat and fever: uncontrolled twisting movements of neck, trunk, arms, or legs: unusual bleeding or bruising: unusual facial expressions or body positions: yellow eyes or skin.

Stop taking this medicine and **get emergency help immediately** if any of the follow-ing effects occur: Convulsions (seizures: difficulty in breathing: fast heartbeat: high fever: high or low (irregular} blood pressure: increased sweating: loss of bladder control:
muscle stiffness (severe): unusually pale skin: unusual tiredness.
This medication may cause your skin to be more sensitive to sunlight than it is normally. Exposure to sunlight, even for brief periods of time, may cause a skin rash, itching, redness or other discoloration of the skin, or a severe sunburn.
Tardive Dyskinesia (lip smacking or puckering, puffing of cheeks, rapid or fine worm-like movement of tongue, uncontrolled chewing movement, uncontrolled movements of arms and legs may occur and may not go away after stopping use of the medication). **See PDR, USPDI** or US Hospital Formulary Service for all-inclusive list of side effects,

Perphenazine (Trilafon)?

Perphenazine is an anti-psychotic medication in a group of drugs called phenothiazines (FEEN-oh-THYE-a-zeens). It works by changing the actions of chemicals in your brain.

Perphenazine is used to treat psychotic disorders such as schizophrenia. It is also used to control severe nausea and vomiting.

Perphenazine may also be used for purposes not listed in this medication guide.

What are the possible side effects of perphenazine (Trilafon)?

Get emergency medical help if you have any of these **signs of an allergic reaction:** hives; difficulty breathing; swelling of your face, lips, tongue, or throat.

Stop using perphenazine and call your doctor at once if you have a serious side effect such as:

- twitching or uncontrollable movements of your eyes, lips, tongue, face, arms, or legs;
- tremor (uncontrolled shaking), drooling, trouble swallowing, problems with balance or walking;
- feeling restless, jittery, or agitated;
- confusion, unusual thoughts or behavior;
- feeling like you might pass out;
- seizure (convulsions);
- decreased night vision, tunnel vision, watery eyes, increased sensitivity to light;
- nausea and stomach pain, skin rash, and jaundice (yellowing of the skin or eyes);
- high fever, stiff muscles, confusion, sweating, fast or uneven heartbeats, rapid breathing;
- pale skin, easy bruising or bleeding, fever, sore throat, flu symptoms;
- urinating less than usual or not at all;
- joint pain or swelling with fever, swollen glands, muscle aches, chest pain, vomiting, unusual thoughts or behavior, and patchy skin color; or
- slow heart rate, weak pulse, fainting, slow breathing (breathing may stop).

Less serious side effects may include:

- dizziness, drowsiness, anxiety;
- blurred vision, headache;

"ONE POWERFUL VOICE"

- sleep problems (<u>insomnia</u>), strange dreams;
- <u>constipation</u>;
- dry mouth or stuffy nose;
- breast swelling or discharge;
- changes in your menstrual periods;
- weight gain, swelling in your hands or feet;
- impotence, trouble having an orgasm; or
- mild itching or skin rash.

This is not a complete list of side effects and others may occur. Tell your doctor about any unusual or bothersome side effect. You may report side effects to the FDA at 1-800-FDA-1088

What is the most important information I should know about perphenazine (Trilafon)?

Stop using this medication and call your doctor at once if you have twitching or uncontrollable movements of your eyes, lips, tongue, face, arms, or legs. These could be early signs of dangerous side effects.

Perphenazine is not for use in psychotic conditions related to <u>dementia</u>. Perphenazine may cause heart failure, sudden death, or pneumonia in older adults with dementia-related conditions.

Do not use perphenazine if you have liver disease, brain damage, bone marrow <u>depression</u>, a blood cell disorder, or if you are also using large amounts of alcohol or medicines that make you sleepy. Do not use if you are allergic to perphenazine or other phenothiazines.

Before you take perphenazine, tell your doctor if you have severe depression, <u>heart disease</u> or <u>high blood pressure</u>, liver or <u>kidney disease</u>, severe <u>asthma</u> or breathing problems, history of seizures, Parkinson's disease, past or present <u>breast cancer</u>, adrenal gland tumor, <u>enlarged prostate</u> or urination problems, <u>glaucoma</u>, low levels of calcium in your blood, or if you have ever had serious side effects while using <u>chlorpromazine</u> or similar medicines.

Before taking perphenazine, **tell your doctor about all other medications you use.**

"ONE POWERFUL VOICE"

There are No "Safe" Psychiatric Drugs

Prozac & Other Antidepressants

By: Peter R. Breggin, M.D. From: Prozac & Other Antidepressants

There are no "safe" psychiatric drugs. Each has numerous harmful short term and largely unknown long term effects. Each psychiatric drug which was originally heralded as the new "safe" wonder drug, was found to have severe harmful side effects, including addiction, and withdrawal symptoms, among others.

Psychiatric drugs obtain their result by causing brain dysfunction. **Prozac is no different**, despite the claims of numerous misguided and misinformed proponents. The recent approval by the FDA allowing Prozac to be given to children of *any age* spells a major disaster for future generations.

The Fundamental Principle of Psychiatric Treatment

The brain-disabling principle applies to all of the most potent psychiatric treatments - neuroleptics (antipsychotics), antidepressants, lithium (drug which sedates – also see Note), electroshock, and psychosurgery (brain surgery).

The principle states that all of the major psychiatric treatments exert their primary or intended effect by disabling normal brain function. Neuroleptic (antipsychotic) lobotomy, for example, is not a side effect, but the sought-after clinical effect. It reflects impairment of normal brain function.

Conversely, none of the major psychiatric interventions correct or improve existing brain dysfunction, such as any presumed biochemical imbalance. If the patient happens to suffer from brain dysfunction, then the psychiatric drug, electroshock, or psychosurgery will worsen or compound it.

If relatively low doses produce no apparent brain dysfunction, the medication may be having no effect or producing a placebo effect. Or, as frequently happens, the patient is unaware of the impact even though it may be significant.

Anyone familiar with the behavior of people drinking alcohol knows how easily a slightly intoxicated person may deny being impaired or even claim to be improved. Most people coming off cigarettes become abruptly aware of missing the sedative and tranquilizing effects that previously were taken for granted.

Iatrogenic (Treatment-Caused) Helplessness

Brain dysfunction, such as a chemical or surgical lobotomy* syndrome, renders people much less able to appreciate or evaluate their mental condition. Surgically lobotomized people often deny

"ONE POWERFUL VOICE"

both their brain damage and their personal problems. They will loudly declare, "I'm fine, never been better," when they can no longer think straight.

Sometimes they deny that they have been operated on, despite the dime-size burr holes in their skulls palpable (capable of being touched or felt) beneath their scalp. Superficially, the denial looks so sincere that pro-lobotomists cite it to justify the harmlessness of the treatment.

Even without the production of brain dysfunction, the giving of drugs or other physical interventions tends to reinforce the doctor's role as an authority and the patient's role as a helpless sick person.

The patient learns that he or she has a "disease," that the doctor has a "treatment," and that the patient must "listen to the doctor" in order to "get well again."

The patient's learned helplessness and submissiveness is then vastly amplified by the brain damage. The patient becomes more dutiful to the doctor and to the demoralizing principles of biopsychiatry (biological psychiatry). Denial can become a way of life, fixed in place by brain damage.

Suggestion and authoritarianism are common enough in the practice of medicine but **only in psychiatry does the physician actually damage the individual's brain in order to facilitate control over him or her**.

I have designated this unique combination of authoritarian suggestion and brain damage by the term iatrogenic helplessness. Iatrogenic helplessness is key to understanding how the major psychiatric treatments work.

There is little or no reason to anticipate a physical treatment in psychiatry that will control severely disturbed or upset people without doing equally severe harm to them. If psychosurgery, electroshock, or the more potent psychiatric drugs were refined to the point of harmlessness, they would approach uselessness. In biopsychiatry, unfortunately, it's the damage that does the trick.

Clarifying a Confusing Point

Whether or not some psychiatric patients have brain diseases is **irrelevant to the brain-disabling principle of psychiatric treatment**. Even if someday a subtle defect is found in the brains of some mental patients, it will not change the damaging impact of the current treatments in use.

Nor will it change the fact that **the current treatments worsen brain function rather than improving it**. If, for example, a patient's emotional upset is caused by a hormonal problem, by a viral inflammation, or by ingestion of a hallucinogenic drug, the impact of the neuroleptics is still that of a lobotomy. The person now has his or her original brain damage and dysfunction plus a chemical lobotomy.

"ONE POWERFUL VOICE"

NOTE: The soft drink 7Up, contained lithium citrate until it was reformulated in 1950, whereas Coca Cola contained cocaine, which remained an active ingredient until 1901.

Letter of Resignation from the American Psychiatric Association

Source: Biopsychiatry Illuminated, December 4, 1998, From: Loren R. Mosher, M.D., To: Rodrigo Munoz, M.D., President of the American Psychiatric Association (APA)

Dear Rod,

After nearly three decades as a member it is with a mixture of pleasure and disappointment that I submit this letter of resignation from the American Psychiatric Association (APA). The major reason for this action is my belief that I am actually resigning from the American Psychopharmacological Association. Luckily, the organization's true identity requires no change in the acronym.

Unfortunately, APA reflects, and reinforces, in word and deed, our drug dependent society. Yet it helps wage war on "drugs". "Dual diagnosis" clients are a major problem for the field but not because of the "good" drugs we prescribe. "Bad" ones are those that are obtained mostly without a prescription. A Marxist would observe that being a good capitalist organization, APA likes only those drugs from which it can derive a profit -- directly or indirectly.

This is not a group for me. At this point in history, in my view, psychiatry has been almost completely bought out by the drug companies. The APA could not continue without the pharmaceutical company support of meetings, symposia, workshops, journal advertising, grand rounds luncheons, unrestricted educational grants etc. etc. Psychiatrists have become the minions of drug company promotions.

APA, of course, maintains that its independence and autonomy are not compromised in this enmeshed situation. Anyone with the least bit of common sense attending the annual meeting would observe how the drug company exhibits and "industry sponsored symposia" draw crowds with their various enticements, while the serious scientific sessions are barely attended.

Psychiatric training reflects their influence as well: the most important part of a resident's curriculum is the art and quasi-science of dealing drugs, i.e., prescription writing.

These psychopharmacological limitations on our abilities to be complete physicians also limit our intellectual horizons. No longer do we seek to understand whole persons in their social contexts -- rather we are there to realign our patients' neurotransmitters. The problem is that it is very difficult to have a relationship with a neurotransmitter - whatever its configuration.

So, our guild organization provides a rationale, by its neurobiological tunnel vision, for keeping our distance from the molecule conglomerates we have come to define as patients. **We condone and promote the widespread use and misuse of toxic chemicals that we know have serious long term effects** ... and serious withdrawal syndromes.

"ONE POWERFUL VOICE"

So, do I want to be a drug company patsy who treats molecules with their formulary? No, thank you very much. It saddens me that after 35 years as a psychiatrist I look forward to being dissociated from such an organization. In no way does it represent my interests. **It is not within my capacities to buy into the current biomedical-reductionistic model heralded by the psychiatric leadership as once again marrying us to somatic medicine. This is a matter of fashion, politics and, like the pharmaceutical house connection, money.**

In addition, APA has entered into an unholy alliance with NAMI (The National Alliance for the Mentally Ill) - (I don't remember the members being asked if they supported such an association) such that the two organizations have adopted similar public belief systems about the nature of madness.

While professing itself the "champion of their clients" the APA is supporting non- clients, the parents, in their wishes to be in control, via legally enforced dependency, of their mad/bad offspring: NAMI with tacit APA approval, has set out a pro-neuroleptic drug and easy commitment-institutionalization agenda that violates the civil rights of their offspring.

For the most part we stand by and allow this fascistic agenda to move forward. Their psychiatric god, Dr. E. Fuller Torrey, is allowed to diagnose and recommend treatment to those in the NAMI organization with whom he disagrees. Clearly, a violation of medical ethics. Does APA protest? Of course not, because he is speaking what APA agrees with, but can't explicitly espouse.

He is allowed to be a foil; after all - he is no longer a member of APA. (Slick work APA!) The shortsightedness of this marriage of convenience between APA, NAMI, and the drug companies (who gleefully support both groups because of their shared pro-drug stance) is an abomination. **I want no part of a psychiatry of oppression and social control.**

"Biologically based brain diseases" are certainly convenient for families and practitioners alike. It is no-fault insurance against personal responsibility. We are all just helplessly caught up in a swirl of brain pathology for which no one, except DNA, is responsible.

Now, to begin with, anything that has an anatomically defined specific brain pathology becomes the province of neurology *(the science of nerves and the nervous system; especially of diseases affecting them)* (syphilis is an excellent example). So, to be consistent with this "brain disease" view, all the major psychiatric disorders would become the territory of our neurologic colleagues.

Without having surveyed them I believe they would eschew responsibility for these problematic individuals. However, consistency would demand our giving over "biologic brain diseases" to them. The fact that there is no evidence confirming the brain disease attribution is, at this point, irrelevant.

What we are dealing with here is fashion, politics and money. This level of intellectual /scientific dishonesty is just too egregious (extraordinary in some bad way) **for me to continue to support by my membership.**

"ONE POWERFUL VOICE"

I view with no surprise that psychiatric training is being systematically disavowed by American medical school graduates. This must give us cause for concern about the state of today's psychiatry. It must mean -- at least in part -- that they view psychiatry as being very limited and unchallenging.

To me it seems clear that we are headed toward a situation in which, except for academics, **most psychiatric practitioners will have no real relationships -- so vital to the healing process -- with the disturbed and disturbing persons they treat. Their sole role will be that of prescription writers -- ciphers in the guise of being "helpers".**

Finally, why must the APA pretend to know more than it does? DSM IV (Diagnostic and Statistical Manual of Mental Disorders) is the fabrication upon which psychiatry seeks acceptance by medicine in general. Insiders know it is more a political than scientific document. To its credit it says so -- although its brief apologia is rarely noted. DSM IV has become a bible and a money making best seller -- its major failings notwithstanding. It confines and defines practice, some take it seriously, others more realistically. It is the way to get paid.

Diagnostic reliability is easy to attain for research projects. **The issue is what do the categories tell us? Do they in fact accurately represent the person with a problem? They don't, and can't, because there are no external validating criteria for psychiatric diagnoses.** There is neither a blood test nor specific anatomic lesions for any major psychiatric disorder. So, where are we? APA as an organization has implicitly (sometimes explicitly as well) **bought into a theoretical hoax.** Is psychiatry a hoax -- as practiced today? Unfortunately, the answer is mostly yes.

What do I recommend to the organization upon leaving after experiencing three decades of its history?

1. To begin with, let us be ourselves. Stop taking on unholy alliances without the members' permission.
2. **Get real about science, politics and money. Label each for what it is -- that is, be honest.**
3. **Get out of bed with NAMI and the drug companies**. APA should align itself, if one believes its rhetoric, with the true consumer groups, i.e., the ex-patients, psychiatric survivors etc.
4. Talk to the membership -- I can't be alone in my views.

We seem to have forgotten a basic principle -- the need to be patient/client/consumer satisfaction oriented. I always remember Manfred Bleuler's wisdom: **"Loren, you must never forget that you are your patient's employee." In the end they will determine whether or not psychiatry survives in the service marketplace.**

Loren R. Mosher, M.D

"ONE POWERFUL VOICE"

May 2, 2012 6:26 PM

Crooked Doctors - 107 charged in Medicare fraud busts

(AP) MIAMI — Federal authorities charged 107 doctors, nurses and social workers in seven cities with Medicare fraud Wednesday in a nationwide crackdown on unrelated scams that allegedly billed the taxpayer-funded program of $452 million — the highest dollar amount in a single Medicare bust in U.S. history.

It was the latest in a string of major arrests in the past two years as authorities have targeted fraud that's believed to cost the government between $60 billion and $90 billion each year. Stopping Medicare's budget from hemorrhaging that money will be key to paying for President Barack Obama's health care overhaul.

Health and Human Services Secretary Kathleen Sebelius and Attorney General Eric Holder partnered in 2009 to increase enforcement by allocating more money and staff and creating strike forces in fraud hot spots.

On Wednesday, hundreds of federal agents fanned out around the country, raiding businesses, seizing documents and charging 107 suspects in Miami, Los Angeles, Houston, Detroit, Chicago, Tampa, Fla., and Baton Rouge, La. The government suspended payment to 52 providers as part of the investigations.

"When President Obama took office he asked Attorney General Holder and me to make fraud prevention a cabinet-level priority," Sebelius said in remarks prepared for a news conference in Washington.

Among those arrested Wednesday were the owners of two community mental health centers in Baton Rouge, charged with billing $225 million in their scams. Hoor Naz Jafri and Roslyn Dogan allegedly recruited vulnerable patients, including elderly people, drug addicts and the mentally ill. Patient charts were doctored to show services that were billed to Medicare but often never given, according to an indictment.

Authorities suspended their companies in May 2011, but the pair continued billing Medicare after purchasing another fraudulent company, according to the indictment. When feds shut down that company, the pair tried to sell their "beneficiaries" to other providers in an attempt to keep making money.

During the investigation, federal authorities tried to put a hold on the company's bank account. Dogan asked to visit the U.S. Attorney's Office to review and copy documents that had been seized as part of a search. After the visit, "Dogan and co-conspirators bragged that, while pretending to copy files, they actually stole incriminating documents from the files and later destroyed them." Dogan referred to herself as a "smooth criminal," according to the indictment.

Another co-conspirator bragged to Dogan and others that he had a "bonfire with fabricated notes that law enforcement officers had failed to seize during the search," according to the indictment.

"ONE POWERFUL VOICE"

They could face life in prison if convicted. A woman who answered the phone at one of the companies hung up and an email to the company was not immediately returned. Five others were charged in connection with the Baton Rouge scam, capping a six-year investigation.

"The results we are announcing today are at the heart of an administration-wide commitment to protecting American taxpayers from health care fraud," said Attorney General Eric Holder. "We are determined to bring to justice those who violate our laws and defraud the Medicare program for personal gain.

More than 50 defendants were also arrested in Miami in unrelated scams totaling $136 million involving community mental health centers and home health care agencies. A handful of those arrested also had criminal backgrounds, according to federal agents.
Community mental health centers are the latest trend in Medicare fraud, which has developed more complex schemes over the years, moving from medical equipment and HIV infusion fraud to ambulance scams, as crooks try to stay one step ahead of authorities. The scams have also grown more sophisticated using patient recruiters who are paid kickbacks for recruiting patients, while doctors, nurses and company owners coordinate to make it appear they are delivering medical services which they are not.
"Medicare fraud also exposes some of our most vulnerable citizens to identity theft, and, in some cases, endangers patients' lives," said Gary Cantrell, Deputy Inspector General for Investigations for HHS. "The indictments announced today demonstrate that we're fighting back."

Wednesday's arrests come as top lawmakers appealed to health care professionals in the private sector to help combat Medicare fraud. Six members of the Senate Finance Committee, led by Ranking Member Orrin Hatch (R-Utah) and Chairman Max Baucus (D-Mont.), announced a bipartisan effort to begin soliciting ideas from interested stakeholders in the health care community looking for a fresh perspective and potentially solutions that may have been overlooked.

"To date, numerous efforts have been made to reduce fraud, yielding a mixed record of successes and failures," according to the letter.

Sebelius said her agency and the Justice Department have more than quadrupled the number of strike teams around the country, charging hundreds of individuals with Medicare fraud. Medicare fraud has been a hot button issue as federal officials have repeatedly come under fire for seemingly staying one step behind the criminals, using outdated technology and not coordinating efficiently with law enforcement. But Sebelius touted a new data system that will allow authorities to spot trends in billing patterns more quickly, which will ideally stop payments before they go out the door. The Centers for Medicare and Medicaid Services launched a $77 million computer system last summer to serve that purpose, but the program has yielded few results in the early stages and drawn criticism from the Senate Finance Committee.

"ONE POWERFUL VOICE"

9480 Princeton Square Blvd. S., #815
Jacksonville, FL 32256
July 17, 2011

Attorney General Eric Schneiderman
Bureau Of Consumer Frauds And Protection
Office Of The Attorney General
The Capitol Albany, NY 12224-0341

Dear Attorney General Schneiderman:

Respectfully. The trouble with this Psychiatric Case is that in all the time I have taken to contact with the people Officially In Charge, over the past several decades of my involvement, of taking care of the business of rectifying the great error occurring here, of our Society Allowing, and thereby, to the toll of human suffering for its being allowed, the grievous mistake; that the mistake has never been taken care of, of the great Injustice.

This Psychiatric Injustice affects a flagrant mass of people, hereby termed as Mental Patients, (respective of whether that that are genuinely Mentally Ill or not, but as termed to be that way by legally unspecified Medical Diagnosis,) and thereby to be rendered over to the State's Mental Wards on Doctor's Signatures, without the slightest contest of Due Process Rights under law in the sense of Miranda Legislation and the Constitutional Rights of the 4th, 5th, and 6th Amendments afforded to Criminal Law Legalities; but not so to the poor Psychiatric Patients who fall into the legal morass of 7th Amendment Civil Law Psychiatric, and otherwise known as Mental Hygiene Law, which has no apparent rights other than to be processed as Mental Patients and left to the arbitrary discretions of the Doctors by the State's Mental Health Attorneys as to the length of their incarcerations and to the terms of their treatments under law; and who are thereby allowed to be legally Force Treated with what are known to be crippling and deadly Psychiatric Chemicals of lethal condition and consequence to anyone's sound mental and physical health over the long run, and that are very excruciatingly painful in the uncomfortable sense to endure.

The issue here is that Without Due Process that this is a criminal matter in the terms of Kidnapping, Deadly Chemical Assault, Manslaughter, and Extortion by the unscrupulous Medical Profession who enslaved the public to their Diagnosed Mental Illnesses. And who, of these Doctors, have been and are "making a living" off of this "Captive Market" of their "Collective Diagnoses" in Conspiracy, and in conjoining with the bitter hypocrisy of Pharmaceutical Manufacturers operating in collusion with The Federal Food And Drug Administration; which the Legal Conspiracy To is what I need to bring to your attention.

In the meaning of intent that: with the function of The Attorney General being To Defend The State, to point out to you, that The State is thereby Obligated To Be Error Free in its treatment and dealing with the population. And whereby, if the State, If Known To Be In Error, when the error is egregious and obvious, then It is The Obligation of The Attorney General "To Correct The Error" and not to play the part of the protector of the state, as it has always been doing, against the legitimate grievance of the public.

Most Sincerely,
Gary L. Koniz

"ONE POWERFUL VOICE"

9480 Princeton Square Blvd. S., #815
Jacksonville, FL 32256
December 13, 2009

The Honorable John Roberts
Chief Justice of The Supreme Court
Supreme Court of the United States
Washington, D.C. 20543

Dear Chief Justice Roberts:

On behalf of myself and the total of the Combat Veterans I represent, please do intervene with our case matter being here presented, "in indigent circumstances," to you, and to the rest of the Honored Members of The Supreme Court for Deliberations and Ruling of your Judgment, regarding the errant ways of psychiatric handling; and for the sake of every of our fellow Americans as well; for Justice to prevail in Defining The Rights of The Psychiatrically Accused, and for the Legal Terms of Diagnoses and Safe Conduct of Treatment in the name of American Civil Liberty; and to the stipulation of Due Process Rights of Mental Hygiene Law to be included under Miranda, the same as with the Penal Laws, and To The Legal Protection of Safe and Beneficial Treatment.

And for the sake of the Nation, in judging the grievous weight of this error to be determined; that We cannot have two systems of justice here, side by side, the one "Just" in the setting of fair minded and impartial deliberations of trial proceedings for the accused; and the other, to be described as "Mental Hygiene Law," under Medical Guise of Civil Law; Not Covered by The Constitution; and being conducted as a, "Criminal Communist Tyranny," in dictation over the lives and the very souls and well-being of a poor suffering population; who are, without recourse to Legal Benefit, through medical malpractice and legal malfeasance, forced to endure indefinite commitment and forced chemo-treatment with deadly chemicals and other versions of deadly treatment in the name of medicine; that in all fair conscience upon the Nation which cannot be condoned to exist here in The United States of America, by a rational and law abiding civilization.

Thank you so very much for your urgent and timely attention to this Appeal for Psychiatric Reform. Which We cannot stress to you enough how desperate the nation is for change, and how frightfully aghast that the population looks upon our government for its acceptance of the error; ongoing now for over half a century. That, in a sense, has abdicated our American Constitution to a Communist Fascism without legal challenge.

I am offering you my own case for display, to be taken for the whole of what is the matter here with the tragic setting; that, without Due Process to confront the injustice, is based upon False and Fabricated Testimony, (in all regards;) that in turn is then used as the basis of Confinement based to a Mis-Diagnosis of Paranoid Schizophrenia, (that cannot be overruled,) that is then used as the grounds for Forcing Disabling Treatment.

Most Faithfully Regarding,

Gary L. Koniz - Corresponding
Veterans of the Vietnam War

"ONE POWERFUL VOICE"

9480 Princeton Square Blvd. S., #815
Jacksonville, FL 32256
May 15, 2012

Leon E. Panetta
U.S. Secretary Of Defense
U.S. Department Of Defense
1400 Defense Pentagon
Washington, D.C. 20301-1400

Dear Secretary Panetta:

   This case that I am herein submitting to you for urgent corrective action, is vital to the security and well-being of The American United States that seems to be coming to a head now in the state of mafia war siege and concurrently with the overthrow of The American United States, to what that an ongoing Psychiatric/Psychotropic War has played a roll.

   The case has to do with two separate incidences of Human and Civil Rights Due Process Violations that occurred against myself on two separate directly related mafia incidences of foul play in the era of late 1986 at a the Hudson River State Psychiatric Hospital for The Insane, that is located in Poughkeepsie, NY, to where I was literally kidnapped by police and taken without ever seeing a judge or an appointed attorney.

   The incidences of Violent Foul Play, against my person, occurred while I was working then at that time with the local newspaper, The Poughkeepsie Journal, and closely with its City Editor Roury Williams when I was the Press Agent and head-strong reporter and photographer for the Poughkeepsie School District back in the early '80's and accidentally inadvertently tangled with the existing Organized Crime of the local Italian/Jewish/Black Mafia, and their Mafia Police, (New York City Mob Connected) with their Hippy Draft Dodger entourage, over the issue of Drugs and Paraquat laced Marijuana being back then epidemic in The Poughkeepsie High School; that included White Slavery Prostitution and Organized Pornography as well, and to direct foul play. Which was my work related assignment to investigate and "to get to the bottom of" in responsible School District Intervention. Only to find out in doing undercover reporting work and the making the rounds of the local police stations, that it was they, the Local and State Police, who were dealing the drugs and who were themselves the protecting the Major Crime Organization.

   To the points being made respectfully about what happened here; that things like; (1.) Psychiatric Commitment without Miranda Due Process Rights, (2.) Forced Labeling and Medical Subjugation of those Allegedly Diagnosed and Accused of having Mental Illness Disorders Without Legal Definition and Stipulation, and to (3.) Involuntary Forced Treatment with Catastrophically Disabling Anti-Psychotic Pharmacy Chemicals Without Legal Justification; Cannot Possibly Ever Occur, or that Should Not Ever Have Occurred, Here in our United States of America. Which in the terms of what went down constitutes the major crime of Treason Against The Nation for its occurrence and For Its Cover-Up.

Most Respectfully,
Gary Koniz – Correspondent
Veterans Of The Vietnam War

"ONE POWERFUL VOICE"

NEW YORK, Dec. 20, 2010

Latest Terror Threat in US Aimed to Poison Food
Exclusive: The Dept. of Homeland Security Uncovered a Plot to Attack Hotels and Restaurants Over a Single Weekend

By Armen Keteyian

CBS) In this exclusive story, **CBS News chief investigative correspondent Armen Keteyian** reports the latest terror attack to America involves the possible use of poisons - simultaneous attacks targeting hotels and restaurants at many locations over a single weekend.

A key Intelligence source has confirmed the threat as "credible." Department of Homeland Security officials, along with members of the Department of Agriculture and the FDA, have briefed a small group of corporate security officers from the hotel and restaurant industries about it.

CBSNews.com Report: Terror in the U.S.

"We operate under the premise that individuals prepared to carry out terrorist acts are in this country," said Dec. of Homeland Security Janet Napolitano on Dec. 6, 2010.

The plot uncovered earlier this year is said to involve the use of two poisons - ricin and cyanide - slipped into salad bars and buffets.

"ONE POWERFUL VOICE"

Of particular concern: The plotters are believed to be tied to the same terror group that attempted to blow up cargo planes over the east coast in October, al Qaeda in the Arabian Peninsula.

In online propaganda al Qaeda in the Arabian Peninsula has praised the cargo attack, part of what it called "Operation Hemorrhage."

The propaganda says in part, "...attacking the enemy with smaller but more frequent operations" to "add a heavy economic burden to an already faltering economy."

Manuals and videos on jihadist websites explain how to easy it is to make both poisons.

"Initially it would look very much like food poisoning," said St. John's University professor of pharmaceutical sciences Dr. Susan Ford.

She showed how little of each poison could be fatal by putting a small amount of poison in cups.

Armen Keteyian: Are these dosages enough to really harm someone or kill someone?

Susan Ford: Yes, these are 250 milligrams and that is the fatal dose.

Keteyian: So just that much sodium cyanide is enough to kill me?

Ford: Yes, it is.

That leads to a difficult debate: The need to inform the public without alarming it.

Former Homeland Security Secretary Michael Chertoff said, "A threat you might feel is sufficiently specific and credible to tell the people who are professionally involved might not be specific or credible enough to tell the general public."

Chertoff says it's important to let public health officials know that what looks like food poisoning could be a terrorist attack.

On Monday Dept. of Homeland Security spokesman Sean Smith said, "We are not going to comment on reports of specific terrorist planning. However, the counterterrorism and homeland security communities have engaged in extensive efforts for many years to guard against all types of terrorist attacks, including unconventional attacks using chemical, biological, radiological, and nuclear materials. Indeed, Al-Qa'ida has publicly stated its intention to try to carry out unconventional attacks for well over a decade, and AQAP propaganda in the past year has made similar reference.

"Finally, we get reports about the different kinds of attacks terrorists would like to carry out that frequently are beyond their assessed capability."

The fact remains the government and hospitality industries are on alert.

"ONE POWERFUL VOICE"

$375M health care scheme went unnoticed for years

NOMAAN MERCHANT, Associated Press
Updated 01:50 a.m., Saturday, March 3, 2012

DALLAS (AP) — The Texas doctor accused of "selling his signature" to process almost $375 million in false Medicare and Medicaid claims went unnoticed for half a decade by a fraud detection system that some critics say is broken.

Authorities say Jacques Roy and six others indicted for health care fraud certified 11,000 Medicare beneficiaries through more than 500 home health providers over five years. Those numbers would have made Roy's Medicare practice the busiest in the country. But an investigation into Roy and his business practices didn't begin until about a year ago, officials said.

The federal agency that administers Medicare has two sets of contractors: one to pay claims and another evaluating those claims for fraud. U.S. Health and Human Services investigators have found that health officials often have a hard time tracking the work of contractors that are supposed to detect Medicare fraud — estimated by some to reach $60 billion annually.

Federal officials who announced the indictment against Roy and six others in Dallas acknowledged the problems with the system. They contend they have improved data analysis and are working to move away from having to "pay and chase" offenders.
Others say Medicare is still very vulnerable to fraud.

"It's a trust-based system that is ripe for the picking by criminals," said Kirk Ogrosky, a Washington, D.C., attorney at the law firm Arnold & Porter and a former top health care prosecutor at the U.S. Department of Justice.

Roy, 41, a doctor who owned Medistat Group Associates in DeSoto, Texas, faces up to 100 years in prison if he's convicted of several counts of health care fraud and conspiracy to commit health care fraud. Six others, including the owners of three home health service agencies, are also charged.

Roy's attorney, Patrick McLain, said he had yet to review much of the evidence but Roy maintained his innocence. A detention hearing for Roy in federal court was delayed until Monday.

More than 75 of the agencies that used Roy's signature to certify claims also have had their Medicare payments suspended.

Some of those indicted alongside Roy are accused of fraudulently signing up patients or offering them cash, free groceries or food stamps to give their names and a number used to bill Medicare.

"ONE POWERFUL VOICE"

Medicare patients qualify for home health care if they are confined to their homes and need care there, according to the indictment. U.S. Attorney Sarah Saldana said some people supposedly eligible for home care were found working on their cars outside.

Roy is accused of signing off on paperwork for home health services and pocketing much of the fraudulent billings.

Health and Human Services Inspector General Daniel Levinson described Roy's billing on Tuesday as "off the charts." But it was missed for years by Palmetto GBA, the contractor that paid the home health agencies using Roy's signature, and Health Integrity LLC, the agency tasked with catching any irregularities.

A spokesman for BlueCross BlueShield of South Carolina, which owns Palmetto, referred questions about its fraud procedures to the federal Centers for Medicare & Medicaid Services. Officials at Health Integrity did not return a phone message.
CMS health insurance specialist Carmen Irwin said a screening process is intended to investigate complaints, but it can be difficult to immediately pinpoint a single doctor's signature being used so often.

"We're paying a home health agency," Irwin said. "We're not necessarily looking at how many claims are for one physician because we're not necessarily paying a physician on a home health claim."

A report by the HHS inspector general's office issued in November highlights problems with the contractors charged with weeding out fraud. The contractors reported their findings in different ways and sometimes provided incomplete data, the report found. Some of the information turned out to be inaccurate. Inspectors said "the inconsistencies and lack of uniformity we identified" could prevent effective oversight.

Patrick Burns, spokesman for the advocacy group Taxpayers Against Fraud, credited HHS for hiring Peter Budetti, CMS' deputy administrator for program integrity, to upgrade its systems. But Burns said the department still had no excuse for missing obvious problems.

"You can't have 11,000 bills from a single doctor if you're the number one home health provider in the nation," Burns said. "You can't see that many patients. It's not physically possible."

Read more: http://www.seattlepi.com/news/article/375M-health-care-scheme-went-unnoticed-for-years-3369159.php#ixzz1o3z9JlgN

"ONE POWERFUL VOICE"

DSM Criteria for PTSD

In 2013, the American Psychiatric Association revised the PTSD diagnostic criteria in the fifth edition of its Diagnostic and Statistical Manual of Mental Disorders (DSM-5)(1). Listed below are the diagnostic criteria (A-F) specified in DSM-IV-TR (2). We will update this factsheet with the DSM-5 criterion upon copyright approval from the APA.

Diagnostic criteria for PTSD include a history of exposure to a traumatic event meeting two criteria and symptoms from each of three symptom clusters: intrusive recollections, avoidant/numbing symptoms, and hyper-arousal symptoms. A fifth criterion concerns duration of symptoms and a sixth assesses functioning.

Criterion A: stressor

The person has been exposed to a traumatic event in which both of the following have been present:

1. The person has experienced, witnessed, or been confronted with an event or events that involve actual or threatened death or serious injury, or a threat to the physical integrity of oneself or others.
2. The person's response involved intense fear, helplessness, or horror. Note: in children, it may be expressed instead by disorganized or agitated behavior.

Criterion B: intrusive recollection

The traumatic event is persistently re-experienced in at least one of the following ways:

1. Recurrent and intrusive distressing recollections of the event, including images, thoughts, or perceptions. Note: in young children, repetitive play may occur in which themes or aspects of the trauma are expressed.
2. Recurrent distressing dreams of the event. Note: in children, there may be frightening dreams without recognizable content
3. Acting or feeling as if the traumatic event were recurring (includes a sense of reliving the experience, illusions, hallucinations, and dissociative flashback episodes, including those that occur upon awakening or when intoxicated). Note: in children, trauma-specific reenactment may occur.
4. Intense psychological distress at exposure to internal or external cues that symbolize or resemble an aspect of the traumatic event.
5. Physiologic reactivity upon exposure to internal or external cues that symbolize or resemble an aspect of the traumatic event

Criterion C: avoidant/numbing

Persistent avoidance of stimuli associated with the trauma and numbing of general responsiveness (not present before the trauma), as indicated by at least three of the following:

"ONE POWERFUL VOICE"

1. **Efforts to avoid thoughts, feelings, or conversations associated with the trauma**
2. **Efforts to avoid activities, places, or people that arouse recollections of the trauma**
3. **Inability to recall an important aspect of the trauma**
4. **Markedly diminished interest or participation in significant activities**
5. **Feeling of detachment or estrangement from others**
6. **Restricted range of affect (e.g., unable to have loving feelings)**
7. **Sense of foreshortened future (e.g., does not expect to have a career, marriage, children, or a normal life span)**

Criterion D: hyper-arousal

Persistent symptoms of increasing arousal (not present before the trauma), indicated by at least two of the following:

1. Difficulty falling or staying asleep
2. Irritability or outbursts of anger
3. Difficulty concentrating
4. Hyper-vigilance
5. Exaggerated startle response

Criterion E: duration

Duration of the disturbance (symptoms in B, C, and D) is more than one month.

Criterion F: functional significance

The disturbance causes clinically significant distress or impairment in social, occupational, or other important areas of functioning.

Specify if:

Acute: if duration of symptoms is less than three months

Chronic: if duration of symptoms is three months or more

With or Without delay onset: Onset of symptoms at least six months after the stressor

References

1. American Psychiatric Association. (2013). Diagnostic and Statistical Manual of Mental Disorders (5th ed.). Washington, DC: Author.

Schizophrenia:

A. Characteristic symptoms: Two (or more) of the following, each present for a significant portion of time during a 1-month period (or less if successfully treated). At least one of these should include 1-3

1. Delusions
2. Hallucinations
3. Disorganized speech
4. Grossly abnormal psychomotor behavior, such as catatonia
5. Negative symptoms, i.e., restricted affect or avolition/asociality

B. Social/occupational dysfunction: For a significant portion of the time since the onset of the disturbance, one or more major areas of functioning such as work, interpersonal relations, or self-care are markedly below the level achieved prior to the onset (or when the onset is in childhood or adolescence, failure to achieve expected level of interpersonal, academic, or occupational achievement).

C. Duration: Continuous signs of the disturbance persist for at least 6 months. This 6-month period must include at least 1 month of symptoms (or less if successfully treated) that meet Criterion A (i.e., active-phase symptoms) and may include periods of prodromal or residual symptoms. During these prodromal or residual periods, the signs of the disturbance may be manifested by only negative symptoms or two or more symptoms listed in Criterion A present in an attenuated form (e.g., odd beliefs, unusual perceptual experiences).

D. Schizoaffective and Mood Disorder exclusion: Schizoaffective Disorder and Mood Disorder With Psychotic Features have been ruled out because either (1) no Major Depressive or Manic Episodes have occurred concurrently with the activephase symptoms; or (2) if mood episodes have occurred during active-phase symptoms, their total duration has been brief relative to the duration of the active and residual periods.

E. Substance/general medical condition exclusion: The disturbance is not due to the direct physiological effects of a substance (e.g., a drug of abuse, a medication) or a general medical condition.

F. Relationship to a Pervasive Developmental Disorder: If there is a history of Autistic Disorder or another Pervasive Developmental Disorder or other communication disorder of childhood onset, the additional diagnosis of Schizophrenia is made only if prominent delusions or hallucinations are also present for at least a month (or less if successfully treated).

"ONE POWERFUL VOICE"

Paranoid schizophrenia

With paranoid schizophrenia, you're less likely to be affected by mood problems or problems with thinking, concentration and attention. Signs and symptoms may include:

Auditory hallucinations, such as hearing voices
Delusions, such as believing a co-worker wants to poison you
Anxiety and Anger
Emotional distance
Argumentativeness and Violence
Self-important or condescending manner
Suicidal thoughts and behavior

Key symptoms
Delusions and hallucinations are the symptoms that make paranoid schizophrenia most distinct from other types of schizophrenia.

- **Delusions.** In paranoid schizophrenia, a common delusion is that you're being singled out for harm. For instance, you may believe that the government is monitoring every move you make or that a co-worker is poisoning your lunch. You may also have delusions of grandeur — the belief that you can fly, that you're famous or that you have a relationship with a famous person, for example. You hold on to these false beliefs despite evidence to the contrary. Delusions can result in aggression or violence if you believe you must act in self-defense against those who want to harm you.

- **Auditory hallucinations.** An auditory hallucination is the perception of sound — usually voices — that no one else hears. The sounds may be a single voice or many voices. These voices may talk either to you or to each other. The voices are usually unpleasant. They may make ongoing criticisms of what you're thinking or doing, or make cruel comments about your real or imagined faults. Voices may also command you to do things that can be harmful to yourself or to others. When you have paranoid schizophrenia, these voices seem real. You may talk to or shout at the voices.

A person diagnosed with schizophrenia may experience hallucinations (most reported are hearing voices), delusions (often bizarre or persecutory in nature), and disorganized thinking and speech. The latter may range from loss of train of thought, to sentences only loosely connected in meaning, to incoherence known as word salad in severe cases. Social withdrawal, sloppiness of dress and hygiene, and loss of motivation and judgment are all common in schizophrenia. There is often an observable pattern of emotional difficulty, for example lack of responsiveness. Impairment in social cognition is associated with schizophrenia, as are symptoms of paranoia; social isolation commonly occurs. Difficulties in working and long-term memory, attention, executive functioning, and speed of processing also commonly occur. In one uncommon subtype, the person may be largely mute, remain motionless in bizarre postures, or exhibit purposeless agitation, all signs of catatonia. About 30% to 50% of people with schizophrenia do not have insight, in other words they do not accept their condition or its treatment. Treatment may have some effect.

"ONE POWERFUL VOICE"

Adverse Effects of Thorazine (Chlorpromazine)

Note: Some adverse effects of Thorazine (chlorpromazine) may be more likely to occur, or occur with greater intensity, in patients with special medical problems, e.g., patients with mitral insufficiency or pheochromocytoma have experienced severe hypotension following recommended doses.

Drowsiness, usually mild to moderate, may occur, particularly during the first or second week, after which it generally disappears. If troublesome, dosage may be lowered.

Overall incidence has been low, regardless of indication or dosage. Most investigators conclude it is a sensitivity reaction. Most cases occur between the second and fourth weeks of therapy. The clinical picture resembles infectious hepatitis, with laboratory features of obstructive jaundice, rather than those of parenchymal damage. It is usually promptly reversible on withdrawal of the medication; however, chronic jaundice has been reported.

There is no conclusive evidence that preexisting liver disease makes patients more susceptible to jaundice. Alcoholics with cirrhosis have been successfully treated with Thorazine (chlorpromazine) without complications. Nevertheless, the medication should be used cautiously in patients with liver disease. Patients who have experienced jaundice with a phenothiazine should not, if possible, be reexposed to Thorazine (chlorpromazine) or other phenothiazines.

If fever with grippe-like symptoms occurs, appropriate liver studies should be conducted. If tests indicate an abnormality, stop treatment.

Liver function tests in jaundice induced by the drug may mimic extrahepatic obstruction; withhold exploratory laparotomy until extrahepatic obstruction is confirmed.

Hematological Disorders, including agranulocytosis, eosinophilia, leukopenia, hemolytic anemia, aplastic anemia, thrombocytopenic purpura and pancytopenia have been reported.

Agranulocytosis — Warn patients to report the sudden appearance of sore throat or other signs of infection. If white blood cell and differential counts indicate cellular depression, stop treatment and start antibiotic and other suitable therapy.

Moderate suppression of white blood cells is not an indication for stopping treatment unless accompanied by the symptoms described above.

Cardiovascular

Hypotensive Effects — Postural hypotension, simple tachycardia, momentary fainting and dizziness may occur after the first injection; occasionally after subsequent injections; rarely, after the first oral dose. Usually recovery is spontaneous and symptoms disappear within 1 / 2 to 2 hours. Occasionally, these effects may be more severe and prolonged, producing a shock-like condition.

To minimize hypotension after injection, keep patient lying down and observe for at least 1 / 2 hour. To control hypotension, place patient in head-low position with legs raised. If a vasoconstrictor is required, Levophed® *** and Neo-Synephrine® § are the most suitable. Other pressor agents, including epinephrine, should not be used as they may cause a paradoxical further lowering of blood pressure.

EKG Changes — particularly nonspecific, usually reversible Q and T wave distortions— have been observed in some patients receiving phenothiazine tranquilizers, including Thorazine (chlorpromazine).

Note: Sudden death, apparently due to cardiac arrest, has been reported.

CNS Reactions

Neuromuscular (Extrapyramidal) Reactions — Neuromuscular reactions include dystonias, motor restlessness, pseudo-parkinsonism and tardive dyskinesia, and appear to be dose-related. They are discussed in the following paragraphs:

Dystonias: Symptoms may include spasm of the neck muscles, sometimes progressing to acute, reversible torticollis; extensor rigidity of back muscles, sometimes progressing to opisthotonos; carpopedal spasm, trismus, swallowing difficulty, oculogyric crisis and protrusion of the tongue.

These usually subside within a few hours, and almost always within 24 to 48 hours after the drug has been discontinued. In mild cases, reassurance or a barbiturate is often sufficient. If appropriate treatment with anti-parkinsonism agents or Benadryl fails to reverse the signs and symptoms, the diagnosis should be reevaluated.

Suitable supportive measures such as maintaining a clear airway and adequate hydration should be employed when needed. If therapy is reinstituted, it should be at a lower dosage. Should these symptoms occur in children or pregnant patients, the drug should not be reinstituted.

Motor Restlessness: Symptoms may include agitation or jitteriness and sometimes insomnia. These symptoms often disappear spontaneously. At times these symptoms may be similar to the original neurotic or psychotic symptoms. Dosage should not be increased until these side effects have subsided.

Pseudo-parkinsonism: Symptoms may include: mask-like facies, drooling, tremors, pillrolling motion, cogwheel rigidity and shuffling gait. In most cases these symptoms are readily controlled when an anti-parkinsonism agent is administered concomitantly. Anti-parkinsonism agents should be used only when required. Generally, therapy of a few weeks to 2 or 3 months will suffice. After this time patients should be evaluated to determine their need for continued treatment. (Note: Levodopa has not been found effective in antipsychotic-induced pseudo-parkinsonism.) Occasionally it is necessary to lower the dosage of Thorazine (chlorpromazine) or to discontinue the drug.

"ONE POWERFUL VOICE"

Tardive Dyskinesia: As with all <u>antipsychotic</u> agents, tardive dyskinesia may appear in some patients on long-term therapy or may appear after drug therapy has been discontinued. The <u>syndrome</u> can also develop, although much less frequently, after relatively brief treatment periods at low doses. This syndrome appears in all age groups. Although its <u>prevalence</u> appears to be highest among elderly patients, especially elderly women, it is impossible to rely upon prevalence estimates to predict at the inception of antipsychotic treatment which patients are likely to develop the syndrome. The symptoms are persistent and in some patients appear to be irreversible. The syndrome is characterized by rhythmical <u>involuntary</u> movements of the tongue, face, <u>mouth</u> or <u>jaw</u> (e.g., protrusion of tongue, puffing of cheeks, puckering of mouth, chewing movements). Sometimes these may be accompanied by involuntary movements of extremities. In rare instances, these involuntary movements of the extremities are the only manifestations of tardive dyskinesia. A variant of tardive dyskinesia, tardive <u>dystonia</u>, has also been described.

There is no known effective treatment for tardive dyskinesia; anti-parkinsonism agents do not alleviate the symptoms of this syndrome. If clinically feasible, it is suggested that all antipsychotic agents be discontinued if these symptoms appear. Should it be necessary to reinstitute treatment, or increase the dosage of the agent, or switch to a different antipsychotic agent, the syndrome may be masked.

It has been reported that fine vermicular movements of the tongue may be an early sign of the syndrome and if the medication is stopped at that time the syndrome may not develop.

Adverse Behavioral Effects — Psychotic symptoms and catatonic-like states have been reported rarely.

Other CNS Effects— <u>Neuroleptic</u> <u>Malignant</u> Syndrome (NMS) has been reported in association with antipsychotic drugs. (See **WARNINGS**.) <u>Cerebral</u> <u>edema</u> has been reported.

Convulsive seizures (<u>petit mal</u> and <u>grand mal</u>) have been reported, particularly in patients with <u>EEG</u> abnormalities or history of such disorders.

Abnormality of the <u>cerebrospinal fluid</u> <u>proteins</u> has also been reported.

Allergic Reactions of a mild urticarial type or <u>photosensitivity</u> are seen. Avoid undue exposure to sun. More severe reactions, including exfoliative <u>dermatitis</u>, have been reported occasionally.

<u>Contact dermatitis</u> has been reported in <u>nursing</u> personnel; accordingly, the use of rubber gloves when administering Thorazine (chlorpromazine) liquid or injectable is recommended.

In addition, <u>asthma</u>, <u>laryngeal</u> edema, angioneurotic edema and anaphylactoid reactions have been reported.

Endocrine Disorders: <u>Lactation</u> and moderate breast engorgement may occur in females on large doses. If persistent, lower dosage or withdraw drug. False-positive <u>pregnancy</u> tests have been reported, but are less likely to occur when a <u>serum</u> test is used. <u>Amenorrhea</u> and <u>gynecomastia</u> have also been reported. <u>Hyperglycemia</u>, <u>hypoglycemia</u> and glycosuria have been reported.

"ONE POWERFUL VOICE"

Autonomic Reactions: Occasional <u>dry mouth</u>; <u>nasal</u> congestion; <u>nausea</u>; obstipation; <u>constipation</u>; adynamic <u>ileus</u>; <u>urinary</u> retention; <u>priapism</u>; <u>miosis</u> and <u>mydriasis</u>, <u>atonic</u> <u>colon</u>, ejaculatory disorders/impotence.

Special Considerations in Long-Term Therapy: Skin <u>pigmentation</u> and <u>ocular</u> changes have occurred in some patients taking substantial doses of Thorazine (chlorpromazine) for prolonged periods.

Skin Pigmentation — Rare instances of skin pigmentation have been observed in hospitalized mental patients, primarily females who have received the drug usually for 3 years or more in dosages ranging from 500 mg to 1500 mg daily. The pigmentary changes, restricted to exposed areas of the body, range from an almost imperceptible darkening of the skin to a slate gray color, sometimes with a violet hue. Histological examination reveals a <u>pigment</u>, chiefly in the <u>dermis</u>, which is probably a melanin-like complex. The pigmentation may fade following discontinuance of the drug.

Ocular Changes — Ocular changes have occurred more frequently than skin pigmentation and have been observed both in pigmented and nonpigmented patients receiving Thorazine (chlorpromazine) usually for 2 years or more in dosages of 300 mg daily and higher. Eye changes are characterized by deposition of fine particulate matter in the <u>lens</u> and <u>cornea</u>. In more advanced cases, star-shaped opacities have also been observed in the <u>anterior</u> portion of the lens. The <u>nature</u> of the eye deposits has not yet been determined. A small number of patients with more severe ocular changes have had some visual impairment. In addition to these <u>corneal</u> and lenticular changes, <u>epithelial</u> keratopathy and pigmentary <u>retinopathy</u> have been reported. Reports suggest that the eye lesions may <u>regress</u> after withdrawal of the drug.

Since the occurrence of eye changes seems to be related to dosage levels and/or duration of therapy, it is suggested that long-term patients on moderate to high dosage levels have periodic ocular examinations.

<u>**Etiology**</u> — The etiology of both of these reactions is not clear, but exposure to light, along with dosage/duration of therapy, appears to be the most significant factor. If either of these reactions is observed, the physician should weigh the benefits of continued therapy against the possible risks and, on the merits of the individual case, determine whether or not to continue present therapy, lower the dosage, or withdraw the drug.

Other Adverse Reactions: Mild fever may occur after large I.M. doses. Hyperpyrexia has been reported. Increases in appetite and weight sometimes occur. <u>Peripheral</u> edema and a <u>systemic</u> <u>lupus</u> erythematosus-like syndrome have been reported.

Note: There have been occasional reports of sudden death in patients receiving phenothiazines. In some cases, the cause appeared to be <u>cardiac</u> arrest or <u>asphyxia</u> due to failure of the <u>cough</u> <u>reflex</u>.

"ONE POWERFUL VOICE"

9480 Princeton Square Blvd. S., #815
Jacksonville, FL 32256
(904) 730-2055
November 15, 2006

General John Abizaid
Commander, United States Central Command
7115 South Boundary Blvd.
Macdill Air Force Base, FL 33621-5101

General Abizaid:

Concerning The Fate of our United States Service Veterans, past and present, at the hands of, and at the intolerable mercy of, Tyrant Psychiatric; and in a Gathering of Force in Collateral Support with you for The Holy Mission of our United Military Campaign Nationally, To Free America's War Veterans from the deadly grip and torment of psychiatric profiling; this is a case, that The Avowed Enemies To This Nation Have Created; and which our government, to us, has permitted and left unresolved, to coincide; (as termed, "The New Regime," or, The Popular Government of The Liberal Left; comprising The Ideologies of; Atheism, Pandemic Drug Use and The Legalizing of Drugs, Pornography, Gay Rights, Interracial Procreation, Third World Overrun Immigration involving The Economic Downfall of The White Middle Class, and geared in all toward a Racial, Foreign, Ethnic National Plot To Overthrow;) and which in all regards is connected to the freewheeling smuggling and trafficking in The Drugs; Heroin, Cocaine, and other Dangerous Chemical Substances in design being carried on with by certain Non-White and Foreign Ethnic National Elements residing here; being permitted, (in the sense of Non-Aggressive Law Enforcement Procedures Being In Effect To Interdict them,) by the current Liberal Government allowing; and along with immorality of pornography to coincide, being allowed and encouraged to proliferate; (in undermine to the soft underbelly of The Traditional White European American Population, to whose vested interest The United States has always belonged to, in integrity,) To Weaken Us and To Move Us Aside in a slow process of attrition warfare; and involving The Use of Drugs and Chemical Agents available, As Weapons Against Us, to inflict grave physical and mental/emotional harm upon our population; who are then, (as a designed part of the plot in conspiracy,) left prey to an Installed Psychiatric Intake Mental Health System, to "Legally" Finish The Job.

And Make No Mistake About It. This is A War Front in its entirety Against The Innocent White American Population; and particularly The White Males, and specifically targeting Our Returning War Veterans in this case, (and in the case of all recent eras of our Nation's Wars dating to the aftermath of The Korean War,) who represent our Nation's First Line of Defense to such type of warfare and against The Subversive Elements who perpetrate it, being closest involved to The Homefront; who are made into The Primary Targets of this Clandestine and Unconventional Style of Drug-Chemical Warfare Conspiracy for this reason, To Eliminate them, The U.S. Armed Forces Personnel; by inducing psychiatric conditions through the means of Drug Chemical Warfare Perpetration, which are then relegated for and remanded into the custody of psychiatric intake for the complaining of, (or from the induced overt effects of such sabotage occurring by atmosphere and by food and beverage perpetration,) and to "Forced Treatment" with metabolically destructive psychiatric drugs, to be turned into "Chemical

"ONE POWERFUL VOICE"

Zombies," in the guise of medicine, under the present system's, (designed for that purpose,) Mental Hygiene Laws; (of cloak and dagger motive,) without the population, (who traditionally have a trust in the medical profession, and in their government to protect them,) being aware of it.

And of which style of clandestine warfare connected to the use and freewheeling access to Heroin, Cocaine, that goes on, Mafia Warfare Style, and in name to popular liberation fronts, (and that has been going on,) on for generations, even centuries, without anyone being aware of it, to the legitimate population being "Systematically Purged" in that surreptitious manner to psychiatric intake, without having any recourse to Legal Defense of Due Process Rights under the current Mental Hygiene Civil Laws, in protection of their Life and Liberty as guaranteed for each citizen under The Constitution by Law.

And subsequently then to each of their, the victims of this war, in this case being perpetrate against The White European Middle Class Population, being ruinously crippled and maimed; and mentally, psychically, psychologically, and emotionally tormented and destroyed, by the use of deadly "Forced Administration" of Disabling Strong Psychiatric Type Tranquilizer Drugs, (that have been approved for such use by our own Nation's Food and Drug Administration, The FDA.)

And which, in the name of medicine, has nothing to do with The Healthy Healing and Curing of anyone suffering to legitimate and bona-fide Mental Disorders; but only to The En Masse Diagnoses, Labeling, Destructive Debilitations of Treatment, and to The Permanently Stigmatized Ruinations of Psychiatric Histories, of innocent people, and as who are forever thereafter subjected to a psychiatric tyranny of unending subordination and to the loss of personal liberty at issue, (en masse of this war's orientation,) to what Our Nation, in all regards, Is To Stand Corrected For! And along with the idea that our Proud Nation Under God; of The People, By The People, and For The People, can be systematically purged and sacrifice of its members, one by one and en mass, under the dispiriting guise of "Political Correctness," and surrendered of our Traditional Christian Morality and American Standards of Ethics in Values, and of our sustaining Middle Class Economy, and of our Territory to Invading Foreign Mass-Immigration Overrun of every description, in name to voting numbers catering to the animosities of a Drug/Porno Fascist, Third World/Ethnic National/Racial/Foreign Speaking, Political Bloc Coalition, (and by Mulatto-izing The White Population as well, called "The War of Babies,") with the objective eventually To Take Over The United States of America, and to Its Ultimate Breakup and Division amongst themselves for their own kind.

And bearing in mind, that the case is, (and which has always been from its inception of subversive intent in use against The Returning War Veterans beginning in the aftermath of The Korean War, and to the subsequent creation of The Mental Health System during The Kennedy Administration in The Civil Rights years of the early 1960s, and in continuing on in its devastation to this day,) a bitter and very difficult one to resolve; due to the fact of it being, that it involves The Government of The United States and Its Above-Board stance regarding The Laws and Policy Decisions of Its Bureaucracy at all times, in the allowing, legally, of an error to exist, that is never stood corrected for; and so which then continues on, the error, on the footing that the government cannot conceive to have any error, and involving The Bureaucratic Conspiracy associated to the case in Cover-Up, of The Government not being willing To Accuse Itself of Any Error. And so it goes on.

And to the point, in all, discussing of "The Error" with you, of allowing; first off, of The Drugs Condition to proliferate here without sufficient "Aggressive Defensive Countermeasures"

"ONE POWERFUL VOICE"

being put into effect to counter it, the bad situation. That secondly has been allowed to wage unmitigated drug and chemical warfare in use of the illegal drugs and chemicals as weapons Against Us! without our required government intervention to it In Defense. That thirdly has allowed The Veterans Administration Hospitals, (and overall regarding the nation's Mental Health Archipelago,) of State Psychiatric Facilities, and involving their Medical Health Professionals in name to The American Medical Association overall; and in particular centered to the idea of government salaried psychiatric medical staffing, (who, in all, are obligated to operate under the ethics of the doctrine of The Hippocratic Oath,) in our government's allowing them to inflict catastrophic damage of their own discretion upon the innocent lives of our population, and upon the lives of our returning home war veterans, (and in general extending out upon the entire population in that regards of Psychiatric Tyranny Without Rights, to what the people of this nation are being subjected to.) And which has been this way most flagrantly since the era of The Korean War, but which has been allowed to escalate, in disgrace to the sensibilities of our government leaders, in more recent years, (and connected to our leaderships permissive acceptance of Drugs and Chemicals and to the inevitable use of The Drug Chemical Warfare Associated, stood un-intervened to through the years, and ongoing,) and which has destroyed the lives, through psychiatric intake and forced treatment with Thorazine, of over 1,000,000 returning Vietnam War Veterans, and for what was responsible for the deaths of 68,000 Veterans, (who committed suicide resulting from the morbid effects of such forced psychiatric treatment.) And which is now engulfing and destroying "one in three" of our Nation's combat soldiers returning from The Iraqi War.

And, "May God Rest Their Souls," of the maimed, and of the slaughtered slain and valiant returning veterans, who have suffered a war and who have sacrificed their lives for the defense of our Nation, who have all died needlessly at the hands of The Veterans Administration's Psychiatric Medical Profession, (and pertaining for the issue of State Run Psychiatric Facilities as well in their negligence and gross mishandling of our Armed Forces Personnel,) in their treatment of our country's War Combat Veterans as homicidal persons.

And let it be stated; that if there is anyone of the non-medical community who does not comprehend about "The Morbidity Factor," involved with the intake of Strong Tranquillizer Psychiatric Pharmacy, that they should volunteer themselves to take a thirty day, or a sixty day, supply of "Heavy Milligram Thorazine," (called "Meds" in a viciously implied sarcasm by the medical community,) the exact same dosage in strength that The V.A. Doctors prescribe to our returning War Veterans, in "Force Ordered Treatment" to take, (or otherwise to be subjected to forced needle injections of, if they refuse or resist voluntary treatment,) on a permanent basis, and with their being treated in that regard as Mass-Murderers for their assigned duty in National Defense as Combat Personnel, and for their brave sacrifices to the nation, To Be Destroyed by Thorazine, or by such other lethal Strong Tranquiller Class Pharmacy.

And of which Chemicals to speak of; that destroy The Body's Central Nervous System, Induce Brain Damage, and which Slows The Blood Circulation and Cripples The Body's Metabolism causing; "Extremely Uncomfortable States Of Being," (in which a person can't sit down, and can't stand up, can't sleep, and can't stay awake, and spends their hours endlessly pacing back and forth in a neurotic frenzy,) Bizarre Nightmares, Gnarling of The Hands and Feet; Severe Muscle Cramping, and a host of other Adverse Effects and Side-Effects, (and in turning our nation's veterans into "Chemical Zombies,") to the point that no one can endure, nor survive, the Catastrophic Effects of such prolonged sedation without lethal morbidity and

"ONE POWERFUL VOICE"

suicidal depression setting-in; and such then, and in the state of induced chemical pharmacy catatonia, and to the state of Drug Induced Depression, Committing Suicide.

That if there be anyone who would care to verify "The Effects" of these Strong Tranquiller Drugs themselves, let them experience it first-hand by offering to experiment with them on yourself to see what it is they are like.

Does the thought of it frighten you to imagine it?

It is hard to change The Ill-Course in Destiny of a Nation overnight, isn't it?

And as we have been experiencing, as an organizational effort on the part of The Veterans of The Vietnam War and other Military Services Organizations, on our part in attempts, through interactions with our government, involved to The Federal Legislature, and The Executive and Judicial Branches, The Federal Drug Enforcement Administration, The Federal Bureau of Investigation, and with The Military itself, and directly in appeals to The Veterans Administration and to The Food And Drug Administration, to salvage the fate and careers and personal esteem of reputations, and the very lives themselves, of our nation's proud Service Personnel, (pertaining for each and all of our Heroic Returning Combat Veterans, who deserve better,) to turn the tide away from the disgrace, and dishonor, and personal sufferings unto death at the hand of psychiatric, of those who have offered their lives to the service of God and Country, on The Fields of Honor and Valor of this Nations' Wars, to their then, and on their returning home, to their then being, "Made Into Psychiatrics," by The Very Country which they so proudly and so valiantly sought to defend with their lives, (and to the shame and discredit of this country and Its government for allowing it to happen, and for condoning it to occur,) and to these returning veterans being made into Prisoners of War (POW) Status in the nation's Veterans Administration Psychiatric Wards, and others relegated to State Mental Institutions, To Be Lost Forever!" without recourse to The Legal Defenses of the Military Legal Department to speak for them and to intervene in their behalf, divested of liberty and subjected to excruciating and inhumane torments of cruel and dis-functionally rendering and maiming treatment in their own beloved homeland; that is the apparent tragedy, that we as an embodied group, combining The Active Arm of entire Armed Services of The United States, The Standing Militias of this Nation, and together with each our Nation's Veterans Service Organization, Must Put An End To.

And so that, and somehow, and by The Grace of God in beseeching, that there must be some psychology to be brought to bear upon the matter, (of the social conversion sense,) to come to terms with the psychiatric injustice, and to bring it forth into alignment with sensible, and just, and humane American Standards of conduct befitting this nation.

To state, that somehow there must be the correct reasoning, short of the conflagration of war outright to be brought to bear, to convince the arguments for Radical Change To Immediately Occur in the favor of our affected Service Personnel in question, and to relieve the stress and suffering of these veterans, and for everyone else suffering out there to the tyranny of Forced Psychiatric Intake and Treatment Without Due Process of Law Intervening, before indeed that a war does break out for the dire matter, to alter the system of things as they stand condemned by reason for in the present setting.

And for the lack of government intervention to occur on Its own right, and in the words of George Washington, The Father of Our Country, (who would have gone to war for less, in specifying for the just cause against this Psychiatric Tyranny in outrage over the psychiatric injustice and ensuing purge of our population in toll of lives occurring, in debacle of tortured ruination in its wake:)

"ONE POWERFUL VOICE"

"That The Tyranny of Tyrants, by whatever form, Shall Never More Prevail Against Us, As A People, and As A Nation, Unto God, of This Earth."

And with the formidable banner of The Green Mountain Militia Minute Men also instated as our motto in the modern hour to spirit the reasoning of the issue:

"DON'T TREAD ON ME."

That we proceed with the directives of the case, (pertaining for the debacle of psychiatric and connected directly to ongoing toleration of the sustained presence of deadly drugs and chemicals afoot in this nation, which are not being intervened to properly in disposition under The Authority of The Constitution as mandated for In Defense of The Nation,) as for the current "Ill-Practitioning," of the Subversive and Mercantile, (For Profit,) Psychiatric, in Ordered Statement, for them:

To Cease and Desist Immediately.

And to clear-up for what ruination they have caused upon the good people of this Country in their ill-formulated wake in aftermath; by wording of General Amnesty to occur for each of The Psychiatric History Records incurred under The Old Mental Health System Without The Rights Of Due Process; for the behalf of the nation's veterans and for the mainstay of the population who have been and made into innocent psychiatric victims by the injustice by the medical malpractice and misdiagnoses, to the ruinations of psychiatric labeling; and by such manner of Compensation For Injuries Suffered to be paid to these affected individuals in national burden, in consequences of the horrific mass-treatment of the people with these, Approved For By The FDA, known to be metabolically destructive and lethal, psychiatric drugs, in name to the curing of mental illness, which they do not! (and which for what matter in fact, that they "Induce," the describe for mental conditions, these types of pharmacy, which they are touted to alleviate and cure,) in Psychiatric Holocaust.

And for what is to say, that there is no one arguing the point of the existence of true and genuine mental illnesses and disorders in the need for health restoring treatment. But for the Point of Law, "By Just Due Process To Be Rendered For," That Such Diagnoses and Treatment Are To Be Governed Over By A Strict Application In Safeguards Of Law, concerning any diagnoses to be rendered to these alleged conditions; and "To The Terms of Safe and Beneficial Treatment" To Be Treated For With Compassion; and which in all is to be brought swiftly to bear upon the matter, where currently none exists.

And to the words of the great French philosopher, Jean-Jacques Rousseau, (1712-1778,) in mind, (who taught in the years shortly preceding The French Revolution,) and which is an analogous concept to be thought about here in regard to the current malfeasances en mass of psychiatric tryanny; that:

"Power Corrupts – and Absolute Power Corrupts Absolutely," and that: "A Tyrant By Any Other Name Is Still A Tyrant."

That we do here now conceive to analyze about the current setting of corrupt and nefarious power that the current psychiatric setting, termed as Mental Health, has garnered to itself here in this country over the last half century of its intrigue under The Nation's Mental Health System created; of what it has evolved into in sinister context to be regarded, that has been given an unholy power over us about; in The Surrender of our Constitutional Rights of Due Process over to; The Police, and The Courts, and to The Doctors of The Psychiatric Medical Community, (the majority of whom are foreign speaking people,) The Absolute Power of Life Or Death Over The People, without any regard for their Well-Being and to their Rights as Human Beings Under Law. And that this hideousness is to conceive about in the real terms of having fallen into the sinister motives of, Moral Degeneracy, Organized Crime, or to The Hostile and Subversive Intents of; Foreign Enemies, or to Political, and/or otherwise, Racial and Nationalistically Biased and Prejudiced Individuals, in Motives, without any fair minded system of Checks and Balances in place to prevent them from doing anything they want, to anyone they want, in throw-back to the skullduggery and torture of medieval times.

And with no intended disrespect for any honest and well-meaning of the medical practitioners of the psychiatric community, (such as to their having the healing and curative scrupulous intent of best possible interests in their patients in mind, and to their respect for human life and for the principles of Hippocratic Oath of Medicine protecting it;) but for the idea apparent; of what can, and of what does, and what has, gone wrong here, to the legitimate practicing of psychiatric medicine, that has been allowed to fall into corrupt and subversive hands in the name of government allowing, that these "otherwise" honest and law abiding professionals have Remained Silent About! and, Have Not Taken Sides, In Defense of The American People, To Correct For, Under Law, concerning The Malpractice of their fellow physicians, and concerning the safe well-being of the unfortunate people of this nation who are suffering to The Intolerable Circumstance in The Crucible of Legal and Medical Malfeasance Injustice involved at the hands of psychiatric, and without Sufficient Defense of Legal Due Process under The Miranda Legislation, through the lack of corrective safe-guards being put in place, to occur by The Restructuring of The United States Constitution to include for The Rights of Mental Hygiene, in the interests of the public safety and well-being; and with no one to counter with any legal defense in their plight, for these suffering individuals, of regard under the present setting of The U.S. Constitution as the case stands, convicted now in The People's Court of exposure currently, To The Deprivation of Life and Liberty, and To The Extent of Lethal and Excruciating Treatment Being Force Inflicted, and Imposed Without Benefit of Legal Rights of Due Process.

And with strongly worded reiteration, and once again in making the point perfectly clear, that there is no one here arguing the respect for the existence of genuine insanity and for the existence of debilitating mental conditions and disorders apparent, nor of the need for Mental Health Confinement to exist; in Commitment Process and else-wise to oversee The Monitoring of The Mentally Ill, and Socially Disturbed as Outpatients in The Mental Health System; and nor to the care and treatment of The Mentally Challenged and Dis-functional, and for Retarded Persons to be provided for by our government; nor for The Need for Beneficial Treatment to coincide for the treatment of such mental conditions described, and nor for the presence, (worded in the terms of judgment,) in necessity of The Medical Profession and other types of Mental Health Professionals, in making their determinations over these matters, in respect and with scrupulous regard for their ethics and credibility in accordance with The Highest Standards.

But it is in the arguing, To Prevent the Sinister Misuse of Psychiatric Injustice! (as a convenient means of disposing of people,) for the issue in reasoning to occur, that we denounce strongly, (and once again to stress,) that the subject of Mental Hygiene in this Country, Must Ensure and Encumber To! The Stipulation of Legal Due Process to occur for every individual being challenged in that regard of Mental Illness Allegation in Diagnosis, under Mental Hygiene Law, by the means of Two Physician Consent (2PC); for the stating of a Legal Psychiatric Charge to be present, (in wording of Irrational Conduct, or as Posing of a Serious Threat To Themselves or To Others, or to be base to a Medical Diagnosis adhering to the legal criteria

"ONE POWERFUL VOICE"

established for such diagnoses coinciding to the legal definitions for such disorders to be found in The Medical Diagnostic and Statistical Manual of Mental Disorders, Fourth Edition "DSM – IV,") and that all other Rights of Due Process, Under Miranda Legislation, Be Accorded each individual in the regard of their public safety in scrutiny of The Medical-Legal Profession in overall safeguard; such To Safeguard, Defend, and To Protect, The Private Rights of The People from Psychiatric Condemnation under the concepts of Corrupt and Maleficent Terms of Racial/Foreign Intrigues, or Mafia Corruptions.

And in further utterance in the matter of, The People vs. The Current Government of The United States, regarding psychiatric at this or any other time, to the issue of Psychiatric Due Process Rights; that it is to be So Order For also, that The Heading of Psychiatric, which comes under the category of, Civil Law Medical Processing, must, from now on into the future, be regarded for in stipulation to embody, The Same Rights expressed for in The 4th, 5th, 6th, and 14th Amendments to The U.S. Constitution, in safeguards to; Life, Liberty, Property, and The Pursuit of Happiness, and that as are found in Legal Expression included for in The Miranda Rights Legislation accorded to Penal (or Criminal) Law, The Same.

And beyond The Fair and Justified Right to have presented the wording of a Specific Psychiatric Charge to be accountable to, to include as well; for The Right To Have A Court Appointed Attorney, (if indeed a private attorney cannot be afforded,) and to The Due Process Right of a Fair Jury Trial for the matter, and for The Right To Confrontation of Testimony, to include also for The Right To Present Evidence In One's Behalf, The Right To The Presumption of Innocence Until Proven Guilty, (the guilt of which must be proven by Legally Obtained Evidence, by The State, and The Verdict of which must be supported by The Evidence of a Psychiatric Offense Presented before an impartial jury, In Burden Of Proof Upon The State vs. The People, To Indict, (and not the other way around as the case stands now, where The Psychiatrically Accused Must Prove Their Own Innocence, and No Right To Review The Testimony of Their Accusers;) and that the stipulation also contain the wording of The Right of The Accused, under assistance of counsel present, To Be Advised of Their Constitutional Rights and Protected Against Self-Incrimination, and to have The Right Not To Be Endlessly Tried, (in the terms of Labeling Harassment,) For The Same Charge In Perpetual Persecution.

And also, that The Case for Comprehensive Due Process; (which is to govern legally over and to each case of psychiatric disposition, and to the behalves, in Rights Protected, of The Psychiatrically Accused,) that is to include and to specify further, In Rights Protected, for The Right To Safe and Beneficial Treatment, to be such legally clarified and stipulated about, (as to the Types of Treatment that may be Prescribed for, or Force Administered, and under what circumstances in conditions that any such treatment specified may be Force Administered, and for what lengths of time in duration that such Forced Administration may be imposed.)

And also what is to include as well, (in cases other than Forced Administration of such Treatment,) for The Right To Informed Consent, to be worded, in The Presence of Counsel, to be discussed with each individual, to be advised of any Dangerous and/or Harmful Effects and Side Effects that such treatment may incur upon them in consequence, and as to what they may be, (as opposed to their therapeutic advantages, if any, to describe for, of such proposed treatment to undergo;) and to include for, The Right To Refuse Treatment, (as unless it falls into the legal category of Parens Patriea, (or Ward of The State,) under Mental Hygiene Legality, allowing Forced Treatment under the conditioned grounds of a person being deeming legally incompetent in the eyes of the law; which is to include for the circumstances of their being Non-Compos Mentis, Insane, Irrational, Delusional, Mentally Challenged or Dis-functional, or to persons of

"ONE POWERFUL VOICE"

Violently Disruptive Behavior of Serious Threat To Themselves or To Others, as persons under Temporary Hysterias, persons Self-Inflicting Harm, persons Attempting Suicide, Legitimate Medical Emergencies in necessity, Psychiatric Inducing Illnesses or Diseases, (such as Syphilis, Epilepsy, and Rabies,) in derangement in the need of Force Treatment To Cure, and to all other circumstances of such matters of common sense in such regard concerning what Mental Illnesses as are generated by Metabolic Disorders, and Hysterias, that timely treatment would cure in the setting of Parens Patriea; which are the only Legalities of Forced Treatment To Be Allowed in The Discerning Judgment of The Medical Profession and The Court.

And also to be worded; that the issue in reasoning upon Forced Treatment of The Mentally Ill, (or to anyone in the setting of Parens Patriea for that matter,) Is Not In Dispute, (as the case is self-evident of its bona-fide necessity under law in legitimate medical circumstances, and falling into the category of mental incapacitation, as is obvious in its necessity to be given over to medical discretion, To Treat For.)

However to state for the grievous matter of what is in dispute; is that this setting of Legally Forced Psychiatric, Is Not To Be Taken as a Corrupt License By The Medical Profession and by The Courts, To Willfully and Arbitrarily and Capriciously Disposed of Individuals by the means of Forced Chemical, or Surgical, or Shock, Treatment, in that manner, without Appropriate Safeguards of Legal Due Process to occur, (in the nature of Parens Patiea or otherwise;) concerning The Legality of Forced Psychiatric Treatment, (in the stating of What Precise Specific Grounds that it may be administered, and to the wording of Safe and Beneficial Treatment to coincide,) concerning The Human Rights of Persons being subjected to it; who in all regard are never to be made into Human Guinea Pigs as given over to the whims and evil discretions of the medical profession and the pharmaceutical industry To Experiment With People in the name of medicine; who in all regard are to be protected from such experimentation and from treatment with bias or malice.

And in further reiteration of all such Psychiatric Treatment, (whether Forced or otherwise of a voluntary rendering under law,) and by The Wording of Law under Martial Ruling, that Must Be Deemed Justified and Necessary, Beneficial, and Therapeutically Sound, and Which May Not Be Arbitrarily or Subjectively Imposed in The Nature Of Experimentation, or to be condoned Conducted With Bias of Prejudice, or with Malice of Forethought in Name To Corruption, and which Treatment in all regard May Never Be Rendered Without Overview of The Court; and what is incumbent upon The Psychiatric/Medical Community To Carry-Out in The Strictest Morality and Scrupulous Ethics of Their Profession, Whose Business It Is, "To Heal and To Cure," and Not To Maim and Disable and Destroy.

And as we dealing with The Sacred Issue of Liberty here, of what this entire subject is about, regarding the current travesty of Psychiatric Injustice to be looked at and handled in that way of Immediate and Sustained Correction To It; from the standpoint of all of the Innocent Victims, (including The Children,) of The Drug Warfare occurring here in our Society, (that Is Not Being Handled Properly!) and for The Behalf of The Poor and otherwise Psychologically Disadvantaged Victims of Hardship and Oppression, and regarding The Defense Entitled to our Nation's Combat Veterans returning home from War; and for the sake of all of those who find themselves haplessly entrapped in the quagmire of psychiatric suspicion by Manipulation of The Courts, without recourse to Justified Processing Under Law; and with being thereof Forced Into Treatment with deadly chemicals or to other devastating procedures, Without Due Process, and who are Unable To Defend Themselves! under The Tyranny of The Present System as it stands to be corrected, and protected from The Corruption of Psychiatric/Medical Malfeasance, under

"ONE POWERFUL VOICE"

Civil Mental Hygiene Law, (as is currently exempt from The Miranda Legislation and The Protection of Civil Rights Provided for of The U. S. Constitution,) under the sardonic wording of Medical Processing, in Trust To The Judgment of The Doctors' Diagnosis, who may or may not be ethical, and as many doctors have proved themselves to be that way of corruption, for reasons of money, or for other more sinister motives of subversive intent, in preying upon "The Captive Market" of their Psychiatric Diagnoses unto Forced Treatment, and in Conspiracy with The Pharmaceutical Companies to that regard, from what their "patients" cannot escape, to be worded: that Our Present Government, Cannot Continue To Condone, in Allowing The Medical Profession and The Courts "The Uncontested Right" To Order Psychiatric Evaluations of Persons, thereunto to their Being Psychiatrically Labeled, and Ordered Over For "Treatment," (and all the while with Sovereign Immunity Protected From All Personal Responsibility For Liability For Damaged and From Legal Prosecution In Cases of Malfeasance and Dereliction of Duty Charged, under The Terms of Current Mental Hygiene Law,) and in more ludicrous arrangement, of having, "The Burden of Proof," for such travesty, To Reside With The Psychiatrically Accused, (who in all regards Have No Right To A Public Defender Under Mental Hygiene Law, and are for the most part, "Too Poor" to hire an expensive attorney in their own defense; concerning the issue of "2-PC," or, "Two Physician Consent.") And to what that the modern day "Justice System" is making, "a mockery out of," in Ordering Anyone and Everyone falling into their jurisdiction who they may not happen to like, To Undergo a Psychiatric Evaluation by Two "Court Appointed Examiners," and to their dispensing entirely with The Due Process of Law under The Penal System altogether, and rendering people into Psychiatric Custody and to Forced Treatment, (that can occur whether a person is being detained in jail or prison, or in a psychiatric facility, this business of Forced Treatment with Deadly Psychiatric Chemicals, to be treated with anything that they, the doctors, feel like treating those persons with, to the Unending Torment of their patient/victims,) for The Diagnoses of The Court Examiners, Without The Accused Having Any Rights of Contestation in The Case!

And furthermore to be worded in The Revised Martial Setting of Legality Governing To, And Over, The Issue of Psychiatric Reform in This Nation; that it is to be understood, that No Court, nor Any Agency of The Government, or Any Hospital or Psychiatric Facility, May Order For A Psychiatric/Psychological Evaluation To Occur Upon The Person of Any Public Member of The United States, (Under Duress of Compulsion In Penalty,) Without Their Being Present In Legal Writ, to the wording, "Of Just And Probable Cause," In Grounds For Such An Order! Based To The Demonstration of a Psychiatric Charge.

And such then, and as it is stated for; that for what Orders For Psychiatric Evaluation, that may not any longer be further rendered to by capricious and arbitrary terms of demand; and nor to the setting of anyone further then being capriciously and arbitrarily diagnosed, without Due Process; such then to their, anyone's, being permanently ruined over by Psychiatric Labeling and History, without Due Process; such then to their, anyone's, being Subjected To The Loss of Their Liberty by Commitment/Incarceration, and subsequently then to their being "Force Treated," without any Due Process to occur; that Is Not To Occur Further On In This Nation, which is dedicated to The Unalienable Rights of Its Constitution.

And importantly regarding for the entire issue of Psychiatric, with its Medical Civil Law Imperiousness of Forced Treatment coinciding, and to its ruinous labeling in histories of, without any Due Process of Law Occurring for its sake, in the name of justice, and of the many lives at stake affected, (and especially as involves and critically affects the great number of our returning War Veterans, past and present, that it does, to intervene about in their behalves about,) and for

"ONE POWERFUL VOICE"

the countless behalves of the great and substantial numbers of the many such members of our population of the civilian nature presently imperiled, in the regard of The Courts and The Psychiatric Medical Profession holding such Tyranny apparent over the population in Profiteering Conspiracy to The Pharmaceutical Industry, (of that Sinister Setting,) and in "getting away with it," on Medical Sovereign Immunity in grounds pertaining for the abdication by this Nation of 4th, and 5th, and 6th, Amendment Rights to Psychiatric Override under the heading of "Civil Law;" that has become an Evil Thing! (and for the issues of legitimate psychiatric insanities withstanding, as are obvious to concern to,) but for the dire impact of The Stated Evil, in plague upon this Nation, that Psychiatric has become, as a manipulating parasite of huge proportions of context upon us, in prey upon the hapless victims of The Drug War, (and with its Drug Warfare,) As Casualties, and to the victims of life's hardships and travails, who cannot defend themselves, who we, as The Military Override of This Nation Empowered, Must In All Ways of Regard, Defend! And To Defend With Our Lives If Necessary, in the heroic words of Nathan Hale:

"Give Me Liberty or Give Me Death."

Which is to be regarded for in the seriousness of that meaning that it is, and for the sense in setting of its occurring; to the perverse idea of Blatant Corruptions, Misdiagnoses/Mal-diagnoses, Malfeasance/Malpractice (and on the part of The Courts as well,) Criminal Mafia Intrigues of Drug Warfare Manipulation Involvement, Foreign Overthrow Subversions, and to the ideas of any Biases or Prejudicial Discriminations and Persecutions to exist, (of Racial or Ethnic Origin, or otherwise of Feminist or Lesbian/Homosexual or to other perverse Sexual Orientations of intrigues, such as Child Molestation and Incest, and to the nature of Errant Housewives concerning the subjects of Infidelity, Interracial Fornication, combined with Drug Addiction, Pornography, and to Drug Warfare Perpetration, as an "inside job," or as perpetrated by close Family Members that way, upon our returning War Veterans; who represent "America's Last Line of Defense;") and coinciding to the sinister setting of The Entire Society Being Forced Dictated Over By The Subjected Tyranny Of Psychiatric Evaluations in concepts to The Drug/Chemical Warfare Designs of; Communism, Islamism, Fascism, Zionism, Black Makimbo Mafia Voodoo-ism, Mulatto-ism, Third World-ism (of The Latin American Drug Cartel Versions in the modern hour,) Asian-ism; and in all, (in Blatant Mafia Gerrymanderings throughout The Country, in being Heroin and Drug/Pornography Related,) of Criminal Tyrannies, of such magnitude who are relentlessly at us On The Attack! Against The Traditional White European American Heritage; to be replacing The Cherished Values and Sacred Intent of Our Founding Forefathers, of Legitimate Democracy, In "Inverse Political Conspiracy" To Overthrow The Trusted Foundation of Our Nation's Constitution; and To The Idea of Replacing The Justice System With Psychiatric Medical Diagnoses and Forced Treatment, and in design most sinister, and to the inflicting of psychiatric histories and treatment upon our Nation's Poor in replacing The Individual States' Welfare burden with Psychiatric Disability, in transferring the burden on to The Federal Social Security Insurance (S.S.I) Program, (in scheme to reduce The Local Welfare Rolls and Local Tax Burden by forcing Welfare Recipients onto The S.S.I Psychiatric Disability, and onto The Federal Tax Burden at huge taxpayers' expense, regarding the captive market of The Medical/Pharmacy Industry Involved,) and to the permanent ruination employment wise of all of those being subjected to it; and who, in being permanently labeled with psychiatric histories, that no one will ever hire, and to their subsequently then in being permanently made into Wards of The State in unending Tax Burden to the public; and in all

"ONE POWERFUL VOICE"

pertaining for, "The Psychiatric Purging," of Our Nation's Combat Veterans returning to civilian life and to their fate in elimination as a presence of opposition In Defense of Our Traditional American Heritage and Homeland, in modern day Holocaust.

This is a formidable Miscarriage Of Justice in Psychiatric Tyranny Being Allowed under the captioning of "Civil Law Medical Procedure;" and Without Any Rights of Due Process In Justice, and In Violation of Human Rights Standards in The Allowing of Chemical Alteration of Persons In Forced Treatment, and with being solely left up to the judgment of a corrupt and subversive Psychiatric Medical Community to oversee, By Law Allowing; (To Treat People and otherwise To Experiment On Persons, singularly and acting as a group that way in profession,) with anything that they want, (Chemically, or otherwise with Surgery or by Electric or Insulin Shock Treatment, and of what Treatment exposed, that is Physically, Mentally, and Emotionally Destructive and Very Excruciating To Endure!) at the sole discretions of the doctors involved, Without Judicial Overview; while their tormented and suffering patient/victims, in Guinea Pig Status, Have No Legal Defense To Be Able To Refuse Treatment or To Do Anything About Their Situation, Under The Present Law; that is ever threatening to engulf The Entire Nation in its deadly grip, and which The Entire Population could conceivably be subjected to by The Present Context of Law Allowing; that such would bear witness upon the horror; of everyone in the entire context of our society being routinely and mandatorily Force Ordered By The State to undergo Psychiatric/Psychological Examinations, to be governed over strictly by The Diagnoses of Examining Physicians, (who may or may not be at any time, English Speaking Americans, of foreign persuasion,) and for profit, and to The Legal Unspecified and Uncertain Outcomes of Capricious, Arbitrary, and in Subjective Bias of Opinions of Diagnoses; and Without Clarifications of Law To Guide Them! And To The Loss of Life, Liberty, and The Pursuit of Happiness, in Justice Sake to all concerned, and to the uncertainties of Confinement/Commitment, and To Life's Long Subordination To The Medical Profession, (and With The Courts Upholding! To Forced Rendering Of Treatment With Mind-Altering Metabolically Destructive Chemicals, FDA Approved For, Without Public Safeguards In Place For Safe and Beneficial Therapeutic Treatment Legally To Occur,) and For Profit! Without Benefit of Counsel and Without Due Process, Here In Our America! covering all that we have just described and beginning to take hold now as well with the Mandatory Public Psychiatric Screening of our Grade School Children, and to their being permanently scarred by Psychiatric Labeling, (formerly termed as, "Guidance Counseling,") and to be Force Treated with Ant-Psychotic Chemicals, on the say-so of the Examining Physicians in conspiracy; that We Need To Prevent! And Must Prevent! from ever occurring, pertaining for this kind of Psychiatric Devastation Without Justified Due Process, (as to The Legal Validity of Medical Psychiatric Determinations,) affecting upon The Sanctity of The American Public, Who We So Cherish To Defend! "Whose Rights, In The Determinations of Our Wills and of Our Collective Strength, and By Our Common Muster To Correct, and By The Power Of War Protected, Included For Our Stand Against Such Tyranny Apparent, By The Constitution Protected, Which Cannot Ever Be Violated!" And To Stand By The Words:

That, Should This Nation Ever Be Overtaken By Tyrants To It; Which It Has:

"As Is The Right And The Duty Of The People To Overthrow!"

As Is Our Public Necessity to "Militarily Override," Categorically, To The Prevailing Status Quo of Psychiatric Tyranny! in the modern hour of its Malfeasance; To What That The Divine Intervention of Due Process and with Safeguards of Treatment Must Be Ensured For as a

"ONE POWERFUL VOICE"

Military Objective; of what is: **"The Order Of The Day,"** In The Unmitigated Defense of The American People, For What We Appeal.

The American United States Cannot Be Peacefully Surrendered of Its Constitutional Rights, and our vested interests in Standard of Economy, and concerning our Time Honored Heritage of Christian Values, and Systematically Handed Over to Foreign Occupation, in Name To Civil Rights.

And which in all regard as a statement, has nothing to do with all the good and decent people of foreign lands who have come respectfully to this nation to take up with residency and citizenship among us in faith. We welcome each and all of these people, and celebrate their diversity and differences among us, and who only serve to enrich our lives and in the great heart of our nation to be proud of. But that these people cannot be made into wage slaves by the element of greed, and to our impoverishment in their replacing us at our jobs, for the sake of the argument; or to be involved here, in mistaken orientation of the privilege of citizenship, to the smuggling and trafficking in drugs, or to any other concepts of organized crime, or designs to overthrow; to what that our current Liberal Government Appeases.

This deadly scenario can be formidably corrected for by; The Aggressive Military Removal of The Drugs and Chemicals and their use as Drug/Chemical Weapons from the population, Military Forensics Analysis of The Nation's Food And Beverage Supplies, Enactment of Secure Due Process and Safety Rights for Psychiatric, The Enactment of Just Fair Wage Labor and Employment Laws, The Imposition of Realistic Immigration Limitations, and by the imposition of a Social Injunction Against Interracial Procreation To Preserve The Integrity of The Races.

The people of this nation just need to be told what to do, and in some instances, to be intervened to; but strong decisive leadership in command is required in either setting if things are ever to get straightened out properly. But someone needs to take the helm that way of objective discussions, and frankly worded, about the right and the wrong of things.

Along time ago I fought a war for the honor of this nation in Vietnam; and, as with each and every veteran and current members of The Armed Forces of America in that right, and to our individual ordeals of laboring and suffering to any war's outcome, and in the sacrifice of our lives at stake, In The Need of Mutual Respect and Regard to tell you, that we care about what goes on here in our country, to what that we offered and sacrificed our lives to defend. And it matters some to us how things are going here now concerning the things that are not right with the way we are here to be remedied. And to what matters to stand corrected for, that we have a vested interest in defending, and a very personal and private interest in defending, strongly worded. To let you know that, and what we are about, as we offer our support and personal dedication to you in the offer of our assistance to resolve the drug war and other pressing matters of conflict which portend to threaten our beloved homeland and our American way of life.

Please let us know what, if anything, that we can do for you.

And in mention that the enlisted men would like to have the respect of Officer Status associated to their rank beginning at E-6 and above, which would go a long way in bonding the two "disparaging" halves of The Military Together into one harmonious fighting unit, that is now divided into unsettling class discrimination in resentment.

Most Respectfully
Gary L. Koniz
Veterans Of The Vietnam War

"ONE POWERFUL VOICE"

 # Psychiatric Drugs: Thorazine

"People's voices came through filtered, strange. They could not penetrate my Thorazine fog; and I could not escape my drug prison." - Janet Gotkin, testimony before the Senate Subcommittee on the Abuse and Misuse of Controlled Drugs in Institutions (1977)

"It's very hard to describe the effects of this drug and others like it. That's why we use strange words like "zombie". But in my case the experience became sheer torture." - Wade Hudson, testimony before the Senate Subcommittee on the Abuse and Misuse of Controlled Drugs in Institutions (1977)

"Frequent Effects: sedation, drowsiness, lethargy, difficult thinking, poor concentration, nightmares, emotional dullness, depression, despair . . ." - Dr. Calagari's Psychiatric Drugs (1987)

In 1954 the neuroleptic drug, Thorazine, began flooding the state mental hospitals. The neuroleptics are synonymous with tranquilizers and antipsychotics. The neuroleptics are the drug most commonly given to schizophrenics. The psychiatrist would like us to believe that drugs such as Thorazine "cure" the patient by repairing or altering "bad" brain chemistry (whatever that means. . .). But the truth is the drug involves a strong dulling of the mind and emotional functions, and that this is what acts to inhibit or "push the symptoms into the back ground". According to Jerry Avon, M.D.:

"My concern is that people are having their minds blunted in a way that probably does diminish their capacity to appreciate life". (Boston Globe, 1988)

To fully understand the nature and effects of drugs such as Thorazine, it is useful to go back and see what the early research psychiatrists themselves had to say about the drug. The two pioneers of Thorazine, Delay and Deniker, said about small doses of the drug in 1952:

"ONE POWERFUL VOICE"

"Sitting or lying, the patient is motionless in his bed, often pale and with eyelids lowered. He remains silent most of the time. If he is questioned, he answers slowly and deliberately in a monotonous and indifferent voice; he expresses himself in a few words and becomes silent".

In 1954, Canada's Heinz Lehmann described the "emotional indifference" and specifically called it the "aim" of the treatment. Like Deniker and Delay, he found "the patients under treatment display a lack of spontaneous interest in the environment. . .". Contrary to today's psychiatric PR, the early pioneers plainly stated there was no positive cure or reduction of the patient's delusional symptoms or hallucinatory phenomena. With stronger dosages, there is a marked dulling and blunting of the patient's overall awareness, motor control and "thereness". A 1950 textbook candidly reported the "lobotomylike" impact of Thorazine, and in 1958, Noyes and Kolb summarized in *Modern Clinical Psychiatry*:

"If the patient responds well to the drug, he develops an attitude of indifference both to his surroundings and to his symptoms".

The common factor is that the drug strongly reduces awareness and interest with the result the patient doesn't lose their symptoms, they lose *interest* in them.

Thorazine has been called a "chemical lobotomy" because of the similar effects it creates. Briefly, a lobotomy destroys partially or completely all functioning of the frontal lobes. The frontal lobes are unique to human beings and are the seat of the higher functions such as love, concern for others, empathy, self-insight, creativity, initiative, autonomy, rationality, abstract reasoning, judgment, future planning, foresight, will-power, determination and concentration. Without the frontal lobes it is impossible to be "human" in the fullest sense of the word; they are required for a civilized, effective, mature life. Without this "human" aspect a person is incapable of living a rewarding, happy and responsible life.

While the neuroleptics are toxic to most brain functions, disrupting nearly all of them, they have an especially well-documented impact on the dopamine neurotransmitter system. As any psychiatric textbook explains, dopamine neurotransmitters provide the major nerve pathways from the deeper brain to the frontal lobes and limbic system - the very same area attacked by surgical lobotomy. The disruption in the functioning of the frontal lobes results in the same effect - a greatly reduced person with dementia and reduction of awareness of self and the environment. They become "vegetables" - a body with very little mind or personality left.

"ONE POWERFUL VOICE"

While American psychiatrists continue to deny the obvious reality of chemical lobotomy, many European psychiatrists often acknowledge it openly, even in public and to the press. They can argue and play word games all they like - Thorazine is an extremely dangerous drug which does chemically what a lobotomy does surgically.

> *"The blunting of conscious motivation, and the inability to solve problems under the influence of chlorpromazine (Thorazine) resembles nothing so much as the effects of frontal lobotomy. . . Research has suggested that lobotomies and chemicals like chlorpromazine may cause their effects in the same way, by disrupting the activity of the neurochemical, dopamine. At any rate, a psychiatrist would be hard put to distinguish a lobotomized patient from one treated with chlorpromazine."* - Peter Sterling, neuroanatomist, article *Psychiatry's Drug Addiction*, New Republic magazine (March 3, 1979)

Like surgical lobotomy, chemical lobotomy has no specific beneficial effect on any human problem or human being. It puts a chemical clamp on the higher brain of anyone. Therefore, the drugs can be used to subdue anyone.

In *Tranquilizing of America* (1979), Richard Hughes and Robert Brewin state:

> *"When used on a large population of institutionalized persons, as they are, they can help keep the house in order with the minimum program of activities and rehabilitation and the minimum number of attendants, aides, nurses, and doctors".*

Again, there is no hiding the obvious real purpose of the drug. It saves money for the institutions and makes the people more manageable. Neuroleptic use is not rare or unusual. In fact,

> *"On many psychiatric wards the neuroleptics are given to 90 to 100 percent of the patients; in many nursing homes, to 50 percent or more of the old people; and in many institutions for persons with mental retardation, to 50 percent or more of the inmates. Neuroleptics are also used in children's facilities and in prisons."* - Peter Breggin, *Toxic Psychiatry*

Neuroleptics have been used in the Soviet Union to quell political dissidents. Russian poet, Olga Iofe, was imprisoned and forcibly drugged. She was singled out for "treatment" after protesting against the resurgence of Stalinism. In *Soviet Psychoprisons*, says political scientist Harvey Fireside, "The massive drugs she was forcibly given were, in Dr. Norman Hirt's opinion, 'in fact a chemical lobotomy', in light of reports that, on her release, Iofe 'appears to be permanently damaged, an altered person' ".

On February 16, 1976, *U.S. News and World Report* quoted another Russian dissent who had been forced to take neuroleptics, in this case Haldol, "I was horrified to see how I deteriorated intellectually, morally and emotionally from day to day. My interest in

"ONE POWERFUL VOICE"

political problems quickly disappeared, then my interest in scientific problems, and then my interest in my wife and children". The reader might assume he was given mega-doses of some especially deadly drug. On the contrary, "I was prescribed haloperidol (Haldol) in small doses."

The neuroleptics are also used in tranquilizing darts for subduing wild animals and in injections to permit the handling of domestic animals who become viscous. The psychiatrists continue to attempt to explain the mechanics of the neuroleptics as an alteration, for the better, of bad brain chemistry. The veterinary use of neuroleptics so undermines their antipsychotic theory that young psychiatrists are not taught about it. Peter Breggin, M.D., psychiatrist, points out clearly that the purpose of Thorazine is to alter and disable normal brain functions. It is actually the HARM caused by the drug which produces the effect.

> *"The brain-disabling principle applies to all of the most potent psychiatric interventions - neuroleptics, antidepressants, lithium, electroshock, and psychosurgery. . . the major psychiatric treatments exert their* primary or intended effect by disabling normal brain function. *Neuroleptic lobotomy, for example, is not a side effect, but the sought-after clinical effect. Conversely, none of the major psychiatric interventions correct or improve existing brain* dysfunction, such as *any presumed biochemical imbalance. If the patient happens to suffer from brain dysfunction, then the psychiatric drug, electroshock, or psychosurgery will worsen or compound it."*

The psychiatrists continue to promote and attempt to educate the public into believing Thorazine and other drugs "help" correct a mental disease. This is so far from the truth. That they even believe this themselves is meaningless. Whether or not some psychiatric patients have brain diseases (which has still never been verified - it's only a theory) is irrelevant to this brain-disabling principle. Even if someday a subtle defect is found in some mental patients, it will not change the damaging effect of the current treatments in use by psychiatry. Nor will it change the fact that the current treatments *worsen* brain function rather than improving it. If, for example, a person's emotional upset is caused by a hormonal problem, by a viral infection, or by ingestion of a hallucinogenic drug, the impact of the neuroleptics is still that of a lobotomy. The person now has his or her original brain damage and dysfunction *plus* a chemical lobotomy.

In summary, Thorazine, and all neuroleptics, cause chemical lobotomies with no specific therapeutic effect on any symptoms or problems. Their main impact is to blunt and subdue the individual. They also physically paralyze the body, acting as a chemical straightjacket. Additionally, these drugs are the cause of a plague of brain damage effecting up to half or more of long-term patients. Psychiatry refuses to accept these criticisms despite a large amount of evidence to the contrary. The psychiatric industry cannot tolerate dissemination of the truth as this strikes at the very core of their theoretical foundation (which is largely false).

"ONE POWERFUL VOICE"

As mentioned in other articles in this site, psychiatry and modern psychology have <u>redefined the meaning of the word "psychology"</u>, and completely ignore addressing the person's actual problems they have with life and their own minds. The entire realm of personality, including thought, concentration, intention, imagination, goals, hopes, and dreams are omitted from the psychiatric approach. Dealing with these areas directly through counseling, support groups, religion or alternative methods such as meditation or visualization techniques, has been forgotten. The result is a complete attempt to control behavior ONLY, with absolutely no regard for the person themselves. It should be no surprise psychiatric methods actually inhibit and harm the basic aspects of the human personality which it's very nomenclature ignores and denies.

<u>Psychiatry is a modern day belief system</u> not dissimilar to the religious structures of the Spanish Inquisition. The psychiatrists are the High Priests, they tolerate no criticisms, will never alter their views despite all evidence to the contrary, and will fight relentlessly to maintain their positions of power and authority. What makes it worse though is that psychiatric theories, parading as "science", have insinuated themselves in nearly all aspects of modern society - <u>government</u>, law, <u>medicine</u>, sociology, social services, and <u>education</u>. Their influence is dulling the overall awareness and ability of the entire society.

(Much of the information in this article came from chapter 3 of Peter Breggin's classic expose on psychiatry, <u>Toxic Psychiatry</u>.)

What side effects may occur?

Side effects cannot be anticipated. If any develop or change in intensity, inform your doctor as soon as possible. Only your doctor can determine if it is safe for you to continue taking Thorazine.

- *Side effects may include:*
  Abnormal secretion of milk, abnormalities in movement and posture, agitation, anemia, asthma, blood disorders, breast development in males, chewing movements, constipation, difficulty breathing, difficulty swallowing, dizziness, drooling, drowsiness, dry mouth, ejaculation problems, eye problems causing fixed gaze, fainting, fever, flu-like symptoms, fluid accumulation and swelling, headache, heart attack, high or low blood sugar, hives, impotence, inability to urinate, inability to move or talk, increase of appetite, infections, insomnia, intestinal blockage, involuntary movements of arms and legs, tongue, face, mouth, or jaw, irregular blood pressure, pulse, and heartbeat, irregular or no menstrual periods, jitteriness, light-headedness (on standing up), lockjaw, mask-like face, muscle stiffness and rigidity, narrow or dilated pupils, nasal congestion, nausea, pain and stiffness in the neck, persistent, painful erections, pill-rolling motion, protruding tongue, puckering of the mouth, puffing of the cheeks, rapid heartbeat, red or purple spots

"ONE POWERFUL VOICE"

on the skin, rigid arms, feet, head, and muscles (including the back), seizures, sensitivity to light, severe allergic reactions, shuffling walk, skin inflammation and peeling, sore throat, spasms in jaw, face, tongue, neck, mouth, and feet, sweating, swelling of breasts in women, swelling of the throat, tremors, twitching in the body, neck, shoulders and face, twisted neck, visual problems, weight gain, yellowed skin and whites of eyes

Special warnings about this medication

You should use Thorazine cautiously if you have ever had: asthma; a brain tumor; breast cancer; intestinal blockage; emphysema; the eye condition known as glaucoma; heart, kidney, or liver disease; respiratory infections; seizures; or an abnormal bone marrow or blood condition; or if you are exposed to pesticides or extreme heat. Be aware that

Thorazine can mask symptoms of brain tumor, intestinal blockage, and the neurological condition called Reye's syndrome.
Stomach inflammation, dizziness, nausea, vomiting, and tremors may result if you suddenly stop taking Thorazine. Follow your doctor's instructions closely when discontinuing Thorazine.

Thorazine can suppress the cough reflex; you may have trouble vomiting.
This drug may impair your ability to drive a car or operate potentially dangerous machinery. Do not participate in any activities that require full alertness if you are unsure about your ability.

This drug can increase your sensitivity to light. Avoid being out in the sun too long.
Thorazine can cause a group of symptoms called Neuroleptic Malignant Syndrome, which can be fatal. Some symptoms are extremely high body temperature, rigid muscles, mental changes, irregular pulse or blood pressure, rapid heartbeat, sweating, and changes in heart rhythm.

If you are on Thorazine for prolonged therapy, you should see your doctor for regular evaluations, since side effects can get worse over time.

"ONE POWERFUL VOICE"

9480 Princeton Square Blvd. S., #815
Jacksonville, FL 32256
December 3, 2009

Robert S. Mueller, III - Director
Federal Bureau Of Investigation
935 Pennsylvania Avenue, N.W.
Washington, D.C. 20535-0001

Dear Director Mueller:

Thank you for your review of my information. I always to like to recall the days back in the
early 90's when William S. Sessions was the Director of The F.B.I. and I worked under Senator
Daniel Patrick Moynihan directly and with The Federal Aviation Administration in assistance
efforts to resolve The Drug War and The Drug Terror going on without anyone to recognize
what it is, and still is! And the Nation' Speed Limit then out on the Interstates, and since The
Vietnam War, was a restricted 55 mph and a far cry form what we are able to drive at, of 70 mph
+ now in these times; to indicate how the sensibilities over irrational conditions can change for
the better --- but not so far as Psychiatric is concerned, involved as it is with its built-in
corruptions of intrigues with nobody of The Justice Department looking-on in responsibility, and
who are boldly replacing our guarantees of protection under our United States Constitution with
a Tyranny of Horror in having the ability to Disable as well as to Permanently Incarcerate its
Victims without the slightest sense of Justice in Due Process of Law to occur.

I was not guilty of any of the assertions attributed to me, as disclosed for about in the attached
records of the three separate occasions of my involvement with Psychiatric, as a bystander,
which were written down about without my knowledge and used as evidence against me without
my having the opportunity to confront my accusers in a Court Proceeding, which were attributed
in part as a conspiracy of drugs and lies to put me away and discredit any testimony as I would
have in that respect from being given credence; and attribute also in part, and on the part of the
doctors, to satisfy the description of their Diagnosis concerning my of Paranoid Schizophrenia, a
very serious and complicated condition, that was then in their fabrications used as justifications
for their use of disabling and crippling chemical pharmacy. And to what in all that I am the
innocent victim of, in both regards, to be left with no recourse by to take up with the defense of
myself, and this country, my nation, on my own; and to what that I was only out to serve, and to
save, from the unseen perils of an Unconventional Warfare being waged with the means and the
use of Drugs and Chemicals in maiming fashion, that I am soliciting your help with to restore a
sense of decency and order here to resolve, and for the sake and regard of the suffering
population, who the Drug Enemies to us are able to destroy with the help and assistance of
Psychiatric as their ally to finish off the job.

Most Sincerely,

Gary L. Koniz
Veterans Of The Vietnam War

"ONE POWERFUL VOICE"

New York Review Of Books
January 15, 2009

Drug Companies & Doctors: A Story of Corruption

By Marcia Angell

No one knows **the total amount provided by drug companies to physicians**, but I estimate from the annual reports of the top nine US drug companies that it comes to **tens of billions of dollars a year**. By such means, the pharmaceutical industry has gained enormous control over how doctors evaluate and use its own products. Its extensive ties to physicians, particularly senior faculty at prestigious medical schools, affect the results of research, the way medicine is practiced, and even the definition of what constitutes a disease.

Many drugs that are assumed to be effective are probably little better than placebos, but there is no way to know because negative results are hidden. One clue was provided six years ago by four researchers who, using the Freedom of Information Act, obtained FDA reviews of every placebo-controlled clinical trial submitted for initial approval of the six most widely used antidepressant drugs approved between 1987 and 1999—Prozac, Paxil, Zoloft, Celexa, Serzone, and Effexor. They found that on average, placebos were 80 percent as effective as the drugs. The difference between drug and placebo was so small that it was unlikely to be of any clinical significance. The results were much the same for all six drugs: all were equally ineffective. But because favorable results were published and unfavorable results buried (in this case, within the FDA), the public and the medical profession believed these drugs were potent antidepressants.

Clinical trials are also biased through designs for research that are chosen to yield favorable results for sponsors. For example, the sponsor's drug may be compared with another drug administered at a dose so low that the sponsor's drug looks more powerful. Or a drug that is likely to be used by older people will be tested in young people, so that side effects are less likely to emerge. A common form of bias stems from the standard practice of comparing a new drug with a placebo, when the relevant question is how it compares with an existing drug. In short, it is often possible to make clinical trials come out pretty much any way you want, which is why it's so important that investigators be truly disinterested in the outcome of their work.

Conflicts of interest affect more than research. They also directly shape the way medicine is practiced, through their influence on practice guidelines issued by professional and governmental bodies, and through their effects on FDA decisions. A few examples: in a survey of two hundred expert panels that issued practice guidelines, one third of the panel members acknowledged that they had some financial interest in the drugs they considered. In 2004, after the National Cholesterol Education Program called for sharply lowering the desired levels of "bad" cholesterol, it was revealed that eight of nine members of the panel writing the recommendations had financial ties to the makers of cholesterol-lowering drugs. Of the 170 contributors to the most recent edition of the American Psychiatric Association's Diagnostic and Statistical Manual of Mental Disorders (DSM), ninety-five had financial ties to drug companies, including all of the contributors to the sections on mood disorders and schizophrenia. Perhaps most important, many members of the standing committees of experts that advise the FDA on drug approvals also have financial ties to the pharmaceutical industry.

"ONE POWERFUL VOICE"

In recent years, drug companies have perfected a new and highly effective method to expand their markets. Instead of promoting drugs to treat diseases, they have begun to promote diseases to fit their drugs. The strategy is to convince as many people as possible (along with their doctors, of course) that they have medical conditions that require long-term drug treatment. Sometimes called "disease-mongering," this is a focus of two new books: Melody Petersen's *Our Daily Meds: How the Pharmaceutical Companies Transformed Themselves into Slick Marketing Machines and Hooked the Nation on Prescription Drugs* and Christopher Lane's *Shyness: How Normal Behavior Became a Sickness*.

To promote new or exaggerated conditions, companies give them serious-sounding names along with abbreviations. Thus, heartburn is now "gastro-esophageal reflux disease" or GERD; impotence is "erectile dysfunction" or ED; premenstrual tension is "premenstrual dysphoric disorder" or PMMD; and shyness is "social anxiety disorder" (no abbreviation yet). Note that these are ill-defined chronic conditions that affect essentially normal people, so the market is huge and easily expanded. For example, a senior marketing executive advised sales representatives on how to expand the use of Neurontin: "Neurontin for pain, Neurontin for monotherapy, Neurontin for bipolar, Neurontin for everything." It seems that the strategy of the drug marketers—and it has been remarkably successful—is to convince Americans that there are only two kinds of people: those with medical conditions that require drug treatment and those who don't know it yet. While the strategy originated in the industry, it could not be implemented without the complicity of the medical profession.

Some of the biggest blockbusters are psychoactive drugs. The theory that psychiatric conditions stem from a biochemical imbalance is used as a justification for their widespread use, even though the theory has yet to be proved. Children are particularly vulnerable targets. What parents dare say "No" when a physician says their difficult child is sick and recommends drug treatment? We are now in the midst of an apparent epidemic of bipolar disease in children (which seems to be replacing attention-deficit hyperactivity disorder as the most publicized condition in childhood), with a forty-fold increase in the diagnosis between 1994 and 2003. These children are often treated with multiple drugs off-label, many of which, whatever their other properties, are sedating, and nearly all of which have potentially serious side effects.

Melody Petersen, who was a reporter for *The New York Times*, has written a broad, convincing indictment of the pharmaceutical industry. She lays out in detail the many ways, both legal and illegal, that drug companies can create "blockbusters" (drugs with yearly sales of over a billion dollars) and the essential role that KOLs play. Her main example is Neurontin, which was initially approved only for a very narrow use—to treat epilepsy when other drugs failed to control seizures. By paying academic experts to put their names on articles extolling Neurontin for other uses—bipolar disease, post-traumatic stress disorder, insomnia, restless legs syndrome, hot flashes, migraines, tension headaches, and more—and by funding conferences at which these uses were promoted, the manufacturer was able to parlay the drug into a blockbuster, with sales of $2.7 billion in 2003. The following year, in a case covered extensively by Petersen for the *Times*, Pfizer pleaded guilty to illegal marketing and agreed to pay $430 million to resolve the criminal and civil charges against it. A lot of money, but for Pfizer, it was just the cost of doing

"ONE POWERFUL VOICE"

business, and well worth it because Neurontin continued to be used like an all-purpose tonic, generating billions of dollars in annual sales.

Christopher Lane's book has a narrower focus—the rapid increase in the number of psychiatric diagnoses in the American population and in the use of psychoactive drugs (drugs that affect mental states) to treat them. Since there are no objective tests for mental illness and the boundaries between normal and abnormal are often uncertain, psychiatry is a particularly fertile field for creating new diagnoses or broadening old ones. Diagnostic criteria are pretty much the exclusive province of the current edition of the *Diagnostic and Statistical Manual of Mental Disorders*, which is the product of a panel of psychiatrists, most of whom, as I mentioned earlier, had financial ties to the pharmaceutical industry. Lane, a research professor of literature at Northwestern University, traces the evolution of the DSM from its modest beginnings in 1952 as a small, spiral-bound handbook (DSM-I) to its current 943-page incarnation (the revised version of DSM-IV) as the undisputed "bible" of psychiatry—the standard reference for courts, prisons, schools, insurance companies, emergency rooms, doctors' offices, and medical facilities of all kinds.

The problems I've discussed are not limited to psychiatry, although they reach their most florid form there. Similar conflicts of interest and biases exist in virtually every field of medicine, particularly those that rely heavily on drugs or devices. It is simply no longer possible to believe much of the clinical research that is published, or to rely on the judgment of trusted physicians or authoritative medical guidelines. I take no pleasure in this conclusion, which I reached slowly and reluctantly over my two decades as an editor of *The New England Journal of Medicine*.

One result of the pervasive bias is that physicians learn to practice a very drug-intensive style of medicine. Even when changes in lifestyle would be more effective, doctors and their patients often believe that for every ailment and discontent there is a drug. Physicians are also led to believe that the newest, most expensive brand-name drugs are superior to older drugs or generics, even though there is seldom any evidence to that effect because sponsors do not usually compare their drugs with older drugs at equivalent doses. In addition, physicians, swayed by prestigious medical school faculty, learn to prescribe drugs for off-label uses without good evidence of effectiveness.

It is easy to fault drug companies for this situation, and they certainly deserve a great deal of blame. Most of the big drug companies have settled charges of fraud, off-label marketing, and other offenses. TAP Pharmaceuticals, for example, in 2001 pleaded guilty and agreed to pay $875 million to settle criminal and civil charges brought under the federal False Claims Act over its fraudulent marketing of Lupron, a drug used for treatment of prostate cancer. In addition to GlaxoSmithKline, Pfizer, and TAP, other companies that have settled charges of fraud include Merck, Eli Lilly, and Abbott. The costs, while enormous in some cases, are still dwarfed by the profits generated by these illegal activities, and are therefore not much of a deterrent. Still, apologists might argue that the pharmaceutical industry is merely trying to do its primary job— further the interests of its investors—and sometimes it goes a little too far.

Physicians, medical schools, and professional organizations have no such excuse, since their only fiduciary responsibility is to patients. The mission of medical schools and teaching

"ONE POWERFUL VOICE"

hospitals—and what justifies their tax-exempt status—is to educate the next generation of physicians, carry out scientifically important research, and care for the sickest members of society. It is not to enter into lucrative commercial alliances with the pharmaceutical industry. As reprehensible as many industry practices are, I believe the behavior of much of the medical profession is even more culpable. Drug companies are not charities; they expect something in return for the money they spend, and they evidently get it or they wouldn't keep paying.

So many reforms would be necessary to restore integrity to clinical research and medical practice that they cannot be summarized briefly. Many would involve congressional legislation and changes in the FDA, including its drug approval process. But there is clearly also a need for the medical profession to wean itself from industry money almost entirely. Although industry–academic collaboration can make important scientific contributions, it is usually in carrying out basic research, not clinical trials, and even here, it is arguable whether it necessitates the personal enrichment of investigators. Members of medical school faculties who conduct clinical trials should not accept any payments from drug companies except research support, and that support should have no strings attached, including control by drug companies over the design, interpretation, and publication of research results.

Medical schools and teaching hospitals should rigorously enforce that rule, and should not enter into deals with companies whose products members of their faculty are studying. Finally, there is seldom a legitimate reason for physicians to accept gifts from drug companies, even small ones, and they should pay for their own meetings and continuing education.

After much unfavorable publicity, medical schools and professional organizations are beginning to talk about controlling conflicts of interest, but so far the response has been tepid. They consistently refer to "potential" conflicts of interest, as though that were different from the real thing, and about disclosing and "managing" them, not about prohibiting them. In short, there seems to be a desire to eliminate the smell of corruption, while keeping the money. Breaking the dependence of the medical profession on the pharmaceutical industry will take more than appointing committees and other gestures. It will take a sharp break from an extremely lucrative pattern of behavior. But if the medical profession does not put an end to this corruption voluntarily, it will lose the confidence of the public, and the government will step in and impose regulation. No one in medicine wants that. This section outlines the wide range of treatments and therapies for mental illnesses and their symptoms. The most common types of treatment are medications and talking therapies. There are also various complementary therapies and electroconvulsive therapy.

The primary treatment for mental illness is usually medication, which is either taken orally or by slow release injection. Medications have been developed to relieve different symptoms, so that one may be taken for something specific, or more than one in a combination to deal with different symptoms at the same time. Medications can be categorised according to their function: Medications:

antipsychotics, to relieve symptoms of psychosis
antidepressants to relieve symptoms of depression
mood stabilisers to moderate extreme mood changes

"ONE POWERFUL VOICE"

benzodiazepines, for the relief of anxiety

Whilst medications are often effective, they can also cause variable side effects, so it is important to find a medication that works for you with minimum disruption. A review of medication being taken should be carried out by a doctor annually or as needed. The second most common type of treatment is talking therapy. This kind of therapy is used to help the client become autonomous and develop effective coping habits and problem solving skills. There are different models of talking therapy which have particular goals, and the client should be referred to a method of therapy relevant to their needs. These models include:

cognitive behaviour therapy, which changes problematic patterns of thinking or behaviour

cognitive analytical therapy, which focuses on improving the client's coping habits so that future problems are easier to deal with

dialectical behaviour therapy, which focuses on learning how to react normally to emotional triggers

psychotherapy is based on the client using their own insight to solve current problems
family intervention, which engages the family unit as part of the therapeutic process

creative therapies (e.g. art and drama) to deal mainly with emotional conflicts

counselling, which is about being able to talk without fear of judgement or criticism
Other therapies

Other treatments for mental illness include complementary therapies, to be used alongside more conventional treatments such as medication and therapy.
Electroconvulsive therapy may also be used in some cases, but is not common.

"ONE POWERFUL VOICE"

Psychiatry: An Industry of Death

Psychiatry: An Industry of Death is a museum in Hollywood, Los Angeles, California, USA, as well as several touring exhibitions.[1] It is owned and operated by the Citizens Commission on Human Rights (CCHR), an anti-psychiatry organization founded by the Church of Scientology. The organization holds that mental illness is not a medical disease, and that the use of psychiatric medication is a destructive and fraudulent practice. CCHR's views on psychiatry are a reflection of the position held by L. Ron Hubbard, the founder of Scientology, whose writings express a very strong viewpoint against psychiatry.[5][6] CCHR advocates that there is no biological evidence to support psychiatric theories of mental disorders.

The museum is located at 6616 Sunset Boulevard, Los Angeles, California and entry to the museum is free. The opening event on December 17, 2005[3], was attended by well-known Scientologists, including Priscilla Presley, Lisa Marie Presley, Jenna Elfman, Danny Masterson, Giovanni Ribisi, Leah Remini, Catherine Bell, and Anne Archer, and is "a display holding psychiatry to blame for the deaths of Ernest Hemingway, Del Shannon, Billie Holiday, Kurt Cobain, Spalding Gray and just about every other entertainment celebrity who did not happen to die of strictly natural causes."
The museum is dedicated to exposing what it describes as "an industry driven entirely by profit" and provides "practical guidance for lawmakers, doctors, human rights advocates and private citizens to take action in their own sphere to bring psychiatry under the law." It has a variety of displays and exhibits that highlight physical psychiatric treatments, such as restraints, psychoactive drugs, shock therapy and psychosurgery (including lobotomy, a procedure not used widely as a treatment since the early 1970's) with which psychiatrists have attempted to treat mental problems.

The CCHR has lobbied for legislative reform on mental health issues. The group has organized media campaigns against various psychiatrists, psychiatric organizations and pharmaceutical companies, including Eli Lilly, the manufacturer of Prozac. One campaign is said to have caused a major fall in sales of Prozac, causing considerable commercial damage to the company.
The group campaigned against the use of Ritalin for the treatment of attention-deficit hyperactivity disorder, a disorder which the organization dismisses as nonexistent. The campaign was part of the Ritalin class action lawsuits against Novartis (the manufacturer of Ritalin), CHADD, and the American Psychiatric Association (APA); all five lawsuits were dismissed in 2002.

In 2004, the CCHR sponsored a bill requiring doctors to provide patients with information about a medication's side effects before prescribing any psychotropic drugs, while also mandating a legal guardian's signature.[3] Opponents of the bill argued that these additional procedures might discriminate against mentally-ill patients while delaying treatment.[3] The bill attracted widespread disagreement from the medical establishment, including the Massachusetts Department of Mental Health, who opposed it on the grounds that it compromised informed consent.[3] The Massachusetts Psychiatric Society also opposed the bill, believing that it would interfere with the doctor-patient relationship.

"ONE POWERFUL VOICE"

Psychiatric treatments are harmful. All psychiatric treatments are harmful. Psychiatric drugs, ECT (electric shock) and brain surgery (lobotomy) each harm the individual and society. This sometimes goes against what we have been taught or indoctrinated into believing, and also against what we would often like to believe. Taking a pill as a "cure" obviously is easier than confronting and dealing with the actual personal reasons for one's difficulties with their own mind and life. The alternative requires personal responsibility, control and can take time, but the final results far exceed the quick fix (drugs, shock, etc.). In fact, the "psychiatric" methods "fix" nothing at all and actually make things worse.

The field of psychiatry is rooted in German experimental psychology, racist eugenics theories, and anti-human materialistic *opinions* parading as scientific facts. The promotional activities and tremendous profits of the major drug companies and affiliated financial interests play no small part in understanding the development and success of modern psychiatry. The result of modern psychiatric theories and methods is the denial of everything comprising man's "inner" personality of thoughts, feelings, values, hopes, dreams, intentions, goals, and ultimately, life itself.

Much of modern education and all aspects of the social sciences are rooted in flawed modern theories of psychology. This has had and continues to have disastrous effects on individual people and society.

The links to information here supply a formidable basis of knowledge leading towards an accurate and true understanding of what psychiatry *really is*. Your local psychiatrists will never refer you to this information.

Do not base your opinion only on what members of the psychiatric field tell you. Liquor manufacturers will not tell you their products cause liver damage, are the source of numerous automobile related deaths every year, and encourage you to cease drinking liquor. Similarly, no psychiatrist will tell you psychiatry harms people and that you should avoid it at all cost. Even if he or she knew or suspected this, he or she couldn't endure the loss of income, status and authority this would entail.

Psychiatry and the affiliated major drug companies form a huge money making enterprise (business) which can tolerate no criticism. Each psychiatrist has gone to school for many years, spent much money on their "education" (which I consider to largely be indoctrination into nonsense), and invested a good part of their life towards their "profession". It isn't easy for anyone, regardless of one's field, to flush years of education, expense, time spent in their field and one's source of a very good income down the toilet, much less also to confront that what one does for a living is fundamentally harmful to other people and society. Don't argue or even discuss the facts with them. Most of them won't listen, and instead will defend their opinions to the end while sarcastically and "authoritatively" criticizing the proponents of the truth.

"ONE POWERFUL VOICE"

PSYCHIATRIC FRAUD INVESTIGATION
INV. NO.: USA-040199101
DATE: JULY 10, 2001
STATUS: ONGOING AND DEVELOPING
COUNTRY: UNITED STATES

SUBJECT: PSYCHIATRIC FRAUD

NAME OF INVESTIGATION: PSYCHIATRIC FRAUD, MENTAL HEALTH PARITY

BACKGROUND OF INVESTIGATION:

Mental health insurance fraud is rampant and the industry itself in urgent need of reform. One recent scandal saw $229 million in claims fleeced from Medicare. Demands to establish mental health insurance parity are undermining health care reform in a system already desperately in need of change.

Tragic and avoidable deaths from psychiatric restraints occur regularly nationwide. Investigative reports published by *The Hartford Courant* in 1998 and early 1999 documented 151 restraint deaths in institutions across the U.S. since 1988. Further reports of deaths abound. Victims have been of all ages, although the majority were between adolescence and their late 20s. A research specialist at the Harvard Center for Risk Analysis, commissioned by the *Courant*, estimated that the actual number of restraint-related deaths, since many go unreported to authorities, is between 50 and 100 each year.

According to industry observers, those figures indicate that hundreds or perhaps thousands are assaulted and harmed but live through the ordeal.

During the early and mid-1990s, close to 1,000 surviving ex-patients of one of the nation's then largest chains of psychiatric facilities—National Medical Enterprises (NME)—filed lawsuits charging that various hospitals and psychiatrists illegally imprisoned them in order to cash in on their insurance monies. Many of the patients were children or teen-agers when admitted and were subjected to abuse, including frequent use of restraints—sometimes for weeks at a time. Nearly 700 of those civil suits have since been settled for $100 million.

The proliferation and abuse of restraints could be more intimately linked to insurance fraud than previously thought. Recent evidence suggests that restraint use may be claimed under "intensive care" for a higher rate of reimbursement.

Widespread Fraud & Abuse

While overwhelming evidence of deaths from psychiatric restraints is spurring U.S. Senate hearings and House legislation in 1999, these are far from the only abuses that lie in the wake of psychiatric fraud.

A federal criminal investigation into NME found that tens of thousands of patients around the country were given unnecessary treatment by psychiatrists in order to illegally collect insurance money. NME paid out $379 million to settle the criminal charges in 1996, and got out of the psychiatric business. NME's well-publicized catastrophe with psychiatric fraud, however, did not deter the practice elsewhere.

"ONE POWERFUL VOICE"

Medicare announced in September 1998 that it was expelling 80 community mental health centers after federal investigators found that the program to provide psychiatric services to the elderly was riddled with fraud. According to a report by the U.S. Department of Health and Human Services, during 1997 alone, 90 percent of Medicare's payments to community mental health centers—$229 million—went to psychiatrists' "unallowable and questionable services."

All told, psychiatric fraud has cost taxpayers a conservatively estimated $20 billion in the United States alone, and as much as $40 billion. The cost in terms of human lives and misery is incalculable.

Fatter Funds

Despite the overwhelming evidence of psychiatric fraud and concomitant abuse, federal and state legislators are relentlessly bombarded with demands to mandate fatter insurance funds for psychiatry under the banner of "mental health parity." To not provide the same benefits for mental illness as exist for physical illness, the parity argument goes, is to discriminate against those who have mental disorders.

Patients' advocates and psychiatric industry watchdogs agree that discrimination is a serious problem for those labeled as mentally ill—but it is perpetrated by the psychiatrists themselves. Discrimination is manifest far more often in the denial of fundamental rights and competent medical treatment to psychiatric patients than in any perceived disparity of insurance benefits. And the results, including deaths, are far more serious.

Further, insurance industry experts and economists state that mandated health insurance benefits (of all types) are a significant cause for increasing lack of health insurance coverage, and are already pricing up to 10.2 million Americans out of the health insurance market.

The "Grass Roots" Lobby

The front-line entity pushing mental health insurance parity is the National Alliance for the Mentally Ill (NAMI). On the surface, NAMI is a support group concerned with eradicating the social stigma attached to those suffering from severe mental disorders. The group is found in the lead of an ostensibly "grass roots" media and legislative campaign for parity and against discrimination.

The campaign steers clear of the well-founded concerns of patients' advocates and industry observers that more access to insurance funds will mean yet more fraud and abuse, not to mention an increasing burden on employers and consumers.

From an investigation of NAMI's agenda, one might conclude that it has little room to address such concerns, nor can it afford to. The "grass roots" movement has an organized headquarters and chapters in each state, professional PR services, streams of pre-packaged, just-add-water media and lobbying instructions for members—and campaign sponsorship from multi-billion dollar pharmaceutical firms whose drugs dominate the psychiatric industry for "treatment" of mental disorders.

And where the psychiatric lobby has failed to convince government to subsidize psychiatry outright, NAMI campaign literature and statements make it apparent that they developed a strategy of circumvention.

Scientific Deficiency

"ONE POWERFUL VOICE"

To achieve insurance parity, the psychiatric industry has to position mental illness on a scientific par with physical illness, which opens the door to equal benefits.

Psychiatrists, however, have often been balked in government funding efforts because their claims about mental illnesses and cures simply lack scientific merit. The medical-scientific community widely acknowledges the deficiency, as do some in the psychiatric community. Even the former acting director of the National Institute for Mental Health (NIMH), Rex Cowdry, stated candidly of "mental illness" before U.S. House of Representatives Appropriations Subcommittee hearings, "We do not know the causes. We don't have methods of `curing' these illnesses yet."

Claims about the efficacy of psychiatric drugs prescribed to "cure" the "chemical imbalances" in people's brains also lack proof. In one study in 1998, researchers Irving Kirsch of the University of Connecticut and Guy Sapirstein of Westwood Lodge Hospital, Massachusetts, analyzed 19 prior studies on antidepressants and sedatives involving 2,318 patients. Their findings ruled out that any chemical balance in the brain is restored through the drugs.

"We do not really know anything about this business of the brain. We are just at the borderline of how it even works chemically," says Dr. Walter Afield, nationally eminent psychiatrist and examiner for the American Board of Psychiatry, who currently serves as Medical Director of the Neuropsychiatric Institute in Tampa, Florida. "Yet a doctor gives a drug to someone, and when it has a side effect, balances it with this other drug, and so on, and it gets to be so much hocus-pocus."

Widespread Psychiatric Fraud

The result has been the widespread use of psychiatric drugs to treat a variety of mental "illnesses" created "by" psychiatrists. Supporting this is a health care industry in which billions from government, taxpayers, insurance companies and employers have continued to be sucked into a black hole. Treatment has been reduced to a five or ten minute visit in which the psychiatrist prescribes expensive drugs, which the patient must then continue to take for an indeterminate period of time, or until his insurance money runs out.

Driven by the bottom line, the practice within the industry has proliferated. So have instances of fraud and law enforcement crackdown. In the wake of such investigations have come evidence of further abuse, brutal use of restraints, violence at the hands of hospital workers trusted with the care of the mentally ill, often resulting in death.

With the continuing explosions of evidence of rampant fraud and abuse in the industry has also come countless individuals and families who have been betrayed by psychiatry, including tens of thousands who grieve the deaths of their children, relatives or friends from psychiatric treatment.

Editorial Office
Freedom Magazine
6331 Hollywood Blvd, Suite 1200
Los Angeles, CA 90028
editor@freedommag.org

"ONE POWERFUL VOICE"

9480 Princeton Square Blvd. S., #815
Jacksonville, FL 32256
May 5, 2012

Warren S. Lacy - Editor in Chief
Colonel, U.S. Army (Ret.)
Military Officer Magazine
201 North Washington Street
Alexandria, VA 22314-2539

Dear Colonel Lacy:

From: gary.koniz@hotmail.com

To: bcotterell@tallahassee.com; diocese@dosafl.com; bobbienord@gmail.com;
bob@bobblackdistrict4.com; charles.mcburney@myfloridahouse.gov;
cindy.holifield@jacksonville.com; pueschel@cxp.com; editorial@nytimes.com;
yrbb@tvc.cbs.com; graymoorcenter@atonementfriars.org; frank.denton@jacksonville.com;
me@glennbeck.com; hparker@flaflcio.org; hill.tony.web@flsenate.gov; apnyc@ap.org;
info@klauder4congress.com; jholland@coj.net; dao@nytimes.com;
klenihan@poughkee.gannett.com; koflaugh@comcast.net; alvarez@nytimes.com;
louisrose@yahoo.com; mimatthews@dos.state.fl.us; mccarron@flacathconf.org;
news@firstcoastnews.com; nick.waller@wctv.tv; rcolenso@atpco.com;
floridafamiliesunite@yahoo.com; info@doveworld.org; rtemplin@flaflcio.org;
bobyjo@cfl.rr.com; russell_harper@ibew177.org; taylorteaparty@hotmail.com;
sallylbaptiste@att.net; evening@cbsnews.com; sshinske@poughkee.gannett.com;
tim@goooh.com; tltompk@bellsouth.net; chair@duvaldemocrats.org;
vcannon@votenassau.com; vote@bakercountyfl.org; nolasco_victor@hotmail.com;
phillipminer@comcast.net; gunnar.paulson@floridaea.org

CC: benedictxvi@vatican.va; carol.boone@jacksonville.com; caffertyfile@cnn.com;
mike.clark@jacksonville.com; communications@afge.org; americanway.editor@aa.com;
engel@aliciapatterson.org; larry@larryhagman.com; warrenl@moaa.org; loudobbs@cnn.com;
dob@buffalodiocese.org; mcnews@hqmc.usmc.mil; oped@csps.com; mostre@vatlib.it;
nightly@nbc.com; cns@catholicnews.com; mtp@nbc.com; oreilly@foxnews.com;
onyourside@firstcoastnews.com; pb_metro@pbpost.com; pilot@aopa.org;
senator@rockefeller.senate.gov; mmsullivan@buffnews.com; opinion@seattletimes.com;
editors@washingtonmonthly.com; woodwardb@washpost.com

Subject: Press Release: Full National Policy Platform Text
Date: Sat, 5 May 2012 05:32:30 -0400

The following is a Free PDF Download of our Platform which is available on demand at:
http://www.lulu.com/items/volume_74/10897000/10897297/17/print/10897297.pdf

"ONE POWERFUL VOICE"

Gary L. Koniz
Journalist Correspondent
Democratic Labor Party Candidate
4th Congressional District, FL
U.S. House of Representatives

9480 Princeton Square Blvd. S., #815
Jacksonville, FL 32256-8310
(904) 730-2055
gary.koniz@hotmail.com

The Candidate is a Corresponding Freelance Journalist with 40 years of career experience in journalism covering the important and pressing social and political issues agendas of the hour and long range important national and local topics to be resolved, who is currently running for Congress, as a "Hands On" approach to Sound Government Management for this election of 2012 as a Democratic Labor Intensive Candidate for Florida's 4th District U.S House of Representatives; with a primary focus as a Labor Rights Activist and Economist, stressing the importance of accepting a well-regulated economy centered to the Productive Middle Ground, "The Golden Mean" of Supply and Demand, that concedes the workers with enough "Consumer Purchasing Power" to generate the production of goods and services, create jobs, and support the government tax structures on all levels of their necessity; with an attempt to salvage our economy and help the people of our district and nationally to survive economically; and among other vital and necessary interests of state to be resolved, guarded, and protected. And which are not "Political Issues" of appeasing the public vote; but Firm Line Policy issues of "Yes or No," to be reasoned forth and forcefully mandated for the Public Good by strong intelligent leadership. In submissions currently to The Times Union, of Jacksonville, FL, The New York Times, New York, NY, CBS Evening News, New York, NY; Associated Press, New York, NY, and for other Newspapers, Magazines, and Radio Involvement.

I – and others – have described my leadership style as aggressive, personal, consultative, and managerial. I strive to treat all people fairly and respectfully and to a model of civility. People have described me as fair, balanced, hardworking, patient, and willing to listen to and consider conflicting viewpoints. I value clear, open, honest, and frequent communication, and have a quiet sense of humor that I exercise often in my work.

We are indeed a great Nation unto God, The Creator Of All Things in our principles. We have accomplished much in our history together and as yet have much still left to accomplish faithfully in the undertaking of our Nation's Moral, Social, and Governing Values. Doing so will require that we sustain and grow our vitality and notable demand for quality and excellence – including, becoming more "people focused" in orientation.

Sincerely and Best Regards,

Gary L. Koniz – Correspondent
Veterans Of The Vietnam War
MOAA No. 02786399

"ONE POWERFUL VOICE"

9480 Princeton Square Blvd. S., #815
Jacksonville, FL 32256
(904) 730-2055
September 11, 2008

Warren S. Lacy - Editor in Chief
Colonel, U.S. Army (Ret.)
Military Officer Magazine
201 North Washington Street
Alexandria, VA 22314-2539

Dear Colonel Lacy:

Thank you so very much, with great relief, for your recent letter of support from Military Officer Magazine on the subject of Combat Related Veterans Psychiatric Devastation, as it is occurring, and of the past sense, to be prevented and remedied; and to thank you also for your most gracious and polite concern regarding your ongoing lobby efforts as an organization in our behalf, as you indicated for, and to the advisement of the upcoming Forum being sponsored for by The Military Officers Association of America (MOAA) that you have scheduled at The Hyatt Regency on Capitol Hill in Washington, D.C. on September 17th, 2008 entitled: "Keeping Faith With Wounded Warriors," that I would like to express each of our heartfelt gratitude to you for doing.

I would here also like to thank you for involving us with Captain John Plehal (USN Ret.) Deputy Director, currently serving matters, MOAA, who is in charge of the arrangements with the event and who has made his willingness known to us to present our recommendations to the panel being convened on the Post Traumatic Disorder situation and what to do about it and to all of our sustained efforts to resolve the crisis.

Which, simply stated, has to do with the issues of Psychiatric Labeling itself, and by its very nature life threatening, and to the "Forced Use" of Disabling Chemical Pharmacy Treatment (termed "Meds,") that is the outright killer, inducing of the actual physical, emotional, and mental ruination of these Veterans to the point of suicide where they don't care to live-on here in The America that they each served to defend any longer.

In this regard it is of great help to us to be put in touch with the 2:00 - 3:15 Panel Moderator, Colonel Jack Jacobs, and with other panel members, especially with Dr. James B. Peake, (The U.S. Secretary of Veterans Affairs;) that is entitled "Challenges and Handling of PTSD / TBI / Depression ... What Comes Next?" So that we can communicate with them directly about what is going on, as Wars go, which you don't see this one occurring from your office window and need our direct veterans input to see things in perspective from the point of view behind the locked ward doors of psychiatric.

We need the coverage to this and to the reasoning made for "Affirmative Action" to being taken for the case of caring for the Mental Health of these Veterans who are now in psychiatric detention custody and being subjected to treatment; to ensure that proper treatment for each of them is occurring, and for their recovery to our recommendations for the proper labeling and treatment being made in name to; Bed Rest, Convalescence, Counseling, and Therapy, with a Sound Nutritional environment, removed from the Chemical Devastation setting of Strong Tranquillizer Drugs; such as with Thorazine and other versions of Neuroleptic Pharmany, (or

"ONE POWERFUL VOICE"

also known as Mind-Altering Psychotropic Pharmacy Medications,) which are approved for use by The FDA but which actually induce the Mental Illness Conditions that they are touted to alleviate to such suffering and destructive ends that their victims are reduced to utter ruination and suicide.

We feel there is, and there has been a conspiracy here afoot concerning our nation's Combat Veterans at the hands of Psychiatric Labeling and Forced Chemical Treatment, (to what that the subject of Medical/Pharmaceutical Corruption plays only a small part of,) and that in overall effect is bent on destroying us, (in Purge Condition, and taken for what it is in its cumulative its aggressions towards us in that way,) in the vein of our being regarded by the civilian element as Programmed Killers, and otherwise for the motive of our being involved with National Security and Defense, to be eliminated. That is an issue for everyone connected to the military to be alarmed over and to take action about, to what we count our blessings for your sympathy of support and encouragement.

The problem then being, that there is a destructive and life threatening lethal situation occurring to our country's fine brave soldiers at the hands of this nation's psychiatric community concerning there labeling and "forced use" of metabolically disabling chemicals in their treatment of the weary Veterans for Combat Related Stress and Depression Disorders; that requires of its very nature to be corrected, and to our necessity then being to exact how then it is that this correction to occur to save the remaining veterans presently suffering to such treatment, and to restore their integrity of well-being and to those veterans who have already been maimed by past treatment from the system in error to have allowed the mentally ill stigmatization, and catastrophic chemical induced ruination to have occurred to the veterans of past and present wars at the hands of psychiatric that has totally destroyed and turned these men into suicidal zombies with the likes of Thorazine. So let us here together, as to include everyone in our military sphere of reference, begin to analyze the problem from the stand-point of correcting it, and to begin by asking ourselves the question, who is "the person or persons" responsible to us for the continued existence of this psychiatric debacle, who has, or have, the power in command decision to clarify and to sternly alter the situation with a Cease and Desist Order; to the Food and Drug Administration and to The Psychiatric Medical Community.

And so it is that we must proceed with determined Affirmed Action to be especially "Protective Over" these surviving Veterans in the aftermath of War. And who are not, per se of the issue, to be destroyed by careless and unthinking civilians, and especially by those of a biased foreign nature or who have gender related issues, (and with being participated in on the part of law enforcement, medical doctors, and administrators, on the active collaborating level,) and which involves the home setting of family members of these veterans also being told by the doctors that the Veterans Are Not Safe To Be Around and Cannot Be Trusted, in creating Veterans Homelessness, and which as well as involves their civilian employment work situations that same way of Joblessness occurring;) and who of these people are on remote control in sway to the brain washing propaganda being put out against our returning Veterans by The Media, and perhaps in real biases of prejudices and with outright fear regarded of these service personnel whom have been deemed "Brain Damaged" from Combat, and Programmed Professional Killers, by The Media, and who the civilian factor feels threatened by, for this reason to be removed from society over and destroyed. And who may be being destroyed as well for more sinister motives of removing these veterans from society by the means of clandestine psychiatric warfare (both by the destruction of self-esteem of the psychiatric labeling, and from the catastrophic disabling effects of pharmacy drug chemicals being used which are force administered across the

"ONE POWERFUL VOICE"

board, "As A Precaution," to disable everyone entering psychiatric,) and preventing our trained War Veterans from uniting in the inevitable common defense of their homeland which they otherwise be involved to.

And which the takeover of this nation by drug mafias would be one example of, (or for pornography motives,) and with pornography moving in on the estranged housewives and family members in the absence of the Veterans who then return home to be lethally sabotaged with "Drugs and Chemicals" at the hands of these "Pornography Rings," being one of the key protagonists in the mysterious illness war upon us. And for other matters presently being held by "Political Correctness," override to name in being spoken about, (and not to distract from the resolution of the Veterans Case, in that way of blockage to mention,) but which need to be named as the established factions in longstanding and more recently at war with us whom we know to be avowedly in adversity to The American United States; and whoever who would have motive that way to be "taking out" our Returning Veterans; as to the case of Islamic Terrorists, Asian Hostilities, and coordinated Black Power "Black Drug Mafia" Militants, (who involve themselves with the White housewives in the Veterans absence and to the perpetration of Drug-Chemical Warfare upon them on their return,) and most decidedly of the Neo-Fascist Movement or otherwise known as The Italian Mafia to be named, and for the Zionist Heroin Mafia Cartels Internationally, (who are no strangers to politics and to the high intrigues of state involving media censorship, key legislation, government finances, and pharmacy chemicals production;) and to their use of Drug-Chemical Warfare overall upon the entire population to induce anxiety, depression, schizophrenia, and mental other illnesses, as well as for many other listed physical maladies such as, attention deficit disorder, chronic fatigue, panic disorder, erectile dysfunction, cardiac arrhythmia, enlarged prostate incontinence, blurred vision, and chronic respiratory distress, to name some maladies.

Let us avow here to put an end to this psychiatric devastation in conclusion and to every square inch of the ground to be covered here; studied, observed, experienced, and otherwise subjected to, to pass judgment upon. It's a lengthy discussion of its necessity and I thank you so very much for indulging me of your time to inform you thoroughly of the situation. This is a crucial undertaking. I will also be involving us at every step of the way with General Franklin L. Hegenbeck, The Superintendent of our U.S. Military Academy at West Point, NY, who is as well overseeing the project to its just conclusion; and also with W. Lee Rawls, Senior Counsel to the Director with The F.B.I., to cover the criminal prosecution side of the case involving Grounds for Commitment, Forced Chemical Treatment, and the efficacy (or lethality) of such Treatment, to what Thorazine is not efficacious in any way to; and with Lt. General Martin Dempsey, who is the current Acting Commander for United States Central Command, and with Mr. Bob Woodward, the Associate Editor - Investigative Unit - with The Washington Post, in mutually involved Task Force arrangement, to resolve the problem in conscience as a Military Objective for the welfare of our Veterans, to the key phrase being, "Affirmative Action."

Gary L. Koniz - Correspondent
Veterans Defense Committee
Veterans of the Vietnam War

"ONE POWERFUL VOICE"

9480 Princeton Square Blvd. S., #815
Jacksonville, FL 32256
October 26, 2008

Warren S. Lacy - Editor in Chief
Colonel, U.S. Army (Ret.)
Military Officer Magazine
201 North Washington Street
Alexandria, VA 22314-2539

Dear Colonel Lacy:

    I do wish to convey my heartfelt appreciation and deep regard to you for the gracious effort put forth on your part of The Military Officers Association Of America (MOAA) and together with The United States Naval Institute (USNI) to co-host the incisive forum conference, "Keeping Faith with Wounded Warriors and Their Families," in Washington D.C. recently in outreaching to our nation's Wounded Veterans, (of wounds seen and unseen;) and with expressed gratitude for including me in the coverage and review of this event and for supplying me with the formal transcript of this forum to study. And it is indeed with a special sense of reverence as a Veteran that I can relate to this project on the subject of Wounded Warriors, and for our moral obligation as a Nation to serve the interests and to the pressing needs of our Veterans in keen indebtedness to each of them personally. I am very proud of your efforts there of The MOAA to host this event, and proud of each of the distinguished Panel Members who devoted of their personal time, and their knowledge, and eminence, to participate and to contribute with their authority for the greater understanding of our concerns to the many areas of Veterans' Needs.

    I was pleased also to observe the dedication to the overall sincerity of the conference on the Vital Necessities of Interest to our Veterans ranging the full spectrum of crucial Reinforcement and Support and to the sense of Coordinating Team Work involved to provide them with the best possible care and treatment; from a detailed description of the living conditions and bureaucratic frustrations of Walter Reed Hospital in the past year, that led to the comprehensive legislation we have in place today; for Increased Veterans Benefits and Services available through The Veterans Administration (VA) and The Department of Defense (DOD) involving each of the Veterans with a "Seamless" (or Smooth Process) Reintegration or Integration Transition back into Civilian Life; in providing them with counseling and help finding Employment, and for special outreach for our Native Americans living on remote reservations, and with Shuttle and Air Taxi Services for our Rural Veterans, and for the reinstating the Priority Group 8 Coverage, (or Veterans Co-Pay,) that has been suspended since 2003 due to overloads, and for special handling of Covert Missions to process them for Service Connected Disabilities, and with sympathetic discussion to the concept of "The Long War" involving the Veterans in several tours of duty of extended exposures to Multiple Blasts and Carnage, involving them with Acute Concussions and Emotional Damage to Traumatic Events, Traumatic Brain Injury (TBI), Post Traumatic Stress Disorder (PTSD), Depression, Amputations, and overall to the concept framed of these events of "Polytruama" involving our Veterans with Multiple Physical Wounds, Blindness, Loss of Hearing, Burns, Scars, Amputations, TBI, PTSD, Depression, Anxiety, and other Psychological Health Disturbances, such as Grief and Remorse involving to the grave Psychological Repercussions of War and necessitating the need for increased Mental Health Care

"ONE POWERFUL VOICE"

and Treatment for our Veterans by expanding Community Based and Veterans Mental Health Centers and overall to the Upgrading of Veterans Mental Health System (with 4 Billion being allocated for The Veterans Mental Health 2009 Budget,) providing Veterans with (1-800-342-9647) and other Suicide Prevention and Veterans Help Hotline Numbers, and with advertising for The Veterans encouraging them to seek help, and addressing the need to "De-stigmatize" the process of Mental Health Treatment to provide the best relief and care for our Veterans through a Process of Rehabilitation in a Holistic Approach to healing (as worded by the current Secretary of Veterans Affairs, Dr. James B. Peake).

That perhaps to quote Brigadier General Wayne W. Hoffmann, AUS (Ret.) Former President and Trustee Military Chaplains Association and Assistant Chief of Chaplains U.S. Army Reserve best comes to terms with the subject, that; "The horrors of war are not fully seen in the battle, but in the harvest of agonies which results. These are the ones behind closed doors, that no one sees, and no one reads about, and no one thinks about."

For what regard with honored reverence that we should all bow our heads over, for the severity and the magnitude of the actual suffering involved here to war, and of what it means, surely to serve in the field of combat, and to offer one's life, for one's Country; and for all our Nation's soldiers, sailors, marines, and airmen, that have been injured physically, mentally, emotionally, and spiritually, by its horrors, to be helped to recover.

But, we didn't get to the heart of the problem, (in the meaning of "we" as a body of soldiers,) did we, which was for the immediate and "Unconditional Reform" of The Veterans Psychiatric Intake situation, in The Meaning, To Save The Lives, and the Quality of Life, Of Our Veteran Warriors who are being subjected to "The Pogrom" that has been, and which is continuously being waged upon our Returning Service Personnel to brand them as "Killers" and to put up "Social Barriers" in obstacle to their pursuits in life, and to remove them from society and otherwise to debilitate them by Psychiatric Means; (and in this manner of clandestine torture and maiming to their outright murder.)

To what reform that we have asked The Secretary "To Correct" the "Unwise" labeling of our returning from war soldiers as "Mental Patients," and with all that that entails in the way of stigmatizing them, as to the incurrence of the hysterias in which our society views and abhors and fears the idea of mental illness (being the least of the problems, in the vein to their being labeled,) that in similar analogy is akin to someone to being labeled to be a "Witch;" (that isn't just to the stigma involved, but to the lethal aspect of it also,) who then becomes a hapless individual to be persecuted and put to death. Which is the travesty that we, as an enlightened civilization engaged to the fighting of wars have surrendered the individual fates of our returning Veterans to, to their being handed over to hysteria as mentally ill, for the issue of PTSD, and therefore by the rendering of them to Mental Health to their being perceived of as "Deranged Killers" in the eyes of society, and to their unconstitutional and inherently illegal disposition to Indefinite Psychiatric Commitment, "At Will," of The Medical Examiners, (called Two Physician Consent, or 2PC) without any Due Process of Law to occur for the sake of the innocently accused.

(And it is with No Offense Intended) to clarify in behalf of the imminent defense of our Veterans being Psychiatrically Evaluated, that the preponderance of these Psychiatric Doctors practicing at our Nation's VA Hospitals and else-way of the State Psychiatric Facilities to where our Veterans are being taken and confined, have been imported here as outsourced foreigners, with foreign degrees, (and with many of these being females in fear prejudice towards males;) and once again to add With No Offense Intended, but who are left as the sole determiners of our

"ONE POWERFUL VOICE"

returning American Veterans' fates, in charge of the Diagnosis and Commitment Process, (and who are operating in harried Overcrowded Understaffed Warehoused Conditions as it is,) but who possess only a very limited and basic comprehension of The English Language, and who can't communicate effectively in English to be able to thoroughly understand its sophisticated nuances To Be Able To Competently Evaluate Our Returning Combat Veterans, (who have fought and suffered for this Nation,) and to reasoning of what our Veterans need to talk about, about what is troubling them. And concerning these foreign physicians in charge, to the idea of their also being able to Order "The Forced Treatment" of our Veterans with Thorazine and other disabling Psychiatric Drugs, and also "At Will" of these attending physicians, (Without Due Process) who are able to cripple our Veterans for their being labeled and diagnosed as Mental Patients, and to then to effectively destroy them with sedation drugs to the point of suicide or to being left to die homeless in the streets; which we cannot allow to proceed further in this destructive manner of treatment without intervening.

Therefore, that it is that we asked of you, The MOAA, in name to The Secretary of Veterans Affairs, James B. Peake, (in the first instance,) for the polite rendering of; Bed Rest, Convalescence, Counseling, and Therapy, in a sound Nutritional Setting, (which in Dr. Peake's own words about related to as "Rehabilitation";) but "Convalescence," and "Counseling," is the right wording to address the situation of replacing The Negative Stigmatization associated to Mental Health, in the allowing our Veterans To Recover From The Horrors of War in the Holistic Approach, Without Stigma, (and in the second instance,) in the absence of destructive Chemical Agent Pharmacy, currently labeled as "Medication;" that In Truth Are Not So! (in the meaning of their being therapeutically beneficial,) but which in point of fact are very deadly; emotionally, physically, and mentally, metabolically maiming drugs, which induce excruciatingly Uncomfortable States of Being that are very painful to endure; in which a person can't sit, can't stand, can't lie down, can't sleep, and can't stay awake, and in which forces one to pace around back and forth under the effects of these drugs for intolerable lengths of time on end, (and which Motor Restlessness induced by the tranquillizer drugs themselves, is then used as in indication of a person's "agitated" mental state, to require further treatment about with these so called Medications which induced the condition in the first place.) And which of these drugs as well, causes sexual dis-function impotence in the males, a flat affect and loss of personality in a zombie like vegetative state, visual disturbances, severe painful cramping, spasms, and twitches of the body, astral sleep disturbances resulting in garish nightmares inducing insomnia, bowl and bladder incontinence, loss of strength and mental alertness; and other "aggravated" side effects, in all which render our Veterans Unemployable, Unable to Perform their Matrimonial Obligations, Socially Withdrawn and Unfit for Society to the point of suicide. To what that we must have intervention to and to deal affirmatively with the aggressions of a mishandled medical, pharmaceutical, and administrative bureaucracy upon us, that no one seems to be capable of challenging.

Gary Koniz - Correspondent
Veterans Of The Vietnam War

"ONE POWERFUL VOICE"

9480 Princeton Square Blvd. S., #815
Jacksonville, FL 32256
November 11, 2008
Veterans Day

Warren S. Lacy - Editor in Chief
Colonel, U.S. Army (Ret.)
Military Officer Magazine
201 North Washington Street
Alexandria, VA 22314-2539

Dear Colonel Lacy:

Thank you so much for your concerned recent letter of involvement and interest, of November 4, 2008, and once again for your continued support and caring assistance provided to us and to our great concern, mutually rendered, for the safety and well-being, to the proper conduct of psychiatric intake and treatment, of our returned and returning Veterans from the Field of Combat Duty in Foreign Lands, these days. And I appreciate for your passing on my Positional Paper on the subject addressing the issues involved, (as were brought up at the recent MOAA/USNI forum, "Keeping Faith with Wounded Warriors and Their Families," that was held in Washington D.C. on September 17, 2008: moaa.org/serv_prof_forum_transcript.htm,) to your MOAA's Professionalism Section, (who sponsored the event,) and to your MOAA's Government Relations Department, which follows legislation and activities having to do with military health care.

But the issue is, and still remains, as it always has, to date, that no one of The Power Structure responds to our appeals and who otherwise are unwilling to help with the case (financially or of Professional and Legal Muscle,) regarding the psychiatric devastation occurring to our comrades in arms who are returning from Combat in Afghanistan and Iraq, and mindfully of the Vietnam War Era and of The Veterans of The Gulf War and Bosnia in past years to be spoken for. To what that these brave men have been left as hapless victims of a tragedy beyond comprehension to the problem of saving their lives at the hands of psychiatric about, and who really don't know how to proceed and with no way "to get at" the situation, without the Proper Authorities to Intervene in their behalf.

To what resolution that we have summoned the testimony of Doctor James B. Peake, our current Secretary of Veterans Affairs, to clear-up for us, (and to his predecessors to have called upon, and else-way of the professional testimony of many others in the Legal and Established Medical and Legislative Communities over the years, to come forth in support of the truth in these matters,) and in support of The Covenant between our Nation and each of its Veteran Soldiers To Protect and Defend, to substantively collaborate on the subjects of the Legal Validity of Psychiatric Intake and Labeling, and to the Safety and Efficacy of the Psychiatric Treatment to occur, and not vaguely worded: that these men are Soldiers who have been programmed and trained "to kill," and who therefore can't be trusted, to be taken into custody and Force Treated with the deadly chemical Thorazine, or other deadly drugs, "At Will" of the attending physicians in say so, "as a precaution." For what that there must be serious psychiatric grounds, of a life threatening and irrational nature to legally document about in justification for such matters to occur.

"ONE POWERFUL VOICE"

And to what gravity that we also asked of Secretary Peake, to conclusively testify and render a formal decision in verdict "On The Safety and Efficacy" of each of the specified Psychiatric Pharmacy Chemicals being put out and approved for by The Food and Drug Administration, (FDA;) and used in the present treatment of our Veterans; (which you can access for yourselves as described for in The Physicians' Desk Reference, PDR,) as to each of their Effects, Side Effects, Adverse Reactions, and Contraindications, as we have asked Secretary Peake for his credibility of either "approval" or "disapproval" to use for on several occasions already, whose judgment holds the key to the underhanded warfare we are suffering to, and to which you hold the power of journalistic inquiry over.

We ask that our Veterans, (for their sake of their suffering to combat related Stress Disorders,) that they be treated the same as for any other innocent victims of a tragic and catastrophic disaster; be they naturally occurring or manmade; such as for those who survived Ground Zero of 9/11, or High School and College Shooting Massacres, or of an Airliner Disaster; and who dazed and bewildered, and suffering grief for the loss of loved ones, are given comforting aid and solace by caring Health Professionals, and otherwise treated humanely and in compassion for their sufferings; and with not being labeled as "mentally ill persons" (just because it was "Mental Health Professionals" who cared for them,) and to be put in the same category of the public devaluation as insane persons of an irrational and threatening nature are perceived under the heading of Psychiatric.

And thereby to our Veterans being prejudiced and persecuted against, for the labeling of psychiatric being attributed to them by the careless handling of the medical profession and hospital administrations. To what they are pathetically innocent of; (and what of, that there are truly insane and mentally disturbed persons in our society to deal with to be sure;) but that our Veterans deserve to be "honored" with the utmost care and respect, and with no less concern than any Health Professional would regard and treat the victims of a civilian tragedy; and who, "As Victims," are not in any-wise misconstrued to be deranged and insane, but only truly in the need of Health Professional Guidance "in the moment" of processing their traumatic experience, to include for grief, remorse, and mourning.

And let us be sensible here. The Doctors just can't attribute labels such as; Paranoid, Delusional, Schizophrenic, Manic/Depressive, to people, in contrived stigmas, falsely imposed by their rigid autocracy on anyone seen as different, and put them down as official "Medical Diagnoses" and to the idea of "Forced Treatment" with Thorazine and other lethal drugs mis-approved for by The U.S. Government; without legal substance, defined for and verified, to coincide. As to state for the situation occurring at our VA Hospitals; that imposes diagnostic labeling as a condition for anyone being admitted and treated, the labeling of Schizophrenia being a common thumbnail to attribute everyone to.

The legitimate condition of Schizophrenia, as describe for about in The Diagnostic and Statistical Manual of Mental Disorders, Fifth Edition, (DSM V,) is characterized by; disorganized thoughts, bizarre beliefs, hallucinations, social withdrawal, and inability to communicate, persisting over a relatively long period of time of several months; certain of which symptoms are induced by the Psychiatric Drugs themselves. That quite frankly about it all, that we may need to organize around private Para-Military lines to resolve.

Most Sincerely,
Gary L. Koniz
Veterans Of The Vietnam War

"ONE POWERFUL VOICE"

9480 Princeton Square Blvd. S., #815
Jacksonville, FL 32256
May 26, 2009

Warren S. Lacy - Editor in Chief
Colonel, U.S. Army (Ret.)
Military Officer Magazine
201 North Washington Street
Alexandria, VA 22314-2539

Dear Colonel Lacy:

This case is not going to resolve without formal Congressional Oversight in Third Degree Intervention, to go over the key points with you involved here with the two letters I received, (as attached,) in behalf of The Secretary of Veterans Affairs, General Erik K. Shinseki; from, Deborah K. McCallum, Assistant General Counsel for the Department of Veterans Affairs, of May 15, 2009, regarding the documented harmful effects of the Neuroleptic Antipsychotic Drugs such as Thorazine, also called Chlorpromazine; and the circumstances under which persons could be "Force Treated," with such drugs, and as to the availability of any Legal Defense Resources provided for Veterans Legal Assistance being forthcoming from The VA, to challenge Diagnoses, Commitment Processing, and to the use of "Forced Treatment;" (to what Ms. McCallum responded to in her letter with her reply that: "Regretfully, we are unable to determine exactly what you are requesting;" and continued from there with a paragraph explaining the parameters of The Freedom of Information Act, FOIA;) which, though informative in its way, had no bearing on the critical urgency of assisting and protecting our Veterans from the perils of Mental Health.

And in response from Dr. Ira Katz, Deputy Chief Patient Care Services, Officer for Mental Health for The Veterans Administration, of May 22, 2009, in addressing the concerns in alarms of proper VA Conduct regarding the routine psychologically maiming labeling of our Veterans as Mentally Ill Mental Patients for their reporting to the V.A. Health Care Centers with Post Combat Related Maladies, to be Warehoused, and Diagnoses en masse, with Mental Disorders, and thereunto treatment for their diagnosed conditions with deadly Neuroleptic and Psychotropic Antipsychotic Chemicals, (that Dr Katz defends in his letter, as the "The Potential Side Effects" involved with the use of "any" medications;) and which Dr. Katz maintains, in speaking for the behalf of The Veterans Administration and The Pharmaceutical/Medical Industry, that such deadly Antipsychotic Drugs: "have been proven effective and even lifesaving over decades of research and practice for thousands, if not millions, of persons suffering with psychotic disorders," and further on to state: "With proper medications and other psychological supports people who in previous eras might have spent their lives in mental institutions are now able to live successful and satisfying lives;" that is unrealistically misleading.

Normal people are not going to be able to live out successful and satisfying lives on Antipsychotic drugs, (and which incidentally have to be paid for, and along with their expensive Doctor's visits for their monthly evaluations and prescriptions, at a person's own expense,) and especially our Veterans, who have offered their lives in the defense of our Nation and our commitments abroad; and who, in straightforward and pointed terms of reasoning, Do Not Need To Be Made Into Victims sacrificed to the Sacred Cow Mentality of Mental Health behaving in a

"ONE POWERFUL VOICE"

tyrannical fashion of Communist Fascist abuse (in the meaning of it being conducted for Criminal, Corrupt Economic, and for Personal Maniacal Motives,) and operating beyond the scope of Dr. Katz' personal overview to the Operations of The VA Health Care Centers, and beyond his ability to control, concerning the dangers confronting our Veterans at the hands of State Run Psychiatric and Mental Health Facilities, and as ordered for by The Courts under the current Justice System's use of Forced Psychiatric Evaluations and Psychiatric Commitments to replace the burden of the Court System, and also involving Social Services in that regard, and concerning "Forced Treatment," in psychiatric oppression over the lives of the public, that especially adversely affects the plight of our of our Combat Veterans, (to whom that this Nation looks to as the forward line of its Homeland Defense Security,) and to the ruination of their lives, physically, spiritually, mentally, and emotionally, from the crippling effects of psychiatric labeling and treatment, voluntary or otherwise, of the idea of psychiatric malfeasance; being allowed, and condoned, and supported for, by the Medical Profession, and by the Government of The United States, in direct violation of our U.S. Constitution.

In the first place being: that there is no Due Process, (other than Medical Evaluation under Mental Hygiene Law,) for Mental Health disposal, (in the terms of Equality Under The Law, as for the Legal Rights set forth and defined for the Penal Laws in protection of the public from tyrants;) No Right To The Presence of a Defense Counsel, No Right To Remain Silent, No Right To Be Presumed Innocent until Proven Guilty, (and quite the opposite, that the Psychiatrically Accused are Presumed Guilty and have to prove their own innocence;) No Trial by Jury, No Right to Confrontation of Testimony, and No Right To Refuse Treatment, (in the manner of drugs, shock therapy, and surgery, all at the disposition of a Medical Committee;) as General Counsel was asked to elaborate on.

And in the second place, that Dr. Katz' statement: "of persons going on to lead successful and satisfying lives" in conjunction with their mind altering, brain cell destroying, and physically and emotionally debilitating Antipsychotic Drug treatments, applies only to insane raving lunatics; and not to our beleaguered Veterans suffering from Posttraumatic Stress, Combat Fatigue, Grieving, Remorse of Combat, Homelessness, (and resulting Exhaustion and Malnutrition,) and overall Depression, and who have been, and are being placed into the same category, of being irrationally and violently mentally ill, with the catastrophically insane (to whom that it might prove useful to be able and allowed, under the effects catastrophic sedation with such Anti-psychotic drugs, to live out their lives in Vegetative Zombie State on "the outside," under the tortured effects of these drugs, and as opposed to being permanently confined in such conditions to a mental facility. And to what obviously that these people, (as Dr. Katz envisions,) are not going to be able to live out "successful, satisfying lives," in stable self-supportive conditions.

The tragic part about it being that there are "Insane People," violent, hysterical, manically deranged, demented idiot people, who are irrationally insane beyond the ability to be reached, and dangerously unpredictable in their threat of bodily harm to themselves and others, to be dealt with; but who are not to be confused with our Veterans who are placed in with these types, and all under the one heading of "Mental Health Psychiatric."

Gary L. Koniz – Secretary Correspondent
Veterans Of The Vietnam War Organization

"ONE POWERFUL VOICE"

9480 Princeton Square Blvd. S., #815
Jacksonville, FL 32256
October 12, 2009
FOIA Request 09-062

David N. Donahue – FOIA Officer
Office of the General Counsel
Department of Veterans Affairs
811 Vermont Avenue, N.W.
Washington, DC 20420

Dear Mr. Donahue:

Most respectfully worded; but it is most important here for you to resolve our case as we have it detailed, that seems a major impasse with you, as it is an obstacle everywhere over the dispensing of Psychiatric information; but that is still a major case in the Nation to resolve, (and to the spirit of befriending people, and of our affected Veterans, in showing appreciation to them for their sacrifices and services rendered to Nation,) to be providing them with the very best Health Care Services available, and to your adopting our suggestions and recommendations of how to conduct things, as we have passed-on to you, when they are offered for the reason of making improvements over failing policy, (which you seem bent on maintaining in your direct stonewalling of our request: "for an overall statement, from The Veterans Administration, regarding of the safety of the Anti-Psychotic Drugs, termed Neuroleptic and Psychotropic Strong Tranquillizers," which you term "Matters," and to the overall saving of lives,) which is the objective here, and not to an excursive rendering of the purview of FOIA Processing of Requests, or to the lack thereof; and to factor in to the successful conclusion, to care for the lives and well-being of our beloved Veterans, in safeguarding them from these harmful drugs, and otherwise to be setting down The Nation's Standards for the Conduct for Psychiatric Due Process Rights, and to Guaranteed Safe Treatment, (also at the hands of "State Facilities," and from Foul Play occurring beyond the abilities of the Veterans Administration to handle,) and for the sake of the general population of Americans as well, who suffer under the Psychiatric Scourge of Criminals and Foreign Intrigues, although Americanized. Which, as is being maintained, that is connected with the sources and corruptions of illegal drugs into the country and for other motives of aggressions; as Is The Case being presented.

Please, do then try and make the effort to work with us, and as well as with the rest of the militarily, as ultimately whose case it is to oversight, and over the power structure in persuasion. That I am not just writing to you to pass on our views in information about, but to convince you Militarily to be providing us with the Department of Veterans Affairs Intervention that we need "to conclude" with our business of psychiatric destruction. That ironically as is all too apparently "obvious" to us, but not so to yourselves there of the Medical-Legal Arms of The V.A.; to what we are not playing word games with you over. We asked you for specific information related with The Safety of Psychiatric Pharmacy.

Gary Koniz – Correspondent
Veterans of the Vietnam War

"ONE POWERFUL VOICE"

9480 Princeton Square Blvd. S., #815
Jacksonville, FL 32256
(904) 730-2055
February 13, 2010

Bob Woodward
Assistant Managing Editor
Investigative Unit
The Washington Post
1150 15th Street, N.W.
Washington, D.C. 20071

Dear Mr. Woodward,

So good to write to you again. How have you been? I've been well and in good health.

We're dropping pressing the case with the V.A. until they come around, (and they have as far as we know,) so as not to pin any of the brass down in the awkward embarrassment of being guilty of mass murder, past and present, and other atrocities of treatment.

In the meantime I was wondering if you would be interested in doing an article in feature of: Lieutenant General Franklin L. Hagenbeck, US Army, who is the Superintendent of the United States Military Academy at West Point, NY 10996, my friend, that would be a biography and tenor and duty of his rank and command regarding the security and interests of The United States and philosophies on training and morale, with photographs. I would be most happy to conduct the interview on your behalf if you would permit me.

I am here offering my service to the nation, in Military Advisory Capacity, to be of call to the confrontation pertaining for the increase in drugs trafficking here domestically and affecting the health and well-being of the average American citizens who deserve better interface with the lawful authorities to intervene, and under authorized use of military power in coordination of protection with civilian law enforcement as required for by The U.S. Constitution: "To Provide For The Public Defense From All Enemies Foreign And Domestic." The United States is being overrun and overthrown by alien and antithetical forces, (Drug Mafia Corruption, and Economic Criminals, being two examples of the setting,) without a shot being fired in defense of The American Posture of The America, and The Americans, who fought WWI and WWII, and verging now on WWIII. Let us be sensible here and declare our soil and territory to be sacred to us, and not to surrender it.

Sincerely,

Gary Koniz – Correspondent
Veterans of The Vietnam War

"ONE POWERFUL VOICE"

RE: Your Recent Letter

I would also like to know how I can "order" a copy of Military Officer Magazine to have for my own reference of review of your interests and to possibly tailor future articles to.

From: **Warren Lacy** (WarrenL@moaa.org)
Sent: Wed 4/07/10 8:26 AM
To: Gary Koniz (gary.koniz@hotmail.com)

Dear Mr. Koniz:

The magazine's Editorial Review Committee vets all story queries and unsolicited manuscripts sent to MOAA for possible publication in the magazine. This group considers the association's policies and the magazine's future needs when reviewing requests. Ms. Nero simply was passing on the committee's decision.

When it comes to reporting on wounded warrior issues, MOAA has its own internal experts in the Government Relations and Benefits Information Departments. We generally defer to them for help in covering such issues. We also employ a nationally-credited writer, Tom Philpott, to conduct most of our senior leader interviews. In addition, as you can imagine, we receive many more article queries each month than we can print. Competition is tough.
For these reasons, we are not able to accept your proposals, including the one you outline, below. As for subscribing to *Military Officer* Magazine, you certainly may do so. You may call MOAA's Member Service Center from 8:00 a.m. to 6:00 p.m. Eastern time at 1-800-234-6622 to purchase a subscription.

Sincerely,
Warren

Warren S. Lacy
Colonel, U.S. Army (Ret.)
Director, Publications
Editor in Chief, *Military Officer* magazine
Military Officers Association of America (MOAA)
201 N Washington St, Alexandria, VA 22314-2539
(800) 234-6622 x105; (703) 838-8105
editor@moaa.org www.moaa.org

One Powerful Voice.®   For every officer at every stage of life and career.

"ONE POWERFUL VOICE"

9480 Princeton Square Blvd. S., #815
Jacksonville, FL 32256
April 6, 2010

Warren S. Lacy - Editor in Chief
Colonel, U.S. Army (Ret.)
Military Officer Magazine
201 North Washington Street
Alexandria, VA 22314-2539

Dear Colonel Lacy:

I am kind of baffled by your two recent letters from your Assistant Editor Ms. Willow Nero in mention of my query to you for possible publication of: (and here you say, legislative correspondence,) without naming what specific materials they are, as I have sent in a lot of material over the recent span of years to you and to the Military Officers Association of America, to digest and don't know which one, or ones, she is referring to.

I specifically wanted to do an interview article with the Superintendent of West Point Military Academy, Lt. Gen. Franklin Hagenbeck, in Command Setting, and my friend, that would be a biography and tenor and duty of his rank and command regarding the security and interests of The United States and philosophies on training and morale, with photographs; to be conducted as an interview on behalf of the Military's Orientation on the Wounded Warrior Program and how it relates to the devastation of Psychiatric Intake to resolve affecting our Veterans, past and present, and to their treatment with destructive chemicals concerning our Nation's Proud Veterans to be disgraced by; and mentally, psychologically, and physically tortured, maimed, and scarred by, to the point of mass Suicide, that I was hoping to attract some Command Decision Making about involving The Veterans Administration to straighten the matter around to where it needs to be in the proper Military Code of Honor to Set Right in perspective by an inclusion in your Military Officer Magazine to enlighten America's Military Officer Corps about.

Please then in that urgency of regard if you would let me know what specifically fits your needs in this matter, either editorial way or feature length interview article way, I would be most happy to tailor my approach to suite your needs. We would like to take care of this psychiatric business at this juncture in time while the issues are still timely and fresh with General Eric Shinseki the Secretary of Veterans Affairs. We have been dropping pressing the case with the V.A. until they come around voluntarily, (and they may have already as far as we know,) so as not to pin anyone down in the awkward embarrassment of being guilty of mass murder, past and present, and for other atrocities of maiming treatment, that nothing is going to go away about concerning the necessity for resolution, only in the deeper magnitude of time of doing it now instead of at a later date and to a greater degree of tragedy that could have been avoided with your help to correct this peril, as I have been in relentless appeals to you about over the years. How is it that no one, including yourself, understands this in responsibility to get it cleared up?

This is a most tragic and difficult situation to resolve, involving mistakes made by the Administration, which changes hands of the years to years, over the issue of psychiatric, but not so of the errors which continue on; to what everyone pays mindless subservience and obeisance to in conceiving the government to be infallible, (Approved By The FDA and so forth;) that the

"ONE POWERFUL VOICE"

public is at odds with and which The Administration Defends itself against the public interest about concerning its errors needing to be corrected. That over the course of years I have tried to "spoon feed" you and every one of the MOAA on the facts of the matter, (and which has amounted scores of articles and two books in print since I began with you,) that I hope "by now" you realize what the errors are needing to be fixed and what needs to be done by the authority of the Administration to fix them.

And which errors are, as I have pointed out to you many times, and upon the theme expressed to them, ("that wars are not fought and endured in duration without emotions, and without memories of tragic events associated to them, and without shock of repeated blasts, and without the long lasting effects of the rigors of fatigue from the arduous demands of combat placed upon our fine and gallant Service Men and Women, under the stress of sheer terror, fear, and horror;") that there is not any need to make psychiatrics out of our Veterans over to be thought of as insane and dangerous mentally ill persons by the society to be feared and made into homeless persons by such labeling, and to be condescended to by the labeling and thought to be inferior, devalued, and unemployable persons in psychological maiming, when the polite wording of Best Rest/Convalescence in Labeling, would do nicely for the Veterans and their families to be able to live with.

And secondly of the errors; that the pharmacy, called "Meds," being used "to treat" our Veterans with, are deadly, and not therapeutic as the public is led to believe by the Veterans Administration. And who, as to the public, believes that, (that these type of drugs are necessary and therapeutic,) because it is "The Government" who they trust that is telling them that; (and as I have displayed the evidence to you to the contrary many times over on how deadly these chemicals are in their Effects, Adverse Effects, and Paradoxical Reactions, (inducing the exact symptoms which they are supposed to alleviate,) that is listed about them; which every medical doctor knows, and which The Federal Food And Drug Administration knows, and which every Veterans who has ever been Force Treated with those types of Anti-Psychotic Neuroleptic Drugs such as Thorazine, knows about firsthand about to tell you about, of those remaining who are left alive from the effects of such treatment to tell about it. Let us proceed together then in solidarity, and always with the thought that these are our Veterans Lives on line for the proper outcome of the case.

I do respect you and your position with regard to the publicizing of our investigations and judgment for resolution of our Veterans Psychiatric affairs in relation to the format of your Military Officer Magazine; who no one is attempting to second guess you over; but this is not a "competition" is it, concerning this matter. It is a Raging War being waged against our Nation's Veterans, being conducted by Organized Crime, (if I have to spell it out for you, concerning a Captive Market Pharmaceutical and Medical Industry Money Interests, and by Other Motives of Hostility feeding off the present government's position to the psychiatric destruction of our returning from War Combat Veterans,) that you need to regard to be a War and respond accordingly in your way of it and utilizing the talent of the personnel that you have assembled to martial the course of the nation by. Whether I do the job or you do is irrelevant to us as long as the job "gets" done, and get done it will.

Gary Koniz - Correspondent
Veterans of The Vietnam War
RE: Veterans Lives On Line

"ONE POWERFUL VOICE"

From: **Warren Lacy** (WarrenL@moaa.org)
Sent: Thu 4/08/10 6:06 AM
To: Gary Koniz (gary.koniz@hotmail.com)
Cc: Willow Nero (willown@moaa.org); MSC (MSC@moaa.org); legis (legis@moaa.org)

Dear Mr. Koniz:

Thanks for your note. We'll consider your comments for the "Your Views" department of
Military Officer magazine.

I've also forwarded your note to MOAA's Government Relations Department for their
consideration. Under the leadership of MOAA's Board of Directors, they manage the
association's legislative campaigns, and they author the "Washington Scene" department of the
magazine.

Sincerely,
Warren

Warren S. Lacy
Colonel, U.S. Army (Ret.)
Director, Publications
Editor in Chief, *Military Officer* magazine
Military Officers Association of America (MOAA)
201 N Washington St, Alexandria, VA 22314-2539
(800) 234-6622 x105; (703) 838-8105
editor@moaa.org www.moaa.org

One Powerful Voice.®   For every officer at every stage of life and career.

9480 Princeton Square Blvd. S., #815
Jacksonville, FL 32256
June 16, 2010

Warren S. Lacy
Colonel, U.S. Army (Ret.)
Editor in Chief
Military Officer Magazine

Dear Colonel Lacy,

I am writing to let you know that I have sent you a Hard Cover Copy of the book, "The Call To Order," that should be arriving any day now to your office as I have just received word that your order has shipped. Please take it to heart for the work involved in the tenor of accomplishing the goal of freeing up every one of our Nation's Veterans from the scourge of psychiatric injustice being inflicted upon them, that the discussions in the book, (and with many of its letters addressed to you,) document and provide the detail substance of the evidence to. I would appreciate it if you would think of it as "your" book, and not "a" book to be sent off somewhere for someone else to look at and review, "or not." I am sending it to you for the purpose for you to have and for you to read and to learn what I know from. That way then that the two of us can think together on the resolutions of the topics to resolve that lay ahead of us; which is the important element.

Thank you, Sir, from the depths of my heart so much for your kind assistance and intercession to me, and each of our Veterans, on this topic. I have sent other copies of the book out to many notable people besides yourself including General Franklin Hagenbeck The Superintendent of West Point Military Academy, Robert Redford of The Sundance Institute, Secretary of State Hillary Clinton, The Nixon Library, The New York Time Book Review, Secretary of Veterans Affairs Eric Shinseki, and Margaret Engel, Director of The Alicia Patterson Foundation, and among others, with limited funding permitted.

On the other matter about your Military Officer Magazine, I received my first copy of it, June 2010, several weeks ago, and was quite pleased with the overall professionalism of its presentation. I enjoyed seeing the photo of you in fromtheeditor comments section to finally know what you look like and to have a sense of rapport with you in that way. I enjoyed the discussion of Tricare featuring Rear Adm. Christine Hunter, USN, and the many other fine and informative articles. I did however sense that while the magazine provided informative substance on many topics of military interest, to add, that it did seem to "lack" a defining position of objective and purpose; as to why we serve, and what it means, to us, and to the nation, to serve, to the offering of our lives for the defense of The United States and its people, to be a proud officer and soldier to, and of what it means to be a soldier concerning the issues of involvement with the country's defense in the modern times, and as to include for articles trouble shooting on what precisely is wrong with the way things are in the modern era of the Nation and what needs to be done about them to make the magazine "more spirited." I hope I have stated this right for you.

Gary Koniz
Veterans of the Vietnam War

"ONE POWERFUL VOICE"

9480 Princeton Square Blvd. S., #815
Jacksonville, FL 32256
June 16, 2010

Warren S. Lacy
Colonel, U.S. Army (Ret.)
Editor in Chief
Military Officer Magazine

Dear Colonel Lacy:

I have done some more thinking today about what I wanted to relate with you about my feelings towards your magazine, and what struck me most, and besides what I already have told you, which was for the feeling of having a sense of "Duty" to perform, and a sense of "Vigilance," in filling the void of what I sensed about the magazine, (and while being very informative,) that is seeming to "lack" a defining position of objective and purpose; (that makes the magazine read like a social newsletter for the VFW,) without the guts of a defining Military Ambition as to why we serve, and what makes us proud to serve, and what it means, to us, and to the nation, to serve, to the offering of our lives on line for the defense of The United States and its Heritage, and its People, to be a proud officer and a proud soldier to, to protect and defend, and in that line of the reasoning of "Making Us Special," of what separates us from the common citizens of what it means to be a soldier concerning the issues of our sacrifice and or our concerns for the security of the Nation and our ongoing involvement with the country's defense at any time, as Veterans and as Active Duty Soldiers alike, and particularly in the modern times of what it is to be on active duty and in harm's way. In the way that seeing the Helmeted Face of an exhausted Tactical Combat Officer in the field looking out from the cover of your magazine at the readers would make you feel, in that Spirit of Duty, and Vigilance, and Sacrifice, of what it means to be a Military Officer in the service of our Country.

And so I began to feel about it, that the Military Officer Magazine needs to become more of a "Tactical Beacon," for its readers, to include for more articles emphasizing what the ordeals of the battlefield are, and trouble-shooting on what the strategic needs of our nation are and what our service priorities ought to be, and to expertly pin point precisely what is wrong with the way things are in the problem eras with articles on the psychology and history of wars and the social conflicts that produced them, and about the problems we are having, as soldiers, past and present, of having to deal with these matters, and oriented towards the healing of the Nation and of what needs to be done about our own domestic social and cultural problems, and as they involve us Internationally with the problems of other Nations to resolve and head-off wars about, to head them off before they start, and in that way to make the magazine "More Spirited."

I hope to have stated this right for you, which in no means is meant to disparage the fine and sensitive intelligent informative tone of your current edition, but only to oriented it to a more stronger and more aggressive position in the security defense of our Nation.

Gary Koniz
Veterans of the Vietnam War

"ONE POWERFUL VOICE"

9480 Princeton Square Blvd. S., #815
Jacksonville, FL 32256
November 11, 2010

Warren S. Lacy
Colonel, U.S. Army (Ret.)
Editor in Chief
Military Officer Magazine

Dear Commander Lacy:

I do enjoy the excellent Military Officer Magazine that you and your professional staff put out each month; and thank you for your service to us in that way to have developed. However, and for the Ask The Doctor column written by Doctor Joyce Johnson USPHS-Ret., and perhaps for your Washington Legal Department to handle as well, concerning the Veterans Post Traumatic Stress issue being mishandled inappropriately by The Department Of Veterans Affairs and by Civilian Mental Hygiene Facilities in their blanket coverage of the ongoing crisis without Due Process and without Legal Definitions, and without Safe Legal Clarifications of Pharmacy, for the attributing of Mental Illness Conditions, (and lethal to their suicidal consequences in psychological maiming and to the Veterans' Cohabitation in civilian society, and medically speaking concerning the reasoning of Forced, or otherwise Ill-Advised, Treatment, with deadly Thorazine and other types of Neuroleptic and Psychotropic Anti-Psychotic Chemicals in mass use,) that your Staff there Has Not Heeded The Warning to take-up with, in taking our side, against the obvious Legal and Medical errors here being committed in mass-atrocity in the self-righteous name of Medical Psychiatry, and to the side of the Veterans who are having to suffer the consequences and repercussions of their Military Combat Service to be Murdered Outright on their return home by Doctors, who may as well be the Communist Insurgency, or The Viet Cong, forcing their lethal pogrom execution style tactics of Diagnosis and Treatment on the returning Veterans who have been grievously physically, (in the terms of sheer exhaustion,) psychologically, and mentally traumatized by Combat; The Unseen Wounds of War. Who, we have urged you To Speak For.

And to let you know what precisely we have been up against, to comment on a recent viewing of a new Television Series entitled, Hawaii 50 (that aired on Monday, November 1, 2010,) concerning the ongoing Propaganda being put out by the Media, (and with being perpetrated by Some Entity in particular on a methodical basis ongoing since the Vietnam War in connection to Mental Health Program here in America,) in which the returning from war Veteran is portrayed as an Unstable Homicidal, who Is Prone To Violent Episodes, suffers from Black Outs, and who his Family Fears To Be Around, and who needs to be on his Clorpromazine, (Thorazine,) Meds, (a Medication commonly used for the treatment of Post Traumatic Stress, as the T.V. Show makes the point of.)

In the meantime, the daily T.V. Soap Opera Y&R is opening teaching Drug Warfare to the housewives on how to put poisons and drugs into people's food and beverages.

Gary L. Koniz – MOAA No. 02786399
Veterans Of The Vietnam War

"ONE POWERFUL VOICE"

9480 Princeton Square Blvd. S., #815
Jacksonville, FL 32256
November 25, 2010

Warren S. Lacy - Editor in Chief
Colonel, U.S. Army (Ret.)
Military Officer Magazine
201 North Washington Street
Alexandria, VA 22314-2539

Dear Colonel Lacy:

The time is at an end now with the patience for those in our discussions with the Veterans Administration Officials there in Washington, (and as the job we have required connected to the ongoing Psychiatric Slaughter of our Veterans In Arms ought to have been done, by now.) I would therefore appreciate your signal of allied defense officially from the standpoint of my discussions on the issues with you and to the solidarity reasoning of the Military Officers Association Of America, (MOAA,) and with backing of Military Officer Magazine as a formidable engine of inquiry, with The Military Order now to be put in effect for The Psychiatric Reform to occur to its required conclusion.

We are at an end with the idea of being polite and for the element of protocol when being met with an ignorance of obstinate intrigue from the V.A. Medical and Legal Staff, (as they have repeatedly displayed to us in the past, in our being evasively side-stepped and run-around, in covering up the atrocity; of Inappropriate Psychiatric Labeling, and for more serious Harmful Effects of the Medications Prescribed, that are touted to the Veterans to be necessary and therapeutic, but which in effect are actually quite deadly, to be redressed; which issues are being skirted around, rather than being treated in a proper and constructive way of handling, <u>to remedy the situations occurring</u>, that is the goal.

And who everyone involved, and otherwise standing-by with powers to assist, are thereby being in direct conspiracy to it, (the slaughter by mental, psychological, and physical maiming and with resulting suicide of our innocent Veterans,) that is costing our brave soldiers in arms their well-being and the safety of their lives at stake for the say so and the sake of someone's corrupt and sinister administrative venue regarding psychiatric labeling and pharmacy mis-treatment, and/or, to its Sacred Cow "Do No Wrong," Cover-Up, (on the part of the V.A., The FDA, and the Pharmaceutical/Medical Industry.)

This is a Criminal Matter of concern Verging Treason, and not about the Medical Profession always being honest and forthcoming and saint-like in their dealings with our Veterans; but about their being corrupt and economically manipulative in conspiracy, (as a Psychiatric Captive Market of diagnosis and treatment to be plundered,) and/or for more sinister motives of conquest by foreign powers, to be disabling and destroying our Nation's Reserves of Military Strength. That I keep spoon-feeding you the evidence about, and that somehow is not being treated with the proper alarm and reaction to date.

Gary Koniz - Correspondent
Veterans of the Vietnam War

"ONE POWERFUL VOICE"

9480 Princeton Square Blvd. S., #815
Jacksonville, FL 32256
December 17, 2010

Warren S. Lacy - Editor in Chief
Colonel, U.S. Army (Ret.)
Military Officer Magazine
201 North Washington Street
Alexandria, VA 22314-2539

Dear Colonel Lacy:

We had another incident of Enemy Propaganda this week, on Tuesday night, 12/14/10, on the T.V. Series NCIS Los Angeles, which airs on CBS each week at 9:00 p.m. EST; The incident depicted a Combat Veteran recently returned from the war in Afghanistan who was reported to be suffering from Post-Traumatic Stress Disorder from his experiences there; the symptom of what being; a Confused and Befuddled Mental State, Agitation, Irrational and Unpredictable Behavior, and reoccurring Black Outs complete with Hallucinations of Combat during which time that the Veteran cannot remember anything; and who may revert to his trained combat killer mode and murder everybody in thinking that he is still in combat; and also that the Veteran was "Off his Meds," (the Strong Anti-Psychotic Tranquillizers used to treat PTSD as the show describes,) used to Control the PTSD Symptoms, in explaining why the Veteran had now become deranged.

I previously reported this Enemy Propaganda occurring on a Hawaii Five O episode, 11/01/10, that depicted a deranged Veteran, suffering from PTSD, and off his "Meds," holding hostages at gunpoint to force police to investigate that he didn't kill his wife in a Blackout. Needless to say, to cost to our Veterans lives, of this kind of systematic and fear inducing propaganda programming of the population, (and the same as what our Vietnam Veterans experienced in our era of war's aftermath,) of having the public, (and that is to say, the family members, wives, friends, and coworkers, of our returning from war Veterans, and the society in general,) to being programmed in blatant Brain Washing of the population by these T.V. shows and movies, to believe that they are being forced to cohabitate with, irrational deranged and catatonic murderers who have been programmed to kill by the Military, and who need to be on their deadly Sedation Tranquillizer Meds at all times, in order for the Veterans to be able to live safely in society. That has been, and is resulting in, the needless; Homelessness, Joblessness, Social Rejection, Despondency, and Desperation facing our returning Veterans, and to their overall sense of futility and en masse Psychiatric Intake resulting to be Treated with Thorazine and other descriptions of such Neuroleptic Drugs in use, for the safety of society, and to their eventual Suicides.

We need to investigate "Who" is responsible for this type of enemy propaganda being put out, and speak with the Producers and Executives in charge of content of these TV Shows to let them know the damage they are contributing to in an already ugly situation.

Gary Koniz – Secretary
Veterans of the Vietnam War
MOAA No. 02786399

"ONE POWERFUL VOICE"

9480 Princeton Square Blvd. S., #815
Jacksonville, FL 32256
December 19, 2010

Warren S. Lacy - Editor in Chief
Colonel, U.S. Army (Ret.)
Military Officer Magazine
201 North Washington Street
Alexandria, VA 22314-2539

Dear Colonel Lacy:

There are all kinds of ways psychologically to phrase things in searching out the correct way to persuade a proper course of action to be taken. Chewing people out never works good. Mewing to people, that is, playing up to their egos, is also likewise ineffective. And discussing things straightforward with certain people of stranded intelligence, "the head in the sand types," and "the tunnel vision programmed," who place their trust in the authority of others, doesn't work either. What does work, is honest reasoning cogently presented by a determined leader to sway the proper course. And so you see, that sending women to Washington to lobby for a male perspective of Post Traumatic Stress Disorder, is not the way to convince the arguments in need of correction, due to the fact that it is the males who the women fear to be around, and who would just as soon sway the argument against the Veterans being injured by Social Rejection and Persecution, and Pharmacy Sedation Treatment; and anymore than we could send a man to Washington to argue for improved feminine hygiene conditions on the battlefield and for the treatment of resulting infections from unsanitary conditions in combat.

I just cannot believe that an entire session of the meeting with President Obama, Secretary Shinseki, and MOAA President Vice Adm. Nrob Ryan Jr., went down without "one mention" of the Pharmacy Issues, and Rights of Mentally Accused, and the Social Persecutions, and their Causes, occurring to our Returning Veterans. And what do you suppose is the reason for the oversight?

Subject: RE: Washington Scene Rebuttle - October Edition
Date: Sun, 19 Dec 2010 12:49:16 -0500
From: WarrenL@moaa.org
To: gary.koniz@hotmail.com
CC: legis@moaa.org
Dear Mr. Koniz:
Thanks for your note. We'll consider your comments for the "Your Views" department of Military Officer magazine.

I've forwarded your note to MOAA's Government Relations Department for their consideration. Under the leadership of MOAA's Board of Directors, they manage the association's legislative campaigns.

"ONE POWERFUL VOICE"

Best wishes, and thanks for your support of Military Officers Association of America.

Warren
******
Warren S. Lacy
Colonel, U.S. Army (Ret.)
Director, Publications
Editor in Chief, *Military Officer* magazine
Military Officers Association of America (MOAA)
201 N Washington St, Alexandria, VA 22314-2539
(800) 234-6622 x105; (703) 838-8105
editor@moaa.org www.moaa.org

One Powerful Voice.®   For every officer at every stage of life and career.

   I thank you and respect you very much for your Sunday Workday reply to me on the urgent matters at hand concerning our Veteran Domestic Safety and Security as I have set fourth in detail for you to assist us with in resolving.
   Thank you for your determined offer of assistance and for the forwarding on of my message on to the appropriate departments within the structure of The MOAA Organization for response.
   It is heartfelt to see that you work the 24-7 routine at all hours of the day and night as I do in the battle against ignorance and obstinacy that is overpowering us and prevailing in detriment against our American Efforts to survive, and against an ill-tide, to the ultimate break-up of The United States predicted.
   What you discuss of the gloomy Economic Picture is directly tide into, in the Battle For American Soil, the plight of the returning soldiers from the Nation's long a prevailing wars who are being systematically removed from society by the means of social rejection and psychiatric attrition, that is coordinated in its Unconventional Warfaring Attack with the overall Economic Destruction of The American United States, in the same sense as you indicated for about in your October Issue "fromtheeditor" Column, (and with a quite handsome and neatly groomed picture of yourself there by the way to reflect on, concerning your always inspiring thoughts,) that in this particular issue had to do with The National Debt being now virtually untenable and verging bankruptcy at 13 Trillion dollars, with Foreign Powers holding 65% of the Marker over us ON Eventual DEMAND of TERRITORY; that was predicted" as well, by everyone decades ago to do some Preventive Maintenance about through the years concerning Deficit Spending.
   To what that you are now calling on everyone in The MOAA to lend a strong hand with in resolving; that in a likewise situation too about, related to the matter of the Disabling and Suicide Extermination of our Veterans at the hands of a calculated psychiatric plot, that we too have also predicted the continuing devastation to occur to our Nations War Veterans, and contributing to the breakup of The United States by the weakening of our Military Reserve Defenses; to what, as well as you regarding predictions over budgetary concerns, that we too have an ax to grind concerning the lack of appropriate response to our pleas for defensive assistance, concerning the ongoing needless, AND PREVENTABLE! Psychiatric Holocaust currently and in the past being perpetrated against the innocent lives of our returning from war Veterans, in the name of

"ONE POWERFUL VOICE"

Government Supremacy over the Rights of its Citizens without relief of response from our elected offices to the resolution of this matter. For you to call for a hand from the pulpit of your monthly column about, for the entirety of MOAA's to stop playing protocol politics and to render our Veterans the assistance their direly require to this Social War Theater of social injustice, persecution and psychiatric devastation to reform as well.

I have enclosed here now as well, with the solution to the overall economic madness, (if anybody is willing to relinquish their ego's enough to harken to ideas not their own, to adopt a new solution in approach to the economy about,) that is called "Full Faith Certificate" Barter Agreement for "Fiat Monetary Issue," direct from The U.S. Treasury, on demand of necessity; for Government Services Rendered, to provide Full Employment to The Population, and to cover for All Types of National Emergency Contingencies to be issued. Which, as we see it, is the only way that we are ever about to salvage The United States as it has existed in American Hands. Which is predicted to collapse into many separate individual Nation States, and perhaps not of its overall structure, but devoid of the American People who "used to" inhabit it. The whole Southern "Breadbasket" by the way, and States like Alabama for example, is, and has been for decades, been left under a sustained and prevailing Sedation-Poison Chemical Warfare Attack, as the prevailing state of general alcoholism, (in their pathetic attempts to override the effects of this type of Sedation-Poison Warfare,) and everyone's Enlarged Prostate Glands and Urinary Urgency will attest to; that needs the present state of the Liberal Government Protocol Policy of Nonintervention to be overridden by Military Forensics to get to the bottom of pronto. Anybody who is on Drugs or Alcohol will not be able to ascertain the effects of this clandestine warfare and will always believe that the ill effects they experience as a result of this type of warfare, not benign, are something in the nature of the bad effect of their use of Drugs and Alcohol that they are responsible for. So, it is a bad "Double Bind" situation that requires to be intervened to from the outside.

Gary Koniz Secretary
Veterans of the Vietnam War
MOAA No. 02786399

"ONE POWERFUL VOICE"

United States Constitution

The United States Constitution is hereby created to read as follows:

Article 1. - Declaration Of Rights.

Section 9. –Right To Solvency To Issue Currency.

    -----Section 1: Be it hereby resolved that The Economy of The United States is to be henceforth conditioned to Spontaneous Fiat Issue Monetary Generation on demand, to be known as Full Faith Certificate, that is to be issued in necessity to meet the urgent criteria in demands of The Nation's Economy in these times in service to the population, to provide for ample and sufficient government, to sustain life, preserve the environment, and to provide for the general well-being, that is critical to the future of our great Nation.

    And by which initiation of such Special Issue that is defined to be redeemed on barter agreement, is required for in the modern era also to pay off the current National Deficit in crisis, and to Balance The Federal Budget on into the future by its conditioned necessity, as to supplant and offset for any current and future budgetary deficit conditions to exist due to any taxation shortfall to occur involving the private sector, and that is also to be used in addition to supplant existing individual State's Budgets in crisis, and therefore also to the emergency contingencies of each State's Local, County, and Municipal Government Budgets necessities, to be allocated for existing and future crises in the overall of the event of taxation shortfall in which to accomplish the objectives of government and to sustain the public well-being.

    And that this special and prioritized Fiat Monetary Issue Resolution, is hereby established to replace the current and at the present hour outdated National Economic Taxation Policy, as applies to The Government Taxation Method in budgetary foundation based to the unsound Supply and Demand Theory of The Private Sector Economy, and to the failings and shortcomings of Private Taxation Method in that regard, that has never been viably suitable, and is no longer remotely adequate to meet the absolute and necessary criteria of The Nation's Governmental Budgetary Requirements and respective of The Individual State's Budgets as well, and that as such is hereby so to be reinforced and augmented by The Special Fiat Monetary Issue in arrangement.

    -----Section 2: And that the concept of Special Fiat Monetary Currency Issue, as named Full Faith Certificate, as shall be so resolutely adopted by The Nation of The United States of America, and as is based to sound foundation of Barter Economic Policy in contingency, is to be issued in spontaneity as it is required for by the empowered Enactment of Congress, and in lieu of there being to exist sufficient taxation in shortfall deficit to occur in the year to year of The Government's Budgetary Necessity, to any level of The U.S. Government, Its Individual States, and to Each State's Local County and Municipal Governments, to conduct and manage The Government's Business by, from wherewithal to derive such necessary taxation from the private sector economy, heretofore the basis for such derived taxation and to the cause of our Government's present suffering in condition of deficit spending and to the dire loss of Government Services Provided to our U. S. Population, based to The Private Taxation of The Nation's Private Sector Gross National/Domestic Product, derived from the production of goods, commodities, and services rendered, through private business and corporate taxes, personal

"ONE POWERFUL VOICE"

income tax, property tax, sales tax, excise tax, luxury tax, estate taxes, and by various other taxes and tariffs imposed, specifying in priority of The Government's need to support itself, and to engage in the necessary Projects and Programs of State of redeeming Social Benefit to our population, and to provide for Disaster Relief in needed times, and for Defense Priority, and to provide subsidies for Law Enforcement, and for needed subsidies concerning Government Employment in providing for The Nation's Unemployed in special care, and for generous subsidies to The Nation's Agriculture, Education, National Public Health Care Needs, and to subsidize Businesses which are essential To The Public Interest requiring prioritized subsidy in special times. This is a practical measure to ensure a harmonious economy, and for the safety and security of the society overall, the idea of providing necessary subsidies for the sake of survival.

To what that the previous private sector taxation resources, based to the supply and demand mercantile theory economy, have not been able to provide for in total wherewithal of such responsible government management, and with having left The Government, whose responsibility it is in obligation of service and care provided to Its People, in the dire position taxation revenues shortfall to meet with these crucial Government Necessities in expectations, that The Issue of Special Fiat Monetary Full Faith Certificate is hereby mandated for in this critical hour to override.

-----Section 3: That, The Federal Treasury thereunto and by the authorization of The Congress of The United States to be so conducted, and under the rigorous process of monitor by The Nation's Federal Reserve Board, shall oversee the special occurrence issuances in generation of such Full Faith Certificate Currency in the year to year, to thereon be allowed and able to, on such writ of Authority by Congress, to issue Primary Character Currency Generation as needed, allowable in sound barter economic compatibility as legal tender, that is to be backed in surety of The Entire Value In Worth of The United States, conceived as The Federal Government, The Individual State's Governments, and of each State's Local County and Municipal Governments, of redeeming Barter Quality Theory of Enhanced Collateralization similar in cognition to the era of Gold and Silver Standard Currency Redemption Issue, and such supplanting the current Supply and Demand Economics Private Taxation Method of securing Government Revenues, in pledge of The Entire Worth of The Government's combined assets in substantial negotiable worth in barter agreement; of lands, projects, real estate properties in holdings, all products, goods, equipment, technologies, and production capabilities belonging to The United States, and pledging the employment services of The Government, and all commodities holdings of The Government, including gold and silver and other precious metals, and to specify further to all and any future acquisitions and developed resources of The Government which are to be offered in collateral.

-----Section 4: In furthering the conditions in requirement to Fiat Issue Currency Generation, it is also to be reasoned that in order to promote the general well-being and to preclude run away inflation as a result, termed Hyper-Inflation, occurring by the regular and periodic release as required, of Primary Issue Currency, named Full Faith Certificate, that The Nation's Federal Reserve is to establish and to maintain in scrutiny and by Its policy Directives Enforced, to The Federalized Standardization of The Wage/Price Index.

And that this measure is to be conducted and carried out by strict and binding Federal Mediation Arbitration in the year to year, conditioned to regulate and stabilize The Nation's Wages, by uniform parity agreement based to The Federal Government's (GS) General Schedule Wage Standards, and else way by special arrangement of union negotiated wage scales

"ONE POWERFUL VOICE"

specifically conducted, to set the yearly wages for each category of employment to exist in America, in index of The Prevailing Wages to be set and monitored for to coincide with each sector of private employment categories. And that such Prevailing Wages for each Job Description to exist are to be posted by The United States Department Of Labor, which is to undertake the responsibility for enforcement.

This arrangement is also to regulate for a Fair Price Index Agreement, in Government Stipulation to every Cost Essential Necessity To Survival of The Public Well-Being in the interest of the public need, to do with, food, shelter, clothing, fuel, transportation, household necessities, vital services, insurance, medical and dental services, and other Cost Essentials, and what does not specify for any luxury items to be included. And that The Pricing to these Cost of Living Essentials are to be regulated by mediation as with the wage index, in similar cognition, as The Utilities, Telecommunications, The Postal Service, and Public Transportation Services Are Regulated, and conceived to have license to operate, In The Public Interest, under Federal Government Supervision.

-----Section 5: Further, it is to be understood that as Government Services in Foundation, possess their own and inherent intrinsic value in barter agreement, in mandate to be issued for to be covered by Special Fiat Issue Generation in contingency basis to any type Government Employment as deemed necessary which may be specially issued for in lieu of sufficient taxation provided to meet such need, based to the Intrinsic Barter Value of Services Rendered, as are worth their own value in remuneration.

And that as The Services of The Government on any level of Its functioning in operations can always be sustained to any and every and all necessity contingency, by Fiat Issue Resolution, to maintain every event of Government Payroll and Benefits to be me in providing for The Nation's Government Workers, that as well, and when necessary is to include for also, that The Special Fiat Issue for Services Rendered, can also be used To Provide Basic Employment to The Population Suffering Unemployment, for survival and to promote for the general well-being, through Government Service Positions, and else way to supplant the need for work among the population with Special Fiat Resolution Funding, sponsoring employment to Government Building and Construction Projects, and to the repair and maintenance of existing projects on into the future.

This measure is also designed to reduce the individual tax burden and the private corporate/business tax burden to a realistic and feasible sum based to a responsible public alignment of private obligation to such taxes in support of government.

That in supplement to such basic and feasible private taxation, to what that all other necessary fiscal financial needs in contingency of The Government of The United States, to any of Its levels, are to be met with Special Issue Fiat Currency Full Faith Certificate Generation as required. The objective being To Provide The Nation Permanently With Government, Government Services and All Necessary Social Programs of Benefit and Productivity To The Population, that as such cannot be subject to capricious taxation methods of finance on into the mature outcome in future of America.

-----Section 6: The concept of our National Debt, by such Full Faith Certificate Fiat Monetary Resolution Act, is hereby permanently dissolved.

"ONE POWERFUL VOICE"

United States Constitution

The United States Constitution is hereby created to read as follows:

Article 1. - Declaration Of Rights.

Section 2. - The Right To Equal Justice.

-----The Seventh Amendment defining, Civil Law, is hereby clarified of its ambiguity of Rights, pursuant to the wording of The Ninth Amendment retaining All Rights of The Constitution to the people, in that All Rights of Due Process of Law inherent to the workings of The Fourth, Fifth, Sixth, and Eighth Amendments to The U. S. Constitution are to be accorded the same foundation of legal integrity concerning the framework of Civil Law in insurance of safeguard for The Rights of The People as they pertain for their Civil Liberties. In Specification:

-----Section 1: That anyone duly acquitted and found innocent of a crime under the statutes of Penal Law cannot therefore under any circumstances be retried for the same crime under Civil Law, (or to be twice tried for the same crime under Federal Jurisdiction,) in accordance with The Rights of The Fifth Amendment.

-----Section 2: The Fifth Amendment stipulation that no person: "shall be compelled in any criminal case to be witness against himself," is hereby clarified to stipulate for and to include for any non-criminal Civil Law matters as they pertain to self-incrimination, and as well is to extend and to guarantee The Right Against Self Incrimination to persons from being compelled to so testify against themselves, in penalty of monetary fine or incarceration, before convened Congressional Committee Hearings and Grand Jury proceedings, and is to preclude inquiries in mandatory disclosure in direct questioning of self-incrimination testimony, to the aspect of the questioning itself, in all regard whether Penal or Civil, Congressional Committee, or by Congressional Authority of Government Agencies.

-----Section 3:That The Medical Terminology Technicality of Mental Hygiene Psychiatric Law that falls under the heading of Civil Law, Two Physician Consent, 2PC, Commitment Procedure, on Medical Grounds, in that no crime has been committed under Mental Hygiene Law to be charged for and thereby to be accorded the protective safeguards of Miranda Rights Legislation to be prosecuted for and processed fairly for under The Constitutional Rights accorded to Criminal Penal Law Legal System under the protection in Rights To The People, of The Fourth, Fifth, Sixth, and Eighth Amendments to The U.S. Constitution, and reinforce by the protection of The Miranda Legislation, is hereby clarified of Its Civil Law Constitutional Rights, in meaning to have the same Rights of Due Process as are and have been established under Penal Law, in guarantee to the people of:

The Right to have a clear definition of a Formal Psychiatric Charge being present in grounds for anyone to be labeled for and to have any specified medical psychiatric condition, or for the offense of irrational behavior labeling being levied against an individual, and in grounds thereby for any psychiatric evaluation process mental illness labeling to be attached to anyone, or for any process of Two Physician Consent,

"ONE POWERFUL VOICE"

2PC, Psychiatric Commitment Procedure to be conducted. And that such definition of charge is also to precede any Court or Government Agency Order for the disclosure of personal and private psychiatric history records to be produced.

The Right to The Fourth Amendment guarantee of privacy in regard of doctor patient confidentiality and invoking to The Due Process Right of Probable and Sufficient Cause In Grounds, is to be present and justified to a specific itemized search and disclosure in mandatory request for Specific Information only of any existing psychiatric history records, regarding The Rights of Government Agencies, as for the specified psychiatric history to be scrutinized, to any private request or public government agency order for, or court authority mandatory order for the scrutiny of anyone's psychiatric medical history records to be revealed. That is not to be construed by court order or by congressional authority concerning government agencies, to be a total and all intrusive invasive invasion of an individual's records history involving The Right To Privacy, but is to be issued only as order for records disclosure pertains selectively and relevant to the specified psychiatric charge of inquiry at hand.

The Right to strict legal definition for any psychiatric labeling terms to be applied to anyone.

The Right to strict legal determinations based to demonstrated facts of observed and defined behavior, in the presence of any attorney for such alleged psychiatric labeling being attributed in legal attachment of a psychiatric condition or involving psychiatric incarceration to anyone to be valid.

The Right to Counsel, to be provided for at government expense if need be, by The Examining Government Agency or by The Court of Jurisdiction, for any alleged psychiatric matter of consequence being attributed to anyone, involving the loss of liberty, property, licensure, employment, or privilege.

The Right to have an Attorney present during questioning to any psychiatric examination/evaluation/interrogation, and to be present during psychiatric commitment processing and to any court proceedings.

The Right to Remain Silent in presumption of innocence until proven guilty to any psychiatric charge in a bona fide court of law.

The Right to Confrontations of any accusing testimony against the accused in virtue of The Sixth Amendment.

The Right to a Jury Trial provided in a timely way in accordance with The Sixth Amendment for any specified psychiatric accusation labeling being imposed, whether involving commitment or not.

The Right to clearly established and legally defined medically safe and beneficial therapeutic treatment to be imposed for legitimate psychiatric conditions.

The Right to Informed Consent in the presence of legal counsel concerning the discussion and patient awareness of adverse effects, reactions, and harmful side effects in short and long-term use of psychiatric chemicals involved with any psychiatric treatment to occur.

The Right To Refuse Treatment, and Against Forced Treatment on Medical Discretion, in the presence of legal counsel, except in matters As Prescribed By Law to be applied for necessary medical emergency procedure in concern to imminent crisis of hysteria, and for violent and disruptive behavior in being in threat to oneself or others requiring emergency medical treatment in judgment.

"ONE POWERFUL VOICE"

The Right against any form, including psychological, of cruel and inhumane treatment to occur, concerning physical, mental, or emotional abuse, to include electro-shock treatment, surgical procedure, and pharmaceutical experimentation, in virtue of The Eighth Amendment.

The Right to reasonable and soundly defined Statute of Limitations in established Legal Age Limits for the mandatory disclosure of previous psychiatric condition labeling history records, or to the disclosure of legally carried-out psychiatric commitment history records, based to the nature and severity and to the extent of such psychiatric conditions in legal stipulation and to the length of time of such conditions in interval, to be imposed for mandatory disclosure of records, not to be in excess of a reasonable and prudent time interval regarding the public removal of stigma and liability of such records history; which in most instances is to be worded, to any current treatment for any serious ongoing psychiatric condition, or to within the past three years concerning The Public Record.

-----Section 4: A Uniform Statute of Age Limits pertaining for employment application concerns and to government licensing matters is also to be instated for The History of Criminal Arrests and Convictions Records conveyed under Penal Law depending to the severity and nature of the crimes committed and not to exceed The Statute of Limitation for any crime or offense, if any. Infractions and Violations are to be absolved from the public record in three years, misdemeanors in five years, and most felony records after a span of ten years, depending on the nature in severity of offense not stipulated for to a greater time interval by a Court Of Law.

-----Section 5: It is also worded that no person shall be infringed upon or denied their Vested Right To Voting Citizenship in The United States due to conviction of a Felony Offense after said offense is duly discharged and the person is free and clear of any probation or parole.

And in all regard that it is the inherent nature of this Nation in standard of integrity and in principle of fair and humane conscience not to discriminate against any persons and to prevent any such discrimination from occurring. Which extends as well to the prevention of needless discrimination in bias of prejudice occurring to anyone on account of their prior criminal conviction or psychiatric history in this Nation, as it is deemed reasonable and prudent to dissolve these matters.

And that each person is to have The Right to a Self-Fulfilled Destiny instilled in the reverent promise of hope in opportunity of success and of healing recovery from stigma, and to the actualization of their highest potentials among the population of The United States to the outlook of being deemed and classified as good, solid, useful, and productive citizens in the eyes of society, and in the spirit of good will, without the infringement of bias, discrimination, and alienating prejudice of social stigma and concerning the hardship of sanctions to such records history being permanently attached to anyone in constant reminder of being negatively classified in downgrade of second class inferior citizenship, to be conceived in permanent ruin to their lives, as to stigma of social embarrassment, and with critical jeopardy of their livelihood and well-being affected, being imposed upon them.

The Second Chance Amendment is included in a series of ten new Amendments to our U.S. Constitution, featured as a major theme of The Epic Novel, "The Call To Order." Available at: http://www.lulu.com/content/paperback-book/the-call-to-order/6663590

"ONE POWERFUL VOICE"

9480 Princeton Square Blvd. S., #815
Jacksonville, FL 32256
January 9, 2011

Warren S. Lacy - Editor in Chief
Colonel, U.S. Army (Ret.)
Military Officer Magazine
201 North Washington Street
Alexandria, VA 22314-2539

Dear Colonel Lacy:

On the subject matter of, "Don't Ask – Don't Tell," let us state that: Homosexuality Constitutes, "Conduct Unbecoming." It is not allowed in the military, has never been allowed, and will never be allowed. So it seems now ridiculous that the sickness of homosexuality has taken over the entire United States Government and our Military, and who are now all demanding, under the threat of forceful retaliation, for Homosexuality to be made lawful to become totally out in the open about it, and even to the point of being allowed to be engaged in of their depraved acts in Military Barracks with impunity.

As I have found out from my research and psychoanalysis discussions with the men, that this sickness comes from the prevalence of Heroin Addiction that is rampant upon a society, and from the male's addictions to their own sticky orgasms acquired, without proper counseling in those matters, from puberty, to be conjured time after time in the days, and to their filthy habit of jerking themselves off on the toilet and sticking carrots up their rectums after their bowl movements and then licking off and sucking on the the fecal matter on the carrots while they indulge their fantasies and achieve their sensual orgasms as a pastime, and as to what that Homosexuality consists of in the literal sense.

And over time, of which pastime with their fantasies of anal and genital fixations in entertaining themselves in the mind with such thoughts attached to their orgasms that would then turn to rumination of mental fantasy around their orgasms to the arousal of the sickness of homosexuality with other men in their fantasies of imagination, and to their depraved desires for other forms of perverted eroticism to heighten the sensations their orgasm, and to the cult of Sado-Masochism, of needing to receive and to inflict pain, and in these times of Gay Pornography to the experience of cruel and sadistic Torture Snuff Movie Thrill Killing Homosexual Ritual Eroticism for pastime, as voyeurs, or as acting participants, and as a group for the pleasure of it; who are known to each other in their conspiratorial preying on the healthy population who become their hapless victims.

And of these Homosexuals, who hold the entire Nation Hostage In Coercion to their threats to engage in the use of the Tactical Terrorism of Drug Poison Warfare "To Out Their Foes" if their demands are not met. And such that has been and is the bane of men everywhere and the curse of all generations from time immemorial passed on, from father to son, and from one generation to the next in its ignorance, as the older men indoctrinate the younger ones at puberty into the practice of homosexuality. And from such memories of shame as no man can escape, that can't be made right by their en massing together as a group, or by banding together as a political/military front, to dominate the society. And who cannot escape from their shame in their efforts for acceptance as a Rights Movement to make themselves seem decent and respectable, which they can never hope to achieve.

"ONE POWERFUL VOICE"

So, let us say, that what is considered, and which literally is, depraved in a private sense as a pastime, is not therefore to be sanctified and to be given the glorified credence of acceptance by being named "Gay Pride," and worse to be condoned for by The U.S. Military as a Military Standard, just because Gay People want to be open about it, and of such depravity, to do it together. That somehow just does not make it work, does it?

Let us perceive it then and call it then, for what it is, that men do with each other, as Gay People, that they want to call, "Gay Pride," and, "Gay Solidarity," with themselves; that is as an utterly depraved condition for the men to fornicate with their partners in the rectum, can you imagine? and then to suck-off the fecal matter there on the phallus and to suck their perverted sexual partners off to climax in their mouths, and call it Gay Rights.

Let us also have sway with the reasoning that Gay People, and like the propaganda of the effeminate Jewish Rabbis presented to the American Public, as opposed to the Evil Types of Mafia Heroin and Pornography Jews, who are like the Evil Italian Mafias, going unchallenged by the American Nation; that Gay People as well are not all peaches and cream effeminate couples holding hands together in Gay Love and wanting society to accept them openly as normal and to sanctify their unholy and unhealthy sodomite relationships, as matrimony.

Some, and perhaps the mainstay of these Gay People are violently sadistic sodomites who are aggressively vicious, and many of whom are pornographers and pedophile criminals, and all are sick in their heads with personality disorders. Who, and like the concept of Drug Users banding together, cannot be trusted with Rational Command over Normal Personnel, and who would promote their Gay Comrades over the capabilities of Honorable Soldiers, and who would grant special privileges for Homosexual Favors, and punish certain others to try and force them to the will of their Homosexual Aberrations.

And perhaps that the words of The Holy Bible state for the matter most appropriately:

"If a man lies with a male as he lies with a woman, both of them have committed an abomination; they shall be put to death, their blood shall be upon them." Leviticus 20:13

And so it needs to be stated to these people, To Give It Up! the awful and depraved and filthy habit of their obnoxious homosexuality, like any other Bad Habit of Addiction, which Can Be Extinguished in time, and to become real men again in their own eyes.

Those desiring true inner peace of mind, and I would speak sensibly to everyone that way, therefore, needing to break the spell of this ill-fated cycle of Homosexuality, and to break the link in the chain of futility of their eternal Self-Loathing and Self-Flagellating Guilt of remorse that leads them to death, over their inability to control themselves and to conduct themselves properly as men, that is caused by the improper misuse of the sex organ, that such relentless depravity induces; who would do well to practice the discipline of self-control, and with it to extinguish in a real way their tendencies to jerk themselves off as a daily exercise, the crux of the matter, and with it, that Control of The Self, that all the urges of homosexuality will go away to be left healthy again with the inner strength of fulfilling the stature of a properly conducted life that the feeling of being in the control over one's body brings to be infused with the sane confidence necessary To Command.

Gary L. Koniz – Correspondent
Veterans Of The Vietnam War
MOAA No. 02786399

"ONE POWERFUL VOICE"

The Earth's Axis has dramatically shifted due to the melting of the polar ice caps and the redistribution of weight and mass over the surface of the planet and the influence of the gravitational pull of the moon. All of our Zodiac signs have changed.

A series of articles would be useful here, discussing what's in store for our U.S. Military Operations as we shift our emphasis from Wars to Humanitarian Relief Missions, to prepare for in advance of the event, as Catastrophic Floods, Drought, Severe Weather, as Tornadoes and Hurricanes, Earth Quakes, and other Natural Disasters Predicted, Tidal Waves and Solar Flares, wreck havoc on the planet. The Earth's Poles may even flip entirely of gargantuan proportions, as has happened several times in the past. Get the verifiable details at: http://www.divulgence.net/.

Your January Issue was very informative reading with a lot of detailed and direct helpful information, to lend a hand to, to chew on.

That was a very nice job and tactical approach to the idea of handling our problems together as an organization on your part to commend you for initiating. Let's see how it will all progresses for everyone to take and active interest in, and incidentally, looking to your magazine for direction and to you for solid corp inspiration.

Date: Thu, 20 Jan 2011 07:22:13 -0500
From: WarrenL@moaa.org
To: gary.koniz@hotmail.com

Dear Mr. Koniz:

Thanks for your note. The magazine's Editorial Review Committee will consider your suggestion.
Please understand that – with 360,000 actively engaged members – we receive many excellent story ideas. Unfortunately, we have space to print only a few. It's a highly competitive environment!

Best wishes, and thanks for your support of Military Officers Association of America.

Warren
******
Warren S. Lacy
Colonel, U.S. Army (Ret.)
Director, Publications
Editor in Chief, *Military Officer* magazine
Military Officers Association of America (MOAA)
201 N Washington St, Alexandria, VA 22314-2539
(800) 234-6622 x105; (703) 838-8105
editor@moaa.org www.moaa.org

One Powerful Voice.®   For every officer at every stage of life and career.

"ONE POWERFUL VOICE"

Dear Colonel Lacy,

Thank you for the reassuring note of confidence, and ever appreciated for your way of softening approach in psychology to everyone to understand and appreciate for the competitive spirit of the initiative ideas that you are beset with each month to have to decide on and relative to the temper and the format of each month's focus, depending. And in such regard of focus, that I am curious though, in your mention of "lag time" in your Editor's December Issue Remarks, concerning submissions, as to just how much specific time is it to allow for in consideration when submitting or in querying an article? And would it be possible to learn what each month's focus of interest is dedicated to, so that one may structure articles to suite the need of the month's dedication.

What I would personally like to see, would be for Military Officer Magazine to become the voice of Rational Command concerning the problems that we are facing together as a Nation and as The American People, and importantly to engage the pragmatic issues of problem solving together, in putting our heads together, as One Powerful Voice, for the project, and to the successful managing of our Society, pertaining for social attitudes to appreciate resolving, and for the proper managing of our Government Affairs. With you at the helm, as to say of the great statesman and commander that you are in the lead of the intent, and with the input and direct involvement of all 360,000 actively engaged members to draw solutions from, for us as a group to be able to make things happen in the right way here.

I do Thank you always for allowing me the personal time with you to contribute, and even to be looked over by you and your staff is a means of influence to an end, because the ideas that are presented lodge there in your heads to be drawn from and relied on at some point in time, or even for someone just to have formed an opinion because of an idea put forth that passed through them to form a judgment with their point of view is important. Your own ideas expressed in your column are that way of mighty influence and which are taken to heart by your many devoted and admiring readers to follow out and importantly to act on.

Sincerely and Best Regards,

Gary L. Koniz – Correspondent
Veterans Of The Vietnam War
MOAA No. 02786399

What you need to understand about The Drug War, and about the concept of Mafia Pornography coinciding to it, that is being allowed and even encourage to flourish here on both accounts; is that it involves us, the citizenry, in a Real War, attacking us with the condition of Drug Warfare, at close range involving our "Loved Ones" and "Family Members," and to the Physical and Mental Maladies that such a Warfare induces, and for the Psychiatric Intake of the population of that regard to be finished off by legally to their demise with Lethal Psychiatric Style Pharmacy while the Legal Authorities motivate the Afflicted Population into its Intake and "Look-On." That, for the sake of our lives and the lives of our loved ones at stake, that needs to be intervened to properly and in a lifesaving timely way, that we, as civilians are unable to intervene to ourselves on our own to defend our lives about. And who therefore have to complain directly to the authorities, who in certain instances may be themselves involved with the criminal conspiracy.

"ONE POWERFUL VOICE"

And not only do we have to contend with the issue of Drugs and Pornography in their raw motives of viciousness of foul play occurring to us, but also which involves certain Ethnic and Racial Motives For War using the corruptions and addictions of Drugs and Pornography as a War Machine against the innocent population, "to whittle us down," inch by inch, in a sustained and dramatically forcible Attack taking place at a glacier speed in slow motion over centuries, and against the larger mass of an unsuspecting host population in objective to defeat it by being systematically replacing it and which goes on barely perceptibly. That involves "The Intake" and "Initiation" of the population into the use of Hard Drugs and Pornography, (to what they have to prove "Their Loyalty To," by murdering a family member or friend, or loved one, by Drug Warfare, to obtain their drug supply, and otherwise to be blackmailed and coerced in extortion to the behest of their Drug Suppliers to do their bidding, whatever that may be, (as to indicate as to whoever is supplying their addicting drugs to someone, having The Power over the craving of their addictions, to involve them with The Active Warfare Arm of their Enemy Aggressions.

And on the topic of The Pornography Mafia that once they have anyone in their grip, (and they begin very young with the homosexuals on the young boys beginning at the age of puberty, and with the young girls too that way who their addict mothers initiate into child pornography,) to what that they become "The Property" of the Pornography Ring for all time to come after that and from what they can never escape from. So that, The Pornography Ring, (and who all know who each other are to themselves, but not so the "outsiders" to,) can essentially "gang-up" on anybody and do them in with foul play, and that is especially sinister and lethal to the households; the parents, relatives, and the siblings, involved with these individuals, to able to "Hit" with Drugs and Chemicals and Poisons, for the sake of the Ethnic or Racial Motives of the advancing Army. And that is particularly heart-felt regarding the plight of the young girls who are inducted and who become the prisoners of a Pornography Mafia when it comes time for them to fall in love and get married, who then have to "bump-off" their boyfriends or husbands at the behest.

And let us here have The Reasoning Right about The Miscegenation of the Black Heroin Mafia and concerning their sense of Inter-Racial Marriage being used as a means to Wage War By Assimilation of The White Race to create The Race of Mulattoes in The Islamic Design of Conquest, by coercive means of forcible aggressions against the White Females, involving their entrapment to the use of Heroin and Cocaine, and other means of White Slavery Prostitution, to attack the White Males by with Drugs and Poisons.

Subject: RE: Article Series Query?
Date: Fri, 21 Jan 2011 06:49:20 -0500
From: WarrenL@moaa.org
To: gary.koniz@hotmail.com
Dear Mr. Koniz:

Our guidelines for writers are posted at http://www.moaa.org/pubs_guidelines.htm . Generally, feature articles are scheduled six months in advance. Features are usually locked in three months in advance of the issue date. We typically don't focus monthly content on narrow themes. Having a very diverse membership, we like each issue to cover a variety of topics that would appeal to readers with different interests.

"ONE POWERFUL VOICE"

Best wishes,
Warren

Warren S. Lacy
Colonel, U.S. Army (Ret.)
Director, Publications
Editor in Chief, *Military Officer* magazine
Military Officers Association of America (MOAA)
201 N Washington St, Alexandria, VA 22314-2539
(800) 234-6622 x105; (703) 838-8105
editor@moaa.org www.moaa.org
One Powerful Voice.®   For every officer at every stage of life and career.

Dear Colonel Lacy,

Thank you, Colonel Lacy for the information. I will certainly look over your website as you recommend. In the meantime let us all put our heads together and solve the problem of The National Debt and the overall Economy of our United States in first priority of business. Just running a series of articles saying how the Nation's current and future economic woes will negatively affect our Military Benefits doesn't satisfy the argument of how "to fix" the problem. To do that we need as an Organization to come up with the solution and to take matters in hand to Take Over and to Successfully Manage the government to ensure our imminent survival, and to prevent The United States from being mis-managed again in the future. Your personal time with me is appreciated.

Sincerely,
Gary Koniz

Dear Colonel Lacy: January 24, 2011

    With all due reverence in respect to you, but I wrote that letter entitled, Don't Ask, Don't Tell, to you personally, for the shock value of its effect. And I hope that it did impact you, and to those to whom you may have passed it on to; as the refined sentiments of language discussing such depravity of what constitutes being a Gay Soldier, of what it really is, doesn't seem to register properly to frankly discuss the subject as we see it, to have a sensible understanding of coming to terms of an organizational decision about it.

    You don't like the language associated with the description of what precisely that the Gay Homosexual Activities consist of, (which your General Council Major Joseph Lynch stated to me of such language: "that does not comport with the fundamental Standards of Decency, and as such is not up to the Professional Standards of The MOAA,) but yet you condone, as an organization, and as Soldiers in defense of a Nation, to uphold to the views of a Liberal Homosexual Government in power, to the praise and reinforcement of the outright sodomy and

"ONE POWERFUL VOICE"

fallacious activities of Homosexuality themselves, (that are as clearly, "Conduct Unbecoming," as we see it; as the language describing it.) And which you as an organization don't have the strength to condemn, and are now allowing, to the weakening of our Military's Moral Fiber and our Ability To Defend, to be dividing our military over the antagonisms of Gay and Non-Gay personnel, to what that you wish to embrace the concept of depravity and perverted Homosexuality as a Normal Aspect of Military Life, as The Position of The MOAA. And which doesn't quite move you, does it, to state for it in a benign way of holding hands that way of skirting the actual sense and meaning of it, of what being Gay really is; which is a totally revolting and ugly concept.

Second, on the issue of my eligibility to your MOAA Membership that your General Counsel Major Joseph Lynch brought up, to point out to you that I asked you as a writer if I could subscribe to your Military Officer Magazine, to view its contents over time and discuss on the topics being brought to your readers' attention, (and which I have been doing.) That you told me to go ahead and do, and which I did, and for what that the membership and assigned membership number came with the subscription. It was not my intent to deceive anybody. If you want to change anything about my status, please do so. Cancel my subscription if you want. You are really not into taking up with any business of mine, as I have judged to date, and over the period of five years or more now, and otherwise to be ignored other than in a placating way of passing my information on to a dead end, (and concerning the critical defense of our Nations Combat Soldiers from Psychiatric desecration and suicide, and concerning the ongoing Drug Chemical Warfare to what that The Gays are a part of, having vowed "to out" their foes.) I had, and still do have, many serious issues on-going to take up with you about our Nation's Defense and about the Sound Rational Functioning of our U.S. Military as a Journalist Correspondent.

Gary L. Koniz – Correspondent
Veterans Of The Vietnam War
MOAA No. 02786399

Franklin L. Hagenbeck - Superintendent
Lieutenant General, US Army
United States Military Academy
West Point, NY 10996-5000

Dear Commander Lacy:

We, as a Society, are not going to get at the nature of the sexual error of what is bothering everybody without talking about what it is, and like any problem to discuss, to indicate ways of what to do about it to correct any misfortune besetting the situation. Both the Ancient Greeks and the Roman Civilizations fell to Homosexuality and, morally bankrupt, and that is in having no pride and self-esteem in themselves and lacking their manly fortitude and family values, having become immoral and pagan in their nature, were overrun and conquered over by Barbarian Hordes. As History is our teacher. And with that to ask you what I wrote about the sexual nature needing discussion that you found to be so offensive as to reprimand and censor me about. And I know it had nothing to do with retirement benefits being cut on the focus of your topics.

But and especially so to do with the psychiatric disabling injustice matter, to the loss of a travesty of American Combat Veterans Lives in injustice, as I have detailed extensively to you

"ONE POWERFUL VOICE"

these past many years, with lives "On Line" each day for its swift resolution, and with lives having "Been Lost" due to the inaction on the part of the MOAA and its members, that I feel you need not to remain as "flip" about what it is I have been discussing, with you to be passing it on as a "competitive market item," and not to be siding with it to the nature of its dire seriousness to be directing both the resources of the MOAA and the Military Officer Magazine about, and 360,000 Members strong, and as a collective body to Intervene strongly worded in the case matter at hand.

And for what that I am not going to let you pass on it either, in skirting your military responsibility with the issues of our case, ethically, morally, and tactically speaking, in defense of American Veterans Lives, to remark that you will always know that we asked you directly and personally for your assistance and support.

Sincerely,
Gary Koniz

"ONE POWERFUL VOICE"

9480 Princeton Square Blvd. S., #815
Jacksonville, FL 32256
February 18, 2011

Warren S. Lacy - Editor in Chief
Colonel, U.S. Army (Ret.)
Military Officer Magazine
201 North Washington Street
Alexandria, VA 22314-2539

Dear Colonel Lacy:

I received your letter of 01/20/11 in from Major General Joseph G. Lunch, (Ret.) the MOAA's General Counsel and Corporate Secretary terminating my membership in the MOAA and also terminating my subscription to Military Officer Magazine; to what I really have no problem with the idea, as for the MOAA as an organization, but for what that you gave me the go ahead to do with in the first place, as a Journalist, and Acting In The Public Health Service as a Drug War Correspondent, and Psychiatric Health Care Professional in aid to our Nation's Veterans, to review the magazine that I take exception, and with the reasoning for his doing so, which violates my First Amendment Rights.

And with apology to you for needing to bring the subject up again, but I still have not received a formal wording in apology as I requested for the mistakenly applied censure of my material, on the topic of Don't Ask, Don't Tell. The censorship for what that had to my use of certain mature adult discussion content on what precisely the term homosexual had to state to do with; and which was wholly taken out of context. Which censorship, suborning libel, impugned the honorable intentions of my good character, in labeling my scholarly treatise on the need for homosexuality Reform to be "not in comportment with the fundamental standards of decency and good taste befitting a profession organization;" and which undermined all the sincere efforts that I have made through the years with you and with the MOAA to resolve the tragic case of the travesty of Psychiatric Malfeasance concerning the fate of our Returning Combat Veterans; and which reprimand also in error discredited me in implying that I falsely misrepresented myself as an Officer in applying for a subscription to Military Officer Magazine, that came with its membership with The MOAA, which you personally gave me the go ahead to do in urging me to subscribe to, as I had only asked you if I could get a copy of your magazine, as a Journalist, to look it over for content reference. And for what request in response from you that has not been forthcoming to date. What is like the way of our government's behavior in general, when confronted by something in its path that it needs to correct, in taking the evasive way-out, to stone-wall and ignore the complaint into submission until it either goes away, or the complainant is forced to hire the expense of an attorney to press the judgment in court.

That being said, I have tried hard to straighten out with you over the course of time some of the bad situations occurring concerning our American Policies on Social Diplomacy in attempting to shape and to deal with our command attitudes toward Drugs, with its Drug Warfare coinciding, Feminist/Housewives Drug Sabotage, (as it affects our Veterans and in regards to the American Male entity overall,) Racial and Ethnic Mafia Wars involved with the use of Drugs Trafficking and Sabotage, Pornography (in perilous undermine of our Nation's Morality, Miscegenation, Homosexuality, Psychiatric Reform, (and especially so to do with the psychiatric

"ONE POWERFUL VOICE"

disabling injustice matter, to the loss of our American Combat Veterans Lives in tragedy, as I have detailed extensively to you,) the American Economy, and our American Heritage and Sovereignty; To Reform these critical social agendas and not to continue on to appease and to placate them to the eventual results of blood wars outright; (and to cite example of what is happening now in Egypt regarding Social Uprisings of what can happen here in The United States if certain blood feuds are not settled properly and promptly,) that we urgently need to deal with.

There are, and have been, some very serious issues which we need to get resolved with The V.A., as I wrote you personally over, and to the life threatening setting; having to do with Thorazine Treatment, and other types of Strong Anti-Psychotic Tranquillizers, being administered without concern to the safety of the lives of each of the Veterans being exposed to such treatment; and as well, having to do with "Improper Routine Labeling" of our Veterans with "Mental Disorders" that they do not have, (and without proper Legal Clarification, as I asked you for,) for the sake of filling out report forms to be "put down" where it says, "reason for admission," needing a Diagnosis to justify the patient's being allowed to remain in The V.A. Health Care System; (which sadly isn't for the rigors of being homeless and malnourished as a result of their affiliation with the killer side of combat duty for the sake of the Nation,) and who otherwise are normal people suffering from what anyone would suffer from in remorse of combat; of having to kill and to maim other human beings, and to profound grief in suffering for the loss of their countrymen in witness to deaths off their friends, and for trauma of experienced tragic events, (the same as civilians faced in the aftermath of 9/11, and who weren't banished to subterranean agonies of the Mental Wards and forced to endure deadly Chemo-Treatment for their being victims of a tragedy, but not so of our Proud Veterans who served their Country At Arms,) and as a consequence to be left feared and rejected by society, suffering with homelessness and joblessness and with having marital problems, (as other people do, who need only counseling, "To Fix," what the problems are, and Not Chemo-Treatment To Wipe Them Out!,) as a consequence of their military bearing in being left estranged from their civilian counterparts in society and only needing to be mended over properly; with Bed Rest, Convalescence, Counseling, Nurturing Therapy, and Good Nutrition, and to be shown respect and caring support, to heal. Which instead, you are ruining their lives over, permanently, and with many, to suicide, for your diagnoses, labeling, and pharmacy.

You need to be informed that the Rules of Conduct have changed by Formality of Congressional Oversight Committee in adjudication over the case matter of Psychiatric Malfeasance; that we are no longer appealing politely in good order about in the former meaning of bureaucratic protocol, but in the straightforward language of good common sense by Direct Military Order, TO CEASE AND DESIST, with the mismanagement of psychiatric; and to do what we have detailed for you to do thus far to the Veterans Administration in your charge to carry out the necessary reforms in protection and safeguard of our Nations Veterans. Regarding in first sense of meaning to the altering of the stigmatizing nomenclature of the "Psychiatric," Mental Wards, to the benign setting of; "Bed Rest, Convalescence, Counseling, and Therapy," in Wards to be named, "Seclusion Recovery;" that is furthermore to be protected by a strict protocol of "Safe Treatment," to be conducted, stressing Medical Nutrition, Rest and Recuperation, and to the Discontinued Routine Use of Disabling and Proven Harmful Anti-Psychotic Chemo-Treatment. You need to do the job promptly, as this is not a "Cover-Up" matter to be tolerated, but a Corrections Issue; involving the safety and lives of our fellow Veterans.

"ONE POWERFUL VOICE"

The Psychiatric Medical/Pharmacy Industry no longer has "the power" to diagnose and to treat-destroy anyone they personally choose to with any drug chemical, surgery, or electro-insulin shock treatment they arbitrarily determine, and with Sovereign Immunity from civil and criminal prosecution as is currently built in to their present practices. And that they are no longer to have the personal tyranny of power over the freedom and the lives of our Veterans, (in Captive Market Condition,) to confine anyone they choose to indefinitely and to set the terms of their release, contingent to continued treatment with drugs, under the current terms of Mental Hygiene Law regarding Commitment and forced treatment, without any Substantive Due Process of Law and in the name of Medicine, as is being carried out against our Veterans, Communist-Purge Style, in Rights Violations.

And for the record, that according to a news release of recent statistics, 75,000 Veterans are today homeless, of whom 40,000 of these are disabled, and all soon to be made into psychiatrics for the sake of their homelessness, with being then labeled as being psychiatric, for the sake of needing a label associated in order for them to be provided with nurturing care and shelter, with no provisions being made by The Veterans Administration to address this area of crisis, of Veterans Homelessness, and Joblessness, with one to care and no one of a military posture to respond to their aid in appropriate defense as it should be. This issue does not end by ignoring the problem along the lines Officer Class Solidarity. All the meetings, and seminars, and magazine articles in discussions about the seminars and meeting on your part, "talking at the problem," and arguing for more funding and programs, does no good unless the problem itself is solved.

Which for the record to add also, that there are all too many numerous cases to cite; of flagrant medical malpractice, medical fraud, kickback complicity with the pharmaceutical companies, and medical moral corruption involving political, pornographic, and drug conspiracies, to organized crime. The Constitutional Rights to Due Process cannot be allowed to continue to be abridged in the face of such corruption just because the legal rendering of Mental Hygiene happens to fall under Medical Non-Criminal Civil Law.

And with all due reverence in respect to you, but I wrote the frankly descriptive article entitled, Don't Ask, Don't Tell, for the shock value of its effect. As the refined wording of language of the perverted depravity of what constitutes being a Gay Soldier, of what it really is, doesn't seem to register properly to objectively discuss the subject as it is, to have a sensible understanding of coming to terms of an organizational decision about it.

You take offense with the language associated with the description of what precisely it is that the Gay Homosexual Activities consist of, (which your General Council Major General Joseph Lynch (Ret,) states: "that the language and tone does not comport with the fundamental Standards of Decency of a Professional Association.) But yet you condone, as an organization, for the Military, and as Soldiers in defense of a Nation, to uphold to the views of a Depraved Homosexual Front in power, to the praise and reinforcement of the outright sodomy and other perverted activities of Homosexuality, (that are as clearly, "Conduct Unbecoming," as we see it; as the language describing it,)

Gary Koniz - Correspondent
Veterans of the Vietnam War

"ONE POWERFUL VOICE"

9480 Princeton Square Blvd. S., #815
Jacksonville, FL 32256
(904) 730-2055
March 26, 2011

Warren S. Lacy - Editor in Chief
Colonel, U.S. Army (Ret.)
Military Officer Magazine
201 North Washington Street
Alexandria, VA 22314-2539

Dear Colonel Lacy:

   I did write and apologize to you for the misunderstanding of the frank content of my discussion of one of my correspondences on the nature of the homosexuality concern in national magnitude. That I asked you for "permission to speak freely," about, during the melee over your magazine's and the Military Officers Association of America's, (MOAA's,) acceptance the government's overriding command to our military of forcing the inclusion of the mentally sick homosexual "gay" element of sadistic perverts into the ranks of our military to harass and intimidate and offend the normal moral sensibilities and routine in manly pride of our military life, that we need to take a united stand against.
   From Wikipedia, the free encyclopedia: Sodomy laws in the United States, which outlawed a variety of sexual acts, were historically pervasive. While they often targeted sexual acts between persons of the same sex, many statutes employed definitions broad enough to outlaw certain sexual acts between persons of different sexes as well, sometimes even married persons. During the 20th century, the gradual liberalization of American sexual mores led to the elimination of many sodomy laws. The Supreme Court upheld the constitutionality of these laws in Bowers v. Hardwick in 1986, but reversed this decision in 2003 with Lawrence v. Texas, invalidating sodomy laws in fourteen states (Alabama, Florida, Idaho, Kansas, Louisiana, Michigan, Missouri, Mississippi, North Carolina, Oklahoma, South Carolina, Texas, Utah, and Virginia). Members of the U.S. Armed Forces may still be prosecuted for sodomy under special criteria.
   Statute Section 47 - Uniform Code of Military Justice, Subchapter X, Punative Articles- Sec. 925. Art. 125. Sodomy
   (a) Any person subject to this chapter who engages in unnatural carnal copulation with another person of the same or opposite sex or with an animal is guilty of sodomy. Penetration, however slight, is sufficient to complete the offense.
   (b) Any person found guilty of sodomy shall be punished as a court-martial may direct.
   And which judgment on the part of our government is also to offend the nation's morals in the condoning of criminally illegal homosexual activities of sodomy and other actions considered in the standards of normal human psychology in our society to be depraved, (and what that I pointed out in my letter to you personally about,) and in objection to your passive acceptance of these activities to set the standard of deviant character behavior in our nation's youth for the mothers of our nation to regard our military as a corrupter of their children, by its abject acceptance of gay homosexuality.

"ONE POWERFUL VOICE"

This impasse of a situation about the homosexual issue and as for other Veterans matters of consequence to us, needs to be cleared-up; to point out and to emphasize that we are in a war for our lives against us over these unchallenged propaganda issues aggression.

We also need to mention to you and to the MOAA for immediate response, that we had a recent breach of National Veterans Security on the Monday night, March 14, 2010 edition of the T.V. show, "Harry's Law," entitled "The Fragile Beast,' (and "yet" another breach of this issue in its methodical, systematic, and relentless negative propagandizing being perpetrated deliberately by an "un-named" entity; and whether being done by the Gay Hollywood Element, of by a Foreign or Domestic National Enemy in control of Hollywood Productions,) that is designed to create "fear" and "mistrust" in the eyes of our civilian population toward the returned from combat Veterans. Who the nation is being systematically programmed to regard as deranged and irrational killers by these distorted portrayals of our Veterans on these popular T.V. shows, for the purpose to make our Veterans into homeless men and eventually into psychiatric patients to be disposed of with zombie-like chemicals such as Thorazine and other deadly Psychiatric Drugs.

The episode of "Harry's Law," depicted a Situation in which a Veteran who was recently returned from the war in Iraq, was holding his estranged and "Illegal Latino Alien," wife captive in a locked room in the basement of his house because the woman had left him for another Illegal Alien man due to the Veteran's deranged and abusive behavior as a result of his Post Traumatic Stress; which the Veteran said he was doing because he wanted keep his wife from leaving him and also that holding her prisoner was better than killing her for being unfaithful to him, which he stated he felt like doing because of his Post Traumatic Stress Condition. The lawyer on Harry's Law was urged not to contact the police, by the Illegal Alien boyfriend, in solicitation of public sympathy to harbor aliens, because the Illegal Aliens would be deported if the police were called in.

The Harry's Law show also then stated that thirty percent of the Veterans returning from the wars in Iraq were suffering from aggressive behavior and homicidal urges symptomatic of Posttraumatic Stress; and which the show convinced the Veteran about "to get help" for his Post Traumatic Stress at the excellent facilities of V.A. Hospital, and in other words to be made into a Zombie there at the V.A. by the Thorazine Treatment.

The show also featured the conspiracy of acceptance of black-white fornication, Miscegenation, and of the fostering of the continuing of this interbreeding absorption idea and annihilation of the White Race to our Total Extinction, here in America, to cease to exist, (and like what happened in the Sub Continent of India over seven thousand years ago, only here.) Which, Harry's Law did offer an "objection to" on the grounds that the Black Man was "too young" to be dating "the older" White Lady. That is now one of the "story lines" of the show. We need a Military Policy Statement from your magazine to deal with this and with the other crisis issues named. Budget cuts effecting Veterans Benefits aren't the only concerns to be stood up for in call for mass action of the MOAA.

You can contact CNBC about the Harry's Law show at the following: Brian Steel, Vice President, Public Relations, 201-735-4778 | Brian.Steel@nbcuni.com

Gary L. Koniz – Correspondent
Veterans Of The Vietnam War

"ONE POWERFUL VOICE"

9480 Princeton Square Blvd. S., #815
Jacksonville, FL 32256
March 5, 2011

Norb Ryan Jr. – President
Vice Admiral, USN-Ret.
Military Officers Association Of America
201 North Washington Street
Alexandria, VA 22314-2539

Dear Admiral Ryan:

And with all due reverence in respect to you, but I wrote the frankly descriptive article entitled, Don't Ask, Don't Tell, essentially for the shock value of its effect in manly exasperation. As the refined and polite wording of skirted language of the perverted depravity of what constitutes being a Gay Soldier, of what it really is, doesn't seem to register properly to objectively discuss the subject as it is, to have a sensible and realistic understanding of coming to terms with its nature as an organizational judgment about it.

I also wrote the article in the stance of a doctor administering to a grave abnormality in our American, or in any, Society, and of any age, of the subject of male homosexuality to deal with, and to the nature of right and wrong about it, and to provide instructional and constructive and objective criticism about it so that those who are still suffering their affliction with the perverted side of their humanity in futility, will man-up and take up their yoke of personal responsibility to correct the condition within themselves and not to be banding together in forming up perverted armies to further the condition along in their efforts to make it seem acceptable, to themselves, and to society, by forcing it upon us.

And which we have called for them "to extinguish" that side of themselves instead, for their own good, and for the good of those around them in the trashed sense, who too as well are forced to suffer from the physical and psychological effects of their being "Gay," (and for the sake of needing a euphemistic label associated to their perversity in order for them to be accepted and to be provided with nurturing care and shelter,) by Society, and by The Military; which They Shall Not Be, Not In This Era, nor any other; and forever to remain in the terms of previous eras to it, of being in the meaning of the Homosexuality Condemned by God, as an utterly immoral and depraved Abomination. That we are asking them who are abandoned to the homosexuality to relinquish the habit and to be men again in their own eyes and in our eyes who have to live with them in sufferance.

Second, on the issue of my eligibility to your MOAA Membership that your General Counsel Major General Joseph Lynch has severed, to point out to you that I asked Editor Warren Lacy as a writer if I could obtain a copy of Military Officer Magazine, to view its contents and discuss on the topics being brought to your readers attention, (in Veterans Advocate Cases;) to what he told me that I could subscribe to, and which I did. And for what that the membership and assigned membership number came with the subscription.

Gary L. Koniz – Correspondent
Veterans Of The Vietnam War
MOAA No. 02786399

"ONE POWERFUL VOICE"

9480 Princeton Square Blvd. S., #815
Jacksonville, FL 32256
December 14, 2011

Warren S. Lacy - Editor in Chief
Colonel, U.S. Army (Ret.)
Military Officer Magazine
201 North Washington Street
Alexandria, VA 22314-2539

Dear Colonel Lacy:

In wishing you the very best for this Season's Holiday Spirit, to add that words cannot convey my gratitude for your support over the years and for your involvement with the case of our Nation's Veterans, brave soldiers of our Nation's Wars, who are left suffering in the aftermath of their patriotic service, to be properly cared for concerning their period of adjustment, and to defend how our Veterans are treated concerning; social rejection, persecutions, and biases, due to hysterical public fears about them; (who are regarded and feared by the private sector to be trained killers,) interrelated with Shell Shock, Post Traumatic Stress, Depression, and other Emotional Disorders, and To Suicide; for our Veterans to be removed from The Psychiatric Rosters about and placed on; Bed Rest/ Convalescence, Nutrition, Counseling and Therapy, without use of Disabling Chemicals.

And, in asking you and our Nation's Military Command if you would kindly support me in my bid for Election to The U.S. House of Representatives 2012 to Florida's 4th CD, to indicate that I would thereby be able to "Take Care of Our Urgent Military Business."

Afghanistan needs the total destruction and the preventive removal of the entire Opium Poppy Crop/Trade, and with it to the ideological and literal defeat of the Taliban Itself; with the destruction of The Poppy Crop, which is the motive for its existence, (the Opium Crop and its Revenues of War,) that has been destroying The U.S. and Europe.

Also to be severely dealt with are the many ongoing, "unconventional under-currents of clandestine wars," and not so subtle, that are threatening us in peril needing to defend against; of the nature of; Racial, Ethnic, Religious, Ideological, Economic, Moral, and Drug War - Drug Warfare, Fronts, (to include the Political Fascism of Drug Related Crime;) that we have to formidably acknowledge as being threats to our Nation's security to confront and defend our Nation against even though they are not being waged with bullets, to take a stand over, with the meaning we undertake with the Oath of Allegiance, "To Defend The United States Against All Enemies Foreign and Domestic." That begins with the absolute necessity of Military Intervention against The Drug Trade and Illegal Immigration and in Defense of American Sovereignty. And, To Defend The Nation's Economy and the Nation's Standards of Morality, (and against the toleration of moral gay liberal degeneration and pornography.) And that we need to have an Intelligent Policy on Miscegenation; (to protect The Races and Ethnic Denominations also from obliteration.)

Gary L. Koniz – Correspondent
Veterans Of The Vietnam War
MOAA No. 02786399

"ONE POWERFUL VOICE"

Chlorpromazine
From Wikipedia, the free encyclopedia

Chlorpromazine (as chlorpromazine hydrochloride, abbreviated **CPZ**; marketed in the United States as **Thorazine** and elsewhere as **Largactil** or **Megaphen**) is a dopamine antagonist of the typical antipsychotic class of medications possessing additional antiadrenergic, antiserotonergic, anticholinergic and antihistaminergic properties used to treat schizophrenia. First synthesized on December 11, 1950, chlorpromazine was the first drug developed with specific antipsychotic action, and would serve as the prototype for the phenothiazine class of drugs, which later grew to comprise several other agents. The introduction of chlorpromazine into clinical use has been described as the single greatest advance in psychiatric care, dramatically improving the prognosis of patients in psychiatric hospitals worldwide. The availability of antipsychotic drugs curtailed indiscriminate use of electroconvulsive therapy and psychosurgery, and was one of the driving forces behind the deinstitutionalization movement.

Chlorpromazine works on a variety of receptors in the central nervous system, producing anticholinergic, antidopaminergic, antihistaminic, and weak antiadrenergic effects. Both the clinical indications and side effect profile of CPZ are determined by this broad action: its anticholinergic properties cause constipation, sedation, and hypotension, and help relieve nausea. It also has anxiolytic (anxiety-relieving) properties. Its antidopaminergic properties can cause extrapyramidal symptoms such as akathisia (restlessness, aka the 'Thorazine shuffle' where the patient walks almost constantly, despite having nowhere to go due to mandatory confinement, and takes small, shuffling steps) and dystonia. It is known to cause tardive dyskinesia, which can be irreversible. In recent years, chlorpromazine has been largely superseded by the newer atypical antipsychotics, which are usually better tolerated, and its use is now restricted to fewer indications. In acute settings, it is often administered as a syrup, which has a faster onset of action than tablets, and can also be given by intramuscular injection. IV administration is very irritating and is not advised; its use is limited to severe hiccups, surgery, and tetanus.

Adverse effects

The main side effects of chlorpromazine are due to its anticholinergic properties; these effects overshadow and counteract, to some extent, the extrapyramidal side effects typical of many early generation antipsychotics. These include; akinesia (inability to initiate movement) and akathisia (inability to remain motionless,) sedation, slurred speech, dry mouth, constipation, urinary retention and possible lowering of seizure threshold. Appetite may be increased with resultant weight gain, and Glucose tolerance may be impaired. It lowers blood pressure with accompanying dizziness. Memory loss and amnesia have also been reported. Chlorpromazine, which has sedating effects, will increase sleep time when given at high doses or when first administered, although tolerance usually develops. Antipsychotics do not alter sleep cycles or REM sleep.

Dermatological reactions are frequently observed. In fact three types of skin disorders are observed: hypersensitivity reaction, contact dermatitis, and photosensitivity. During long-term therapy of schizophrenic patients chlorpromazine can induce abnormal pigmentation of the skin. This can be manifested as gray-blue pigmentation in regions exposed to sunlight.

There are adverse effects on the reproductive system. Phenothiazines are known to cause hyperprolactinaemia leading to amenorrhea, cessation of normal cyclic ovarian function, loss of libido, occasional hirsutism, false positive pregnancy tests, and long-term risk of osteoporosis in women. The effects of hyperprolactinemia in men are gynaecomastia, lactation, impotence, loss of libido, and hypospermatogenesis. These antipsychotics have significant effects on gonadal hormones including significantly lower levels of estradiol and progesterone in women whereas men display significantly lower levels of testosterone and DHEA when undergoing antipsychotic drug treatment compared to controls. Antipsychotic drugs may cause priapism, a pathologically prolonged and painful penile erection, which is usually unassociated with sexual desire or intercourse. Although this effect is rare it is a potentially serious complication that can lead to permanent impotence and other serious complications.

Even therapeutically low doses may trigger seizures in susceptible patients, such as those with an abnormally low genetically determined seizure threshold, presumably by lowering the seizure threshold. The incidence of the first unprovoked seizure in the general population is from 0.07 to 0.09%, but in patients treated with commonly used antipsychotic drugs it reportedly ranges from 0.1 to 1.5%. In overdose, the risk reaches 4 to 30%. This wide variability among studies may be due to methodological differences. The risk is greatly influenced by the individual's inherited seizure threshold, and particularly by a history of epilepsy, brain damage or other conditions. The triggering of seizures by antipsychotic drugs is generally agreed to be a dose-dependent adverse effect.

Tardive dyskinesia and akathisia are less commonly seen with chlorpromazine than they are with high potency typical antipsychotics such as haloperidol or trifluoperazine, and some evidence suggests that, with conservative dosing, the incidence of such effects for chlorpromazine may be comparable to that of newer agents such as risperidone or olanzapine.

A particularly severe side effect is neuroleptic malignant syndrome, which can be fatal.[20] Other reported side effects are rare, though severe; these include a reduction in the number of white blood cells—referred to as leukopenia—or, in extreme cases, even agranulocytosis, which may occur in 0.01% of patients and lead to death via uncontrollable infections and/or sepsis. Chlorpromazine is also known to accumulate in the eye—in the posterior corneal stroma, lens, and uveal tract. Because it is a phototoxic compound, the potential exists for it to cause cellular damage after light exposure. Research confirms a significant risk of blindness from continued use of chlorpromazine, as well as other optological defects such as color blindness and benign pigmentation of the cornea.

Cardiotoxic effects of phenothiazines in overdose are similar to that of the tricyclic antidepressants. Cardiac arrhythmia and apparent sudden death have been associated with therapeutic doses of chlorpromazine, however they are rare cases. The sudden cardiovascular collapse is attributable to ventricular dysrhythmia. Supraventricular tachycardia may also develop. Patients on chlorpromazine therapy exhibit abnormalities on the electrocardiographic T and U waves. These major cardiac arrhythmias that are lethal are a potential hazard even in patients without heart disease who are receiving therapeutic doses of antipsychotic drugs. In order to quantify the risk of cardiac complications to patients receiving therapeutic doses of phenothiazines a prospective clinical trial is suggested.

"ONE POWERFUL VOICE"

9480 Princeton Square Blvd. S., #815
Jacksonville, FL 32256
(904) 730-2055
July 12, 2008

Franklin L. Hagenbeck
Lieutenant General, US Army
Superintendent
United States Military Academy
West Point, NY 10996-5000

Dear General Hagenbeck:

Respectfully, I was wondering perhaps if you would find it in your sentiments at this time to connect the beleaguered and remaining Veterans of our U.S. Armed
Forces with decent Military Attachment Positions in cutting through some Red Tape; either here in The United States in covering the various elements of Civil Strife domestically and particularly with involvement to The Illegal Immigration concern, and expressly in involved coverage to The Drug War ongoing, (and perhaps to say of the ongoing Civil Wars in undercurrents here at large here, involving Racial Issues, Zionism, Neo-Fascism, Labor and The Economy, and to add stability to our nation about,) and otherwise to cover overseas positions with in securing our U.S. Interests abroad.

And in speaking for myself, at the age of 62, and with a great deal of personal experience of my own as an Analyst in the field Drug Warfare and Drugs Intervention, (and as a Vietnam War Veteran with Military Experience within the ranks of the civilian population of The United States in insight, and to the field of occupational endeavor of journalism,) that I do have a lot to offer and The Plan To Save Our Country in the way of common sense Intelligence if there might be found a place for me within your Military scope of organization. This would also be for the sake of reasoning that we Veterans need substance in our lives at this time in the form of government recognition in order to fulfill our lives, and who of us have already offered them To The Defense of Our Nation in sacrifice, (or at least that we seem to be longing for that type of recognition at this time, not to be confused with the overzealous idea of patriotism, but with the genuine concerns for the survival and the future of our America and its people at odds now with many enemies, and with many false ideologies, to destroy it, and us along with it in collateral damage as the Nation collapses,) to what we need coordination to conduct Para-Military Organization involving The Civilian Factor in the field of Drug Enforcement and to coordinate with The Military and with Domestic Law Enforcement involved with Drug Enforcement Activities and Approach and with Illegal Immigration, and as well with Terrorist Concerns here locally in our individual State and as well as Nationally and Internationally. This would also give us the clout we need to conduct ourselves formally with our nation's political leaders and to enhance our position among the hostile civilians.

Gary L. Koniz
Journalist Correspondent
Veterans Of The Vietnam War

"ONE POWERFUL VOICE"

9480 Princeton Square Blvd. S., #815
Jacksonville, FL 32256
August 21, 2008

Superintendent Franklin L. Hagenbeck,
Lieutenant General, US Army
United States Military Academy
West Point, NY 10996

Dear General Hagenbeck,

Colonel Warren S. Lacy (Ret.), the Editor in Chief of Military Officer magazine published by The Military Officers Association of America (MOAA), has sent me (the attached) notice of an upcoming major conference event to take place on September 17, 2008 at The Hyatt Regency Washington on Capitol Hill in Washington D.C. entitled: 2008 Defense Forum – Keeping Faith With Wounded Warriors and Their Families – in response to my editorial inquiry of "Affirmative Action" regarding the fate of our combat soldiers past and present who have, and who have had, the misfortune to be involved with Psychiatric Intake, to be treated as deranged killers by the Veterans Administration Hospitals involving State Psychiatric Facilities also, and to their Medication at such Facilities with Thorazine and other destructive Chemical Pharmacy to their unending ruination and risk of suicide; that we need reclassified to a benign non-psychiatric de-chemicalized setting of Best Rest/Convalescence, Counseling, and Therapy.

Dr. James B. Peake, the current Secretary of Veterans Affairs, is going to be present for The Panel Discussion on Posttraumatic Stress Disorder (PTSD,) Traumatic Brain Injury (TBI,) and Depression and we would very much appreciate it if you or someone of your concerned involvement could attend this conference in peer command magnitude of influence and to pose the following questions to Dr. Peake in examining scrutiny:

What is the percentage and numbers of U.S. Combat Veterans Psychiatric Intake dating from The Korean War to the present? What percentage of these were treated with Strong Tranquillizer Class Drugs; and of these, what numbers committed suicide?

Do you personally approve of and declare safe for use the Strong Tranquillizer Class Drugs, such as; Thorazine, Prolixin, Navane, Trilifon, Congentin, Lithuim, Loxitane, and others of the Neuroleptic or Psychotropic Pharmacy description for use in the treatment of Post Traumatic Stress and Depression or to the treatment of any mental illness.

What are Effects of these drugs, both for short term and long-term use. And, were any of these drugs developed from Human Experimentation in Research Studies involving Veterans in such Experimentation at any time in their history that you know of.

Are there any situations where you feel these drugs could be appropriately used and if so, what would they be? What are the Legal Criteria in which you feel that Veterans could be legally "Force Treated" or "Chemically Restrained" with such pharmacy? And   what are the legal grounds that Mental Disorders can be legally ascribed to anyone, with treatment, and what Legal Services are available Veterans to challenge such diagnoses?

Gary L. Koniz
Veterans of The Vietnam War

"ONE POWERFUL VOICE"

9480 Princeton Square Blvd. S., #815
Jacksonville, FL 32256
December 7, 2008

Superintendent Franklin L. Hagenbeck,
Lieutenant General, US Army
United States Military Academy
West Point, NY 10996

Dear General Hagenbeck:

In wishing you and your Staff there at West Point our well wishes for this Christmas; that It has been nearly a year now since you wrote me last in personal communication in signing your name as "Buster," (that I gratefully admire,) in regard to The Work I sent you entitled, "The Orders Of The Day," in coverage of concern over the treatment, on returning home, of our Nation's Veterans, past and present, to being relegated into the category of Psychiatric Mental Patients, (and having to do with Media Propaganda in fear inducement that way,) insinuating the suspicions and rejections of society towards our Veterans, and to their unnecessary intake into psychiatric and to treatment thereafter with deadly chemicals by The V.A. Hospital Administration and else-way by State Psychiatric Facilities also; and to what that the Veterans have no say in the matter, (as to any Due Process of Law available,) for the sake of their being labeled, forcibly committed, and forcibly treated,) with any drug chemical, electric or insulin shock treatment, or surgery, at the whim of any Medical Psychiatrist under the Nation's current Mental Hygiene Law.

To what that I have exhausted the past year over; to you, and to The Secretary of Veterans Affairs, Dr. James B. Peake, and to The Military Officers Association of America (MOAA,) under the direction of Colonel Warren Lacy (Ret.), The Editor and Chief of Military Officer Magazine, and to The U.S. Navel Institute's "Wounded Warrior Program," and as well as to The Commander of United States Central Command, The Director of The F.B.I., The Director of The C.I.A., and to our Legislators and The Media, in an attempt to bring this matter under scrutiny to justice and reform; for the health and well-being of our Nation's Veterans, and to save their lives, from the deleterious effects of psychiatric treatment, and from suicide, (and in particular from their treatment with the Neoroleptic, or Strong Tranquillizer, Anti-Psychotic Drugs, as I previously named for you: such as; Thorazine, Prolixin, Navane, Trilifon, Congentin, Lithuim, Loxitane, and others of that Classification,) and which I petitioned to Secretary Peake on an ongoing basis about, to clarify for, of his personal decision, as to whether or not that any of these particular drugs, are adjudged by The Veterans Administration, to be safe for use; and which in all has not been responded to. And that now we are being told that Secretary Peake is now to be replaced, (and all of our labors in continuity to exhaustively explain the position to Secretary Peake about, to be lost,) by the current Obama Administration, to replace Secretary Peake with General Eric K. Shinseki, former Army Chief of Staff.

Most Respectfully
Gary Koniz
Veterans of The Vietnam War

"ONE POWERFUL VOICE"

9480 Princeton Square Blvd. S., #815
Jacksonville, FL 32256
Independence Day
July 4, 2009

Superintendent Franklin L. Hagenbeck
Lieutenant General, US Army
United States Military Academy
West Point, NY 10996

Dear General Hagenbeck:

What we need is closure to the Veterans Psychiatric Case, black and white, cut and dry, to what there is no in between of compromise; not with the scruples of professional medical and legal ethics, resting on the foundation of The Constitution, nor with the safety involving the lives and well-being of countless numbers of healthy and well-meaning Veterans suffering psychiatric intake for the sake of domestic difficulties experienced, (such as homelessness, joblessness, marital problems, Post Traumatic Stress, Grief and Mourning, and Remorse of Combat,) as a consequence to their brave service to their beloved Nation, and with the legalities of the situation, (which, as we have been stressing for, in obviousness.) As involve The Legal Standards and Medical Technicalities to coincide with respect for the Medical Diagnosis of a stated Mental Condition, and under what conditions; that such Diagnoses may be Legally Imposed upon anyone. And which as well also involves The Legal Conditions of what that a person can be charged with a Mental Disorder sufficient to Commitment under 2PC, Two Physician Consent, Mental Hygiene Law. And what are the Legal Grounds in which a person can be Treated under Voluntary Informed Consent, (as to the nature of what must be told to them beforehand.) And what are The Terms involved with Forced Treatment with Mind Altering and Metabolically Disabling Psychiatric Pharmacy, or otherwise Force Treated with Shock Treatment, or Medical Surgery. And what are The Rights of The Mentally Accused to Due Process under The Constitution. That we have not in all of our persistent inquiries after; to The Veterans Administration, United States Central Command, The U.S. Supreme Court, The Federal Bureau Of Investigation, and The U.S. Attorney General, been able to arrive at straight answers to. And so then to the serious question in closing to the case, as to what are we going to do about it in lieu of proper official action?

Because, you cannot have the rendering of Psychiatric this way, the way that it is, as it is being conducted and condoned for by the current Representation of The United States Government, Militarily Convened, because it is Unconstitutional to have it the way it is; (and in the meaning of its being a Communist Dictatorship in tyranny over the safety and the lives of the public and to the disgrace and well-being of our proud Veterans.) Which to be psychiatrically accused of, and indefinitely detained for without Due Process, is one thing bad enough, but to be Forcibly Treated for and Destroyed over is a blatant atrocity.

Most Respectfully
Gary Koniz – Correspondent
Veterans of the Vietnam War

"ONE POWERFUL VOICE"

9480 Princeton Square Blvd. S., #815
Jacksonville, FL 32256
(904) 730-2055
October 10, 2008

Robert S. Mueller, III – Director
Federal Bureau of Investigation
935 Pennsylvania Avenue, N.W.
Washington, D.C. 20535-0001

I need money to work with most importantly to resolve our case. I know that it is an impasse with you as it is an obstacle everywhere over the Money Issue; but it still is a major necessity in life, (and to the spirit of befriending people and showing appreciation for services rendered, when they are offered for the reason of making improvements over policy and to saving lives;) and to factor in the successful conclusion to save the lives and well-being overall all of our beloved Veterans, and for the sake of the general population of Americans in this regard under the psychiatric siege of a foreign involvement although Americanized, as yet not disclosed; which, as I have stated in the past, that I have been footing the bill alone over to accomplish, and to no relief in sight in torment of finances; that I am asking you resourcefully if you will help me out with in Tactical Assistance.

This is the case here as I am currently presenting it. You can see what it costs me to "put it out" just in the terms of stamps, paper, envelopes, and printing ink cartages, to resolve this grievous matter, and FOR which concern of urgency that I have been for many years in the process of detailing for everyone in positions of possible influence of relentless appeals of pursuing the project and in the undertaking to my own personal exhaustion.

If you want the job done, it will be resolved of this crisis in intervention over the power structure in enforcement. I am not just writing to pass on information, but to convince you to be providing us with the enforcement alliance intervention assistance we need "to conclude" our business with psychiatric; which ironically is all too apparently "obvious" to us, but not so to the Medical-Administrative Industry. That once rectified in those terms that we may then "go quietly home and about our business" in a metaphorical way of putting it. And until what day then, that The Major Case is Still At Large, as it is here detailed and described for in plain straightforward meaning of urgency in the matter of its necessity being cleared up and correct of its criminal malfeasance of duty in that regard of "dirty business." We are not dealing with scrupulous medical ethics under Hippocratic Oath, but with straightforward tyranny and abuse of privilege and power and corruption.
We do always respect and thank you in indebtedness for all of your timely assistance.

Most Respectfully Yours

Gary L. Koniz
Journalist Correspondent
Veterans of The Vietnam War

"ONE POWERFUL VOICE"

Military Officers Association *of* America

February 18, 2010

Gary L. Koniz

9480 Princeton Square Blvd S, #815 Facksonville, FL 32256

Dear Mr. Koniz:

Thanks for your letter we received February 17, 2010, proposing a feature article on LTC Franklin Hagenbeck. I've passed your query to the magazine's Editorial Review Committee. That group vets story ideas and sets the magazine's lineup.

Please understand that we receive many excellent article queries each month, but we have space to act on only a few. We do our best!

Again, thanks for your continuing interest in and support of Military Officers Association of America.

Best wishes,

Warren S. Lacy
Colonel, U.S. Army (Ret.) Editor in Chief
Military Officer magazine

201 N. Washington Street
Alexandria, VA 22314-2539
800.234.6622 phone
www.moaa.org

One Powerful Voice°

9480 Princeton Square Blvd. S., #815
Jacksonville, FL 32256
February 22, 2010

Franklin L. Hagenbeck
Lieutenant General, US Army
Superintendent - 646 Swift Road
United States Military Academy
West Point, NY 10996

Dear General Hagenbeck:

   You see here that we have a letter of endorsement from Commander Warren S. Lacy, Colonel, U.S. Army (Ret.) in direct invitation to submit the proposed feature article, and with several photographs about yourself, (of the history and tenure in ideology of your position there as Superintendent,) the History Of and Indomitable Military Spirit of West Point, with photographs, (that sometimes on blustery days in the late Fall of the year after the leaves have fallen and the trees are stark and bare, and the sky is overcast with low gray clouds impending snow, that has brought tears to eyes of many strong willed mortal men for the slain and fallen soldiers of our Nation's Wars,) and to your outlook on the current wars going on in the way of sacrifice, and your testimony to their objectives; and particularly regarding your feelings and ideas concerning Afghanistan for the destruction and the total preventive removal of the entire Opium Poppy Crop/Trade, and with it to the ideological and literal defeat of the Taliban Itself; which is the motive for its existence, (the Opium Crop and its Mass Addictive Revenues of War,) the scourge of nations.

   We would also be very pleased concerning your policy on the discontinuation of the sadomasochistic yearly ritual of Plebe Hazing, in the ego defacement of the old era, to be replaced with the modern format of Solid Morale Building along the lines of Discipline and Mutual Respect for the Soldier, the Officer, and Leadership Based On Mutual Honor.

   We also would be interested to have a statement regarding the modern "under currents of clandestine wars," of the nature of; Ideological, Economic, Moral, and Drug Warfare Fronts; and having to do with Military Intervention to The Drug Trade, Immigration and American Sovereignty, the Nation's Economy, Pornography and the Nation's Standards of Morality, and Miscegenation; which play a military roll in the future of our Country.

   And most importantly concerning your respect for The Military Officers Association Of America, (MOAA's,) Fallen Warrior Program, for a statement about "The Aftermath of War," and how our Veterans are treated, and as to how you are instructing your future Officers to program the returning soldiers to civilian life and the adjustments to be made; concerning social rejections, biases, persecutions, and fears, against them, and for other matters of Shell Shock, Post Traumatic Stress, Emotional Disorders, and Suicide; for our Veterans to be removed from The Psychiatric Rosters about and placed on; Bed Rest/ Convalescence, Nutrition, Counseling and Therapy, without use of Disabling Chemicals.

Most Reverently Yours,
Gary L. Koniz - Correspondent
Veterans of The Vietnam War

"ONE POWERFUL VOICE"

April 26, 2010

Dear General Hagenbeck:

"The Call To Order" is a book about our loyalty to The United States that men have fought and died and gave their life's blood for along the scene of many gory battles. What it is here that I am trying to impress upon you, is that there are several very deadly situations going on to the detriment of our Nation that no one is seeming to pay any attention to; primarily for the reason in motive that they don't appreciate in concern of what the nature of the problems to surmount are all about; and then, and even in knowing that, of their having to face the insurmountable task of trying to figure out what to do about it in a collective and concerted common sense approach to go about challenging the obstacles in our path and to surmount them;   The principle problem being to us the psychiatric devastation to our Veterans; that I, for one of course, don't blame anyone for their lack of participation on either of both accounts. But I do find fault with those who I have taken the time to educate, and over the length of several years now, for not coming at least to the foreground of the battle field to display themselves to the enemy for the compelling virtue of strength and honor among soldiers, bravely worded, not to leave anyone behind, abandoned, and in the meaning to be left stranded in the hands of psychiatric killers in the vein of unconventional warfare, to be maimed and tortured and ultimately demised by, by suicide or by physiological complications using prescription drugs and psychological devaluation warfare instead of bullets to kill off not just our Veterans, and easy prey, but also several generations of the population along with them, while everyone stands idly by to it. The book, as of May 1, 2010, is finished, but not the work it bears witness to the readers of it to undertake; that being to finish the job that we started.

The concept here being, however, that we are not dealing with "Paper Case Law" being presented, but with the real workings of the Bill of Rights of The U.S. Constitution in formality as it affects the public; that no person shall be deprived of Life, Liberty, or Property, without Due Process here in this Country. And that is to the point being about my case: that there is No Court Record to be found regarding of my case, and that I was completely deprived of Due Process and forced into Chemo-Treatment against my will.

Nobody it seems is defending The United States of its Sacred Heritage in this matter, of our Constitutional Rights since the Country has begun "deteriorating" in the aftermath of Vietnam and The Civil Rights War in the meaning of our being mass-invaded by foreigners as we speak, in a passionate meaning of Patriotism, To Defend, and before a Real Bloodshed War for The Ideology of The United States and its Territory breaks out, and after they have turned everybody into Chemical Psychiatrics without Due Process.

To what that The Veterans of this Nation are seeking Just Restitution about with The Veterans Administration, and with State Facilities, concerning The Due Process Rights and Safe Treatment Violations with the terms of Psychiatric, and dating back into the 1970's to be resolved, regarding the ill-advised use and forced treatment of Thorazine and other harmful Anti-Psychotic Chemicals; and for the benefit of our Veterans who lost their jobs, their marriages, their families, and ways of life as a result of such treatment, and who now need a hand financially, and in their declining senior years, to survive.

In the History of the Indomitable Military Spirit of West Point, (that sometimes on blustery days especially in the late Fall of the year in New York State after the leaves have fallen and the trees are stark against an overcast sky with a chill is in the air, that it is that has brought tears to eyes of many strong willed and brave mortal men for the slain and fallen.

"ONE POWERFUL VOICE"

9480 Princeton Square Blvd. S., #815
Jacksonville, FL 32256
(904) 730-2055
July 4, 2010

Franklin L. Hagenbeck
Lieutenant General, US Army
Superintendent - 646 Swift Road
United States Military Academy
West Point, NY 10996

Dear General Hagenbeck:

I wanted to touch base with you for the 4th of July Tradition in relating to you that the job of saving our Veterans Lives from the tyranny and wrongful abuse of psychiatric devastation is still not being done completely and is yet to be accomplished to call it a day with; and non-bloody combat to us, like other methods of unconventional warfare such as economic destruction, drug addiction, personal demoralization, and character assassination. Which I list the D.W.I. Law at the end of this message to you as one type of warfare that is being done on a "slow" and grand scale of all the time in the world to a specific end, by several entities in particular, and which we need to defend ourselves to.

I also wanted to tell you that The Interview with Military Officer Magazine is still open to you if you should decide that you want to do it along any lines of discussion to would care to relate to with your fellow Officers on the welfare and dense of The Nation.

I painted the mural you see here, myself, of the deer, and the mountains, and sky, in the Mess Hall at Camp Boone Okinawa, Japan, where we were for seven months building a storage facility before being sent to Vietnam. The Officers table is seen in the foreground. Behind the mural is where the cooks slept. I painted it from the cover of a Field and Stream Magazine and it took me three weeks to paint. They had asked for an artist volunteer to do it for the Commanding Officer. I mixed the colors for it myself.

1. Photo of our Camp Boone sign facing North toward Naha, Okinawa.
2. Our Camp in its entirety. The Mess Hall is the building at the far back left.
3. Our Work, drilling, and blasting, and excavating, Fire In The Hole, to create the storage facility for the build-up for Vietnam, which we pushed out into the sea.
4. Our Camp near Long Binh, along Highway 15, in South Vietnam.
5. Our Company Road - 6. b, my tent area.
6. Photo of myself and bulldozer doing Preventive Maintenance.
7. Storage Area we created on arrival in Vietnam. The Red Dust and The Red Mud.
8. On arrival at Bear Cat, near Vung Tau, near the coast. Mourning out dead.
9. Our work at Bear Cat. One Operated, while another rode along and stood watch. Somehow we survived. But we had already resigned ourselves to die. And such was the meaning of, "Service," to us, to have a special interest in Our Nation for.

Most Respectfully Yours,
Gary L. Koniz - Correspondent
Veterans of the Vietnam War

"ONE POWERFUL VOICE"

9480 Princeton Square Blvd. S., #815
Jacksonville, FL 32256
December 14, 2011

Franklin L. Hagenbeck
Lieutenant General, US Army
Superintendent - 646 Swift Road
United States Military Academy
West Point, NY 10996

Dear General Hagenbeck:

In wishing you the very best for this Season's Holiday Spirit, to add that words cannot convey my gratitude for your support over the years and for your involvement with the case of our Nation's Veterans, brave soldiers of our Nation's Wars, who are left suffering in the aftermath of their patriotic service, to be properly cared for concerning their period of adjustment, and to defend how our Veterans are treated concerning; social rejection, persecutions, and biases, due to hysterical public fears about them; (who are regarded and feared by the private sector to be trained killers,) interrelated with Shell Shock, Post Traumatic Stress, Depression, and other Emotional Disorders, and To Suicide; for our Veterans to be removed from The Psychiatric Rosters about and placed on; Bed Rest/ Convalescence, Nutrition, Counseling and Therapy, without use of Disabling Chemicals.

And, in asking you and our Nation's Military Command if you would kindly support me in my bid for Election to The U.S. House of Representatives 2012 to Florida's 4th CD, to indicate that I would thereby be able to "Take Care of Our Urgent Military Business."

Afghanistan needs the total destruction and the preventive removal of the entire Opium Poppy Crop/Trade, and with it to the ideological and literal defeat of the Taliban Itself; with the destruction of The Poppy Crop, which is the motive for its existence, (the Opium Crop and its Revenues of War,) that has been destroying The U.S. and Europe.

Also to be severely dealt with are the many ongoing, "unconventional under-currents of clandestine wars," and not so subtle, that are threatening us in peril needing to defend against; of the nature of; Racial, Ethnic, Religious, Ideological, Economic, Moral, and Drug War - Drug Warfare, Fronts, (to include the Political Fascism of Drug Related Crime;) that we have to formidably acknowledge as being threats to our Nation's security to confront and defend our Nation against even though they are not being waged with bullets, to take a stand over, with the meaning we undertake with the Oath of Allegiance, "To Defend The United States Against All Enemies Foreign and Domestic." That begins with the absolute necessity of Military Intervention against The Drug Trade and Illegal Immigration and in Defense of American Sovereignty. And, To Defend The Nation's Economy and the Nation's Standards of Morality, (and against the toleration of moral gay liberal degeneration and pornography.) And that we need to have an Intelligent Policy on Miscegenation; (to protect The Races and Ethnic Denominations also from obliteration.)

Most Reverently Yours,
Gary L. Koniz - Correspondent
Veterans of the Vietnam War

"ONE POWERFUL VOICE"

9480 Princeton Square Blvd. S., #815
Jacksonville, FL 32256
June 25, 2011

Department Of Veterans Affairs
St. Petersburg Regional Office
Re: File No. 24 891 327
P.O. Box 7000
Bay Pines, FL 33744

To Whom It May Concern:

This affidavit is to serve to plead my request for Substantive Due Process to occur (and that is to state to be allowed to explain myself and the details of my case properly in perspective to any judgments being made in result of the survey of my records, On The Grounds that Not Everything Being Stated About Me In The Records Is True And Accurate, whether in Testimony About Me, or as Doctor's Medical Opinion Diagnosis, that are made up to satisfy the Physician's Diagnosis, or Rubber Stamped,) and prior to any decision being made to my claim for Disability Compensation for Lost Income due to Permanent Disability Damages Suffered from the effects of sustained Treatment with the Chemicals; Loxitane, Cogentin, Thorazine, Trilafon, and Navane. Which were the drugs that I was Force Treated with, (or ordered to take under the threats of Forced Treatment.) The Adverse Effects of Treatment I Received for being a Vietnam Veteran to be disabled, then further complicated the suffering of the Posttraumatic Stress Disorder, that onset with me in the aftermath of our surrender of South Vietnam to the Communists in 1975, and which lasted veritably for fifteen years. We were also at and during that time under the siege of a Drug-Chemical Warfare that was rampant upon us and to the Nation being conducted and carried out by The Hippie Draft Dodger Drug Movement that needs to be pointed out. That in all bears consideration with you in perspective to my case needing to be understood correctly in order for you to properly evaluate my legitimate claim appeal.

And which also needs your understanding of PTSD: that Wars are not fought without emotion in the terms of grieving, mourning, and remorse of combat for the taking of lives, and to the ordeals of combat in 18 hour days and sleepless nights on end without rest in sheer physical exhaustion, the unmitigated fear and terror and excruciating horrors of the battlefield, and from the neurological and psychological effects of repeated blasts. All of what culminate, upon separation, and even unto years later when the psychological blockade wears thin and the Veterans are left with the stark reality of the War. That is then further complicated by the Veterans Alienation from Society from the effects of the Social Programming of Population to Fear the Returning Veterans as Brain Damaged Killers who have been programmed to kill and who could kill again in a fugue state while sleepwalking in the night. And what has left the returned home again Veterans to face rejection, homelessness, joblessness, despair, depression, alcoholism and drug addiction.

Gary L. Koniz
Veterans of the Vietnam War

"ONE POWERFUL VOICE"

9480 Princeton Square Blvd. S., #815
Jacksonville, FL 32256
May 1, 2009

Warren S. Lacy
Colonel, U.S. Army (Ret.)
Director, Publications
Editor in Chief, Military Officer magazine
Military Officers Association of America (MOAA)
201 N Washington St, Alexandria, VA 22314-2539
(800) 234-6622 x105; (703) 838-8105
editor@moaa.org www.moaa.org

Dear Colonel Lacy:

Thank you so much for your recent letter and continuing strength of solidarity to our cause of Veterans Affairs in concern to Appropriate Psychiatric Handling, and to their being returned safely home from Combat to Civilian Life to a "Seamless Transition." That is not so seamless in the hostile real world of negative media programming, fearful public attitude in opposition, and to the outright disposal of our Veterans by government and medical malfeasance in misconduct of gross negligence pertaining for their outright mishandling of psychiatric intake and treatment in dire need to be rectified to the secure the dignity and emotional well-being of our Veterans returning safely home, and to their being provided for in the future with therapeutic safe healing of their Stress Disorders.

The V.A., and as their Deputy Chief Office for Mental Health, Dr. Ira Katz has stated, can write and say that the public "is coming around" to the acceptance of the diagnosis of mental disorders in a benign way, like having diabetes. But the truth of the matter is that the public doesn't accept it, especially in the case of the Veterans. And quite the opposite, that the population is being programmed to believe that each Veteran is potentially a deranged and violent killer and to be viewed as a dangerous threat, who must be put away and rendered incapacitated by chemical treatment for the public safety.

To what that, "Place No Head Above Your Own," as the saying is stated, and which is The Military's General Prudential Rule in avoidance of imminent danger, is The Order.

A case in point of this being the television soap opera called, Y&R, The Young and The Restless, which airs every weekday on CBS at 12:30 p.m. and which can be taped to watch later in the evening. That has become, on the part of its producers and writers, an Inter-Racial show advocating the nonchalant acceptance of Mixed Racial Affairs and Marriage; and to the use of drugs and poisons, in providing instructional training for the housewives, to play pranks or to inflict serious harm to unsuspecting males on the show.

That I mention, in prefacing and concerning the Interracial Affairs idea, which needs to be ruled on by the military as a firm policy not to be condoned, in heart and sanctity to preservation of the racial identity and heritage, of The White Race and The Black African Race, and to the innate racial desires and right of self-determination in governing; (and in being weighed conjunction to the Drug Warfare design;) versus the mixed identity, and often warfaring hostile pursuits, of the resulting issue of the Mulatto Caste, being an alienated mixture of White and Black, and as having to do with the mixed caste nature of the ingrained Islamic hatreds of the White Race, continuing from the history of The Moors (710 to 1482 A.D.,) in their occupation of

Western Europe, as it relates to The Spanish Inquisition and the Crusades of that Era in World History to save the White Race from the forced incursion of the Moorish Heroin Drug Culture into White Society of the time, and to the drug warfare problems they faced with the White Women then, many of whom were burned at the stake for their part in the betrayal, in similar condition as we also face as a society in these modern times of racial confrontation in ideology, with being forced upon us to accept and allow; of the one side programming the tolerance and adaptation to Drug Use, Promiscuous Morals, and Interracial Mixing, and of the other side, of the White Race Defending against it, and often in the manner of Backlash inducing discrimination, for the sake of Racial Preservation, and of The White Race, as such to be viewed now as an "Endangered Species," living in fear of annihilation, to cease to exist altogether, and be rendered like The Sub-Continent of India, if Inter-Racial Procreation here in the United States were carried out to the extreme of total assimilation.

Which is being told like it is. That has become for us now, a Political-Military Issue of being forced to witness an amassing of numbers through immigration overrun and racial assimilation, and being achieved through a means of forced intimidation of Social Domination in Stockholm Syndrome effect to embrace the Ideology and Cultural Influences of Heroin Drug Use, Pornography, Prostitution, and Inter-Racial Co-Mixing.

And concerning what has been happening to our Veterans, in one setting of regard, to their being sabotaged by means of Drug Perpetration, and using the females, who do the traditional food preparation, in a forced arrangement of coerced black-mail, as an "inside job" of it in the deadly conflict of a Race War, using drugs and chemicals; or to the matter of Pornography moving in as well; and also to do with the media inducing fear into the women in brainwashing them to be Sedating their men into docility, or to their doing so for purely personal Women's War Feminist motives in use of Drugs and Poison to inflict serious physical harm and psychological damage at the hands of these women, and to the Veterans developing, "mysterious maladies," as are always being reported about during our modern war era settings, as in "Gulf War Syndrome;" (which are easy to identify in the terms of Drug Sabotage properly understood,) or to the Veterans being labeled with Paranoid Schizophrenia and forced to take Thorazine for their saying so.

And for example, that on the Monday April 13, 2009 episode of Y&R, one of the characters went berserk in a "Fugue State" (described about in the Webster's Dictionary as "a disturbed state of consciousness characterized by acts that are not recalled upon recovery,") stemming from a psychological re-injury of an early childhood trauma, in which the character, in what Fugue State, hallucinates that he is in an imaginary place and that he sees his imaginary enemy, and begins to attack those around him in thinking that they are that person. Which is what is being programmed in mass hysteria into the public who have been and are continuing to be, brainwashed into believing, that the returning Combat Veterans, have been programmed to kill, and might sleep walk about in such a Fugue State and murder the household in believing that they are the enemy.

The need "to be put away" for which, is then further reinforce later in the show by a Courtroom scene where the character is being arraigned for going berserk and robbing banks at gun point while in the "Fugue State" that the character then jumps up and becomes irrational and begins to violently attack people in the courtroom in hallucinating again that he is someplace else. To what that his older brother and defense council on the show cites to the judge, (as to the not-so-subtle propaganda being implanted into the public's brains,) that his brother is suffering

"ONE POWERFUL VOICE"

from "Post Traumatic Stress Disorder" and needs to be placed in a psychiatric facility for treatment where he can get some help.

Which was granted and to the character then being placed in a padded room and rendered comatose by injections with a Strong Tranquiller. Which only serves in example, to reinforce to the public that removal and Hospitalization and Treatment with Thorazine for our returning Veterans is appropriate, (and who are suffering tragically with Post Traumatic Stress Disorders,) as it relates to the public's attitude, and especially the attitudes of the fearful housewives, towards the incoming and returning home Veterans who are suffering through no fault of their own from the rigors of combat.

The symptoms of Posttraumatic Stress Disorder of these Veterans are of a Vacuous Shock Affect and Depression to be treated for with respect, compassion, and dignity.

In what regard for intercession that our ongoing requests to The Veterans Administration for Proper Administrative Handling to this critical matter of Labeling and Treatment, have gone basically un-responded to, and of what few times that there have been responses, that are not provided to us in an intelligent manner of reply, (in the way of patronizing side-stepping, and polite "down talking" of the issues.) For what problems that we must have intelligent solutions to, or to face the crucible of social stigma, being discarded by society as "Mental Patients," and to a horrifying chemical maiming and death as a result, as we have raised and have addressed these issues, to each of the prior Veterans Affairs Secretaries in succession from the Vietnam War, and of recent history extensively with Dr. James B. Peake, and presently to the current Secretary General Eric Shinseki's, in addressing the need for a decisive verdict in Accountability and with Faith of Trust for The V.A. to act responsibly regarding the destruction of our returning home Combat Veterans through the V.A.'s warehousing policy of General Diagnosis with Schizophrenia and to prevailing use of heavy sedation with Strong Tranquillizer Drugs; such as Thorazine, Navane, Prolixin, Loxitain, Trilifon, and others, as to whether the Neuroleptic Drugs being mass administered by the Veterans Hospitals, (and elsewhere of the State Mental Health Facility settings to our Veterans also,) and to their, "Forced Treatment," or to "Ill-Advised Consent" to Treatment, Are Safe To Use; or, if in fact and indeed whether or not that these Drugs are lethally harmful to persons; and if so for the V.A. to formally acknowledge this crucial detail and to conclude with such disabling business on a permanent basis. And also that we need for the V.A.'s General Counsel to define under what circumstances allowed by law can any of our Veterans ever be "Force Treated," against their will with these drugs? And to define for us the legal resources available for Legal Counsel To Be Provided to Veterans by The Veterans Administration, (or for the Right to Counsel under Miranda Legislation secured,) concerning The Rights of our Veterans To Challenge Psychiatric Diagnosis, 2PC (Two Physician Consent,) Commitment Procedure, and otherwise for their Miranda Rights of Due Process to be clarified and protected, as they relate with the Non-Criminal Mental Hygiene Law.

We need our inquiries addressed under the Freedom of Information Act; which have not been forthcoming to this date. And that we do have urgent business here to take care of right now, and unresolved from our extensive coverage and briefing of the first Keeping Faith with Wounded Warriors and their Families Forum, (of September 17, 2008,) with Secretary James Peake to resolve, of the same timely issues ongoing to General Shinseki, concerning the obvious in documented harm of statistics occurring as a direct result and consequence of the psychiatric intake labeling and stigmatizing, and to the use of deadly drug chemicals being administered; which we need all available means presently at our disposal to address and to bring these matters in crisis to the attention of the Federal Government, and to the Justice Department, as to legally

"ONE POWERFUL VOICE"

handle our specific request for intervention on the Injustices of Psychiatric Diagnosis Labeling, Unsafe Forced Treatment, and Violated Rights of Due Process as we have called to be resolve.

That in way of reference to my qualifications to reason on, to mention here, that I am a College Graduate educated as a "Faith Based Psychologist" and "Medical Nutrition Specialist" with Advanced Certificate Training and Hands-On Clinical Experience Interned as a Psychotherapy Aid in the real time dynamics of a Psychiatric Facility in Holistic Psychology to effectively "heal people," and also educated with extensive Para-medical, Para-Legal background in Psychiatric Pharmacology and Mental Hygiene Law.

And with what tools on the issues here defining legitimate treatment of mental health issues; as problems with causes to be pragmatically worked out, handled, dealt with, and solved; to get at the sources of, and to seek remedies for, the problems, (and not as to be "masking them over" (as the Medical Doctors do,) with disabling chemical drugs, (termed facetiously as, "Meds," which heal no one;) but to provide remedies for; in a holistic way of applying sound nutritional practice, for a proper diet to be clinically provided and individually taught as a course of treatment, and coinciding to a regimen of physical fitness exercise and self-discipline, (not to over eat, and to have a proper sense of a healthy sexuality, as affect one's psychological health in the need to be structured in order to feel better and to a good state of mind in the strength of internal fortitude, and coinciding to the elimination or avoidance of "bad habits," the likes of alcohol, drugs, and tobacco,) being the foundation to a healthy mind; to go along with group workshop therapy sessions relating and talking-out one's problems with one's peers, and along with professional one on one guidance counseling to provide insight into the mind for healthy personal, family, and social relationships to be instilled, and in being educated to the handling of conflicts and stress anxiety, as to be provided with working tools of the mind; and for the individuals to form a good positive outlook on life with conviction to a positive work ethic in orientation towards survival, as a way of structuring and ordering one's life, and as another foundation block to good mental health in keeping to a sound faith regime of responsibility to oneself and one's family, and to the avoidance of negative thoughts and actions leading in consequence to the bad karma, depression of guilt in wrongdoing, in avoidance of all wrongdoing, not to do wrong, and otherwise to do good works and to atone for past misdeeds and indiscretions, and to the overall concept of "doing good." Of which regimen, foundationally applied, that can basically "heal anybody" suffering with emotional and stress disorders, (provided they are not due to an organically induced mental illness,) given the proper nutrition, the proper incentives to heal, the proper amount of bed rest and time to recover, and time to detox from society.

The tragic setting here, is that the Neuroleptic Drugs, Strong Tranquilizers, such as Thorazine, being currently used to render Post Traumatic Stress Disorder victims into a comatose and vegetative existence in excruciatingly uncomfortable states of being, (and not to the sense of trying to treat anyone to heal them of their disorders, but for the sake of warehousing to be mass sedating them to be disposed of, to be rendering persons sedated for the purposes of mass control, and for other motives more sinister concerned with National Security, having to do with the medical/pharmacy industry, (for corrupt financial gain motives in the maintaining of a "captive diagnosis market," from whom no one can escape, except to remain on the "medications prescribed;" which becomes to them a chemical prison,) and/or for personal corrupt and maniacal motives; with the Medical Pharmacy Industry oriented in gross negligence of error in judgment to the force administered use of neuroleptic pharmacy, across the board, being administered to everyone, in total desecration of our Veterans, who have served our Nation

"ONE POWERFUL VOICE"

proudly and bravely and heroically in point of honor, and who don't deserve to be treated as Mentally Ill Persons, in seriousness of the grievance being addressed; to wit: that these drugs, and the psychiatric labeling associated to them, are destroying people and not healing them.

And as your MOAA Assistant Director of Government Services, Ms. Cassidy Scott Vreeland has mentioned to me at your forward of request, of a second Wounded Warrior Forum to be held this upcoming September to participate in. But the war, our way, needs to be over by then in its urgency. And with wars being what they are to the people that they affect who are seeking alliances to defend themselves against, let us all then labor together and be mindful that time is of the essence in this regard to the safety and well-being of our returned home Veterans, and to repair the damage to those already injured, of those of past wars, who have suffered to the psychiatric disposal system, to whom "next September" is a long and costly time in deadly toll of lives away; and once again which will only produce "more talk" to be "talking at" the problems without solutions.

The Psychiatric Medical Industry not only has "the power" to diagnose and to treat-destroy anyone they personally choose to with any drug chemical, surgery, or electro-insulin shock treatment they arbitrarily determine, and with Sovereign Immunity from civil and criminal prosecution to do so built in to their current practices; but to realize for also, that they also have the maniacal personal power over the freedom of the lives of every individual who they do diagnose, (in Captive Market arrangement,) to imprison anyone indefinitely, to set the terms of their release, and to do with whatever they want to under the current heading of Mental Hygiene Law regarding commitment and "to the terms of treatment," without any real Due Process of Law and in the name of Medicine. Which is taking place, Communist Bloc Style, "here," in our United States of America, without anyone of the entirety of the legal and legislative functions to defend against.

Which for the record to add that there are all too many numerous cases to cite; of medical malpractice and fraud, medical kickback complicity with the pharmaceutical companies, medical monetary corruption, and with ties to political, pornographic, and drug conspiracies to organized crime, that do periodically surface to come to light. To the point being; that how can anyone be denied their God Given and Constitutional Rights to Due Process in the face of such subversion and corruption just because the legal rendering of Mental Hygiene is worded to fall under the Medical Clause of Civil Law; which demands a Congressional Investigation and Government Oversight to monitor.

The Lives of our Veterans are on-line for the swift and determined resolution of this case, which has been destroying and taking the lives of our Veterans in great numbers.

One Powerful Voice.® For every officer at every stage of life and career.

Most Respectfully,
Gary Koniz
Veterans of the Vietnam War

"ONE POWERFUL VOICE"

9480 Princeton Square Blvd. S., #815
Jacksonville, FL 32256
November 2, 2009

Timothy H. Graham, J.D., LL.M., CIPPIG
VHA FOIA Officer – (19F2)
Department of Veterans Affairs
810 Vermont Avenue, N.W.
Washington, D.C. 20420

Dear Agent Graham:

Thank you so much for being in contact officially from The VHA with me. I appreciate the sincerity and detailed length of your letter in useful information and Am indeed grateful for your expertise of defining and in clarifying the parameters of the Freedom Of Information Act FOIA for us. I was thinking perhaps though, that my questions posed to the Office of the General Counsel should not have been formulated under the heading of a FOIA Request, but posed straightforwardly as legal questions to be answered for in the seriousness of their necessity to be answered, as they affect our Veterans wherever they happen to be, and as to whether or not that they are involved directly with The Veterans Health Administration, or find themselves being regarded as Veterans with Civilian Courts and Psychiatric Facilities; for whose regard we appeal.

The legal answers to our questions posed are most important in helping to safeguard their individual lives; that are too often, too poor, to afford private medical advice and counsel. And which are also up against a barrier of ingrained biases and preconceived prejudices, both from the stand point; of being Veterans, (in the public hysterias over our job function,) and from the stigmatized labeling of mental illnesses; which can be justified or otherwise, depending to the state of the scruples of the doctors; acting out of corrupt financial, personal biased, or scientific experimental research motives, and/or for the motives of The Health Care Facility in Warehoused Precautions to Diagnostic Labeling for the Purpose of Sedation Restraint, administered for the perceived safety of the Hospital Staff, and not for the treatment in particular necessity of the persons being handled; that we asked for the availability of Legal Representation from The V.A. about?

They are really very straightforward questions to be answered, (as I have enclosed, addressed to The U.S. Attorney General Eric Holder;) for clarification of Due Process Rights, Grounds for Diagnostic Labeling, Commitment, Forced Treatment, and Informed Consent, with the lives of our Veterans "life on line" for your adjudications of our case.

I would also like to note that in future responses; that it would be helpful if you would make quote of and directly refer to the questions specifically asked in your return replies for legal clarity; and not just to say, "your questions posed, as of such-and-such a date."

Most Sincerely Regarding,

Gary L. Koniz – Corresponding
Veterans of the Vietnam War

"ONE POWERFUL VOICE"

9480 Princeton Square Blvd. S., #815
Jacksonville, FL 32256
November 24, 2009

Ira Katz, MD, PhD
Deputy Chief Patient Care Services
Officer for Mental Health
Veterans Health Administration
810 Vermont Avenue, N.W.
Washington, D.C. 20420

Dear Doctor Katz,

    I need you to be aware of our appeal for concession to our en masse damage report on the part of The Veterans Administration; that occurred during and in the aftermath of The Vietnam War with over 1,000,000 Combat Veterans reporting to The V.A. for Psychiatric Treatment; and as occurred to myself on two occasions; the first in 1982, that I was misrepresented in being attributed with the symptoms of Paranoid Schizophrenia about; (ie; hallucinating, hearing voices, and being irrationally fearful of people out to get me, and being abusive to my family; which I was neither of;) and misdiagnosed as such and subsequently then mistreated with 200 MG of Thorazine, and later with the drug Trilifon, after the Thorazine induced severe Hypotension in me, and for what that we, and virtually the entire Ward of patients, of some fifteen to twenty men, had to sit each morning connected to Blood Pressure Monitors to determine if we could continue on with the Thorazine Group Experimentation being held as a Clinical Trail, and for me that was on top to the complications that I was already suffering from (seeing red spots in my vision and crippled from severe cramping in my legs in being hobbled from the effects of Forced Treatment at a Psychiatric Facility in South Caroline, called G. Werber Brian, in Columbia South Carolina, to where in 1982, (and just prior to my reporting afterwards to the Albany V.A.,) that I was taken by police in Chains from General Hospital as they asked me if I was a Vietnam Veteran and said they weren't taking any chances, after getting sick and nearly collapsing on the road trying to hitchhike back to New York, and for complaining that I had been drugged while visiting my brother, and had been dropped off in Columbia by him and abandoned. That I came to the Albany, NY V.A. about on making my way home to New York State, for assistance in relief to be treated for the adverse effects of the drug treatment Loxitane and Cogentin, that I was forced to take already in my system and being taken as the psychotic symptoms of the condition, and only to be labeled with Schizophrenia from over the effects of, and in Contraindication complications with the effects of the medication already in my system, to then being put on Thorazine and Trilifon by the VA in Medical Malpractice; that left me among "The Walking Dead," and discharged as Disabled by Doctor Byung Kim, who mis-treated me, and of what treatment that left me; mentally, physically, and emotionally, dysfunctional.

    And in all, in direct testimony to relate about the experience; that most of the men being treated suffered from comatose flat affect syndrome of their treatment, myself among them, and some suffered with pathetic uncontrollable incontinence, and some had bad convulsive seizures biting their tongues, as I witnessed. And in tragic note, that my own personal room-mate there on the Psychiatric Ward 10B in The Albany, NY Veterans Health Care Center, and with whom I had become close intimate friends with, told me one day several weeks into our Thorazine

Treatment and while standing in the doorway to our room with as sad and forlorn an expression as I had ever seen, that: "Maybe I can get a job in a sheltered workshop somewhere." And then went home that weekend on weekend pass and shot and killed himself in the head with a 22 rifle. That, Dr. Kim, and after telling us that our friend had taken his own life that weekend, wanted to know on the following Monday morning during our group conference after breakfast, how we all felt about it. And at what point that I became convinced to leave the V.A. and checked out.

But too late for the effects of the catastrophic sedation I experienced; and as a result of which in trying to Self-Medicate and revive myself over the effects of it with Alcohol over the years, that in 1988 I was admitted for a D.W.I. Rehab (to what I was entitled;) to prevent a Felony Conviction; that I was denied my rights to treatment for the program to, "for not listing myself as a psychiatric," <u>which I denied being</u>, and to which that they were going to force me into dual compliance with in having to stay up in the psychiatric ward, (and to more Chemo-Treatment,) if I wanted to continue on to complete the Rehab Program. Which I refused, and was subsequently forced out to leave the program, that ultimately left me to have the permanent Felony Conviction to my record instead of the lighter record of a Misdemeanor; and which has affected my gainful employment and with my FAA Pilot Licensing in jeopardy through the years ever since in having to list.

What this drama completely lacks is the understanding, and the comprehension, of the facts about the raging "Drug War" that engulfed this Nation at the time of The Vietnam Conflict, and concerning The Hippie Draft Dodger element, using Drugs and Chemicals such as LSD, PCP Angel Dust, Speed, Barbiturates, and the Hard Drugs, Cocaine and Heroin, as their weapons; that is to be "dropping drugs," (and The Poisons that the drugs are "Cut" with, Cyanide with the Heroin, and Strychnine Rat Poison with the Cocaine,) on unsuspecting persons to cause them to suffer the effects of the drugs, adverse effects, and the after effects withdrawal symptoms of the drugs, and to manipulate them into believing that they are truly physically or mentally ill to get help for; that had trouble coming across with a Foreign Asian Doctor whose command of English was superficial.

I never said I smoked marijuana on occasion as Dr. Kim reported about me. I said that on occasion I inadvertently ran into marijuana smoke in the air from my family's use of it and was compromised. As for instance of the incident one Christmas morning as I will relate about to show what it was like to be in the Generation Gap with the Hippy Mafia, as they were called, and to what that my brothers and sisters were involved with, who I turned in to the Police for drug dealing, (as was indicated about in my record by Dr. Kim as an example of my psychotic behavior in need of treatment;) that as I had come home to visit with my family that year over the Holidays, and as I went upstairs to my room to relax a bit after opening presents and having breakfast, that when I opened the door to my room I found all my siblings, my two younger brothers, and two younger sisters, and their related spouses and significant others, sitting around smoking from a Marijuana Pipe.

My other previous admission mentioned, in 1977, and in 1982 as discussed, had to do with Drug Warfare Sabotage; and for what that I was labeled as Paranoid Schizophrenic.

Gary L. Koniz – Correspondent
Veterans Of The Vietnam War

"ONE POWERFUL VOICE"

9480 Princeton Square Blvd. S., #815
Jacksonville, FL 32256
December 1, 2009

John H. Thompson
Acting General Counsel
Department of Veterans Affairs
810 Vermont Avenue, N.W.
Washington, D.C. 20420

Dear Mr. Thompson:

Please do take an active interest in our case, as defined by my case, detailed here for you in three parts, all involving Drug Chemical Warfare Style intrigues of Unconventional Warfare stratagem, and otherwise dealing with the public hysterias over Combat Duty, Deranged Veterans, and the safety of the public, and especially family members, on return home of our Veterans; leading to psychiatric intake without Due Process of Law under false and irrational charges and to forced, (or improper voluntary concerning The Veterans Administration's use of Thorazine,) treatment with deadly Antipsychotic Drugs. Which we need a legal and financial resources hand with and for damages from the V.A. in resolving, not just for us, but for the good and sake of the nation and its people who are also being destroyed by psychiatric malfeasance. And in other words, that the charges brought against me here, are not accurate, and that were used as grounds for Diagnosis and Treatment in criminal conduct to be addressed by The General Counsel.

What this drama completely lacks is the understanding, and the comprehension, of the facts about the raging "Drug War" that engulfed this Nation at the time of The Vietnam Conflict, and concerning The Hippie Draft Dodger Rebellion, using Drugs and Chemicals such as LSD, PCP Angel Dust, Speed, Barbiturates, and the Hard Drugs, Cocaine and Heroin, as their weapons; to be "dropping drugs," (and The Poisons that the drugs are "Cut" with, Cyanide with the Heroin, and Strychnine Rat Poison with the Cocaine,) on unsuspecting persons to cause them to suffer, "unknowingly," from the effects of the drugs, adverse effects, after effects, and withdrawal symptoms, and to manipulate them into believing that they are truly physically or mentally ill and urging their victims to get help for; (the help being the debilitating psychiatric treatment,) that has trouble coming across with a Foreign Asian Doctors whose command of English was superficial. Thank you so much for your time spent to resolve this important issue.

I never said I smoked marijuana on occasion as Dr. Kim, (and suffering from the language barrier,) reported about me. I said that on occasion I inadvertently encountered marijuana smoke in the air around me during the height of The Vietnam War Protests, with Marijuana Smoking going on all around me, and from my family's use of it, who I suffered a generation gap with and who I tried to intervene with the police about regarding my family's drug use and drug dealing.

Respectfully,
Gary Koniz
Veterans of The Vietnam War

"ONE POWERFUL VOICE"

9480 Princeton Square Blvd. S., #815
Jacksonville, FL 32256
September 11, 2006

General John Abizaid
Commander, United States Central Command
7115 South Boundary Blvd.
Macdill Air Force Base, FL 33621-5101

General Abizaid:

   Respectfully, Sir. Thank you for your time in review of this discussion on the timely subject
of Military Intervention to The Drug War in defense of United States Soil and our American
Homeland and Way Of Life, and respecting the lives of The American Population at stake and
for their well-being to resolve, that never does get taken care of properly by the existing political
structure in the meaning of being done. This responsibility must rest with The Military: To
Protect The People.
   And which to focus on in particular state of crisis at this time, (and which could just as
urgently speak for every major American City in current siege crisis of The Drugs, but to provide
you with a specific and immediate target objective in Direct Show of Force,) is the priority of
The Drug War as It affects the key American City of Buffalo, NY, (and "Key" in the sense of Its
strategic location in concern to The Electric Power Generation from Niagara that supplies the
entire Northeastern portion of The United States, and for the fact of the already discovered
harboring of The Al Qaeda Terrorist Network there associated with and to the revenues supplied
by The Afghanistan Heroin Connection Trafficking into the region of Western New York and
that is associated as well to the longstanding smuggling operations of the Mafia Terrorist
Organization entrenched and established there, of a specific type, who have been dealing the
heroin and the cocaine and other illicit drugs to the population, to what that The City of Buffalo
is the nucleus for, and longstanding in the grievance that way,) of what is now ongoing in severe
crisis concerning The Drugs Situation there, but in particular in sympathy to the public that has
turned that City's Streets and Its Public Schools into a murderous teenage battleground of gang
violence for the control of The Drug Trade, in sorrowful commentary regarding the tragic apathy
and neglect on the part of our Government in the shirking of Its responsibility to The American
People, regarding the necessary, and required by law, unilateral Drug Intervention to occur.
   And for the grave matter of the setting of the drug related gang violence occurring there in
The City of Buffalo, that is combined with an alarming crime rate prevailing in support of the
drug habits, and from the severe ill-health effects of the prevailing Drug Warfare ongoing at the
hands of the Mafia Terrorist Organization associated to the trafficking and supply of the Heroin
and Cocaine into The City of Buffalo, which has been established there in that region for
decades, and which even boasts, (and according to "The Hard Copy Reporting" of The Buffalo
News, The City's local newspaper,) having a "Needle Exchange Program," (that even supplies
up to "50 Clean Needles" at a time to responsible clients operating legitimate "Crash Pads," for
addicts, in return for an even count of "Dirty Needles,") and "Street Runners" posted
conveniently in the drug neighborhoods to facilitate the purchase the heroin and cocaine and
other drugs to drive-by customers from the surrounding areas, that has been causing Buffalo's
businesses and jobs to leave and Its residents to flee the area. And what, of Buffalo's Troubles

"ONE POWERFUL VOICE"

that way, is further being aggravated by The City having to increase Its taxes in order to compensate for the loss of revenue that the dwindling population, related to the drugs, has caused, that is causing even more people to leave and to the point now where The City, and a major city of The United States, is dying.

And in all what is in direct connection as well with the uncontrolled flood of illegal, or otherwise, Foreign Immigration Overrun of the Nation occurring there who are replacing the established American Population to their jobs and otherwise forcing everyone to compete to a substandard labor market economy and which in turn is further feeding The Cottage Drug Industry Economy dependent to drug income for survival.

And it would help now to analyze Al Qaeda's alleged motives for their hatred towards The United States and The West, that are directly Heroin and Drug Traffic related and are connected at issue with the supply of Heroin being grown and produced currently in Afghanistan, to what that their Terrorism is a distraction to The Intervention Of, with the intention of dominating coercion in appeasement to their trafficking, and to disrupting the ability of governments to intervene by displacing manpower and financial resources away from the drug flow, and who therefore are encouraged to continue on with their campaigns of violence.

Which bring us to the crucial issue as to why is it then that we are allowing The Poppy Growers in Afghanistan and The Taliban, (who are declared and avowed International Criminals,) to continue on in cultivating their Poppy Fields and dealing their Opium-Heroin into the heart of Europe, and The United States, to fuel Al Qaeda and otherwise Mafia Terrorist Organizations, on the pretext of Official U.S. State Department Policy condoning it, that The Afghanis are an impoverished nation in need of their "Opium Cash Crop."

Which in truth bears out to be a "Liberal Conspiracy," to it on the part of the present Administration. And which for this year of 2006 alone, have already predicted for "a record" bumper crop, while the entire Earth suffers for its being allowed, and while The United States Military and The Militaries of our Allies Abroad, and the entire Forces of The United Nations Assembly, look haplessly on while they should be targeting the cultivation, production, and trafficking of Heroin, Cocaine, and other illicit drugs, and the criminal networks, world-wide, that support them, as a major military involvement. Wouldn't you agree?

What we need, not only in reference to the key City of Buffalo, NY, but for every major American City, and everywhere in The United States Of America, where there is evidence of sustained massive amounts of The Drug Trade occurring in condition imperiling The Nation and linked to spiraling rates of murder, government instability, and lawlessness, is; to regard the drugs Heroin and Cocaine and other mass amounts of Illegal Chemical Drugs, (such as LSD, and Methamphetamine,) as categorical "Weapons Of Mass Destruction," under The Domain of Homeland Security, and to direct The United States Congress, of The Senate and The House Of Representatives, and to be ratified by The President, To Permanently Establish The Jurisdiction for The Removal of All Drugs from U.S. Soil in the hands of The Combined Armed Forces of The United States Military as a major War Effort In Declared Status, equating The War On Drugs with The War On Terror, and giving into the hands of The Military "Special Powers," similar to The War On Terror, under The Articles Of Martial Law established, with which to combat The Drug Mafia Organizations that are currently co-existing with us here in The United States.

These, "Special Powers," would amend The Fourth Amendment, in like manner as with The Patriot Act, to ease restrictions in provision to a General Search Warrant, in easement to Search and Seizure and Wiretap limitations, which are to be based to the wording of, "Obviousness Of

"ONE POWERFUL VOICE"

Suspicion," replacing the unworkable "Probable Cause;" (that has "Undercover Agents" posing as Drug Dealers and Purchasers making "buys" before a search warrant may be issued on "Probable Cause,") and that would make it a "Treasonous Offense," in mandatory, "Death Sentence," for anyone, or any parties in conspiracy, to engage in Major Drug; Growing, Producing, Manufacturing, Smuggling, and Trafficking, at the source, on down to The Mid-line Suppliers. Who in all regards of these treasonous offenders are hereafter to be tried by Military Tribunal Courts and summarily executed.

Persons arrested on Minor Drug Offenses, for Possession and for Petty Street Trafficking in small quantities, are to be rendered "Held In Military Quarantine" and "Organized Into Narc Battalions," for an indefinite period of time, pending their "Rehabilitation," Boot Camp Style, To Society, and depending to their disposition to "Cooperate" with The Authorities in assisting to intervene with the suppliers of these drugs, who are to be "Hunted Down,"
in the seriousness of intent as a lethal threat,
hand to hand, and in the similar manner as the disease of Syphilis is hunted down, and essentially treated as a Health Problem on that level of cooperation.

And what overall newly reformed United States of America Drug Policy, would also include for the provision for economic employment relief for the impoverished populations of the heavily drug infested areas, (to assist in breaking up their dependency to "The Cottage Industry" drug economy,) and for the enlistment of the aid of communities in popular support for anti-drug efforts through the sponsoring of community youth monitoring programs, and through public drug awareness education, in a multi-pillared approach to the otherwise hopelessly pervasive and pandemic American Drug Problem To Overcome.

This Declaration Of War On Drugs! is also to be accompanied by "The Re-Imposition" (that has fallen by the wayside now since The Clinton Administration,) of routine and periodic, "Mandatory Drug Screening," (at specified intervals of every six months, and with random testing,) for All Government Employees, with special priority drug screening in effect for all Law Enforcement Personnel and Elected Political Officials, and that is to specify also for mandatory screening to The Nation's Medical Profession who are licensed by The Government to Practice Medicine, (and to Dispense Narcotics Prescriptions,) to ensure that drug use and conspiracy to drugs trafficking are never in the position to govern over us here.

And which joint action against the onslaught of the drugs here, is to be accomplished, in priority, on The International Level of Cooperation, To Remove The Drugs, Heroin and Cocaine, from The United States at their growing, producing, and refining sources, in utilizing the mobility and power in force of The United Nations, in cooperative coordination Internationally with; The United Nations Office of Drugs and Crime, (UNODC,) The Internationals Police Organization, (INTERPOL,) and The United States Central Intelligence Agency, (CIA.)

And that is Domestically on The Offensive to be handled in simultaneous attack on the drugs, by the immediate placement of sufficient numbers of Federal Troops within The Drug Infested Areas, (going door to door making inquiries, and block by block, as required in certain neighborhoods to gather information, conduct searches, and to make arrests,) to work in unison with The Individual State Units of The National Guards to be fully utilized, and with The Federal Drug Enforcement Administration, (FDA,) The Federal Bureau Of Investigation, (FBI,) The State Police of each individual State, County and Local Municipal Law Enforcement Agencies, and "Involving The Civilian Population Itself," in a combined effort under The Unified Direction of The Military as a War Operation.

"ONE POWERFUL VOICE"

And who are, these civilian counterparts to The Drug War, to be thought of in the same manner to be appreciated as Volunteer Fire Firefighters are who are enlisted to the aid of manpower to assist in putting out forest fires, and who are well thought of and much needed and gratefully appreciated for in the working side by side with the professional firefighters, and in this case taken as professional law enforcement and drug enforcement personnel, (and who, of these public volunteers, to the drugs intervention, are not further on to be regarded, as they are currently, in snide reference about by the existing authorities, who refer to these citizens attempting to assist them, as "Snitches," or as "Informants," in mocking derogation, and who are henceforth to be respected as concerned, patriotic and dedicated citizens,) to be mobilized in Task Force Support, (utilizing public phone hotlines and mail-in addresses for drug source information, and coinciding with the concept of paid Bounty Hunters for information leading to arrests and convictions,) in order to permanently clear-up, and with permanent resolution to keep it cleared, of The Dangerous Drug Situation that has been allowed to transgress here for over the many generations now that it has been tolerated, for The Good and Well-Being of Our Nation.

And to stress once over again, that The Issue Of Drugs is not being handled by the present setting by The Politicians of Our Country, in the gravity that it should be addressed. Which is due to the fact, and bluntly spoken for, that The Big Drug Blocs represents voters who our political leaders, in this or in any other era, would rather court, in the inversion of the prevailing general will electing them into office, than to offend.

This is however, the subject of the drugs, not a Political Objective. It is a War Matter! And It has been a War Matter for as long as the subject has existed in coexistence with the lives at stake, for the removal of these dangerous drugs and chemicals, of every American Citizen.

And to mention along with the issue of The Drug Warfare being ongoing perpetrated by The Drug Element in relentless fashion upon the innocent population to be remedied, and for the sake of the murderous intent in ever present danger of The Drug Mafias themselves as they present themselves upon each citizen of the Nation in intimidating way to silence them, and to threaten whoever attempts to reveal their identities and expose their activities, that has coerced the people in real fear for their lives, into silence, that It Is A Real War and Life-Taking Threatening War to those it is A War To! in the meaning of It, The Drug War, taking our lives, and threatening to take our lives, piecemeal fashion one by one, and en masse in the aspects of Drug Terrorism, and concerning The Terrorism of Mass-Violence, without a unified military stand against It to defend us!

And which We Ourselves Need To Defend About in a state of urgency, in taking on the job that is the responsibility of our Government Authority over us to accomplish.

Furthermore, the issue of The Drugs being present here, is not being handled, and has not ever been handled in the seriousness of extent that it is needed and has been needed to be handled, by the existing Established Law Enforcement Structure of our Government, upon whose responsibility it has been placed To Defend The Population from The Drugs and from The Terrorism and The Corruption, and The Immorality, of The Drugs, under "The Civil Authority" of Police Jurisdiction, who cite "Lack of Manpower," as the main obstacle hindering them.

And while that The Lack of Manpower available to do the job is certainly and obviously the case, and but which however also involves the aspect of blatant and obvious police corruption and conspiracy to the drugs as well, (and which is a fact which has been demonstrated for many times over in its exposures of corrupt police conspiracies to drug trafficking and to the use of drugs themselves,) involving law enforcement personnel addiction to heroin and cocaine use, (who become addicted by the proximity, opportunity, curiosity, in the handling of theses drugs as

"ONE POWERFUL VOICE"

they are forced to do in connection with their police work, and which affects them as well, in the element of addiction, particularly where the aspect of large busts are concerned, in the atmospheric pollution of Drug Atmosphere surrounding the environs of such arrests and involved with the handling of the confiscated drug supply,) and that as well as involves the element of money corruption in their conspiracy to the trafficking in drugs, that has played a major part in Treason Matter in preventing the obstacle in our path of The Drugs from being removed to complete intervention.

And which is one more motive in incentive, (besides lack of manpower,) for the use of The Military to enforce Drug Intervention in this Nation, to override and to oversee the long establish mishandled and corrupted existing efforts of the Local, State, and Federal Law Enforcement, who have not done, and who have "Never Done" their job successfully to date, (and to augment and to bolster those honest and sincere law enforcement agencies and personnel who have been acting legitimately in a dedicated manner in their attempting to do so.)

On the practical edge of what must transpire here, of our United States Agreement, to be, (and yet to remain,) inspirited of the trusted vision of our fore-bearers, encumbering in creed to the physical well-being, security, and safety of our people, and to the sense in well-being of Liberty ensured, as to the safeguarding of The Rights of Our People concerning the physical workings of our United States Constitution as it applies, that must be ideologically concerned for the emotional and physical security of the entire population; it must be made apparent to all that The United States cannot continue-on with Its divided and lackadaisical illusion of competency in paradoxical toleration to The Presence of Drugs on the pretense to the captioning of Tolerance, and to the idea of making drugs legal, on the self-righteous heals of Liberal Left Wing Politics as a religion that everyone must offer their allegiance in adherence to or suffer the punishment of economic and social sanctions for, and much worse in the case of The Drug Warfare Perpetrations, in persecution for decent. To What We Do Not Choose To Go Along With!

And for the reasoning that of what Drugs, and primarily to do with The Heroin, and Cocaine, but involving the other dangerous Street Chemicals and Pharmacy also, are The Primary Cause, involving us and our safety of security domestically, in Many Wars of Drug Related Outbreak Abroad; and besides in being the root cause of many of the population's "mysterious" physical and mental/emotional maladies as a serious health issue, and beside the health issue affecting the population of the ill-consequences involved with blatant addiction; (and to what fact, which most of our current public policy statements of anti-drug appeal on the subject by our government are presented about in that manner of priority, and not in mention of any of the other serious matters which are wrong with the allowing of the presence of the drugs here which are never mentioned about the drugs as if they didn't exist, but they do;) in being responsible for the massive amounts in onslaught of serious crimes occurring in this Nation in relation to it, both from the aspect of violence, and from the thefts ongoing to support the drug habits of those who are addicted, and for the many grievous social corruptions and injustices that the condition Of Drug Use, and The Conspiracy To Drug Trafficking, In Power, perpetuates, engenders, and creates, and for the depraved and sadistic immorality that prevails in relation to Heroin, (particularly concerning for the rampant existence of pornography, the depraved condition of lesbianism and homosexuality among the people, and the liberal attitude towards prostitution rampant,) and for the real danger setting of the population at the mercy of The Drug Mafias across America, that must straight-up Be Severely Stood Up To, and Dealt With, Conclusively, In The Present Context to "The Compulsion of Civil Defense," by Military Authority Override, (and as that there is no Civilian Civil Authority capable of doing the job of removing the population from this ongoing danger,)

"ONE POWERFUL VOICE"

for it to be no longer conceived of as a "Social Medical Condition of Addiction," in that Laissez-Faire context, to be Mishandled Ineptly and/or Corruptly under Civil Authority, (in the meaning of Ad Hoc Enforcement Style, of whoever happens to get caught instead of doing the entire job of what needs to be done everywhere in The Nation that it is needed,) But To Be Accomplished!

Clearly this is a situation that can only be competently and completely handled by Military Authority acting methodically and relentlessly under a Presidential Proclamation of Declared War On Drugs! to such effect, and in full utilization of The Legal and Authorized Constitutional Authority of Martial Law to do so, and without mercy in judgment, To Permanently Eradicate The State of The Drug Siege Condition here, and the criminal individuals who are responsible for its existence to be done away with, in our Nation, which is, and who are, causing direct and serious harm to our population, both from the standpoint of direct use of these drugs being allowed to cohabitate on an ongoing basis, and from the heinous perspective of outright and direct murderous coercive intent upon those who would speak out against it, and concerning the pernicious premeditated sadistic sabotage upon the innocent victims of those coinciding to the use of drugs prevailing, pertaining for the ongoing state of siege of The Drug Warfare occurring, that is premeditatedly designed to inflict grave bodily and mental/emotional harm on the persons en masse to whom the drugs are perpetrated.

And which, (for the mere mentioning Sabotage with a Drug or Chemical to The Authorities, personally conveyed, or for the experiencing of the outright harmful effects of such deliberate sabotage presented,) involves the issue of Psychiatric Intake and Forced Treatment with Catastrophically Disabling Psychiatric Chemical Pharmacy Drugs under Civil Law Commitment Process, and with the authorization of The Federal Food and Drug Administration (FDA) to do so, without The Constitutional Guarantees of Due Process Rights applying, and to what that The Police/Medical Authorities responsible for such catastrophic damage unto the psychiatric murder of these many innocent victims, have "Sovereign Immunity," from arrest, prosecution, and civil damages, to.

And what is a situation that is rife for exploitation by a Corrupt Medical Profession, Corrupt Law Enforcement, a Corrupt Political Structure involving Organized Crime, Mafia Terrorist Groups, and other entities bent on the overthrow of The United States, as you may well determine for yourself in the terms of its monolithic threat to the population at large, regarding the subject of Drug Warfare.

In just taking the example of The Heroin/Narcotics issue alone, as taken directly from the current edition of The Physician's Desk Reference, (PDR) and pertaining for any persons, taking in use, or in being "Hit" with or "Sabotaged" with this drug, or who have the miss-happenstance to be affected with it Atmospherically by the close proximity of a nasal user or users of Heroin; (or which can be accomplish simply by shaking the dust of It in their pocket,) affecting the atmosphere, (like cigarette smoke,) of our domestic home life, work settings, school class room and assembly areas, places of recreational and sports congregation, shopping areas, theaters, restaurants, and taverns and bars, (and deadly in the proximity to alcohol causing "black-outs,") in closed in air supply to the user(s), and that is particularly in threat to air travel concerning "The Re-Circulating Cabin Air" aboard airliners, closed into the fuselage with a Heroin Nasal Snorter or Snorters (in plural) breathing their heroin contaminated air out into the recycling atmosphere, at 35,000 feet, to what effects, this Drug causes:

Psychotic Disorder - Euphoria, Disphoria, Rage - Allergic Reactions (skin rashes, hives, itching,) - Dry Mouth -Urinary Retention -Constipation - Diarrhea -Drowsiness - Confusion -

"ONE POWERFUL VOICE"

Lightheadedness - Nausea - Impaired Concentration - Sensation of Drunkenness - Suicidal Depression - Behavioral Disturbances - Blurred Vision - Double Vision - Quadruple Vision - Choking - Shortness of Breath - Anaphylaxis (Cramping,) - Delirium - Hallucinations - Excitement - Agitation - Increased Sensitivity To Pain (after the analgesic effect has worn off,) - Impaired Breathing - Cessation of Breathing During Sleep (Sleep Apnea,) - Seizures - Muscle Twitching - Sudden Loss Of Consciousness - Facial Flushing - Sweating - Heart Palpations - Drop In Blood Pressure (causing weakness and fainting.)

And as with the threat to America stated of the ill-health inducing effects wrought by the warfaring ways of The Narcotics Element, to include as well all other illegal drugs and chemicals available to use in trafficking on the drug market, that in number have their specifically listed Effects, Side Effects, Adverse Reactions, After Effects, and Withdrawal Symptoms, in issue of their being and therefore available to use as Drug-Chemical Warfare Weapons Against The Innocent Population by those who use and traffic and wield in these illicit drugs and chemicals, who comprise the concept and condition of being The Drug Mafia in its entirety imperiling our society. To what condition that anyone who has access to a Drug or Chemical Agent is thereby free to use that Drug or Chemical with virtual impunity against anyone they care to without fear of apprehension and reprisal.

"Just grind it up and put it in their food," as the popular taunt is rendered. Or, "hit" their atmosphere with it.

Freebasing Cocaine for example causes Panic Syndrome and Cardiac Arrhythmia in the unwary who assume that something psychological or physical really the matter with them, and who are then prescribed with debilitative pharmacy or to surgical procedures by the physicians who profiteer enormously, (and with the pharmacy companies that way as well in kick-back arrangement with the medical industry,) off the drug effects in treating the symptoms of the ongoing and pervasive warfare as if they were physiological maladies of a different biological source entirely.

And such as it is in tactical warfare with every Drug and Chemical Weapon, "At Close Range," in the family or social settings, or involving, "Mass Sabotage," on a public scale, as with the case of The French Mafia producing "Taste Compatible" Psychotropic Chemicals for perpetration to our American Food Supply, (which are Psychiatric Chemicals such as Navane and Prolixin, (and named so for their mind-altering properties,) which were interdicted in our current history by Interpol and reported on by The New York Times; and which have the taste compatibility of Orange Juice, Grape Juice, and other common Household Condiments.

And which of these drug chemicals, cause and are responsible for many of the afflictions being suffered en masse by The American Population, to include:

The outright mental illnesses that these drugs are touted to alleviate, called Paradoxical Reactions by The FDS, of Schizophrenia and Manic Depression, Erectile Dis-function Syndrome, EDS, (Impotence,) Restless Leg Syndrome, RLS, (or listed as Uncomfortable States of Being and Motor Restlessness in The Physicians' Desk Reference,) Hyperactive Bladder, (termed Incontinence,) Prostatism, (or causing the Prostate Gland to enlarge in men,) and of what sedation to the population, to include for the Sedation Effects of Heroin proximity/sabotage also,) that is responsible for alarming rate of Alcoholism among the population in their attempts to "Self-Medicate" to override the sedation, to mention the obvious mass ill-health inducing effects being premeditatedly perpetrated unknown to the people, and which are all being treated at a huge profit by The Medical/Pharmacy Industry.

"ONE POWERFUL VOICE"

And concerning the effects of such Psychotropic Sabotage, are intended in design overall to make the population physically and mentally ill, weak, docile, inept, and unable to prevent their being overthrown; by whatever corrupt and sinister forces about that are attempting to overthrow them, regarding in the for instance, The Ideology of Drugs of Legal Drugs, Pornography, Money Corruption, (in government as well as business,) Criminal Politics, or for other sinister motives in design having to do with Racial and/or Nationalist Ethnic Overthrow, (in the concept of the annihilation of The White Race,) or to overthrow by Foreign Powers, (seeking relief to their over-burgeoning populations, or arable land,) and to combinations of the above in coalition.

Cocaine is always "The Antidote" To Sedation, whether the sedation is the result of Heroin or Pharmacy Chemicals.

And those who know and use Cocaine habitually also need sedation to rest and to sleep. And of which condition of general and pervasive sedation sabotage is easily overridden by those who know and are aware of drug pharmacology. And which explains why The Mafia and Terrorist Organizations afoot are able to function in the climate of general sedation sabotage to the population at large through the availability, to them, of Illegal Cocaine.

This is a conspiracy knowingly to inflict grave mental, emotional, mental, and psychological harm onto the population by the means of this clandestine style of warfare, that can be perpetrated for sadistic personal motives, and/or for purposes of more methodical programming having to do with the elimination of The Drug Opposition in large numbers from the society, and along the lines of Fascist Politics, (or The Politics of Organized Crime,) to the principle of strength in numbers, ("a bundle of sticks that cannot be broken,) and to what is therefore politically described for as, "Fascism," and that goes by other names and for other motives also, (such as "Zionism," and "Black Power,") based to the idea of Controlling The Drug Trade and using The Drugs As Weapons, and besides to the idea of making the drugs legal, (in the sense of The Drug Laws not being enforced and prosecuted for,) by the elected criminal government, and governments, (in being Gerrymandered across The Land and presenting a United Front, quilt-work style, in encompassing the entire Nation over us,) In Power, by eliminating the opposition through surreptitious means of Drug-Chemical Warfare. And to point out, that whoever controls The Source of The Drug Supply, controls the motives and the sinister orientation to attack of those who they have enslaved to its addiction.

And in the eyes the of such government conceived to the meaning of doing nothing about the presence of the drugs and keeping up with the pretense of illegality for the purpose of preventing rivals to the existing established market, that is lucratively based to an established supply system, from competing, to what rivals would diminish the profits to, and to the confiscation and redistribution of the rivals drug supply throughout their own networks. And concerning what stated Drug-Chemical Warfare that cannot be complained of.

The reason that it cannot be complained of, is that the mention of its occurrence in personal ways contains the element of psychiatric penalty and intake; either to one being labeled as a Paranoid Schizophrenic suffering with delusions of persecution, or to the effects of The Drugs and Chemicals perpetrated inducing mental, emotional, and physical ailments, which the persons so inflicted, and being unaware of the secret perpetrations of the drugs or chemicals upon them, seek treatment for, (or are Forced Into Treatment For Under Current Mental Hygiene Law,) for the ailments which have been induced by the drug or chemical being secretively administered to them.

And who, of these hapless and innocent American victims, are then subsequently treated for the symptoms of these drugs and chemicals by physicians, (who should know better,) with

"ONE POWERFUL VOICE"

harmful and destructive pharmacy chemicals, (which themselves can be used for the chemical warfare motives besides,) to induce the symptoms of Schizophrenia, Manic-Depression, Suicidal Depression, Chronic Fatigue, Hypertension, and other symptoms associated to the drugs and chemicals.

Here now is a composite listing of the adverse; physical, mental, and emotional reactions of the currently prescribed pharmacy chemicals that are being used to treat the symptoms of the drug warfare condition here in The United States, as taken directly from The Physicians' Desk Reference, (that is available to physicians also,) and beginning with The Strong Tranquilizers - Phenothiazines Class, Anti-Psychotic, Neuroleptic, Psychotropic, Types of Pharmacy, that are routinely used in mass administration for the treatment of actual, or induced, mental disorders. And which are:

Thorazine (Chlorpromazine,) Haldol (Haloperidol,) Navane (Thiothixine,) Mellaril (Thioridazine,) Loxitane (Loxapine Succinate,) Prolix in (Fluphenazine,) and Trilafon (Perphenazine,) in brief listing not totally inclusive.

Which in and of themselves induce the following; Effects, Side-Effects, and Adverse Reactions: Paradoxical Worsening of Psychotic Symptoms, Aggravation of Schizophrenia - Paranoia, Serious Toxic Effects On Brain (with long term use,) Black-Outs, Visual Hallucination, Amnesia, Deep Sleep, Bizarre Dream States, Headaches, Impaired Concentration, Mental Confusion, Impaired Mental Ability, Listlessness, Weakness, Agitation, Nervousness, Paranoia, Delusions, Depression (Suicidal,) Disorientation, Seizures, Memory Loss (long and short term,) Abnormal Behavior, Euphoria/Disphoria/Rage, Irreversible Amnesia In Elderly, Hypothermia, Fatal Shock, Ataxia (muscle cramps,) Flat Affect (fixed emotionless - mask-like facial expression,) Uncomfortable States of Being (Extreme Motor Restlessness, also known as Restless Leg Syndrome, RLS,) Tardive Diskinesia (grimacing - eye rolling - fly catcher tongue protrusions - fine involuntary wave like movements in tongue - spasmodic movements of face, neck, and extremities,) Hepatitis-like Reactions (with jaundice,) Inability To Move Certain Muscle Groups, Low Grade or High Grade Fever, Sore Throat, Cardiac Arrhythmia (palpations - heart rhythm disorders,) Liver Damage (Jaundice,) Sexual Disorders (Priapism - prolonged and painful erection, Inhibited Ejaculation and Female Orgasm, Impaired Erection, Permanent Impotence, Decreased Libido, Male Infertility, Testicular Disorders - painful swelling - atrophy, Lactation In Females, Menstruation Disorders (cessation - altered timing - severity,) Infertility, Prostatism,) Hemolytic Anemia (impaired production of white blood cells,) Convulsions - Coma, Parkinson-like Disorders (muscle spasms of face, jaw, neck, back, and extremities,) Hypoglycemia (fluctuation of blood sugar levels,) Reye Syndrome (painful discoloration, coldness, numbness, tingling, in hands and feet,) Allergic Reactions (skin rashes, hives,) Asthma, Anaphylaxis Reactions (dangerous allergic reaction - choking - shortness of breath - shock,) High or Low Blood Pressure (prolonged severe drops in blood pressure - weakness,) Impaired Breathing, Sleep Apnea (cessation of breathing during sleep,) Serum Sickness (Fever,) Disulfiram Reactions (stupor - slurred speech,) Lupus Erythematosus-like Reactions (Immune System Disorders - Deterioration, Low Grade Fever, Aching Muscles and Joints, Chest Pains, Enlargement of Lymph Glands,) Epileptic-like Reactions (provoking latent epilepsy,) Diabetes Mellitus, Diabetes Insipidus, Hemophelia-like reactions (Abnormal Bleeding,) Loss of Appetite - Indigestion/Un-digestion - Nausea, Skin Dryness - Psoriasis, Ringing In Ears, Irritation in Tongue and Mouth - Metallic Taste, Vomiting, Diarrhea, Lightheadedness, Dizziness, Drowsiness, Weakness, Tremor, Myasthenia Gravis (Exhaustion - Weakness Effecting, Speech, Eye Muscles, Swallowing, Causing Drooping Eyelids, Spasms of

"ONE POWERFUL VOICE"

Vocal Chords,) Chronic Fatigue (loss of strength in arms and legs,) Extra-Pyramedial Effects (rippling muscular motion,) Eye Damage (Loss of Peripheral Vision Neuritis, Blurred or Double Vision, Color Blindness, Impaired Night Vision, Halos Around Lights, Long Motion Trails - associated to overmedication, Pigmentation of Retina, Deposits On Retina, Nearsightedness, Structural Damage to Lens, Retina, and Cornea, Opacities - Internal Eye Pressure, Glaucoma, Painful Eye Muscles,) Gray to Violet Pigmentation of Skin Exposed To Sunlight, Neuroleptic Malignant Syndrome (Brain Damage,) Orthostatic Hypotension (type of low blood sugar,) Nerve Damage, Incontinence of The Bowl and Bladder, Chronic Constipation and Bladder Retention, Insomnia.

The Drug Cogentin is an Anti-Convulsive/Anti-Parkinsonismoften Agent, that is often prescribed, or forced treated, concurrently with The Stong Tranquilizer Phenozines Class, (which induce Convulsions and Parkinson-like Disorder as a particular side effect of their use.) The Drug Congentin itself induces The Adverse Reactions of; Extreme Rigidity, Aggravated Tardive Diskinensia, Abnormal Behavior, Confusion, Delusions, Hallucinations, Agitation, Male Infertility, Glaucoma, Hypothermia, Muscle Cramps, Myasthenia Gravis, and Depression.

The Anti-Depressant Class of Pharmacy, such as: Sinequan, Elavil, Lithuim, and Prozac, induce the Paradoxical Reaction known as Rapid Cycling (The Conversion of Depression To Mania and Re-Conversion to Depression,) and Black Outs.

Clearly then there is an error here to conceive, of allowing Afghanistan, which we, and other allied forces of The United Nations, control militarily, to continue on with their growing of vast quantities of Opium Poppy, (and 87% of the world's illicit supply according to a recent CRS, Congressional Report Service, document,) by which official State Department figures have estimated, (and by some strange coincidence to know exactly how much is being produced in the year to year, and specifically where It is being grown, in what Provinces there in Afghanistan, without doing anything about it, and down to the precise number of thousands of metric tons of raw opium being estimated,) for processing and for refining into pure grade Heroin, and bound for distribution, to our detriment and peril, throughout Europe and The United States.

Where we here, as to the civilian population in The United States, have to deal with the persistent and dire severity of the consequences of the condition and in detriment to the population, in personal ways of assault with the drug, to whatever degrees of being affected by it, and to the point of Civil War concerning out outright lack of defense to It on the part of our government responsible to us, on an ongoing day-to-day basis.

And in the meaning of being severely affected, beginning with the extremely hazardous and harmful ill-health inducing effects of the drug in pandemic proportions upon the those who have become addicted personally to it, that grows like a cancer blight, and with all the crime and foul play that it generates, to include the issue of the drug warfare upon the innocent population, as we have elaborated.

And which concerning the issue of corruption also that corresponds to the harboring of that drug Heroin in our midst, of its insidious nature to ruin lives and to corrupt societies, and that engenders the psychological effects of Greed and Evil in those who take up with It as an Addictive Habit, that spreads beyond the debased world of the drug culture, in mafia terms of subversion, to our businesses and economy and to our government itself in Its inverted fascism of democracy.

And from what revenues of this diabolical trade that are generated from the trafficking in The Drug Heroin and other drugs, (that cannot be gotten rid of under normal law of the present system, and Drug Weapons of Mass Destruction all,) of what illicit proceeds, that go to fueling

"ONE POWERFUL VOICE"

the outright Al Qaeda Terrorists network against us, a network of terror whose only motive is to create diversion, through the means of terror, away from the intervention to the trafficking of their "Domestic Product," that originates in The Protected Opium Poppy Fields of Afghanistan.

Clearly then there is an error here to conceive to allow the continuation of Poppy Farming there, (and to anywhere, and everywhere else in The World where It is known to grown and be cultivated.)

The following is a list of the major illicit drug producing or drug transit "countries" currently trafficking in Heroin, Cocaine, and other Drugs into The United States, (including certain entities that are not sovereign states):

Afghanistan, Aruba, The Bahamas, Belize, Bolivia, Brazil, Burma, Cambodia, China, Colombia, Dominican Republic, Ecuador, Guatemala, Haiti, Hong Kong, India, Jamaica, Laos, Mexico, Nigeria, Pakistan, Panama, Paraguay, Peru, Taiwan, Thailand, Venezuela, and Vietnam,

This issue also cites, North Korea, and Iran as well as Opium/Heroin Growing/Producing Nations, and heavily corrupted Narco-States, (with Atomic Weaponry Capabilities, to coincide with their Smuggling Routes,) to be wary of also.

Which are, in all regards, and in common sense to do so, to be emphatically, "Militarily Shut Down!" by Joint Resolution of The General Assembly of The United Nations in a Unified and Coordinated Effort.

Pertaining for Thorazine and other Anti-Psychotic Pharmacy, that is not medicine at all but lethal disabling chemicals which have resulted in untold hardships and tens of thousands of Veterans Suicides in despair and deaths from other complications arising from joblessness, homelessness, and from alcoholism, and drug addiction, **(Cocaine here being "the antidote" to catastrophic sedation of the neuroleptic style sedation pharmacy, that no-one can endure in the sustained and prolonged sense without becoming emotionally and psychologically crippled by,)** in attempts to Self-Medicate to Anti-Dote their way back into the semblance of a normal life from the crippling and morbid effects of these drugs. And which is something that we all need to take-up a stand on together about.

Virtually the entire Ward of patients at The Albany V.A. in 1982, of some twenty men, had to sit each morning on awakening connected to Blood Pressure Monitors to determine if we could continue on with the Thorazine Treatment for that day, which was then being conducted as a Clinical Trial; listing effects and side effects and collecting statistics; to what adverse-effects that everyone suffered from comatose zombie-mask-like flat affect syndrome, ticks and twitches, from their treatment, myself among them, and we all suffered with pathetic uncontrollable incontinence, and some had bad violent convulsive seizures biting their tongues, as I witnessed, from the effects of the treatment.

Opium/Heroin is The Mother of All Wars.

Most Respectfully,

Gary L. Koniz
Journalist/Correspondent
for The Buffalo News

"ONE POWERFUL VOICE"

9840 Princeton Square Blvd. S., #815
Jacksonville, FL 32256
(904) 730-2055

Administrative Officer
Office of General Counsel
Central Intelligence Agency
Washington, D.C. 20505

November 24, 2006

The case being presented here is that you are not doing the job, as you should be doing, of removing the Heroin and the presence of other dangerous Drugs and Chemicals from the soil of The United States, and even though that you have the means in government resources and the technology available to do so.

That being the case, you need to know that we intend to stringently oversee the arrangement of your version of government to us, that is unsatisfactory, in ensuring that The United States is maintained by the standards and principles that our guiding forefathers set before us to expect in intent, (concerning the integrity of our government supervision and upholding to the stipulation To Provide For The Common Defense,) until such matters which our present government, and stemming from previous Administrations, has been allowing to deteriorate in disgrace, as to The Drugs epidemic situation continuing-on and concerning the deterioration of our U.S. Economy fallen now into corrupt and subversive hands and with being overrun by Third World Populations, (with no offense intended, but nonetheless,) undercutting our legitimate Middle Class Wage Structure, in version of a Slave Culture, and withal in need to be resolved.

The Drugs, and coinciding with The Drug Warfare and Corruption Issue, affect The Economy, which we depend to for our survival and to the survival of our dependent family loved ones. Which has become a war front to us to remove in our civilian efforts to destroy the condition before it destroys us. War is what it is. You need to remember that we are the ones who ultimately live here and who elect our government, in representation, to serve to us in our best interest. We don't choose to cohabitate with The Drugs you allow, and have been allowing, and we don't wish to be governed over by The Drug Regimes acquiring the corrupt power through The Criminal Inversion of our Political Democracy to rule here, concerning your allowing of The Drugs, Immoral Pornography, The Tyranny of Wage Servitude, Price Gouging To The Cost Essentials, and with No Affordable Health Insurance available for the immediate public, To Prevail! That has become a matter of life and death to us to overturn.

We are particularly concerned with the continued allowing of Opium to still be freely cultivated in Afghanistan, and coinciding with the issue of Free Trade Agreement with The Drug Nations of The Americas and now being proposed with Vietnam, which is an entrenched, "Narco-State," which was responsible for The Vietnam War concerning Its Trafficking in Opium from Laos and The Golden Triangle, and that inviting free and unrestricted trade with Vietnam is inviting a conspiracy to disaster.

Gary L. Koniz
Journalist Correspondent
Veterans of the Vietnam War

"ONE POWERFUL VOICE"

STATEMENT OF

IRA KATZ, M.D

DEPUTY CHIEF PATIENT CARE SERVICES OFFICER

FOR MENTAL HEALTH

DEPARTMENT OF VETERANS AFFAIRS

BEFORE THE HOUSE COMMITTEE

ON VETERANS AFFAIRS

July 25, 2007

Good morning Mr. Chairman, thank you for this opportunity to speak about multiple diagnoses and specifically about the principle that Post Traumatic Stress Disorder (PTSD) frequently coexists with other mental health conditions.

Multiple Mental Health Problems
As of the end of the first half of FY 2007, almost 720,000 service men and women have separated from the armed forces after service in Iraq or Afghanistan, and over 250,000 have sought care in VA. About 95,000 received at least a preliminary mental health diagnosis. Among these, PTSD, experienced by over 45,000 or 48 percent is the most common.

The average veteran with a mental health problem received approximately 1.9 diagnoses. There could be several reasons. First, injuries of the mind, like injuries of the body can be non-selective. Depending upon psychological, physiological, or genetic vulnerabilities, the same stress and trauma can give rise to multiple conditions, for example PTSD and depression or panic disorder. Second, the disorders may occur sequentially. Some veterans with PTSD may try to treat their own symptoms with alcohol and wind up with a diagnosis related to problem drinking. Third, some pre-existing mental health conditions like milder personality disorders may be quite compatible with occupational functioning, even in the military, but may increase vulnerability to stress-related disorders like PTSD or depression.

How does VA deal with this problem?
VA has intensive programs to ensure that mental health problems are recognized, diagnosed, and treated. There is outreach to bring veterans into our system, and once they arrive, there is screening for mental health conditions. For those who screen positive for mental health conditions, the next step is a comprehensive diagnostic and treatment planning evaluation. In this, the question is about what is causing the veteran's suffering or impairment, and what can be done about it. If someone screens positive for symptoms of PTSD, we are interested in whether or not they, in fact have PTSD. But we are also interested in whether or not they have depression, or panic disorder, or problem drinking, or other problems. Which do we treat? We treat them all. Or more significantly, we treat the person, not his or her labels.

Clinical science has advanced dramatically since the Vietnam War. We now know how to diagnose PTSD, and how to treat it. Accordingly, we are hopeful that we can prevent the lasting suffering and impairments that occurred after that war. There is a firm evidence-base for several classes of treatment for PTSD, both psychopharmacological or medication based and psychotherapeutic or talk/behavior based. Specifically, several of the antidepressants that act on the neurotransmitter serotonin have been found to be effective and safe for the treatment of PTSD, and many other medications are currently being studied. Two specific forms of cognitive behavioral therapy, prolonged exposure therapy and cognitive processing therapy appear to be even more effective than the medications, and VA is currently developing high throughput training programs to make them increasingly available within our medical centers, clinics, and Vet Centers. In addition, there is

"ONE POWERFUL VOICE"

increasing evidence for the effectiveness of psychosocial rehabilitation. For veterans for whom there may be residual symptoms after several evidence-based treatments, treatment is available to help them function in the family, in the community, or on the job.

Given that there are a number of effective treatments, how do we decide which to provide?
Actually, the question should be which to offer first and which comes next. The first treatments are usually offered on the basis of both the provider's judgment and the patient's preference. However, we monitor treatments and outcomes, and if the first doesn't work, we modify it.

What happens when patients have more than one condition? The choice of what to treat first depends on the severity of the conditions, the provider's judgment, and the patient's preferences. Plans must allow for combinations or sequences of treatments, as appropriate following Clinical Practice Guidelines or other sources of guidance.

There may have been a time in the past when coexisting conditions may have been barriers to care, when it was hard to treat people with PTSD and alcohol abuse because PTSD programs required people to be sober, and substance abuse programs required them to be stable. This no longer occurs. In fact, there are now evidence based strategies for beginning PTSD and substance abuse treatment simultaneously. One approach, called Seeking Safety was developed in the VA, and is being disseminated broadly.

It may be difficult to diagnose personality disorders in the face of PTSD or other mental health conditions. For patients with relevant symptoms, the clinical approach in VA is to treat the PTSD first. A subsequent step would be evaluate what symptoms or impairments remain, and to plan treatments accordingly.

The message I want to deliver in this hearing is that treatment for PTSD can work. For veterans or others with multiple conditions, treatment may be a multistage process beginning with an evidence based intervention for the most severe of the patient's conditions, and continuing in a way that depends upon the outcome. Overall, the message should be cautiously optimistic.

Thank you for this opportunity to testify. I will be pleased to answer any questions you may have.

"ONE POWERFUL VOICE"

9480 Princeton Square Blvd. S., #815
Jacksonville, FL 32256
May 1, 2009

Ira Katz, MD, PhD
Deputy Chief Patient Care Services
Officer for Mental Health
Veterans Health Administration
810 Vermont Avenue, N.W.
Washington, D.C. 20420

Dear Doctor Katz,

I know that you are an intelligent man, and a medical person of the highest magnitude of integrity and of a sincere and genuine compassion in understanding for the nature of your job function in position, and with a great weight to rest solidly on your shoulders, the weight of the precious lives in the reasoning of our returning from war Veterans, and to discuss for all of our soldiers in uniform in sacrifice of their service for our country, for their trauma and grief and for their emotional suffering en masse of the horrors of combat, and to the wounds of war, both seen and unseen, that they suffer, that the Nation entrusts to you, our Chief Counsel for Mental Health with The Veterans Administration, and to whom that there is no one higher to judge the performance of their care and treatment, to assist and to alleviate the ordeal of our Veterans in remedy and to the safe-keeping and safety of their lives at stake of the issue, for the sake of their diagnostic labeling and treatment, and with regard to their livelihoods and family settings, of their being permanently labeled and scarred by their being known a mental patients, and from the effects of treatment, to their ultimate ruination within the society, and in their own eyes to be tortured over forever, and ultimately then to their not wanting to live anymore.

I overheard my younger sister ask my father one day in a concerned voice; "Why does Gary have to go to the V.A. and take medication."

To what my father replied; "Because he's killed, and he may kill again."

Repeating what was told to him by the Asian Doctor who "Treated Me" with Thorazine at The Albany V.A. Medical Center in 1982, Byung Kim.

And in which that much of their morass, (as you are well aware,) with being brought on also by the effects of their treatment, or torture, as it is described for by those on whom it is inflicted upon, in the form of Anti-Psychotic Pharmacy, either being "Forced" in that rendition of Psychiatry, (and as also termed as, "The Industry of Death,") or upon the ill-informed consent, in ill-advisement of Medical Authority, to take, and to whom, of these Medical Doctors as Health Professionals, that our Veterans are entrusted to, and whom that they are trained To Trust, and who represent as well the outright Authority of The United States, and regarding The Veterans Administration, to obey the orders of about, as in the meaning of Doctors Orders, for the taking

"ONE POWERFUL VOICE"

of these drugs; that we asked you for, (and through the office of the Secretary of Veterans Affairs, General Eric Shinseki,) your statement in evaluation of these Drug Chemicals, (and which we have previously listed for you under the heading of Neuroleptic, and Psychotropic Pharmacy,) as to whether or not that you approve or disapprove of these drugs, and as to whether or not that these drugs in your protective opinion are in fact ultimately harmful, or beneficial and therapeutic, for our Veterans to take, of their short term and long term effects, in side effects, adverse effects, contraindications, and paradoxical reactions, of these pharmacy products; and also under what circumstance that a person can be Force Treated with these drugs, such as Thorazine (Clorpromazine,) and Haldol (Haldoperidol,) and as to the Legal Resources available to challenge, Diagnosis Labeling, Commitment Processing, and Treatment. And for what that you responded in your letter dated, May 22, 2009:

All medications have potential side effects as well as therapeutic effects and chlorpromazine is no exception. Neuroleptic or antipsychotic medications have been proven effective and even life-saving over decades of research and practice for thousands, if not millions, of persons suffering from psychotic disorders. With proper medications and other psychosocial supports people who in previous eras might have spent their lives in mental institutions are now able to live successful and satisfying lives in the community. Chlorpromazine is not much used in VA currently, (only 0.1 % of Veterans received this medication in FY 2008), while other medications with fewer side effects are in more common use.

Patients have the right to accept or refuse any medical treatment or procedure recommended to them. The decision to employ a treatment is the joint decision of the patient and the clinician treating them, with the potential gains and risks of accepting or rejecting treatment made clear. The only situation in which a patient might be compelled to accept a medication, such as an antipsychotic medication, is if there is clear evidence that not doing so would endanger the patient or others. An involuntary commitment procedure would be required for this and there is a statutorily prescribed process that must be followed which is established in 38 C.F.R.17.32(g)(2) along with procedures set forth in VHA Handbook 1004.1 Informed Consent for Clinical Treatments and Procedures. Commitment procedures are regulated by State law and adjudicated by the courts. Involuntary commitment status must be reviewed on a regular basis: once conditions for commitment no longer apply, the involuntary commitment is terminated.

That does not answer our questions, as to whether or not that such described for chemistry products are safe and within the realm of being therapeutically beneficial.

Your reply was that "All Medications have potential side effects," and is not descriptive as to the meaning of their proving, in your eyes, to be, harmful, and ultimately fatal to take over the long run. And as you indicated that only 0.1% of Veterans were administered with Thorazine in fiscal year 2008 but without describing the numbers of Veterans treated in that year, that has no relevance in the sense that one can relate to. Is it 0.1% of a million, or a hundred thousand Veterans being diagnosed and treated with Thorazine, for their alleged Psychiatric Conditions, (as was the case for the Vietnam War Veterans, of whom, 1,000,000 were psychiatrically labeled and treated, most of them with Clorpromzine, in so called "Clinical Trials," either as Force Patients, or without proper Informed Concent, as to the consequences, and of whom that 68,000

"ONE POWERFUL VOICE"

of those committed suicide in numbers, more than the 58,000 who were killed in the war outright.

And with your 38 C.F.R. 17.32(g) (2) on the subject of being provided by the V.A. with legal counsel for the sake of being Psychiatrically Accused and Treated, reading as follows: Which, as you can see, only provides the Veterans with the "opportunity" to consult with their own attorney, or to seek consultation with an independent specialist, (both of which are very expensive to procure, if at all,) and which in no way guarantees that either the private attorney, or the independent specialist, will have "any impact" whatsoever on the determinations, ultimately, of the "multi-disciplinary committee" appointed by the Director of the facility, whose ultimate decision of such "Forced Treatment" is determined by, and not upon any formal adjudication of law, in such an unmitigated and serious matter of one's being potentially destroyed by Chemicals that have a catastrophic effect on a person's mind and body in the altering their matabolism.

(g) *Special consent situations.* In addition to the other requirements of this section, additional protections are required in the following situations.

(1) No patient will undergo any unusual or extremely hazardous treatment or procedure, *e.g.,* that which might result in irreversible brain damage or sterilization, except as provided in this paragraph (g). Before treatment is initiated, the patient or surrogate must be given adequate opportunity to consult with independent specialists, legal counsel or other interested parties of his or her choosing. The patient's or surrogate's signature on a VA authorized consent form must be witnessed by someone who is not affiliated with the VA health-care facility, *e.g.,* spouse, legal guardian, or patient advocate. If a surrogate makes the treatment decision, a multi-disciplinary committee, appointed by the facility Director, must review that decision to ensure it is consistent with the patient's wishes or in his or her best interest. The committee functions as the patient's advocate and may not include members of the treatment team. The committee must submit its findings and recommendations in a written report to the facility Director. The Director may authorize treatment consistent with the surrogate's decision or request that a special guardian for health care be appointed to make the treatment decision.

(2) Administration of psychotropic medication to an involuntarily committed patient against his or her will must meet the following requirements. The patient or surrogate must be allowed to consult with independent specialists, legal counsel or other interested parties concerning the treatment with psychotropic medication. Any recommendation to administer or continue medication against the patient's or surrogate's will must be reviewed by a multi-disciplinary committee appointed by the facility Director for this purpose. This committee must include a psychiatrist or a physician who has psychopharmacology privileges. The facility Director must concur with the committee's recommendation to administer psychotropic medications contrary to the patient's or surrogate's wishes. Continued therapy with psychotropic medication must be reviewed every 30 days. The patient (or a representative on the patient's behalf) may appeal the treatment decision to a court of appropriate jurisdiction.

(3) If a proposed course of treatment or procedure involves approved medical research in whole or in part, the patient or representative shall be advised of this. Informed consent shall be obtained specifically for the administration or performance of that aspect of the treatment or procedure that involves research. Such consent shall be in addition to that obtained for the

"ONE POWERFUL VOICE"

administration or performance of the non-research aspect of the treatment or procedure and must meet the requirements for informed consent set forth in 38 CFR Part 16, *Protection of Human Subjects.*

And, it is in that light then, that we must have the proper Legal Resources and Definitions of Law ensured for the protection of our Men In Arms; as to what exactly constitutes for a, "Legal Definition of a Mental Condition," and under what specific circumstances that anyone may be "Force Treated;" which that you yourself, in being only one man at the helm of a vast and complicated system, with very complex issues to resolve on many levels, cannot possibly hope to control without specific guidelines in place to secure the safety and well-being of everyone who comes into contact with the heading of psychiatric in exposure, and to what that everyone is lumped into a common plight about with the utterly insane and violently irrational over, as to the meaning that being labeled as a "psychiatric patient" is to imply; and whether that they are suffering with remorse of combat, or grieving over the deaths of their comrades, or suffering the loss of their wives on their return, or from anxiety of being jobless and homeless in their suffering, that the wording of psychiatric implies "the worst case scenario" to. Therefore:

Since the Medical Terminology Technicality of Mental Hygiene Psychiatric Law falls under the heading of Civil Law, Two Physician Consent, 2PC, Commitment Procedure, on Medical Grounds, in that no crime has been committed under Mental Hygiene Law to be charged for and thereby to be accorded the protective safeguards of Miranda Rights Legislation to be prosecuted for and processed fairly for under The Constitutional Rights accorded to Criminal Penal Law Legal System under the protection in Rights To The People, of The Fourth, Fifth, Sixth, Eighth and Fourteenth Amendments to The U.S. Constitution, and reinforced by the protection of The Miranda Legislation, is hereby clarified of Its Civil Law Constitutional Rights, in meaning to have the same Rights of Due Process as are and have been established under Penal Law, in guarantee of:

The Right to have a clear definition of a Formal Psychiatric Charge being present in grounds for anyone to be labeled for and to have any specified medical psychiatric condition, or for the offense of irrational behavior labeling being levied against an individual, and in grounds thereby for any psychiatric evaluation process mental illness labeling to be attached to anyone, or for any process of Two Physician Consent, 2PC, Psychiatric Commitment Procedure to be conducted. And that such definition of charge is also to precede any Court or Government Agency Order for the disclosure of personal and private psychiatric history records to be produced.

The Right to The Fourth Amendment guarantee of privacy in regard of doctor patient confidentiality and invoking to The Due Process Right of Probable and Sufficient Cause In Grounds, is to be present and justified to a specific itemized search and disclosure in mandatory request for Specific Information only of any existing psychiatric history records, regarding The Rights of Government Agencies, as for the specified psychiatric history to be scrutinized, to any private request or public government agency order for, or court authority mandatory order for the scrutiny of anyone's psychiatric medical history records to be revealed. That is not to be construed by court order or by congressional authority concerning government agencies, to be a total and all intrusive invasive invasion of an individual's records history involving The Right To Privacy, but is to issued only as order for records disclosure pertains selectively and relevant to the specified psychiatric charge of inquiry at hand.

The Right to strict legal definition for any psychiatric labeling terms to be applied.

"ONE POWERFUL VOICE"

The Right to strict legal determinations based to demonstrated facts of observed and defined behavior, in the presence of any attorney, for such alleged psychiatric labeling being attributed in legal attachment of a psychiatric diagnosis or involving commitment.

The Right to Counsel, to be provided for at government expense if need be, by The Examining Government Agency or by The Court of Jurisdiction, for any alleged psychiatric matter of consequence being attributed to anyone, involving the loss of liberty, property, licensure, employment, or privilege.

The Right to have an Attorney present during questioning to any psychiatric examination/evaluation/interrogation, and to be present during psychiatric commitment processing and to any court proceedings and signing of documents.

The Right to Remain Silent in presumption of innocence until proven guilty to any psychiatric charge in a bona fide court of law.

The Right to Confrontations of any accusing testimony against the accused in virtue of The Sixth Amendment, that under current Mental Hygiene Law there is No Right To.

The Right to a Jury Trial provided in a timely way in accordance with The Sixth Amendment for any specified psychiatric accusation labeling being imposed, whether involving commitment or not.

The Right to clearly established and legally defined medically safe and beneficial therapeutic treatment to be imposed for legitimate psychiatric conditions.

The Right to Informed Consent "in the presence of Legal Counsel" concerning the discussion and patient awareness of adverse effects, and harmful side effects in short and long-term use of psychiatric chemicals involved with any psychiatric treatment to occur.

The Right To Refuse Treatment, and Against Forced Treatment on Medical Discretion, in the presence of legal counsel, [except in matters As Prescribed By Law to be applied for necessary medical emergency procedure in concern to imminent crisis of hysteria, and for violent mania and agitated disruptive behavior in being in threat to oneself or others requiring emergency medical treatment in judgment or relief.]

The Right against any form, including psychological, of cruel and inhumane treatment to occur, concerning physical, mental, or emotional abuse, to include electro-shock treatment, surgical procedure, and pharmaceutical experimentation, [Clinical Trials] in virtue of The Eighth Amendment.

The Right to reasonable and soundly defined Statute of Limitations in established Legal Age Limits for the mandatory disclosure of previous psychiatric condition labeling history records, or to the disclosure of legally carried-out psychiatric commitment history records, based to the nature and severity and to the extent of such psychiatric conditions in legal stipulation and to the length of time of such conditions in interval, to be imposed for mandatory disclosure of records, not to be in excess of a reasonable and prudent time interval regarding the public removal of stigma and liability of such records history. Which in most instances is to be worded, to any current treatment for any serious ongoing psychiatric condition, or to within the past three years in age limit concerning

Gary L. Koniz – Representing
Veterans Of The Vietnam War

"ONE POWERFUL VOICE"

9480 Princeton Square Blvd. S.
Apartment #815
Jacksonville, FL 32256
(904) 730-2055

File No: 24 891 327

S. L. Smith
Service Center Manager
Department Of Veterans Affairs
St. Petersburg Regional Office
P.O. Box 7000
Bay Pines, FL 33744

Dear Mr. Smith:

With all due regard of respect for you and for the volume of work that you and your dedicated staff at The Veterans Affairs Service Center have to contend with; but I have been through all the various points of your requests with you enough already and have sent you in all the text in paper work that you requested from myself and from the various Psychiatric Treatment Facilities which I attended; and with very elaborate discussions to the nature and definition of **Post Traumatic Stress Disorder**, and the catastrophic and permanently disabling **Thorazine Treatment** received at The V.A. Medical Center in Albany, NY (on the dates 4/19/82 to 5/13/92; the records for which you claim you have not received,) and otherwise of catastrophically ruining other descriptions of Neuroleptic Strong Tranquillizers known as Anti-Psychotic Drugs that I was Forced Treated with by the two State Facilities I fell prey to; which were G. Werber Brian Psychiatric Hospital in Columbia, SC, 3/28/82 to 4/13/82; which records you claim you have not received, and prior to my seeking help at the Albany, NY V.A. for the effects of their Forced Disabling Treatment with Loxitane and Cogentin;) and at the later date of my being Committed to Hudson River Psychiatric Facility in Poughkeepsie, NY, <u>which you have received</u>, (on the two consecutive sixty days intervals of Commitment, of 6/23/85 to 8/22/85 and of 12/10/85 to 2/10/86, to be detained **Without Benefit of Due Process** <u>in Violation of my Civil Rights and with no means of an Attorney to defend myself from such commitment and from being Forcibly Treated with the disabling Chemical Navane</u>; that was directly connected to my previous hospitalization by the V.A.;) and for what matters in all <u>that I have already requested that the Records be released for you</u>. To the point, <u>that my case with you is now being "Referred Back" to its original starting point</u> as if I had submitted nothing; that is a product of your **Warehousing Effect** (being understaffed and over worked,) over the decades of my relentless appeals; that have to do with, in first instance:

That, **as I have previously explained at length**, that my appeal to the V.A. for PTSD consideration, (and not just being spoken for, for myself, but for all Veterans who have had to endure and to suffer the hardships, and the rigors, and the carnage of our Nation's Wars being fought, and to say, by them, The Veterans, who make this appeal regarding the nature in definition of Post Traumatic Stress;) that has to do with **the Very Tragic Emotional Nature of War Itself Being, In and Of Itself, The Trauma**; to state that Wars are not fought without

"ONE POWERFUL VOICE"

emotions, (to the nature of the PTSD Symptoms with the Veterans being left in a **Vacuous Dazed State of Suicidal Depression** following their Separation From Service; from shell shock, remorse of combat, unrelenting fear, terror, and horror, and bearing the common grief of all soldiers for their fallen comrades, to be left in real mourning, and with an alienated feeling of being unable to find their place and way among the civilian population. The second part of which being; **that Military Service, in and of Itself, is The Disability**, in that it sets up a **Distrustful Division between the Veterans and Society**, as being viewed as distinct and as separated from the general norms of the social setting among the civilian population who "fears" the returning Veterans en masse, In Profiling, as to their being Trained Killers, and of having Killed, to be feared, as society fears all killers in the general idea of their being deranged. And my point being here, that concerning your original "Denial" of my PTSD claim, on 4/28/86, that it was "**Denied Without Show Cause**;" which I repeatedly requested for in **Due Process Rights** in order to ascertain Precisely Why that my claim was summarily denied to have the facts presented by the Attorney at the New York City Regional V.A..

The other point I make quite strongly to you is this. That the Drug Thorazine is a deadly chemical substance that **Causes Brain Damage** and ruinous **Metabolical Destruction**, that the V.A. never did have any business administering to the Vietnam Veterans of my era with the V.A.'s en masse general order for Thorazine Treatment for Veterans falling in the happenstance of the locked Psychiatric Wards at the V.A. Hospitals; (of which well over 1,000,000 men were treated for PTSD during the Vietnam War and in its aftermath, and of these, to point out, that 64,000 of these brave men committed suicide, as the result of such treatment,) and to the point that I am making for the case of blatant "Malpractice Disability Compensation," and beyond any issue of PTSD, but for the case of the Forced Thorazine Treatment by The V.A. being of Itself Permanently Disabling.) And if you would pay attention to me here **To Acknowledge This**; that The V.A. made an error "**In Its Profiling**" of our returning Veterans **as being murders** and by prescribing to them the most **catastrophic disabling chemical substance Thorazine** there is, reserved for homicidal mental patients. Concerning which treatment that I have personally "lost" over twenty years of my life to the disabling effects of this drug; and disabling in the lingering sense of having lost my way in life; professionally, economically, and relationship wise.

I am pressing the case here for compensation from the effects of the Thorazine Treatment I was Force Treated with at the V.A.; and with appeal for the "**Readjustment**" of your thinking regarding **Post Traumatic Stress Disorder**, as it is officially legally described. I am also requesting **FOIA Verification** of all documents pertaining to my case on file.

Most Respectfully In Regard,

Gary L. Koniz

CC: Department Of Veterans Affairs Secretary Eric Shinseki
       Ira Katz – V.A. Deputy Chief Mental Health Officer
       V.A. General Counsel Will A. Gunn

"ONE POWERFUL VOICE"

DSM Criteria for PTSD

In 2000, the American Psychiatric Association revised the PTSD diagnostic criteria in the fourth edition of its Diagnostic and Statistical Manual of Mental Disorders (DSM-IV-TR)(1). The diagnostic criteria (A-F) are specified below.

Diagnostic criteria for PTSD include a history of exposure to a traumatic event meeting two criteria and symptoms from each of three symptom clusters: intrusive recollections, avoidant/numbing symptoms, and hyper-arousal symptoms. A fifth criterion concerns duration of symptoms and a sixth assesses functioning.

Criterion A: stressor

The person has been exposed to a traumatic event in which both of the following have been present:

The person has experienced, witnessed, or been confronted with an event or events that involve actual or threatened death or serious injury, or a threat to the physical integrity of oneself or others.

The person's response involved intense fear, helplessness, or horror. Note: in children, it may be expressed instead by disorganized or agitated behavior.

Criterion B: intrusive recollection

The traumatic event is persistently re-experienced in at least one of the following ways: Recurrent and intrusive distressing recollections of the event, including images, thoughts, or perceptions.

Note: in young children, repetitive play may occur in which themes or aspects of the trauma are expressed.

Recurrent distressing dreams of the event.
Note: in children, there may be frightening dreams without recognizable content

Acting or feeling as if the traumatic event were recurring (includes a sense of reliving the experience, illusions, hallucinations, and dissociative flashback episodes, including those that occur upon awakening or when intoxicated). Note: in children, trauma-specific reenactment may occur.

Intense psychological distress at exposure to internal or external cues that symbolize or resemble an aspect of the traumatic event.

"ONE POWERFUL VOICE"

Physiologic reactivity upon exposure to internal or external cues that symbolize or resemble an aspect of the traumatic event

Criterion C: avoidant/numbing

Persistent avoidance of stimuli associated with the trauma and numbing of general responsiveness (not present before the trauma), as indicated by at least three of the following:
Efforts to avoid thoughts, feelings, or conversations associated with the trauma
Efforts to avoid activities, places, or people that arouse recollections of the trauma
Inability to recall an important aspect of the trauma
Markedly diminished interest or participation in significant activities
Feeling of detachment or estrangement from others
Restricted range of affect (e.g., unable to have loving feelings)
Sense of foreshortened future (e.g., does not expect to have a career, marriage, children, or a normal life span)

Criterion D: hyper-arousal

Persistent symptoms of increasing arousal (not present before the trauma), indicated by at least two of the following:
Difficulty falling or staying asleep
Irritability or outbursts of anger
Difficulty concentrating
Hyper-vigilance
Exaggerated startle response

Criterion E: duration

Duration of the disturbance (symptoms in B, C, and D) is more than one month.

Criterion F: functional significance

The disturbance causes clinically significant distress or impairment in social, occupational, or other important areas of functioning.

Specify if:
Acute: if duration of symptoms is less than three months
Chronic: if duration of symptoms is three months or more

Specify if:
With or Without delay onset: Onset of symptoms at least six months after the stressor

References
American Psychiatric Association. (2000). Diagnostic and statistical manual of mental disorders (Revised 4th ed.). Washington, DC: Author.

"ONE POWERFUL VOICE"

DEPARTMENT OF VETERANS AFFAIRS
VARO St Petersburg
P O Box 1437
St. Petersburg FL 33731

GARY L. KONIZ

VA File Number
24 891 327

Rating Decision
May 16, 2013

INTRODUCTION

The records reflect that you are a veteran of the Vietnam Era. You served in the Army from August 14, 1964 to August 11, 1967. You filed a new claim for benefits that was received on April 1, 2011. Based on a review of the evidence listed below, we have made the following decisions on your claim.

Letters were sent to you, on April 25, 2011 and November 27, 2012, requesting evidence, and offering assistance in compliance with the 5103 notification and informing you of what evidence is required to complete the processing your claim.

DECISION

1 . Service connection for posttraumatic stress disorder (PTSD) is denied.

2 . Entitlement to compensation under 38 U.S.C. 1151 for crippled nervous system is denied.

3 . Entitlement to compensation under 38 U.S.C. 1151 for amnesia is denied.

4 . Entitlement to compensation under 38 U.S.C. 1151 for impotency is denied.

5 . Entitlement to compensation under 38 U.S.C. 1151 for crippled muscular system is denied.

"ONE POWERFUL VOICE"

GARY L. KONIZ
24 891 327
Page 2

6 . Entitlement to compensation under 38 U.S.C. 1151 for incontinence is denied.

7 . Entitlement to individual unemployability is denied.

EVIDENCE

- Service Treatment Records from August 14, 1964 through August 11, 1967
- Treatment reports from VA Medical Center Albany, NY from April 19, 1982 through June 3, 1988
- Letters from veteran dated May 22, 2009 to April 13, 2013
- Private medical records from Hudson River Psychiatric Center of Poughkeepsie, NY from July 12, 1985 through December 10, 1985
- PTSD Questionnaire received March 7, 2012
- Private medical records from G Werber Bryan Psychiatric Hospital of Columbia, SC from March 28, 1982 through April 6, 1982
- VA examination results from VA Medical Center Gainesville, FL dated September 11, 2012
- Application for individual unemployability received December 12, 2012
- Private medical record from Dr. Charles Cobb of Jacksonville, FL dated May 14, 2012
- VA examination results from VA Medical Center Bay Pines, FL dated May 13, 2013
- There were no treatment records from the VA Healthcare System of jurisdiction

REASONS FOR DECISION

1 . Service connection for posttraumatic stress disorder (PTSD).

Service connection for posttraumatic stress disorder (PTSD) is denied.

Service connection may be granted for a disability which began in military service or was caused by some event or experience in service.

Service connection for post-traumatic stress disorder (PTSD) requires medical evidence diagnosing PTSD in accordance with 38 CFR 4.125 (a); a link, established by medical evidence, between current symptoms and an in-service stressor; and credible supporting evidence that the claimed in-service stressor occurred.

Service Treatment Records from August 14, 1964 through August 11, 1967 show no complaint, diagnosis or treatment for a mental condition. On your separation examination you denied having nervous trouble, depression or excessive worry or excessive drinking habits.

"ONE POWERFUL VOICE"

GARY L. KONIZ
24 891 327
Page 3

PTSD Questionnaire received March 7, 2012 noted you claimed you suffer stress and anxiety due to enemy action in Vietnam. A stressor based on fear of hostile action was conceded and a VA examination was requested.

Treatment reports from VA Medical Center Albany, NY from April 19, 1982 through June 3, 1988 noted that you were diagnosed and treated for paranoid schizophrenia. You made no report of problems associated with your service in Vietnam and no diagnosis of PTSD was provided.

Letters from veteran dated May 22, 2009 to April 13, 2013 noted that you felt that your mental condition in the 1970's through 1996 was PTSD.

Private medical records from Hudson River Psychiatric Center of Poughkeepsie, NY from July 12, 1985 through December 10, 1985 noted that you were diagnosed and treated for paranoid schizophrenia. You made no report of problems associated with your service in Vietnam and no diagnosis of PTSD was provided.

Private medical records from G Werber Bryan Psychiatric Hospital of Columbia, SC from March 28, 1982 through April 6, 1982 noted that you were diagnosed and treated for a paranoid disorder. You made no report of problems associated with your service in Vietnam and no diagnosis of PTSD was provided. Records noted that an informant probably a family member noted that in 1972-1973 you abused marijuana heavily as well as other drugs including LSD.

VA examination results from VA Medical Center Gainesville, FL dated September 11, 2012 noted that you reported being in fear when you left your basecamp on convoys or working on roads. The examiner noted that she reviewed your service treatment records, private psychiatric records in your claim file, performed psychiatric testing and completed an in-person examination. Based on the results of her review, the examiner noted she could make no diagnosis of a mental condition per DSM-IV criteria. She noted that based on CAPS (Clinician Administered PTSD Scale) you did not meet the criteria for a diagnosis of PTSD as you did not satisfy the criteria for Criterion B,C and D under DSM-IV. She also noted you had a perfect score of 30/30 on the Mini-mental State exam.

As the evidence does not show a diagnosis of a current mental condition under the criteria set forth in DSM-IV, service connection for posttraumatic stress disorder (PTSD) is denied.

2. Entitlement to compensation under 38 U.S.C. 1151 for crippled nervous system.

Entitlement to compensation under 38 U.S.C. 1151 for crippled nervous system is denied.

Compensation is payable for any disability which is caused by VA hospitalization, medical or surgical treatment, vocational rehabilitation, compensated work therapy program (CWT), or as the result of having submitted to a VA medical examination. The evidence must show that the veteran's additional disability is actually the result of the VA care. Specifically, carelessness, negligence, lack of proper skill, error in judgment, or similar instance of fault on the part of the

"ONE POWERFUL VOICE"

GARY L. KONIZ
24 891 327
Page 4

Department in furnishing the hospital care, medical or surgical treatment, or examination must be shown; or the proximate cause of disability must be an event not reasonably foreseeable. For training and rehabilitation services or compensated work therapy program, it must be shown that the veteran's participation in an essential activity or function of the training, services, or CWT program provided or authorized by VA proximately caused the disability. Merely showing that a veteran has additional disability is not sufficient to establish causation.

Service connection may be granted for a disability which began in military service or was caused by some event or experience in service.

Service Treatment Records from August 14, 1964 through August 11, 1967 noted no diagnosis, treatment or complaint of nervous system disorder.

Treatment reports from VA Medical Center Albany, NY from April 19, 1982 through June 3, 1988 noted that you were treated with thorazine for paranoid schizophrenia from April 19, 1982 to May 3, 1982. The only side effect of the drug noted while under treatment was orthostatic hypotension.

Private medical record from Dr. Charles Cobb of Jacksonville, FL dated May 14, 2012 noted no dizziness, tremor or numbness/tingling in your extremities.

VA examination results from VA Medical Center Bay Pines, FL dated May 13, 2013 noted a complete review of you claims file to include all available records from VA medical Center Albany, NY. The examiner opined that it is more likely that the your crippled nervous system IS UNRELATED, caused, by or aggravated by medical treatment, rehab program, or participation in a compensated work therapy program activity at VA Medical Center Albany, NY. The examiner reasoned that you wer admitted for the treatment of an acute exacerbation of your paranoid schizophrenia on April 19, 1982 manifested by auditory and visual hallucinations. You were prescribed Thorazine which is an accepted and a necessary treatment for this condition. Alternative agents like Loxitane and Cogentin were not used due to the side effects experienced by you. The hospital discharge continues that you were prescribed Thorazine for from 4/19/1982 to May 3, 1982. The dose given to you was a therapeutic one for your condition. However it was discontinued due to problems with orthostatic hypotension that you developed. No other issues such as the amnesia, crippled nervous system, impotence, incontinence, and enlarged prostate were mentioned during that hospitalization alone or arising from the use of the Thorazine medication. The evidence in your current claims file makes no references to any of the above issues that you have which have been evaluated, diagnosed and treated. As such there may be many reasons why you have your conditions if they do indeed exist aside from the short term use of the Thorazine some thirty years ago. Additionally while it has been mentioned that Thorazine in the medical literature may result in impotence and urinary retention, this would be true only during the time that an individual would be taking this agent. Such conditions would resolve with the cessation of the Thorazine. As far as the enlarged prostate, crippled nervous system, crippled muscle system, and amnesia, no long term effects or complications have been noted to arise either during the use of Thorazine or after it has been discontinued.

"ONE POWERFUL VOICE"

GARY L. KONIZ
24 891 327
Page 5

Supporting pieces of information for this line of reasoning comes from the private sector hospital discharge summary of 8/22/1985 in which you were described by the treating psychiatrist as an individual of perhaps above average intellectual endowment. On 2/10/1986, the hospital discharge summary stated that you had been doing quite well working at IBM after your August, 1985 hospital discharge until 12/85 when you quit taking your medications and had to be admitted once more for the treatment of your chronic paranoid schizophrenia. The importance of these notes after your hospitalization in 1982 was that it demonstrated that there was no compromise of your neurological or musculoskeletal systems since you were able to do ad lib endeavors and be gainfully employed.

Hence, no evidence can be shown that the proximate cause of disability was due to the carelessness, negligence, lack of proper skill, error in judgment, or similar instance of fault on the part of the Department in furnishing the hospital care, medical or surgical treatment or examination for the veteran. Given the level surveillance and prompt attention to address your medical issues as they developed, there was no departure from the accepted levels of medical care or the performance of professional duties expected of reasonable health care providers.

As the VA examiner does not find that any additional disability is actually the result of the VA care, specifically, carelessness, negligence, lack of proper skill, error in judgment, or similar instance of fault on the part of the Department in furnishing the hospital care, medical or surgical treatment, or examination must be shown; or the proximate cause of disability must be an event not reasonably foreseeable, entitlement to compensation under 38 U.S.C. 1151 for crippled nervous system is denied.

3. Entitlement to compensation under 38 U.S.C. 1151 for amnesia.

Entitlement to compensation under 38 U.S.C. 1151 for amnesia is denied.

Compensation is payable for any disability which is caused by VA hospitalization, medical or surgical treatment, vocational rehabilitation, compensated work therapy program (CWT), or as the result of having submitted to a VA medical examination. The evidence must show that the veteran's additional disability is actually the result of the VA care. Specifically, carelessness, negligence, lack of proper skill, error in judgment, or similar instance of fault on the part of the Department in furnishing the hospital care, medical or surgical treatment, or examination must be shown; or the proximate cause of disability must be an event not reasonably foreseeable. For training and rehabilitation services or compensated work therapy program, it must be shown that the veteran's participation in an essential activity or function of the training, services, or CWT program provided or authorized by VA proximately caused the disability. Merely showing that a veteran has additional disability is not sufficient to establish causation.

Service connection may be granted for a disability which began in military service or was caused by some event or experience in service.

GARY L. KONIZ
24 891 327
Page 6

Service Treatment Records from August 14, 1964 through August 11, 1967 noted no diagnosis, treatment or complaint of amnesia.

Treatment reports from VA Medical Center Albany, NY from April 19, 1982 through June 3, 1988 noted that you were treated with thorazine for paranoid schizophrenia from April 19, 1982 to May 3, 1982. The only side effect of the drug noted while under treatment was orthostatic hypotension.

VA examination results from VA Medical Center Gainesville, FL dated September 11, 2012 noted you had a perfect score of 30/30 on the Mini-mental State exam.

VA examination results from VA Medical Center Bay Pines, FL dated May 13, 2013 noted a complete review of you claims file to include all available records from VA medical Center Albany, NY. The examiner opined that it is more likely that the your amnesia IS UNRELATED, caused, by or aggravated by medical treatment, rehab program, or participation in a compensated work therapy program activity at VA Medical Center Albany, NY. The examiner reasoned that you were admitted for the treatment of an acute exacerbation of your paranoid schizophrenia on April 19, 1982 manifested by auditory and visual hallucinations. You were prescribed Thorazine which is an accepted and a necessary treatment for this condition. Alternative agents like Loxitane and Cogentin were not used due to the side effects experienced by you. The hospital discharge continues that you were prescribed Thorazine for from 4/19/1982 to May 3, 1982. The dose given to you was a therapeutic one for your condition. However it was discontinued due to problems with orthostatic hypotension that you developed. No other issues such as the amnesia, crippled nervous system, impotence, incontinence, and enlarged prostate were mentioned during that hospitalization alone or arising from the use of the Thorazine medication. The evidence in your current claims file makes no references to any of the above issues that you have which have been evaluated, diagnosed and treated. As such there may be many reasons why you have your conditions if they do indeed exist aside from the short term use of the Thorazine some thirty years ago. Additionally while it has been mentioned that Thorazine in the medical literature may result in impotence and urinary retention, this would be true only during the time that an individual would be taking this agent. Such conditions would resolve with the cessation of the Thorazine. As far as the enlarged prostate, crippled nervous system, crippled muscle system, and amnesia, no long term effects or complications have been noted to arise either during the use of Thorazine or after it has been discontinued.

Supporting pieces of information for this line of reasoning comes from the private sector hospital discharge summary of 8/22/1985 in which you were described by the treating psychiatrist as an individual of perhaps above average intellectual endowment. On 2/10/1986, the hospital discharge summary stated that you had been doing quite well working at IBM after your August, 1985 hospital discharge until 12/85 when you quit taking your medications and had to be admitted once more for the treatment of your chronic paranoid schizophrenia. The importance of these notes after your hospitalization in 1982 was that it demonstrated that there was no compromise of your neurological or musculoskeletal systems since you were able to do ad lib endeavors and be gainfully employed.

"ONE POWERFUL VOICE"

GARY L. KONIZ
24 891 327
Page 7

Hence, no evidence can be shown that the proximate cause of disability was due to the carelessness, negligence, lack of proper skill, error in judgment, or similar instance of fault on the part of the Department in furnishing the hospital care, medical or surgical treatment or examination for the veteran. Given the level surveillance and prompt attention to address your medical issues as they developed, there was no departure from the accepted levels of medical care or the performance of professional duties expected of reasonable health care providers.

As the VA examiner does not find that any additional disability is actually the result of the VA care, specifically, carelessness, negligence, lack of proper skill, error in judgment, or similar instance of fault on the part of the Department in furnishing the hospital care, medical or surgical treatment, or examination must be shown; or the proximate cause of disability must be an event not reasonably foreseeable, entitlement to compensation under 38 U.S.C. 1151 for amnesia is denied.

4. Entitlement to compensation under 38 U.S.C. 1151 for impotency.

Entitlement to compensation under 38 U.S.C. 1151 for impotency is denied.

Compensation is payable for any disability which is caused by VA hospitalization, medical or surgical treatment, vocational rehabilitation, compensated work therapy program (CWT), or as the result of having submitted to a VA medical examination. The evidence must show that the veteran's additional disability is actually the result of the VA care. Specifically, carelessness, negligence, lack of proper skill, error in judgment, or similar instance of fault on the part of the Department in furnishing the hospital care, medical or surgical treatment, or examination must be shown; or the proximate cause of disability must be an event not reasonably foreseeable. For training and rehabilitation services or compensated work therapy program, it must be shown that the veteran's participation in an essential activity or function of the training, services, or CWT program provided or authorized by VA proximately caused the disability. Merely showing that a veteran has additional disability is not sufficient to establish causation.

Service connection may be granted for a disability which began in military service or was caused by some event or experience in service.

Service Treatment Records from August 14, 1964 through August 11, 1967 noted no diagnosis, treatment or complaint of nervous system disorder.

Treatment reports from VA Medical Center Albany, NY from April 19, 1982 through June 3, 1988 noted that you were treated with thorazine for paranoid schizophrenia from April 19, 1982 to May 3, 1982. The only side effect of the drug noted while under treatment was orthostatic hypotension.

Private medical record from Dr. Charles Cobb of Jacksonville, FL dated May 14, 2012 noted no complaint of impotency.

VA examination results from VA Medical Center Bay Pines, FL dated May 13, 2013 noted a complete review of you claims file to include all available records from VA medical Center

"ONE POWERFUL VOICE"

GARY L. KONIZ
24 891 327
Page 8

Albany, NY. The examiner opined that it is more likely that the your impotency IS
UNRELATED, caused, by or aggravated by medical treatment, rehab program, or participation in
a compensated work therapy program activity at VA Medical Center Albany, NY. The examiner
reasoned that you were admitted for the treatment of an acute exacerbation of your paranoid
schizophrenia on April 19, 1982 manifested by auditory and visual hallucinations. You were
prescribed Thorazine which is an accepted and a necessary treatment for this condition.
Alternative agents like Loxitane and Cogentin were not used due to the side effects experienced by
you. The hospital discharge continues that you were prescribed Thorazine for from 4/19/1982 to
May 3, 1982. The dose given to you was a therapeutic one for your condition. However it was
discontinued due to problems with orthostatic hypotension that you developed. No other issues
such as the amnesia, crippled nervous system, impotence, incontinence, and enlarged prostate
were mentioned during that hospitalization alone or arising from the use of the Thorazine
medication. The evidence in your current claims file makes no references to any of the above
issues that you have which have been evaluated, diagnosed and treated. As such there may be
many reasons why you have your conditions if they do indeed exist aside from the short term use
of the Thorazine some thirty years ago. Additionally while it has been mentioned that Thorazine
in the medical literature may result in impotence and urinary retention, this would be true only
during the time that an individual would be taking this agent. Such conditions would resolve with
the cessation of the Thorazine. As far as the enlarged prostate, crippled nervous system, crippled
muscle system, and amnesia, no long term effects or complications have been noted to arise either
during the use of Thorazine or after it has been discontinued.

Supporting pieces of information for this line of reasoning comes from the private sector hospital
discharge summary of 8/22/1985 in which you were described by the treating psychiatrist as an
individual of perhaps above average intellectual endowment. On 2/10/1986, the hospital
discharge summary stated that you had been doing quite well working at IBM after your August,
1985 hospital discharge until 12/85 when you quit taking your medications and had to be admitted
once more for the treatment of your chronic paranoid schizophrenia. The importance of these
notes after your hospitalization in 1982 was that it demonstrated that there was no compromise of
your neurological or musculoskeletal systems since you were able to do ad lib endeavors and be
gainfully employed.

Hence, no evidence can be shown that the proximate cause of disability was due to the
carelessness, negligence, lack of proper skill, error in judgment, or similar instance of fault on the
part of the Department in furnishing the hospital care, medical or surgical treatment or
examination for the veteran. Given the level surveillance and prompt attention to address your
medical issues as they developed, there was no departure from the accepted levels of medical care
or the performance of professional duties expected of reasonable health care providers.

As the VA examiner does not find that any additional disability is actually the result of the VA
care, specifically, carelessness, negligence, lack of proper skill, error in judgment, or similar
instance of fault on the part of the Department in furnishing the hospital care, medical or surgical
treatment, or examination must be shown; or the proximate cause of disability must be an event not

GARY L. KONIZ
24 891 327
Page 9

reasonably foreseeable, entitlement to compensation under 38 U.S.C. 1151 for impotency is
denied.

5. Entitlement to compensation under 38 U.S.C. 1151 for crippled muscular system.

Entitlement to compensation under 38 U.S.C. 1151 for crippled muscular system is denied.

Compensation is payable for any disability which is caused by VA hospitalization, medical or
surgical treatment, vocational rehabilitation, compensated work therapy program (CWT), or as the
result of having submitted to a VA medical examination. The evidence must show that the
veteran's additional disability is actually the result of the VA care. Specifically, carelessness,
negligence, lack of proper skill, error in judgment, or similar instance of fault on the part of the
Department in furnishing the hospital care, medical or surgical treatment, or examination must be
shown; or the proximate cause of disability must be an event not reasonably foreseeable. For
training and rehabilitation services or compensated work therapy program, it must be shown that
the veteran's participation in an essential activity or function of the training, services, or CWT
program provided or authorized by VA proximately caused the disability. Merely showing that a
veteran has additional disability is not sufficient to establish causation.

Service connection may be granted for a disability which began in military service or was caused
by some event or experience in service.

Service Treatment Records from August 14, 1964 through August 11, 1967 noted no diagnosis,
treatment or complaint of nervous system disorder.

Treatment reports from VA Medical Center Albany, NY from April 19, 1982 through June 3, 1988
noted that you were treated with thorazine for paranoid schizophrenia from April 19, 1982 to May
3, 1982. The only side effect of the drug noted while under treatment was orthostatic hypotension.

Private medical record from Dr. Charles Cobb of Jacksonville, FL dated May 14, 2012 noted no
muscular deficits.

VA examination results from VA Medical Center Bay Pines, FL dated May 13, 2013 noted a
complete review of you claims file to include all available records from VA medical Center
Albany, NY. The examiner opined that it is more likely that the your crippled muscular system IS
UNRELATED, caused, by or aggravated by medical treatment, rehab program, or participation in
a compensated work therapy program activity at VA Medical Center Albany, NY. The examiner
reasoned that you were admitted for the treatment of an acute exacerbation of your paranoid
schizophrenia on April 19, 1982 manifested by auditory and visual hallucinations. You were
prescribed Thorazine which is an accepted and a necessary treatment for this condition.
Alternative agents like Loxitane and Cogentin were not used due to the side effects experienced by
you. The hospital discharge continues that you were prescribed Thorazine for from 4/19/1982 to
May 3, 1982. The dose given to you was a therapeutic one for your condition. However it was
discontinued due to problems with orthostatic hypotension that you developed. No other issues

GARY L. KONIZ
24 891 327
Page 10

such as the amnesia, crippled nervous system, impotence, incontinence, and enlarged prostate were mentioned during that hospitalization alone or arising from the use of the Thorazine medication. The evidence in your current claims file makes no references to any of the above issues that you have which have been evaluated, diagnosed and treated. As such there may be many reasons why you have your conditions if they do indeed exist aside from the short term use of the Thorazine some thirty years ago. Additionally while it has been mentioned that Thorazine in the medical literature may result in impotence and urinary retention, this would be true only during the time that an individual would be taking this agent. Such conditions would resolve with the cessation of the Thorazine. As far as the enlarged prostate, crippled nervous system, crippled muscle system, and amnesia, no long term effects or complications have been noted to arise either during the use of Thorazine or after it has been discontinued.

Supporting pieces of information for this line of reasoning comes from the private sector hospital discharge summary of 8/22/1985 in which you were described by the treating psychiatrist as an individual of perhaps above average intellectual endowment. On 2/10/1986, the hospital discharge summary stated that you had been doing quite well working at IBM after your August, 1985 hospital discharge until 12/85 when you quit taking your medications and had to be admitted once more for the treatment of your chronic paranoid schizophrenia. The importance of these notes after your hospitalization in 1982 was that it demonstrated that there was no compromise of your neurological or musculoskeletal systems since you were able to do ad lib endeavors and be gainfully employed.

Hence, no evidence can be shown that the proximate cause of disability was due to the carelessness, negligence, lack of proper skill, error in judgment, or similar instance of fault on the part of the Department in furnishing the hospital care, medical or surgical treatment or examination for the veteran. Given the level surveillance and prompt attention to address your medical issues as they developed, there was no departure from the accepted levels of medical care or the performance of professional duties expected of reasonable health care providers.

As the VA examiner does not find that any additional disability is actually the result of the VA care, specifically, carelessness, negligence, lack of proper skill, error in judgment, or similar instance of fault on the part of the Department in furnishing the hospital care, medical or surgical treatment, or examination must be shown; or the proximate cause of disability must be an event not reasonably foreseeable, entitlement to compensation under 38 U.S.C. 1151 for crippled muscular system is denied.

6. Entitlement to compensation under 38 U.S.C. 1151 for incontinence.

Entitlement to compensation under 38 U.S.C. 1151 for incontinence is denied.

Compensation is payable for any disability which is caused by VA hospitalization, medical or surgical treatment, vocational rehabilitation, compensated work therapy program (CWT), or as the result of having submitted to a VA medical examination. The evidence must show that the veteran's additional disability is actually the result of the VA care. Specifically, carelessness,

GARY L. KONIZ
24 891 327
Page 11

negligence, lack of proper skill, error in judgment, or similar instance of fault on the part of the Department in furnishing the hospital care, medical or surgical treatment, or examination must be shown; or the proximate cause of disability must be an event not reasonably foreseeable. For training and rehabilitation services or compensated work therapy program, it must be shown that the veteran's participation in an essential activity or function of the training, services, or CWT program provided or authorized by VA proximately caused the disability. Merely showing that a veteran has additional disability is not sufficient to establish causation.

Service connection may be granted for a disability which began in military service or was caused by some event or experience in service.

Service Treatment Records from August 14, 1964 through August 11, 1967 noted no diagnosis, treatment or complaint of nervous system disorder.

Treatment reports from VA Medical Center Albany, NY from April 19, 1982 through June 3, 1988 noted that you were treated with thorazine for paranoid schizophrenia from April 19, 1982 to May 3, 1982. The only side effect of the drug noted while under treatment was orthostatic hypotension.

Private medical record from Dr. Charles Cobb of Jacksonville, FL dated May 14, 2012 noted no complaint of incontinence. You reported having urinary frequency, urgency and incomplete emptying. You were diagnosed with benign prostatic hypertrophy with an element of obstruction.

VA examination results from VA Medical Center Bay Pines, FL dated May 13, 2013 noted a complete review of you claims file to include all available records from VA medical Center Albany, NY. The examiner opined that it is more likely that the your incontinence IS UNRELATED, caused, by or aggravated by medical treatment, rehab program, or participation in a compensated work therapy program activity at VA Medical Center Albany, NY. The examiner reasoned that you were admitted for the treatment of an acute exacerbation of your paranoid schizophrenia on April 19, 1982 manifested by auditory and visual hallucinations. You were prescribed Thorazine which is an accepted and a necessary treatment for this condition. Alternative agents like Loxitane and Cogentin were not used due to the side effects experienced by you. The hospital discharge continues that you were prescribed Thorazine for from 4/19/1982 to May 3, 1982. The dose given to you was a therapeutic one for your condition. However it was discontinued due to problems with orthostatic hypotension that you developed. No other issues such as the amnesia, crippled nervous system, impotence, incontinence, and enlarged prostate were mentioned during that hospitalization alone or arising from the use of the Thorazine medication. The evidence in your current claims file makes no references to any of the above issues that you have which have been evaluated, diagnosed and treated. As such there may be many reasons why you have your conditions if they do indeed exist aside from the short term use of the Thorazine some thirty years ago. Additionally while it has been mentioned that Thorazine in the medical literature may result in impotence and urinary retention, this would be true only during the time that an individual would be taking this agent. Such conditions would resolve with the cessation of the Thorazine. As far as the enlarged prostate, crippled nervous system, crippled

GARY L. KONIZ
24 891 327
Page 12

muscle system, and amnesia, no long term effects or complications have been noted to arise either during the use of Thorazine or after it has been discontinued.

Supporting pieces of information for this line of reasoning comes from the private sector hospital discharge summary of 8/22/1985 in which you were described by the treating psychiatrist as an individual of perhaps above average intellectual endowment. On 2/10/1986, the hospital discharge summary stated that you had been doing quite well working at IBM after your August, 1985 hospital discharge until 12/85 when you quit taking your medications and had to be admitted once more for the treatment of your chronic paranoid schizophrenia. The importance of these notes after your hospitalization in 1982 was that it demonstrated that there was no compromise of your neurological or musculoskeletal systems since you were able to do ad lib endeavors and be gainfully employed.

Hence, no evidence can be shown that the proximate cause of disability was due to the carelessness, negligence, lack of proper skill, error in judgment, or similar instance of fault on the part of the Department in furnishing the hospital care, medical or surgical treatment or examination for the veteran. Given the level surveillance and prompt attention to address your medical issues as they developed, there was no departure from the accepted levels of medical care or the performance of professional duties expected of reasonable health care providers.

As the VA examiner does not find that any additional disability is actually the result of the VA care, specifically, carelessness, negligence, lack of proper skill, error in judgment, or similar instance of fault on the part of the Department in furnishing the hospital care, medical or surgical treatment, or examination must be shown; or the proximate cause of disability must be an event not reasonably foreseeable, entitlement to compensation under 38 U.S.C. 1151 for incontinence is denied.

7. Entitlement to individual unemployability.

Entitlement to individual unemployability is denied.

Application for individual unemployability received December 12, 2012 noted that you are currently employed in maintenance at a local Country Club making $1,800 a month.

A review of your claims file show you have no compensable service connected disabilities.

Entitlement to individual unemployability is denied because the claimant has not been found unable to secure or follow a substantially gainful occupation as a result of service connected disabilities. Service connected disabilities currently evaluated as 0 percent do not meet the schedular requirements for entitlement to individual unemployability. 38 CFR 4.16 provides that individual unemployability may be granted where there is one disability evaluated as 60 percent disabling, or two or more disabilities, one of which is 40 percent with a combined evaluation of 70 percent or more. These percentage standards are set aside only when the evidence clearly and factually shows the veteran has been rendered unemployable solely due to service connected

GARY L. KONIZ
24 891 327
Page 13

disabilities regardless of their individual and combined percentages. Such cases are submitted to the Director of the Compensation and Pension Service for extra-schedular consideration. This case has not been submitted for extra-schedular consideration because the evidence fails to show the veteran is unemployable due to service connected disabilities. (38 CFR 4.16)

REFERENCES:

Title 38 of the Code of Federal Regulations, Pensions, Bonuses and Veterans' Relief contains the regulations of the Department of Veterans Affairs which govern entitlement to all veteran benefits. For additional information regarding applicable laws and regulations, please consult your local library, or visit us at our web site, www.va.gov.

Veterans Wait for Benefits as Claims Pile Up

By JAMES DAO

Published: September 27, 2012

For Dennis Selsky, a Vietnam-era veteran with multiple sclerosis, it was lost documents. It seemed that every time he sent records to the Department of Veterans Affairs, they disappeared into the ether.

For Mickel Withers, an Iraq war veteran with severe post-traumatic stress disorder, it was a bureaucratic foul-up. The department said he received National Guard pay in 2009, though he had left the Guard the previous year, and cut his disability compensation by $3,000. He filed for bankruptcy to protect himself from creditors.

For Doris Hink, the widow of a World War II veteran, it was the waiting. The department took nearly two years to process her claim for a survivor's pension, forcing her daughter to take $12,000 from savings to pay nursing home bills.

These are the faces of what has become known as "the backlog": the crushing inventory of claims for disability, pension and educational benefits that has overwhelmed the Department of Veterans Affairs. For hundreds of thousands of veterans, the result has been long waits for decisions, mishandled documents, confusing communications and infuriating mistakes in their claims.

Numbers tell the story. Last year, veterans filed more than 1.3 million claims, double the number in 2001. Despite having added nearly 4,000 new workers since 2008, the agency did not keep pace, completing less than 80 percent of its inventory.

This year, the agency has already completed more than one million claims for the third consecutive year. Yet it is still taking about eight months to process the average claim, two months longer than a decade ago. As of Monday, 890,000 pension and compensation claims were pending.

Skyrocketing costs have accompanied that flood of claims. By next year, the department's major benefit programs — compensation for the disabled, pensions for the low-income and educational assistance — are projected to cost about $76 billion, triple the amount in 2001. By 2022, those costs are projected to rise nearly 70 percent to about $130 billion.

These are the compounding wages of war, and they are not just the result of recent conflicts. The department is administering pensions for World War II veterans while handling new claims from Vietnam veterans struggling with the multiplying ailments of age. Indeed, nearly a third of all pending new claims are from Vietnam-era veterans, roughly equal to the number from Iraq and Afghanistan war veterans.

"ONE POWERFUL VOICE"

Thanks to superior battlefield medicine and armor, those Iraq and Afghanistan veterans have survived combat at a higher rate. As they return home with more wounds, and perhaps more savvy, the ones who file for disability compensation are claiming on average nearly 10 disorders or injuries each, compared with 6 for Vietnam veterans and fewer than 4 for World War II veterans. Their complex claims are often more time-consuming to process, adding to the backlog.

At the same time, a higher percentage — nearly half — of Iraq and Afghanistan veterans are filing for disability compensation, partly because of the weak economy. That is double the rate for previous wars.

"We're not gaining any ground here," Eric K. Shinseki, the secretary of veterans affairs, acknowledged in an interview over the summer. "Am I impatient? Yes, but I've got a fix."

That fix is the department's "transformation plan," which calls for a new training regimen that Mr. Shinseki says will improve speed and accuracy in processing claims; creation of special teams to handle complex claims; and new digital technology that will replace the current paper-choked system.

When all those pieces are in place by 2015, Mr. Shinseki says that every claim will be processed in fewer than 125 days, with almost no errors — a pledge that veterans' advocates view skeptically.

Current and former front-line workers, who spoke out of frustration with the widespread criticism of their agency, offer a different analysis. The dysfunction, they say, stems from inadequate training and weak management, an excessively complicated process, and assembly line-like performance standards that require them to meet production quotas under threat of demotion or firing. The solution, they say, is clear.

"They need more workers," said Mark Locken, a retired Army artillery officer who worked for the department for three years in Boston before quitting in May because, he said, of the stress.

The history of the backlog, which predates the Sept. 11, 2001, attacks, suggests another source of the problem: a bureaucratic culture with conflicting missions.

On one hand, Department of Veterans Affairs employees are urged to be advocates for veterans. "I tell them: you're going to take care of these young men and women for life," Allison A. Hickey, a retired Air Force brigadier general who is under secretary for benefits, said in an interview.

Yet those workers are also required to be stewards of the public dime, called on to distinguish the truly needy from the less needy from the fraudulent.

That means they must evaluate veterans to determine whether their illnesses or injuries are real, and whether they are the result of military service, or something else. If those problems are

"ONE POWERFUL VOICE"

deemed "service connected," the workers must then quantify their severity and attach dollar values.

Is that traumatic brain injury from high school football or a roadside bomb in Iraq? Is that back injury a 10 percent disability or 30 percent? Is that post-traumatic stress disorder real?

Medical questions without simple answers must be settled by harried bureaucrats and overworked doctors applying black-and-white rules to very gray ailments. Their decisions mean the difference between monthly checks of a few hundred dollars versus a few thousand.

When veterans are not happy with the results, as is often the case, they can appeal, or reapply, submitting new documents and diagnoses to bolster their claims — and adding years to the process.

About half of the current backlog is due to veterans reapplying for denied claims or seeking to increase existing benefits because of new or worsening conditions. So the backlog grows, and along with it, the pessimism of some advocates.

"They are rearranging the decks chairs on a sinking ship," said Katrina Eagle, a lawyer who represents veterans before the agency. "You can hire people and buy new software. But nothing will improve."

Bureaucratic Behemoth

Born from a system that paid pensions to Revolutionary War soldiers, the Department of Veterans Affairs has grown into a behemoth with more than 270,000 employees who maintain 131 cemeteries, operate 152 hospitals and disburse benefits to more than four million veterans. The nation has a total of about 23 million veterans.

Congress, the courts and the executive branch have contributed to the growth by creating new benefits and rights like perennial blooms. Typically, Congress has accomplished that by establishing "presumptive connections" between military service and certain diseases, allowing veterans to seek disability compensation if they received a diagnosis within a certain period.

There are now scores of diseases that are presumed to be the result of, or aggravated by, military service, from anemia to yellow fever. Each time the government adds a new one, thousands of veterans apply for benefits.

In 2010, for example, Mr. Shinseki announced that three diseases — ischemic heart disease, Parkinson's disease and b-cell leukemia — would be considered the result of Agent Orange exposure for veterans who served in Vietnam. As of this week, the department had processed more than 240,000 claims for those diseases filed in just the last two years.

Since at least the 1960s, multiple sclerosis has been on the presumptive list, and in the decades since, tens of thousands of veterans with the disease have received benefits from the Department of Veterans Affairs. Dennis Selsky, 69, is one.

"ONE POWERFUL VOICE"

A Navy reservist from the Philadelphia area who was called to active duty for 10 months in 1968, Mr. Selsky worked as an ordnance specialist on domestic air bases. Two years after leaving the service in 1970, he says, doctors told him he had multiple sclerosis, which Mr. Selsky believes he contracted from working on planes contaminated with the herbicide Agent Orange.

Two years ago, he learned from the National Multiple Sclerosis Society that he was eligible for veterans compensation, applied and was granted the minimum benefit: a 30 percent rating, worth $435 a month. That seemed low to him because, he says, he has tremors, walks with a cane and is losing his vision. So Mr. Selksy, who spent 31 years with Verizon before retiring in 1998, appealed, seeking a 100 percent rating that would pay about $3,000 a month.

Then his problems with the Department of Veterans Affairs began in earnest.

First, the Philadelphia regional office lost part of his file, his wife, Sheila, said. Then it lost authorizations to obtain records from his cardiologist, podiatrist, neurologist and ophthalmologist — more than once. After the office finally obtained those doctors' reports, it still required him to see department doctors to confirm his diagnoses.

Each appointment and lost document has added weeks to the processing, now in its 15th month. So have skeptical department examiners, who have requested additional information on whether Mr. Selsky's heart palpitations and vision loss are related to his multiple sclerosis. "This should be a slam dunk," Ms. Selsky said. "He keeps getting worse, and they keep fighting and fighting and fighting with us. The stress is unbelievable."

Mr. Selsky may have also been the victim of another problem common to claims processing: the chaotic handling of records. Lost or mishandled documents are perhaps the No. 1 complaint about the processing system. Indeed, a 2009 review by the department's inspector general found rampant cases of mishandled mail, including documents being improperly put in shred bins at 40 of the department's 57 regional offices.

Workers who process mail in the Philadelphia regional office, which handled Mr. Selsky's claim, say that veterans' records have for years piled up in gray file cabinets or cardboard boxes because they were thought to lack clear identifying information, like Social Security numbers.

Ryan Cease, a former mail handler at the regional office, said that earlier this year he saw workers who were cleaning up the mail room in preparation for a visit by a senior official tossing records into boxes marked "for shredding."

Suspicious, he and a fellow worker later leafed through the boxes and found numerous records that they believed could have easily been identified.

Mr. Cease, through another employee, sent an urgent e-mail to the department's central office. After an investigation, the department concluded that nothing improper had occurred.

"We have not shredded any documents up there," Ms. Hickey said.

"ONE POWERFUL VOICE"

THE LOST WAR
251

Mr. Cease is not so sure. "I'm convinced," he said in an interview, "that mail was shredded and that the mail was identifiable."

Manpower Shortage Cited

In 2009, Kathryn Kausch learned that her mother, Doris Hink, was eligible for a pension because her husband, who died in 1987, had served honorably during World War II. Ms. Kausch sent in the paperwork, hoping the funds would help pay assisted living costs for her mother, now 89, who has dementia.

The application was rejected because her mother's assets were above the $80,000 threshold. But in a year, those assets had shrunk and Ms. Kausch reapplied in January 2010. That September, the Philadelphia pension office asked for additional documents, and she sent off a fat packet of bank statements, medical invoices and other financial records.

In November, the office notified her that it had not received the documents and was rejecting her mother's application again. But Ms. Kausch produced a receipt showing that the documents had been delivered, and the office acknowledged it had received them. Then she hunkered down to wait. Months passed.

Ms. Kausch began dipping into her savings to pay her mother's bills at an assisted living center. Then in July 2011, Ms. Kausch was laid off from her job at Xerox. Desperate for help, she called her congressman, Representative Michael Fitzpatrick, a Republican from the Philadelphia suburbs. A week after his office made inquiries, her mother's pension was approved.

But Ms. Kausch's problems did not end. Her mother is eligible for $22,000 in retroactive pension payments dating to 2009. But because of her mother's dementia, the department must approve Ms. Kausch as her mother's fiduciary. Though the department has conducted the required interview, it has not filled out the final paperwork, despite calls from Mr. Fitzpatrick's office.

"No wonder our government has such problems," Ms. Kausch, 58, said. "It seems you get lost in this bureaucratic paperwork."

A routine pension claim, undisputed by the department, took nearly two years to process, and only after a congressman's intervention. An equally straightforward fiduciary application is still pending after six months. Why?

Employees and veterans advocates repeatedly point to one reason: a lack of manpower. Though the Veterans Benefits Administration, the division that oversees entitlement programs, has grown significantly in the past decade, to 20,600 employees from 12,150, it still often assigns mandatory overtime to meet workload demands. And because the processing is so complicated, it can take two years before new hires are fully productive, the department says.

With its staff stretched to the limit, the Veterans Benefits Administration supervisors set priorities for processing claims, workers say, with seriously wounded recent veterans, the homeless and terminally ill often rising to the top. Veterans or survivors who are already

"ONE POWERFUL VOICE"

receiving benefits but applying for new ones may, as a consequence, be given lower priority, the workers say.

Another problem, front-line claims workers say, are production quotas that determine whether they will be promoted, given raises, demoted or fired. The pressure to meet those quotas cause some workers to skip complicated, time-consuming files and reach for simpler ones, workers and advocates say.

"Given the choice, they'll go for the thin folder every time," said Gerald T. Manar, a former manager for the Veterans Benefits Administration who now works for Veterans of Foreign Wars.

More processors would make a difference, most experts say. But at a time when both parties are talking about slashing the federal deficit, hiring more employees may be impossible. Since 2004, the department's total budget — which includes health care, administrative costs and entitlements — has doubled, to $127 billion. "New employees hired into a broken system that awards process instead of outcomes will not get us there," Mr. Fitzpatrick said.

For Mickel Withers, a veteran of the Georgia National Guard, the system was not exactly broken. But it was blundering. After serving on a bomb-detection team in Iraq in 2005 and 2006, he left the Army in 2008 with a diagnosis of post-traumatic stress disorder and started receiving $3,080 a month in disability compensation from the Department of Veterans Affairs.

But this May, a check arrived for only $109. The department told him they were docking his compensation because they had determined he received drill pay from the Guard in 2009. Veterans are not allowed to receive both kinds of pay. In fact, Mr. Withers had left the Guard as a sergeant in 2008, but it took the department weeks to confirm that fact. With two children and a wife to support, he had to seek emergency housing assistance from a veterans group to pay rent and filed for bankruptcy to avoid debt collectors.

It was his second bad experience with the benefits system: In 2009, the department overpaid the art school he was attending, then tried to collect the money from Mr. Withers. It took months to resolve that dispute.

"I think they are so overwhelmed over there, they just glance at things," he said. "It doesn't make me feel good about the system."

"ONE POWERFUL VOICE"

Gary L. Koniz
Journalist Correspondent
Independent Workers Party Candidate
4th Congressional District, FL 2014
U.S. House of Representatives

9480 Princeton Square Blvd. S., #815
Jacksonville, FL 32256-8310
(904) 730-2055
gary.koniz@hotmail.com

The Candidate is a Corresponding Freelance Journalist with over 40 years of career experience in journalism covering the important and pressing social and political issues agendas of the hour and other important national and local topics to be resolved currently in submissions to The Times Union, of Jacksonville, FL, The New York Times, New York, NY, CBS Evening News, and other syndicated Newspapers, Magazines, and T.V. and Radio News Agency Sources.

I am currently running for Congress, as a "Hands On" approach to Sound Government Management for this election of 2014 as an "Independent" Democratic Labor Intensive Candidate for Florida's 4th District U.S House of Representatives; with a primary focus on: (1.) "The Legal Protection Of," and, "The Securing Of Veterans Rights," to Compassionate and Beneficial Psychiatric Care and Treatment in our V.A. Medical Centers and regarding State Psychiatric Facilities; and as it pertains to their Protection from the Forced Use of Psychotropic Chemicals and other Disabling Types of Treatment; and: (2.) as a Labor Rights Activist and Economist, stressing the importance of accepting a well-regulated economy centered to the Productive Middle Ground, "The Golden Mean" of Supply and Demand, that concedes the workers with enough "Consumer Purchasing Power" to generate the production of goods and services, create jobs, and support the government tax structures on all levels of their necessity; with an attempt to salvage our economy and help our Nation's Veterans and the people of our district and nationally to survive economically; and among other vital and necessary interests of state to be resolved, guarded, and protected. And which are not "Political Issues" of appeasing the public vote; but Firm Line Policy issues of "Yes or No," to be forcefully reasoned forth and forcefully mandated about for the Public Good by strong intelligent leadership and who are convinced of their power of correct reasoning regarding my active working agendas in process.

It is obvious to all that our modern day Government needs more income revenues in public responsibility to maintain itself than it is capable of taking-in under Supply and Demand GNDP Taxation; and it is also clear that we cannot continue to provide Quality V.A. Health Care being saddled with an untenable National Debt; to what Fiat Issue, based upon the Full Faith Integrity of The United States and Its Amassed Wealth and Resources, is the only Intelligent Solution.

Complete Democratic Labor Party Platform – Free PDF Download
http://www.lulu.com/product/ebook/the-democratic-labor-party-platform-2012/18837994

Superintendent
United States Military Academy
West Point, New York 10996-5000

January 11, 2008

Dear Gary,

Thank you for the copy of your book *The Orders of the Day*, I look forward to reading it. On behalf of a grateful nation, I also salute you for your brave service in Vietnam. I hope you and your family have a happy and prosperous 2008 – all the best from West Point.

Sincerely,

Buster

F. L. Hagenbeck
Lieutenant General, US Army
Superintendent

Mr. Gary L. Koniz
9480 Princeton Square Blvd S.
815
Jacksonville, FL 32256

DANIEL P. MOYNIHAN
NEW YORK

United States Senate
WASHINGTON, DC 20510-3201

September 16, 1997

Mr. Gary L. Koniz
198 Kenville Rd., #C
Buffalo, New York 14215

Dear Mr. Koniz:

I do thank you for taking the time to share your thoughts with me on our national drug policy. As former co-chair of the Democratic Substance Abuse Working Group, I have given the issue of drug abuse and trafficking a great deal of study and attention.

The work of this Senate task force culminated in the passage of the Omnibus Anti-Drug Abuse Act of 1988, which was signed into law by President Reagan. This remarkable piece of legislation committed the federal government, for the first time, to place proper emphasis on treatment and education in its effort to fight the drug problem.

Too often when addicts come to a treatment center and ask for help, they are turned away and told to come back in six months or more. This is how long the waiting list can be. Of all the inexplicable aspects of our response to the drug epidemic, none seems more unforgivable. The Omnibus Anti-Drug Abuse Act committed us to an elemental principle: anyone who seeks treatment for drug abuse should be provided it. This is a fundamental response to any public health epidemic.

If we've learned anything, we've learned that we are in the midst of a public health crisis. Drug use appears to be rising in inner-city neighborhoods where addiction problems are most severe. In addition, a federal survey of American households shows that one million Americans use crack at least occasionally. There is nothing more important in this battle against drug addiction than early intervention with access for all to appropriate treatment. The consequences of inadequate or inappropriate action in this epidemic will continue to be devastating unless we respond immediately.

The 1988 Omnibus Anti-Drug Abuse Act does not ignore law enforcement. The first principle we sought to impose was this: "Take Back the Streets." The minimum requirement to destroy the drug trade is a sufficient police force -- the front line in this

Printed on recycled paper

"ONE POWERFUL VOICE"

September 16, 1997
Page 2

war. It was during the Reagan administration that federal support for street-level law enforcement dropped to $2.9 billion, a
level where it had been 15 years earlier. If we are to succeed
in a return to law and order in our cities, we must provide federal support to local police. The Anti-Drug Abuse Act of 1988
and the Crime Control Act of 1990 both increased authorized federal funding to local law enforcement.

But we must do more to alleviate the drug crisis that faces
our country. One bill of mine, S. 29, would permit coverage of
residential drug treatment for pregnant women and certain family
members under the Medicaid program. There is nothing more pathetic than a drug-addicted infant. And the costs of treating
them are staggering. We ought to do all we can to intervene with
a pregnant mother to stop her drug use. Another bill I have
sponsored, S. 30, would direct the Secretary of Health'and Human
Services to conduct a comprehensive study of the effectiveness of
our federal anti-drug program. We are now spending huge amounts
of funds in our "drug war," more appropriately, our "drug epidemic." We ought to be serious about knowing what works and what
doesn't.

Again, thank you for your interest. Please do not hesitate
to contact me in the future on this or any other matter of concern.

                        Sincerely,

                        Daniel Patrick Moynihan

ALFONSE D'AMATO
NEW YORK

520 HART BUILDING
(202) 224-6542

United States Senate
WASHINGTON, D.C. 20510

October 26, 1989

Mr. Gary Koniz
198 C Kenville rd.
Buffalo, New York 14215

Dear Mr. Koniz:

Thank you for expressing your concern regarding the alcohol and drug abuse epidemic plaguing our society today.

The current wave of violent crime is increasingly associated with illegal drug and alcohol use. In 1988, for example, 90 percent of the male arrestees in New York City tested positive for an illicit drug.

Congress is attempting to address these problems with several anti-drug and anti-crime initiatives, such as S. 1225, the Comprehensive Crime Control Act of 1989. I am proud to be an original cosponsor of that bill.

The Comprehensive Crime Control Act of 1989 seeks to improve our criminal justice system by augmenting law enforcement capabilities, enhancing our abilities to prosecute criminals, and expanding prison capacity. It provides enhanced penalties for firearms violations. S. 1225 also includes a provision for the death penalty for instances of murder for hire, and for hostage taking and espionage where death results.

In order for the government to be effective in its efforts to arrest, prosecute, and incarcerate violent criminals, we need many more law enforcement personnel. S. 1225 provides funding for much needed additional U.S. Marshals, U.S. Attorneys, and FBI agents. It also authorizes additional funds for the Immigration and Naturalization Service to expedite the deportation of convicted criminal aliens. Crimes committed by criminal aliens are rising disproportionately in relation to the general population. This is a trend which must be stopped.

The passage of the Anti-Drug Abuse Act of 1988 will also make significant contributions to the war on drugs. It includes the death penalty for drug-related killings, the appointment of a national drug czar to oversee our war on drugs, and a host of law enforcement, prevention, and treatment initiatives.

"ONE POWERFUL VOICE"

October 26, 1989
Page 2

   We must also pay much more attention to educating young
Americans about the dangers of illicit drug and alcohol use, and
to treating and rehabilitating those who are addicted. That is
why 50 percent of the new funding contained in the 1988 bill is
for education and treatment efforts to reduce the demand for
drugs.

   Again, thank you for expressing your concerns regarding this
problem. Please be assured that I will continue to support comprehensive federal, state and local efforts aimed at stemming
both drug and alcohol abuse.

                              Sincerely,

                              Alfonse D'Amato
                              United States Senator

AD:jd

STATE OF NEW YORK

DEPARTMENT OF LAW

ROBERT ABRAMS
ATTORNEY GENERAL

ALBANY, N.Y. 12224

(518) 474-7134

FRANK R. FIORAMONTI
ASSISTANT ATTORNEY GENERAL
IN CHARGE LEGISLATIVE BUREAU

September 1, 1993

Mr. Gary Koniz
198 C. Kenville Road
Buffalo, New York 14215

Dear Mr. Koniz:

   This will acknowledge receipt of copies of letters sent to
you by United States Senators Rockefeller and Moynihan relating to
health issues and narcotic drugs.

   The Attorney General appreciates your taking time to share
with him the views of these federal officials.

                    Sincerely,

                    FRANK R. FIORAMONTI

"ONE POWERFUL VOICE"

DEPARTMENT OF THE ARMY
US ARMY FORT BELVOIR
FORT BELVOIR, VIRGINIA 22060

January 7, 1992

REPLY TO
ATTENTION OF

Office of the Commanding General

Mr. Gary L. Koniz
198C Kenville Road
Buffalo, New York 14215

Dear Mr. Koniz:

Thank you for sharing your concerns with us at Fort Belvoir. The issues you raise definitely need attention at all levels of government. We will consider them as we make our plans for the future and strive to do the best for our country.

Thank you again for your interest in the security and future of our great nation.

Sincerely,

Gerald P. Williams
Colonel, United States Army
Deputy Commander

"EXCELLENCE THROUGH SERVICE"

"ONE POWERFUL VOICE"

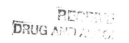

CITY OF BUFFALO
OFFICE OF THE MAYOR

ANTHONY M. MASIELLO
MAYOR

November 19, 1998

Gary Koniz
198 Kenville Road #C
Buffalo, New York 14215

Dear Mr. Koniz: *GARY*:

Thank you for your recent letter dated November 16, 1998.

I appreciate your kind words and comments.

Thank you for taking the time to write.

Sincerely,

Anthony M. Masiello
Mayor

AMM/gh

Thank you so much for your nice kind remarks and words of encouragement. Please keep in touch,

sundance

May 18, 2009

Gary L. Koniz
9480 Princeton Square Blvd. S., #815
Jacksonville, FL 32256

Dear Mr. Koniz:

I am writing on behalf of Robert Redford.

Mr. Redford has asked me to thank you for your kind letter
inquiring about the possibility of him participating with you in
Veterans health issues. While he appreciated the invitation to
participate with you, I am afraid that he is not in a position to
consider involvement. His current film schedule is devoted to
several successive projects. This, along with his ongoing business
commitments, makes it impossible for him to take on any other
obligations.

Mr. Redford did appreciate your thinking of him. He extends his
best wishes.

Sincerely,

Amber Smith

Amber Smith

DANIEL P. MOYNIHAN
NEW YORK

United States Senate
WASHINGTON, D.C. 20510

November 15, 1993

Mr. Gary L. Koniz
198 C Kenville Rd.
Buffalo, New York   14215

Dear Mr. Koniz:

I do thank you for sending me a copy of your letter to General Schwarzkoph regarding Opium. I am glad to have it for my own reference, and appreciate knowing your views on this subject.

Sincerely,

Daniel Patrick Moynihan

Printed on recycled paper

"ONE POWERFUL VOICE"

DANIEL P. MOYNIHAN
NEW YORK

United States Senate

WASHINGTON, D.C. 20510

February 2, 1994

Mr. Gary L. Koniz
198C Kenville Rd.
Buffalo, New York   14215

Dear Mr. Koniz:

I do thank you for sending me a copy of your letter
to Secretary General of the United Nations. I am glad to
have it for my own reference, and appreciate knowing your
views on this subject.

Sincerely,

Daniel Patrick Moynihan

Printed on recycled paper

"ONE POWERFUL VOICE"

DANIEL P. MOYNIHAN
NEW YORK

United States Senate
WASHINGTON, D.C. 20510

January 8, 1990

Mr. Gary Koniz
198 C Kenville Rd.
Buffalo, New York 14215

Dear Mr. Koniz:

    I do thank you for sending me a copy of your letter
to the Federal Bureau of Investigation. I am glad to
have it for my own reference, and appreciate knowing your
views on this subject.

                Sincerely,

                Daniel Patrick Moynihan

"ONE POWERFUL VOICE"

DANIEL P. MOYNIHAN
NEW YORK

United States Senate
WASHINGTON, D.C. 20510

February 21, 1992

Mr. Gary Koniz
198 C Kenville Rd.
Buffalo, New York 14215

Dear Mr. Koniz:

I do thank you for sending me a copy of your letter
to Lt. Gen. Graves. I am glad to have it for my own
reference, and appreciate knowing your views on this
subject.

Sincerely,

Daniel Patrick Moynihan

"ONE POWERFUL VOICE"

DANIEL P. MOYNIHAN
NEW YORK

United States Senate

WASHINGTON. D.C. 20510

December 30, 1992

Mr. Gary Koniz
198 C Kenville Rd.
Buffalo, New York 14215

Dear Mr. Koniz:

Thank you very much for having taken the time to
write and to send the packet of information concerning
the illegal narcotic trade. I am glad to have it, and I
anticipate that it will prove to be of use.

Sincerely,

Daniel Patrick Moynihan

"ONE POWERFUL VOICE"

DANIEL P. MOYNIHAN
NEW YORK

United States Senate

WASHINGTON, D.C. 20510

August 6, 1993

Mr. Gary L. Koniz
198 C Kenville Rd.
Buffalo, New York   14215

Dear Mr. Koniz:

    I do thank you for sending me a copy of your letter
to William S. Sessions. I am glad to have it for my own
reference, and appreciate knowing your views on this
subject.

                Sincerely,

                Daniel Patrick Moynihan

Printed on recycled paper

"ONE POWERFUL VOICE"

DANIEL P. MOYNIHAN
NEW YORK

United States Senate
WASHINGTON, D.C. 20510

January 3, 1995

Mr. Gary L. Koniz
198C Kenville Rd.
Buffalo, New York   14215

Dear Mr. Koniz:

Thank you very much for having taken the time to
write and to send the informative packet of articles on
drug abuse and mental illness. I am glad to have it, and
I anticipate that it will prove to be of use.

Sincerely,

Daniel Patrick Moynihan

Printed on recycled paper

"ONE POWERFUL VOICE"

THE REPRESENTATIVE
OF THE
UNITED STATES OF AMERICA
TO THE
UNITED NATIONS

December 15, 1997

Dear Mr. Koniz:

Thank you for your letters and the material you have
sent to the Mission.

I greatly appreciate your comments on my work as the
U.S. Representative to the United Nations as well as your
support for the United Nations.

I send my best wishes to you and your family.

Sincerely,

Bill Richardson

Bill Richardson

Mr. Gary Koniz,
    198 Kenville Rd., Apt. C,
        Buffalo, NY 14215-2519.

"ONE POWERFUL VOICE"

SHELDON SILVER
Speaker

THE ASSEMBLY
STATE OF NEW YORK
ALBANY

Room 932
Legislative Office Building
Albany, New York 12248
(518) 455-3791

October 1, 1997

Mr. Gary Koniz
198 Kenville Road, Apt. C
Buffalo, New York 14215

Dear Mr. Koniz:

    Thank you for sending me the packet of material on various
issues.

    I appreciate receiving this information, and I have forwarded
it to the appropriate staff.

    Again, thank you for contacting my office.

                              Very truly yours,

                              SHELDON SILVER
                              Speaker

SAM HOYT
Assemblymember 144th District

PLEASE REPLY TO:
General Donovan State Office
Building
125 Main Street, Buffalo
New York 14203
(716) 852-2795

Room 656
Legislative Office Building
Albany, New York 12248
(518) 455-4886

THE ASSEMBLY
STATE OF NEW YORK
ALBANY

CHAIR
Subcommittee on High Speed Rail
and Magnetic Levitation

COMMITTEES
Transportation
Energy
Children and Families
Tourism, Arts & Sports Development
Alcoholism & Drug Abuse

MEMBER
Task Force on Women's Issues
Office of
State-Federal Relations

HONORARY MEMBER
Puerto Rican/Hispanic Task Force

January 9, 1998

Gary L. Koniz
198 Kenville Rd., Apt. C
Buffalo, NY 14215-2519

Dear Mr. Koniz:

I am in receipt of your note dated December 26, 1998. Thank you
for your warm words. I am fortunate to have the confidence of
individuals such as you.

I hope you are having a happy New Year.

Sincerely,

SAM HOYT
MEMBER OF ASSEMBLY

SH:jbm

♻ Printed on recycled paper.

"ONE POWERFUL VOICE"

WEST VIRGINIA

United States Senate

WASHINGTON, D.C. 20510

October 9, 1991

Mr. Gary L. Koniz
198 C Kenville Road
Buffalo, New York 14215

Dear Gary:

Thank you for getting in touch with me recently regarding
the war on drugs. It is very good to hear from you.

Because I recently have heard from so many individuals, I am
afraid that I'm not in the position of replying with a detailed
response. Please be assured that I find it helpful to hear from
people like yourself as I consider the issues that you raised. I
value the advice and ideas that I am getting on this subject, and
appreciate knowing of your interest.

Again, thank you for the effort you made to be in touch. My
best wishes to you.

Sincerely,

John D. Rockefeller IV

"ONE POWERFUL VOICE"

EDWARD M. KENNEDY
MASSACHUSETTS

United States Senate
WASHINGTON, DC 20510-2101

December 29, 2000

Mr. Gary Koniz
9480 Princeton Square Blvd. S.
Apt. 815
Jacksonville, Florida 32256

Dear Mr. Koniz:

I was delighted to receive your warm holiday
greeting, and Vicki and I are very grateful to you for
thinking of us.

One of the most gratifying aspects of public
service is to be remembered by friends on special
occasions. Vicki and I thank you again for your
kindness, and send you our best wishes for the New
Year.

With warmest regards,

Sincerely,

Edward M. Kennedy

EK:PL

"ONE POWERFUL VOICE"

JACK QUINN
30TH DISTRICT, NEW YORK

TRANSPORTATION AND
INFRASTRUCTURE

SUBCOMMITTEES:
SURFACE TRANSPORTATION
WATER RESOURCES AND ENVIRONMENT
RAILROADS

VETERANS' AFFAIRS

SUBCOMMITTEE
HOSPITALS AND HEALTHCARE

JOINT ECONOMIC COMMITTEE

Congress of the United States

House of Representatives

Washington, DC 20515-3230

April 29, 1996

PLEASE RESPOND TO

WASHINGTON OFFICE:
☐   331 CANNON BUILDING
WASHINGTON, DC 20515
(202) 225-3306
FAX: 226-0347

MAIN OFFICE:
☐   403 MAIN STREET
SUITE 240
BUFFALO, NY 14203-2199
(716) 845-5257
FAX: 847-0323

SATELLITE OFFICE:
☐   1490 JEFFERSON AVENUE
BUFFALO, NY 14208
(716) 886-4076

Mr. Gary L. Koniz
198 Kenville Road Apt C
Buffalo, New York 14215-2519

Dear Gary:

Thank you for taking the time to contact me with your concerns about United States. It was a pleasure to hear from you and it is extremely important to know how my constituents feel about the issues that are prominent today. I sincerely appreciate your comments and opinions.

As a member of the 104th Congress, I look forward to facing these and many other challenges I will encounter. I appreciate all of your concerns and be assured that I will include your thoughts in any input I have as these issues come across the Floor of the House.

Again, thank you for contacting me. If I may ever be of any service to you in the future please do not hesitate to contact me.

Very truly yours,

Jack Quinn
Member of Congress

JQ:cm

"ONE POWERFUL VOICE"

DISABLED AMERICAN VETERANS

Building Better Lives for America's Disabled Veterans

April 26, 2000

Mr. Gary L. Koniz
198-C Kenville Road
Buffalo, NY 14215

Dear Mr. Koniz:

Thank you for your recent letter and the thoughtful comments you made. The thoughts of the members of the Disabled American Veterans and its Auxiliary are always essential input to the organization's professional staff.

We will certainly keep your comments and reflections in mind as we move forward in our efforts to do the best possible job for all of America's disabled veterans and their families.

Once again, thank you so much for sharing your ideas and feelings with us.

Sincerely,

GARY WEAVER
National Director of Communications

GW:ajb

"ONE POWERFUL VOICE"

Military Order of the Purple Heart

1782   1932

SERVICE AND REHABILITATION OFFICE, INC.
Syracuse V.A. Medical Center
800 Irving Avenue
Syracuse, New York 13210-2796
(315) 476-7461, EXT. 2488 • FAX (315) 472-2356

November 19, 1999

Mr. Gary L. Koniz
198 C. Kenville Road
Buffalo, New York 14215

I wish to express my thanks to you for taking your time to share thoughts of "Comrades in Arms" and the "Columbine High School Massacre".

Too often the veteran and hopefully not the veteran **to be** are forgotten in this day and age. Your points are well taken and after reading all the letters that you have received from State Senators, United States Congressman, Central Intelligence Agency, Federal Communication Commission and the Clergy I see your ideals are shared with all.

I've enjoyed the pleasure of reading your correspondence and feel privileged that you have shared your thoughts with Mr. Gregory Bresser and myself.

Sincerely,

Lois L. Reinhardt Reyes
National Service Officer
Senior Field Supervisor

LLRR/s

cc: Mr. Gregory Bresser, Service Director
     File

"ONE POWERFUL VOICE"

Military Officers Association *of* America

August 7, 2008

Gary L. Koniz
9480 Princeton Square Blvd. S., #815
Jacksonville, FL 32256

Dear Mr. Koniz:

I am writing in response to your August 3, 2008, letter to the editor.

As we had previously corresponded, I don't know of any additional assistance
MOAA could provide to support your cause. As you know, MOAA already has
an aggressive agenda that supports our nation's veterans and, especially, wounded
warriors from all conflicts. Our lobbying efforts support this goal, and the
association also presents public forums that air such issues and attempt to find
improvements.

FYI, in conjunction with the U.S. Naval Institute, MOAA is presenting its second
wounded warriors forum September 17, 2008. I think this public forum will
discuss many of the issues you mention. You may see more information at
http://www.usni.org/conferences/details.asp?id=23 . I've also included a copy of
the agenda with this letter.

Again, thanks for contributing your thoughts, and thanks for thinking of Military
Officers Association of America.

Best wishes,

Warren S. Lacy
Colonel, U.S. Army (Ret.)
Editor in Chief
Military Officer magazine

201 N. Washington Street
Alexandria, VA 22314-2539
800.234.6622 phone
www.moaa.org

One Powerful Voice.

"ONE POWERFUL VOICE"

DEPARTMENT OF VETERANS AFFAIRS
Office of the General Counsel
Washington DC 20420

SEP - 2   In Reply Refer To:

024T

Mr. Gary L. Koniz
9480 Princeton Square Blvd. S. #815
Jacksonville, FL 32256

Dear Mr. Koniz:

This letter responds to your August 15, 2009, letter addressed to David Donahue, under the Freedom of Information Act (FOIA), 5 U.S.C. § 552, requesting a statement regarding legal resources available for veterans when they want to challenge a medical diagnosis or treatment.

We are referring your request to:

ATTN: Tim Graham/Kellie Robinson
FOIA Officers
Department of Veterans Affairs
Veterans Health Administration (19F2)
810 Vermont Avenue
Washington DC 20420

You will receive a reply directly from that office. You may also contact that office directly regarding your request.

Sincerely yours,

Deborah K. McCallum
Assistant General Counsel

"ONE POWERFUL VOICE"

DEPARTMENT OF VETERANS AFFAIRS
Office of the General Counsel
Washington DC 20420

MAY 1 5

In Reply Refer To.   024T

Mr. Gary L. Koniz
9480 Princeton Square Blvd. S.
#815
Jacksonville, FL 32256

Dear Mr. Koniz:

We have received your April 11, 2009, correspondence addressed to Acting General Counsel, John H. Thompson. A copy of that correspondence is enclosed. Regretfully, we are unable to determine exactly what you are requesting.

If you wish to file a Freedom of Information Act (FOIA) Appeal, please provide us with a letter that clearly outlines what records or documents you are seeking. Please also provide us with copies of any letters that you have sent to or received from the Department of Veterans Affairs in regards to the issue you wish to address.

You can send your appeal letter to:

Department of Veterans Affairs
Office of General Counsel (024)
810 Vermont Ave.
Washington, D.C. 20420

Also, please note that the FOIA is a records statute, implemented to provide access to records already in existence. It neither requires an agency to create a record in response to a FOIA request, nor provides a means to obtain answers to questions.

We hope this information is helpful. We will close this case in 30 days if we do not receive clarification.

Sincerely yours,

Deborah K. McCallum
Assistant General Counsel

Enclosure

"ONE POWERFUL VOICE"

Department of Veterans Affairs
Office of the General Counsel
Washington, DC 20420

October 5, 2009

Mr. Gary L. Koniz
9480 Princeton Square Blvd S. #815
Jacksonville, FL 32256   In Reply Refer To: FOIA Request 09-062

Dear Mr. Koniz:

I respond to your letters dated August 15, 2009, which I received on August 25, 2009 and September 4, 2009. In your letters, you requested under the Freedom of Information Act (FOIA), an overall statement of the safety of the proven harmful effects and side effects of various matters enumerated in the first paragraph of your letter.

The only records I can process to respond to FOIA requests are those which are maintained by the Office of the General Counsel (OGC). I cannot create records in order to respond to a FOIA request. A FOIA request must contain descriptions of the records sought that would enable a professional agency employee familiar with the subject area to locate the record with a reasonable amount of effort.

We have searched our offices and found no records pertinent to your request, other than those provided in my reply to your previous request on July 27, 2009. I am enclosing a copy of that letter.

I believe the aforesaid is in full response to your inquiry.

Sincerely yours,

David N. Donahue
FOIA Officer
Office of the General Counsel

Enclosure

"ONE POWERFUL VOICE"

Military Officers Association of America

January 27, 2009

Gary L. Koniz
9480 Princeton Square Blvd S, #815
Jacksonville, FL 32256

Dear Mr. Koniz:

I am writing in response to your January 21, 2009, letter asking if MOAA can
provide funding for your activities on behalf of military veterans' mental health
care.

Because MOAA operates with dues provided by members for specific programs,
the association must focus its efforts on issues approved by the Board of Directors
and managed by MOAA's Government Relations Department. For this reason, the
association cannot fund third-party advocacy programs, no matter how worthy
they may be.

We appreciate your consideration and wish you the best in your endeavors.

Sincerely,

Warren S. Lacy
Colonel, U.S. Army (Ret.)
Editor in Chief
Military Officer & Today's Officer

201 N. Washington Street
Alexandria, VA 22314-2539
800.234.6622 phone
www.moaa.org

One Powerful Voice.

"ONE POWERFUL VOICE"

DEPARTMENT OF VETERANS AFFAIRS
Veterans Health Administration
Washington DC 20420

DEC 2 2008

Mr. Gary Koniz
Veterans of the Vietnam War   In Reply Refer To:
9480 Princeton Square Blvd. S., #815
Jacksonville, FL 32256

Dear Mr. Koniz:

Your letter to The Honorable James B. Peake, Secretary of Veterans Affairs, was referred to my office for reply. Your letter cited concerns about the quality of mental health care provided to veterans including the use of medications.

Mental Health care provided by the Department of Veterans Affairs (VA) is guided by the principles of recovery and rehabilitation. Recovery focuses on engaging the patient and significant others as partners in their therapy. Skills training, education on mental health and wellness, and peer support are examples of recovery oriented practices. Rehabilitation means a focus on a person's strengths as well as problems; a focus on improving social and occupational function rather than just on symptoms. For veterans with Post-Traumatic Stress Disorder (PTSD), the first line treatments are evidence based forms of psychotherapy: Cognitive Processing Therapy and Prolonged Exposure. Evidence based forms of treatment with medications are employed for those who need more help than that which can be provided by psychotherapy.

Due to funding enhancements, since fiscal year (FY) 2005 3,900 new mental health clinicians have been hired by VA allowing expansion of treatment programs for PTSD, substance use disorders and other serous mental illness. Although the number of veterans treated for PTSD increased from 340,000 in FY 2006 to 390,000 in FY 2007, the frequency of visits per individual veteran increased in FY 2007 an indication that VA's hiring increase is meeting the increase in veterans seeking care for PTSD.

In summary, VA is making effort to provide veterans with mental health services that represent the state of the art in terms of clinical effectiveness and respect for the veteran as a person. Your concern for the well being of our nation's veterans is appreciated.

Sincerely,

Ira Katz, MD, PhD
Deputy Chief Patient Care Services
Officer for Mental Health

"ONE POWERFUL VOICE"

Department of Veterans Affairs
Office of the General Counsel
Washington, DC 20420

July 27, 2009

Mr. Gary L. Koniz
9480 Princeton Square Blvd S. #815
Jacksonville, FL 32256   In Reply Refer To: FOIA Request 09-046

Dear Mr. Koniz:

I respond to your letter dated May 19, 2009, which I received on
June 16, 2009. In your letter, you requested which legal resources are available
to veterans concerning their legal rights to challenge medical diagnosis,
commitment, treatment, histories, and due process rights under Miranda
legislation.

The only records I can process pursuant to FOIA requests are those which
are maintained by the Office of the General Counsel (OGC). I will discuss what
OGC records we have on legal resources but I will need to refer you for the rest
of your request to the Veterans Health Administration (VHA).

You wanted to know the legal resources that are available for veterans
when they want to challenge a medical diagnosis or treatment. All VHA facilities
have a patient advocacy program. The purpose of this program is to resolve any
complaints made by veterans and their families regarding treatment and
diagnosis. I am enclosing a copy of VHA Handbook 1003.4 which explains the
VHA Patient Advocacy Program. If a veteran is not satisfied with the decision
made on his complaint, he may file a clinical appeal on the complaint. I am
enclosing a copy of VHA Directive 2006-057 which explains the appeal process.

You have inquired about the legal resources available for veterans who
are facing commitment. The Department of Veterans Affairs (VA) does not
handle commitment matters. Those matters are handled by State courts. I am
enclosing a copy of 38 C.F.R. §§ 14.701-14.705 which explains the commitment
process.

You wanted to know if there were legal resources that can challenge a
veteran's medical history. Under the Privacy Act, you are entitled to one free
copy of your medical records. If you feel that there are any discrepancies in your

"ONE POWERFUL VOICE"

records, you can request an amendment of any records pertaining to you. 5 U.S.C. § 552a (d); 38 C.F.R § 1.579. If you believe that records in your file are inaccurate or incomplete, you should identify for the Privacy Officer of the facility which documents you believe should be amended, what amendments you believe should be made to them, and enclose any evidence you have of their inaccuracy or incompleteness.

If you have any questions regarding the remainder of your request which is being referred to VHA, you may contact the Veterans Health Administration at this address:

Veterans Health Administration
810 Vermont Ave. NW
Washington, DC 20420
Attn: Timothy Graham

If you are not satisfied with any decisions made on your request, you will be provided appeal rights in the response from VHA.

We believe the aforesaid is in full response to your inquiry.

Sincerely yours,

David N. Donahue
FOIA Officer
Office of the General Counsel

Enclosures

Notice of Appeal Rights: If you consider this response to be a denial of any part of your request, you may appeal by writing to the Assistant General Counsel (024), Department of Veterans Affairs, 810 Vermont Avenue, N.W., Washington, DC 20420. Please include your case number in any appeal. If you wish to request additional records or clarification, please write directly to the person signing this letter. Doing this will not change your appeal rights.

In Reply Refer To:

Mr. Gary Koniz
Veterans of the Vietnam War
9480 Princeton Square Blvd. S., #815
Jacksonville, FL 32256

Dear Mr. Koniz:

Your letter to The Honorable James B. Peake, Secretary of Veterans Affairs, was referred to my office for reply. Your letter cited concerns about two issues: The perception of psychiatric diagnoses as stigmatizing to veterans and use of antipsychotic medications for the treatment of mental disorders.

It is true that a diagnosis of mental disorder can perceived as stigmatizing, but that is an unfortunate situation that is steadily decreasing in our society. It is becoming increasingly clear to Americans that mental disorders have more in common with other medical conditions than not: that persons with mental disorders have strengths on which they can build as well as symptom-related deficits in functioning that can be reduced, if not totally eliminated by modern evidence based therapies. The treatment of mental disorders, as with all other illnesses and injuries, is based on an accurate diagnosis that is defined by the symptoms and problems that characterize the disorder. Evidence based clinical practice guidelines describe approaches to diagnosis and treatment based on scientific clinical evidence. The diagnosis, based as it is on a set of symptoms and problems is essential for proper treatment designed to reduce symptoms and improve patient functioning. An important way to eliminate stigma is to demonstrate that proper diagnosis and treatment are effective in returning a patient to improved health and functioning. Proper treatment for the correct diagnosis is as important for persons suffering with depression as it is for persons suffering from diabetes or hypertension.

As noted in the previous paragraph, treatments tied to diagnoses are described by Clinical Practice Guidelines that are published and regularly updated by professional organizations. Clinical Practice Guides for given diagnoses published by various professional organizations have similar recommendations because they are based on the latest scientific medical literature. The Department of Veteran Affairs (VA) and the Department of Defense (DOD) have joint Clinical Practice Guidelines for Post-Traumatic Stress Disorder (PTSD), Major Depression, Addictive Disorders and for Psychoses such as schizophrenia. Antipsychotic medications have been proven by scientific research and years of clinical practice to be effective and often life saving

"ONE POWERFUL VOICE"

Page 2

Mr. Gary Koniz

treatments for persons suffering from psychotic disorders. Their appropriate use has allowed thousands of persons suffering from serious psychiatric illnesses to live safe, productive and satisfying lives in the community whereas before the development of these medications they would have languished in institutions for years, some for virtually the whole of their adult lives. It is true that no medication is without potential side effects and VA and other clinical practice guidelines carefully note the need to be alert to such problems and to actively monitor patients for their development so quick corrective action, including the possibility of decreasing or eliminating use of a medication, can be taken. Finally, VA holds it essential as part of the orientation of recovery and rehabilitation described in the December 2, 2008 letter you received from our office, that potential side effects and risks of use of a medication as well as anticipated benefits from taking the medication, be presented to the patient. Use of a medication by a patient is based on an agreement between the patient and the health care provider. The only situation in which this might not be the case is in the rare instance when a medication must be administered in an emergency to a patient presenting an active danger to themselves or others. This type of situation is not limited to the treatment of mental disorders and is supported by both ethical and legal opinion.

In closing let me thank you for your concern with the care of our nation's veterans. Be assured that VA health care providers share your concerns about the stigma that has been associated with mental disorders and the importance of eliminating that stigma. Also be assured that VA providers take every care to prescribe only those medications that are necessary for improvement of the patient and only for so long as those medications are needed.

Sincerely,

Ira Katz, MD, PhD
Deputy Chief Patient Care Services
Officer for Mental Health

STATE UNIVERSITY OF NEW YORK
COLLEGE AT NEW PALTZ
ON THE RECOMMENDATION OF THE FACULTY
AND BY VIRTUE OF THE AUTHORITY VESTED IN THEM
THE TRUSTEES OF THE UNIVERSITY HAVE CONFERRED ON

GARY LEE KONIZ

THE DEGREE OF

BACHELOR OF ARTS
SUMMA CUM LAUDE

AND HAVE GRANTED THIS DIPLOMA AS EVIDENCE THEREOF
GIVEN IN THE VILLAGE OF NEW PALTZ IN THE STATE OF NEW YORK
IN THE UNITED STATES OF AMERICA ON THE NINETEENTH DAY OF MAY
ONE THOUSAND NINE HUNDRED AND SEVENTY-FOUR

Chairman of the Board of Trustees

Chairman of the College Council

Chancellor of the State University of New York

President of the College

"ONE POWERFUL VOICE"

NEW YORK STATE
OFFICE OF MENTAL HEALTH

RICHARD C. SURLES, PhD, Commissioner

RICHARD J. GLAVIN, MD, Clinical Director
JAMES R. REGAN, PhD, Director, Community Services
JED BAUMGOLD, MPA, Director, Adminstrative Services
JAMES LEWANDOWSKI, MSW, Director, Quality Assurance

HUDSON RIVER PSYCHIATRIC CENTER
WENDY P. ACRISH, MPS, CMHA
Executive Director

October 28, 1993

TO WHOM IT MAY CONCERN:

This is to verify that Gary Koniz, SSN 115 36 5132 was employed at this facility as a Mental Hygiene Therapy Aide Trainee for the period November 13, 1980 through May 8, 1981.

Very truly yours,

BEVERLY BOSLEY
SR. PERSONNEL ADMINISTRATOR

POUGHKEEPSIE, NEW YORK 12601-1197 · (914) 452-8000
AN EQUAL OPPORTUNITY/AFFIRMATIVE ACTION EMPLOYER

"ONE POWERFUL VOICE"

THE BUFFALO NEWS

Murray B. Light
Editor and Senior Vice President
(716) 849-4455

November 3, 1994

Mr. Gary L. Koniz
198 C Kenville Road
Buffalo, New York 14215

Dear Mr. Koniz:

I will not give you blanket authorization
to reproduce News material. You will have
to be specific and also state the purpose
for each reproduction.

Sincerely,

Murray B. Light

ML:jr

One News Plaza, P.O. Box 100, Buffalo, New York 14240

"ONE POWERFUL VOICE"

International Union of Operating Engineers
Local Unions No. 137, 137-A, 137-B, 137-C, and 137-R
1360 Pleasantville Road
Briarcliff Manor, NY 10510
Telephone: (914)762-1268 Fax: (914)762-7034

GARY KONIZ   Soc Sec Num: 115-36-5132
198C KENVILLE ROAD
BUFFALO, NY 14215

Dear Gary Koniz:

We are updating our computer please provide the following information

Birthdate: _05/01/46_____

If you have any questions, please feel free to call the Fund Office.

Very Truly Yours,

Raymond H. Burgess, Jr.
Fund Administrator

KONI198* 142153048 1500 05 05/10/00
NOTIFY SENDER OF NEW ADDRESS
KONIZ'GARY L
9480 PRINCETON SQUARE BLVD S APT 815
JACKSONVILLE FL 32256-8310

Phone: (904) 730-2055

"ONE POWERFUL VOICE"

"ONE POWERFUL VOICE"

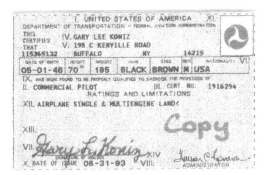

GARY L KONIZ

NUMBER: 01300927

JOINED: 1996 EXPIRES: 07/31/05

Duval County Florida Voter Registration Card

VOTER NAME AND RESIDENCE ADDRESS					BIRTH DATE
GARY L KONIZ					MAY/01/1946
9480 PRINCETON SQUARE BLVD S APT 815					REGISTRATION DATE
JACKSONVILLE FL 32256					MAY/12/2000
POLLING LOCATION			PRECINCT NO		PARTY
COMFORT SUITE SOUTHSIDE/BAYMEADOWS					DEM
8277 WESTERN WAY CIR			05V		
COUNCIL	CONGRESS	SENATE	HOUSE	SCHOOL	OTHER DATA
5	4	1	16	3	12/22/09 5
	103337343				M
FLORIDA REGISTRATION NUMBER					

"ONE POWERFUL VOICE"

Most Sincerely
Gary L. Koniz
Journalist Correspondent
Independent Workers Party Candidate *for*
United States Representative, 4th CD, FL 2014
"United Labor Unifying The Nation"
(904) 730-2055 – Office
gary.koniz@hotmail.com

The Right Formula for Peace and Prosperity in Our Time: "A Fair Deal For Everyone"

The Right Formula for Peace and Prosperity in Our Time: Calls For a Fair Deal Gainful Prevailing Middle Class Wage Legislation with an Anti-Trust Fair Price Cost of Living Regulation Agreement, an Affordable Graduated FICA Payroll Deducted National Health and Dental Care Plan, and for Full Faith Fiat Issue; On Demand, To Fund Our Government and To Preclude Fiscal Deficit by Issuing Taxation Shortfall directly from the Federal Reserve instead of borrowing it at excessively high rates of interest; that will, in all, Produce the Consumer Purchasing Power We Need for Economic Vitality, Growth, and Stability.

It is obvious to us all that our modern day Government needs more income revenues in public responsibility to maintain itself than it is capable of taking-in under Supply and Demand GNDP Taxation; and it is also clear that we cannot continue to incur untenable and catastrophic Nation Debt to what Fiat Issue, that is based upon the Full Faith in integrity of The United States and Its Amassed Wealth and Resources, is the only Intelligent Solution.

Full Faith Certificate Issue to meet the needs of our Government and to Provide for the Public Well-Being; is to be respected in Sound Economic Recovery Policy, as "Legitimate Currency," to augment any Federal Deficit Budget Shortfall; to meet Federal Payroll Necessity, Provide Work for the Nations Unemployed, Fund for Disaster Relief and for other Emergency Crisis Issues affecting; Education, the Environment, and U.S. Agriculture, and to Augment failing City and State Budgets in their own regard of these matters in yearly contingency; and is not designed to replace "Hard Currency," for the purchase of Goods and Services in the Private Sector, that is derived from the Nation's Gross National/Domestic Product Taxation, GNDP, to what the Value of our U.S. Dollars is configured. Hard Currency will be used in all U.S. money dealings with Private Sector Contractors, Foreign Governments, and for the Repayment of our National Debt. Sound Economic Analysis calculates that 1/4 (One Forth) of the Nation's yearly Budget can be supplanted with Full Faith Issue without harm to the Value of the Dollar; (that in turn will be "Reabsorbed," back into the Federal, State, and Municipal Treasuries by taxation to further "Strengthen" our U.S. Budgetary Future,) and as well as to provide Needed Economic Stimulus.

Here is the link to your free eBook *The Democratic Labor Party Platform 2012* (ID #11647902): **http://www.lulu.com/content/e-book/the-democratic-labor-party-platform-2012/11647902**

"That the Earth with All Its Life Abounding Exists in the Eternity of Infinite Time and Space is a miracle beyond comprehension to behold. Let us govern ourselves accordingly." In The End You Will Say, "We Did It Ourselves." Sophisticated Reasoning Is In Order.

"ONE POWERFUL VOICE"

2014 General Election
United States Representative

District	Candidate	Status	Primary	General
1	Miller, Jeff (REP) *Incumbent	Qualified		
	Bryan, Jim (DEM)	Qualified	Unopposed	
	Krause, John E (REP)	Qualified		
	Wichern, Mark (NPA)	Qualified		
2	Graham, Gwen (DEM)	Qualified	Unopposed	
	Southerland, Steve (REP) *Incumbent	Qualified	Unopposed	
	Lee, Luther (WRI)	Qualified		
3	Yoho, Ted (REP) *Incumbent	Qualified		
	Lawson, Howard Term Limits (NPA)	Qualified		
	Rush, Jake (REP)	Qualified		
	Wheeler, Marihelen (DEM)	Qualified	Unopposed	
4	Crenshaw, Ander (REP) *Incumbent	Qualified		
	Shoaf, Ryman (REP)	Qualified		
*****	Koniz, Gary L. (NPA)	Qualified		
	Moser-Bartlett, Paula (NPA)	Qualified		
	Pueschel, Deborah Katz (WRI)	Qualified		

http://www.lulu.com/shop/gary-koniz/forty-thousand-brothers/ebook/product-21258805.html

Louis William Rose: Gary L. Koniz is my favorite candidate. While we do not agree on everything by far, he is courageous in his convictions, does not lie or disseminate, freely debates anywhere on any subject, and is a gracious gentleman in his demeanor and approach to others, especially those with whom he disagrees.

"ONE POWERFUL VOICE"

The Right To Equal Justice Under The Law

-----Section 3: That The Medical Terminology Technicality of Mental Hygiene Psychiatric Law that falls under the heading of Civil Law, Two Physician Consent, 2PC, Commitment Procedure, on Medical Grounds, in that no crime has been committed under Mental Hygiene Law to be charged for and thereby to be accorded the protective safeguards of Miranda Rights Legislation to be prosecuted for and processed fairly for under The Constitutional Rights accorded to Criminal Penal Law Legal System under the protection in Rights To The People, of The Fourth, Fifth, Sixth, and Eighth Amendments to The U.S. Constitution, and reinforce by the protection of The Miranda Legislation, is hereby clarified of Its Civil Law Constitutional Rights, in meaning to have the same Rights of Due Process as are and have been established under Penal Law, in guarantee to the people of:

The Right to have a clear definition of a Formal Psychiatric Charge being present in grounds for anyone to be labeled for and to have any specified medical psychiatric condition, or for the offense of irrational behavior labeling being levied against an individual, and in grounds thereby for any psychiatric evaluation process mental illness labeling to be attached to anyone, or for any process of Two Physician Consent, 2PC, Psychiatric Commitment Procedure to be conducted. And that such definition of charge is also to precede any Court or Government Agency Order for the disclosure of personal and private psychiatric history records to be produced.

The Right to The Fourth Amendment guarantee of privacy in regard of doctor patient confidentiality and invoking to The Due Process Right of Probable and Sufficient Cause In Grounds, is to be present and justified to a specific itemized search and disclosure in mandatory request for Specific Information only of any existing psychiatric history records, regarding The Rights of Government Agencies, as for the specified psychiatric history to be scrutinized, to any private request or public government agency order for, or court authority mandatory order for the scrutiny of anyone's psychiatric medical history records to be revealed. That is not to be construed by court order or by congressional authority concerning government agencies, to be a total and all intrusive invasive invasion of an individual's records history involving The Right To Privacy, but is to issued only as order for records disclosure pertains selectively and relevant to the specified psychiatric charge of inquiry at hand.

The Right to strict legal definition for any psychiatric labeling terms to be applied to anyone.

The Right to strict legal determinations based to demonstrated facts of observed and defined behavior, in the presence of any attorney for such alleged psychiatric labeling being attributed in legal attachment of a psychiatric condition or involving psychiatric incarceration to anyone to be valid.

The Right to Counsel, to be provided for at government expense if need be, by The Examining Government Agency or by The Court of Jurisdiction, for any alleged psychiatric matter of consequence being attributed to anyone, involving the loss of liberty, property, licensure, employment, or privilege.

The Right to have an Attorney present during questioning to any psychiatric examination/evaluation/interrogation, and to be present during psychiatric commitment processing and to any court proceedings.

The Right to Remain Silent in presumption of innocence until proven guilty to any psychiatric charge in a bona fide court of law.

The Right to Confrontations of any accusing testimony against the accused in virtue of The

"ONE POWERFUL VOICE"

Sixth Amendment.

The Right to a Jury Trial provided in a timely way in accordance with The Sixth Amendment for any specified psychiatric accusation labeling being imposed, whether involving commitment or not.

The Right to clearly established and legally defined medically safe and beneficial therapeutic treatment to be imposed for legitimate psychiatric conditions.

The Right to Informed Consent in the presence of legal counsel concerning the discussion and patient awareness of adverse effects, reactions, and harmful side effects in short and long-term use of psychiatric chemicals involved with any psychiatric treatment to occur.

The Right To Refuse Treatment, and Against Forced Treatment on Medical Discretion, in the presence of legal counsel, except in matters As Prescribed By Law to be applied for necessary medical emergency procedure in concern to imminent crisis of hysteria, and for violent and disruptive behavior in being in threat to oneself or others requiring emergency medical treatment in judgment.

The Right against any form, including psychological, of cruel and inhumane treatment to occur, concerning physical, mental, or emotional abuse, to include electro-shock treatment, surgical procedure, and pharmaceutical experimentation, in virtue of The Eighth Amendment.

The Right to reasonable and soundly defined Statute of Limitations in established Legal Age Limits for the mandatory disclosure of previous psychiatric condition labeling history records, or to the disclosure of legally carried-out psychiatric commitment history records, worded, to any current treatment for any serious ongoing psychiatric condition, or to within the past three years concerning The Public Record.

"ONE POWERFUL VOICE"

NATIONAL ASSOCIATION FOR GUN RIGHTS
2014 CONGRESSIONAL CANDIDATE SURVEY
BACKGROUND BRIEFING

Question #1: The Second Amendment

The Second Amendment unequivocally protects an individual's right to civilian gun ownership. Like the First Amendment, there is no question that the right belongs to the individual rather than the state.

Question #2: Firearm Prohibitions and Magazine Capacities

Magazine capacity limits are simply arbitrary restrictions that fail to grasp the nature of firearms and their intended use. Limiting the number of cartridges one firearm can hold at any given time is akin to limiting the number of words a journalist is allowed to print.

Question #3: Veterans' Second Amendment Protection

Over 140,000 military veterans, who have not been found to be a danger to themselves or others, have been denied their Second Amendment rights without due process and that number continues to grow. Our veterans deserve an opportunity to have their rights restored.

Question #4: "Mental Health" Records

Mental health data should be controlled and have oversight by those who are experts in the field of mental illness -- i.e. not local Sheriffs, but trained psychiatrists. The idea of giving mental health data to a national background check system calls into question both the doctor/patient privacy right as well as the ability of non-professionals to determine what is, in fact, mental health data. The term is very ambiguous and one that is not even agreed upon by professionals.

Question #5: Expanded Background Checks

Expanding background checks only assures that in order to exercise Second Amendment rights, one would have to first submit to de facto government-run gun registration.

Simply put, the Brady Bill which established the NICS system is unnecessary. It has created an extraneous bureaucracy that serves only to make the lives of law-abiding gun owners and dealers harder by making them jump through extensive bureaucratic hoops. It does not affect criminals, and there is absolutely no evidence suggesting that the Brady Bill has lowered crime in any way.

Question #6: Lautenberg Gun Ban

Under the Lautenberg Amendment, a citizen can be stripped of his Second Amendment rights simply by being accused of domestic violence charges -- in some cases including spanking a child or grabbing a spouse's wrist. Violent criminals do not take the time to check and see if it is legal for them to carry a firearm; this is yet another law affecting only those who obey the law to begin with.

Question #7: "Gun-Free" School Zones (Criminal Safezones)

To imply that any area can be made "gun-free" without security at every possible entry point is not only disconnected from reality but also ignores the law and the intent of the Second Amendment. Making a school zone "gun-free" only prevents law-abiding citizens from being able to protect themselves in a crisis, while assuring criminals of a soft target with unarmed victims. A person intent on shooting children in a school will not suddenly change their mind because a law has declared it to be a "gun-free" zone.

Question #8: BATFE Reform

The recent events surrounding the colossal failure known as "Project Fast & Furious" by the BATFE have proven beyond a shadow of a doubt that the agency is not only in need of a serious overhaul, but dangerously corrupt to the level of bringing loss of life to other federal law enforcement agents.

Question #9: Patriot Act Amendment

The language from the so-called "Patriot Act" itself and from people such as the Homeland Security director has shown clearly that the act's provisions are directed more at law-abiding citizens of our own country than at any foreign threat. The so-called "Patriot Act" enables law enforcement agencies to label individuals as "terrorists" for actions as simple as buying supplies at a surplus store. This is clearly an infringement on individual liberties and provides little to no value in the actual realm of security.

Question #10: "Gun Trafficking" Legislation

The intention of expanding "gun trafficking" legislation is not to stop or curtail large scale criminal instances of gun trafficking but rather to redefine what gun trafficking is currently understood to be. This redefinition would render the unknowing or negligent gun owner a criminal, on par with career criminals who receive large amounts of money to arm gangs, cartels, and other organized criminal groups. This would result in otherwise law-abiding citizens being imprisoned for federal gun crimes and being subject to obscene penalties.

"ONE POWERFUL VOICE"

Palestine Liberation

As a well-known quote states: **Your first mistake might be assuming that people are rational and/or Ethically and Morally Motivated.** Your second mistake could be assuming that people are eager for change. And a third mistake is in assuming that once someone knows things the way you know them, they will choose what you chose. I have also found this, about "assuming things," to be the case. But I always assume too that there may be a proper chance for changing "people's minds;" with a presentation of reasoning factors, and with that: to change the ways that things are ... for the better, in telling people right from wrong and when they are on a dangerous course and not perceiving things in the way that they need to be perceived in the correct way to stave-off disaster; as is the case of Israel's (The Jewish State's,) refusal to accept our ongoing Appeals, to reverse its holocaust/apartheid attitude towards the Indigenous Palestinians, and to take a benevolent approach towards them; and that failing that, there is the need then to forcibly "take charge," over these affairs where "Injustice Prevails" to reverse their improper course.

As it stands, We are now fast approaching the end of the Jewish State, called Israel, and as it is situated on Palestinian Territory outright; that was founded on Palestinian Soil, and in atrocity, "taken from the Palestinians" by force; (as in Biblical Times;) and for what is the cause of the Hostilities in that region, and concerning what Terrorist Aggressions, for our support, that are occurring to us here in the U.S.. To be understood: that in 1947, the United Nations partitioned Historic Palestine, giving 55% to the Jewish population and 45% to the Palestinian population. The indigenous Palestinians rejected the division of the land on which they had lived and farmed for centuries. At the time of partition, the Jewish population owned less than 6% of Palestine.

Historically, the land of Palestine was populated by a people known as the Palestinians who have always been religiously diverse, with the Muslim majority maintaining friendly relations with their Christian, Jewish, and Druze brethren. At the turn of the 20th Century, a new **Jewish Nationalist Ideology** called **Zionism** was developing. **Zionism** called for the creation of a Jewish homeland in Palestine, and elsewhere. During this time, increasing numbers of Jewish Europeans immigrated to Palestine, causing the Jewish population to grow from a tiny minority to 35% of the population. In 1948 Israel declared its "independence," but chose not to name its borders. Following its founding war of 1947-49 Israel came into existence on 78 percent of Palestine, a percentage it has steadily increased in subsequent years, that continues to this day. The Holy Land, as it is called, needs to be "taken over" at this critical time in our history, and supervised and managed by a **United Nations Peace Keeping Force, and maintained as an International Zone,"** until further notice, or at least for the next "generation," or two, 40 years, until things settle down in the area and the animosities of the immediate setting are forgotten.

Take notice at this time: that The United States, as the Chief Principle Ally and Financial Military Backer of Israel in the Middle-East, **Can No Longer Support and Abide With the continued Israeli Aggressions towards the Palestinians**, and must take the side of the Palestine Liberation Organization, (the PLO,) against Israel, in forcing a "Two State" International Zone in the region, to be Enforced and Supervised over by The U.N., returning Palestine to the original 1947 United Nations Charter Agreement for a Two State System; and in which Jews, Arabs, and other Nationalities abiding throughout the region are Equal Citizens of either State's Territories.

"ONE POWERFUL VOICE"

File:UN Palestine Partition Versions 1947.

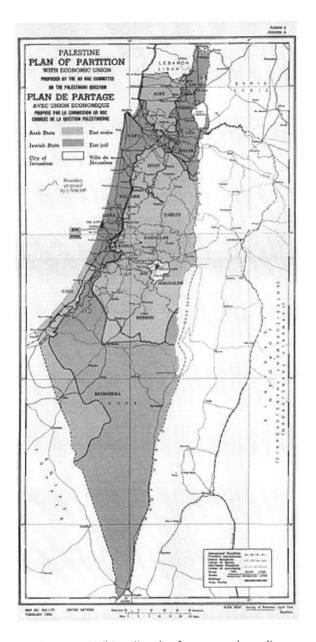

Source: Wikipedia, the free encyclopedia

UNSCOP (3 September 1947) and UN Ad Hoc Committee (25 November 1947) partition plans. The UN Ad Hoc committee proposal was voted on in the resolution.

Date   November 29 1947

Meeting no.   128

Code   A/RES/181(II)

"ONE POWERFUL VOICE"

United States Senate
WASHINGTON, DC 20510-0905

September 23, 2013

BILL NELSON
FLORIDA

Mr. Gary Koniz
9480 Princeton Square Blvd S, Apt 815
Jacksonville, Florida 32256

Dear Mr. Koniz:

Thank you for writing and sharing your thoughts about the Middle East peace process. I share your concerns regarding the need for peace and stability in the region.

The goal of two states living side-by-side in peace and security is long overdue, and I am encouraged that Israelis and Palestinians have agreed to resume direct talks. I believe continued, direct, bilateral negotiations remain the best way to resolve their complex differences, and continued U.S. engagement and leadership is required to help get us there.

Our commitment to Israel should never be in doubt. Maintaining a strong U.S. – Israel partnership is critical. It's a partnership rooted in history, democratic ideals, and steadfast friendship. Furthermore, helping Israel achieve peace with its neighbors while maintaining its security strengthens our strategic interests in the region. I also believe that the United States should continue to support Palestinian moderates and independents as they negotiate with Israel to secure a lasting peace in the region.

Please know that I will continue to monitor the situation closely. If you have any additional concerns, please do not hesitate to contact me again.

Sincerely,

Bill Nelson

P.S. From time to time, I compile electronic news briefs highlighting key issues and hot topics of particular importance to Floridians. If you'd like to receive these eBriefs, visit my Web site and sign up for them at http://billnelson.senate.gov/news/ebriefs.cfm

"ONE POWERFUL VOICE"

Photo by Jennifer Stetler - Sears Portrait Studio – The Avenues Mall – Jacksonville, FL

The Author Gary L. Koniz

"ONE POWERFUL VOICE"

About The Author

The Author Gary L. Koniz is a Freelance Journalist, the son of a Medical Nutrition Specialist, Margaret Fondren Koniz, and a Chemist, Leon F. Koniz, who is currently involved with many of the great Humanitarian and Social Struggles of our day and with troubleshooting the developing crises concerns of state as they affect us imperatively in the context of our Society and within the realm of our ambition and ability as a People Politically to resolve.

He was born in Fort Meade, Maryland in 1946 and was raised and educated in The Mid-Hudson Valley Region of New York State. He was drafted out of high school and served in The United States Armed Forces from 1964-1967 with The Army Corps of Engineers as a Heavy Equipment Operator and fought in The Vietnam War in 1966. After his Honorable Discharge he was fortunate to be taken-in by The International Union of Operating Engineers and worked as a Heavy Equipment Operator for Local 137 for ten years. He also earned a Commercial Pilot License during that time under The G.I. Bill with single and multi-engine land ratings and later worked as a Charter Pilot for a local airport and flew extensively throughout the Eastern and Central United States and Canada, flying passengers and cargo.

In 1970 he began to undertake his college studies and to fulfill his real life's "Calling of God" to be a writer. To accomplish which goal he attended and graduated Summa Cum Laude from The State University at New Paltz, NY with a Bachelor's Degree in English/Humanities and Creative Writing in 1974. After graduation he attended graduate studies for several years and taught Freshman English as a Teaching Assistant at SUNY University before beginning his professional writing career in taking a job as Project Development Team Supervisor, creating employment positions and writing Grant Proposals for The Dutchess County C.E.T.A. Program (Comprehensive Training and Employment Act,) under President Carter's Administration.

Immediately following the conclusion of his successful tenure with the C.E.T.A. Program, in 1979 (having fulfilled his quota of creating over 3,500 C.E.T.A. Job placements for the needy and desperately unemployed and impoverished population in placing them with county-wide not-for-profit agencies locally,) he then took a job with The Poughkeepsie, NY School District in the position of Public Information Officer as a Reporter/Photographer covering school events in connection with the local newspaper The Poughkeepsie Journal. It was with this newspaper that he began doing Freelance Journalism Dispatch Work in Investigative Journalism with this press for the next ten years covering The War On Drugs (becoming involved directly with President Ronald Reagan's Task Force in 1981, "To Break The Cone of Silence Surrounding Organized Crime Activities," regarding The Drug-Chemical Warfare Subversive Terrorism occurring in the aftermath of The Vietnam War.) He was also involved with many other issues of; the Economy, Labor, Humane Appeals, Race Relations, a Proper Moral Code for The Nation, and The Environment, before relocating to Buffalo, NY in 1989.

In Buffalo he became involved with Bishop Henry Mansell of The Diocese of Buffalo on an expansive Christian Social Outreach Project on Government Reform and began to work as an advisor and media correspondent with Senator Daniel Patrick Moynihan on The War On Drugs, and many other vital issue of the hour; that as well involved working closely on all levels of the government with many other Political Leaders, most notably with Senator Alfonse D'Amato, Senator Jay Rockefeller, (with whom he assisted in working on the Senator's 1992 Presidential Campaign Platform as a Policy Platform Speech Writer, and with whom he continues on with to the present day in correspondence,) and Senator Edward Kennedy, (with whom he worked closely with as well on the Drug War.) He also worked closely with, and in conjunction to AFL-

"ONE POWERFUL VOICE"

CIO President John J. Sweeney, on Economic/Labor Issues, and was successfully involving with raising The Minimum Wage; and to the upgrading of The Minimum Wage Law itself to the initiation of a Prevailing Fair Wage and Benefits Legislation based to The Federal Government's General Schedule, (GS) Standards formula, and for Universal IRS Deductible Health Care, (as yet to be accomplished.) He also worked very closely with NYS Congressman Jack Quinn, (in particular,) and with New York State Governor George Pataki, with New York State Senator William T. Stackowski, New York State Assemblyman Sam Hoyt, Erie County Executive Dennis Gorski, The City of Buffalo Mayor Anthony Masiello, with Local, State, and Federal Law Enforcement, with Government Agencies, (most notably The Federal Aviation Administration,) and with The National Guard and Central Command on The Drug War.

During this time (of the decade 1989 – 2000,) he was also directly responsible for the clearing the City of Buffalo's air with The Environmental Protection Agency, (EPA,) regarding the local Bethlehem Steel Mill in stopping it from its burning of low grade coal with high sulfur benzene carcinogens emissions. And he was responsible for the resolution of The Native American Indians' Tax Treaty Case, with New York State's Governor George Pataki, (that was resolved in the favor of The Seneca Indian Nation for New York State not to Tax on their Reservations in Violation of the existing Treaty With The Seneca, in a state of War Crisis.)

The Author also did extensive coaching and air-time psychology work as well as providing literary contributions with the Actor Larry Hagman for many years as a contributing commentator and was instrumental in organizing the final episode of "Dallas," entitled, "The Dallas Reunion," in psychological resolution to the tragic (apparent suicide) ending of the show in relief to his grief stricken fans. He was also a Correspondent, Political Press Agent, and Information News Source Advisor to The Editor of The Buffalo News, Mr. Murray Light, from 1989 – 2000 (and in major contributions to his "War Press" in Policy Confrontation to the Drug War and to other crises of the era.) He was successful in forming a united public army around The Buffalo News in influence and with the ability to generate dynamic social policy change, (in resolution to The Drug War,) before moving to Jacksonville, FL in 2000 where he currently resides with his wife Kathleen and works as a National Correspondent and Lobbyist for; Veterans Affairs, (The Wounded Warrior Program,) Labor Rights, the Economy, and the Environment, and is a Contributing Editorial Policy Writer for many newspapers and agencies; including The Buffalo News, The New York Times, CNN, The Poughkeepsie Journal, The Washington Post, and with The Florida Times Union of Jacksonville, FL. He is also a Contributing Freelance Writer for Military Officer Magazine, and The Catholic News Service.

He became involved with Journalism as a Call of The Spirit to help reform the many ways of errors of humanity In Sympathy to God that has become his life long quest in personal ambition. It is to his belief that we only need to have the proper imprint of guidance in our lives to become the true potential of our divine-selves as human beings and to know God in appreciation of our existence to be healed. And that is all we need to realize, (given to the corrections of any errors,) to persevere. The Candidate plans to continue his work in support of Social Reform, of Inspiring People, and To Enlighten the Ways of Humanity, Offering Hope.

Gary L. Koniz
Journalist Correspondent
9480 Princeton Square Blvd. S., #815
Jacksonville, FL 322556
gary.koniz@hotmail.com
http://www.lulu.com/spotlight/greenskeeper6

"ONE POWERFUL VOICE"

Gary L. Koniz   9480 Princeton Square Blvd. S.,
(904) 730-2055   #815 Jacksonville, FL 32256
                                                 Email: gary.koniz@hotmail.com

S.U.N.Y. New Paltz, New Paltz, NY (1972 - 1974)
B.A. English, with honors - Summa Cum Laude (3.8 cum)
Post Graduate Studies (1975 - 1976)
Teaching Assistantship, S.U.N.Y. New Paltz - Freshmen English, Spring Semester 1975 Dutchess Community College, Poughkeepsie, NY (1970- 1972)
A.A. Degree, with honors (3.8 cum)

SKILLS:
Computer - IBM PC ... Typing ... Math ... Communications Public Public Relations ... Freelance Articles/Journalism ... Research ... Organizing
    Published Author: Books, Short Stories, News Articles, and Essays

VOCATIONAL TRAINING:
I.B.M. Temporary Employment - I.B.M. Main Plant, Poughkeepsie, NY Freight Processor (9/85 – 12/85) IBM Industrial Computer Operator Mental Hygiene Therapy Aid (11/80 - 5/81) Therapy/Counseling Hudson River Psychiatric, Poughkeepsie, NY – CPR - Crisis Intervention Grant Proposal Writing with C.E.T.A. Program, Dutchess County, NY

Public Information Officer (6/78 - 12/78)
In charge of press relations for the Poughkeepsie School District
Created releases - Prepared (typed) and edited - highlighted school activities for "The Poughkeepsie Journal" - Circulation of 80,000

Project Development Team Supervisor (12/77 - 6/78) In charge of developing C.E.T.A. Job Projects for Dutchess County, NY – Supervised 7 employees - Contacted Non-Profit Organizations Prepared Grant Proposals – Exceeded Requirements

Sky Acres Flying School, Billings, NY Commercial, Multi Engine Rating (1968 - 1970) Charter Pilot

MILITARY - United States Army - Specialist 4th Class, Engineers Heavy Equipment Operator - (8/64 - 8/67) – Vietnam Veteran

CONSTRUCTION - LABOR ORGANIZATION -
EMPLOYMENT INTERNATIONAL UNION OF OPERATING
ENGINEERS:
Heavy Equipment Operator (1967 -2000)
LOCAL 137, BRIARCLIFF MANOR, NY - LOCAL 17, WEST SENECA, NY
Greater Buffalo Building And Construction Trades Council - 1992- 2000
New York AFL-CIO, New York, NY – with President Edward Cleary – Policy
AFL-CIO International - with President John Sweeney - 1995-2009
North Florida Central Labor Council – Currently with President Russell Harper
Secretary – International Brotherhood Of Golf Course Maintenance Workers
Union DeerCreek Country Club Maintenance Department

INTERESTS: G o l f – T e n n i s - R e a d i n g – G a r d e n i n g - Current Events - Chess – Aviation
CAREER IN LABOR ADMINISTRATION - REFERENCES AVAILABLE ON REQUEST

"ONE POWERFUL VOICE"

Photo by Jennifer Stetler - Sears Portrait Studio – The Avenues Mall – Jacksonville, FL

Vietnam Veteran Gary L. Koniz and his Wife Kathleen
Behind Every Successful Outcome there is a Kind and Loving Woman

"ONE POWERFUL VOICE"

"ONE POWERFUL VOICE"

"ONE POWERFUL VOICE"

"ONE POWERFUL VOICE"

"ONE POWERFUL VOICE"

"ONE POWERFUL VOICE"

"ONE POWERFUL VOICE"

"ONE POWERFUL VOICE"

"ONE POWERFUL VOICE"

"ONE POWERFUL VOICE"

"ONE POWERFUL VOICE"

"ONE POWERFUL VOICE"

"ONE POWERFUL VOICE"

"ONE POWERFUL VOICE"

"ONE POWERFUL VOICE"

"ONE POWERFUL VOICE"